CONFLICTS THAT CHANGED THE WORLD

CONFLICTS THAT CHANGED THE WORLD

by Rodney Castleden

Futura

A *Futura* Book

First published by Futura in 2008

ISBN: 978-0-7088-0488-9

Produced by Omnipress, Eastbourne

Printed in the EU

Futura
An imprint of Little, Brown Book Group
100 Victoria Embankment
London EC4Y 0DY

Photo credits: Getty Images

CONTENTS

3 RENAISSANCE CONFLICTS

4 CONFLICTS OF THE ENLIGHTENMENT

5 NINETEENTH-CENTURY CONFLICTS

6 WORLD WAR I: 'The war to end wars'

INTRODUCTION

As far back in time as we can see, there has been conflict. Archaeologists have found evidence that people were fighting each other in the Stone Age. The late neolithic settlement built on Crickley Hill in the Cotswolds in 2500 BC was surrounded by earth banks; and those ramparts were crested by wooden palisades which look distinctly defensive – why build ramparts unless you expect somebody to attack you? There were entrance gaps in the ramparts which were presumably closed by timber gates. At each of the entrance gaps, archaeologists found lots of arrowheads sprayed into the interior of the settlement in a fan-shaped pattern, and further in along the line of a street. The settlement was also burnt down. This gives us clear evidence of an incident of tribal warfare, an attack by one group of people wielding torches, bows and arrows on another, fighting to get into a fortified enclosure, firing arrows in through the gates to kill or drive back the defenders, and setting fire to their thatched huts. This is a glimpse of a specific conflict, an armed assault that happened at a particular place on a particular day, 4,500 years ago. Such sharply focused glimpses of long-past conflicts are very rare. The reason for that attack long ago on Crickley Hill can only be guessed at, but in archaic societies tribal warfare has often been triggered by conflicting claims to resources, such as water or land, or by breaches of etiquette, such as failure to pay or return a dowry.

In the Stone Age, the conflicts must always have been small in scale, because the societies themselves were small in scale. As communities have expanded, so have conflicts. Over the centuries, with advancing communications and transport and weapons technology, the scale of conflict has increased. The most conspicuous increase in the scale of warfare came in the nineteenth and twentieth centuries. The Industrial

Revolution brought with it an industrialisation of warfare; the invention of a range of enabling technology allowed an escalation of war. One classic example of this is Lord Kitchener's use of an early machine gun, the Maxim gun, at the Battle of Omdurman in 1898. Using this advanced technology enabled Kitchener and his army to kill 10,000 African warriors while losing only forty-eight of their own men. Kitchener gave a speech after the Battle of Omdurman, thanking the Lord of Hosts for the victory. Really the victory was not down to the Lord of Hosts but to the inventor Hiram Maxim, whose machine guns had enabled a force of 25,000 men to defeat an army twice its size.

The earliest named battle seems to have been the Battle of Megiddo, from which we take the ominous word 'Armageddon'. That took place as early as 1479 BC. The Battle of Kurukshetra, which is central to the Hindu epic *Mahabharata*, may be mythical or it may be historical. It was, according to the epic, part of a dynastic power struggle between rival clans, the Kauravas and the Pandavas, for the throne of Hastinapura. The culminating battle was alleged to have lasted eighteen days and involved huge armies from all over India. Some scholars think, from astronomical details incorporated into the epic, that the battle took place in 3100 BC, but others think it took place in 1200 or 1250 BC; the later date would put it at round about the same time as the Trojan War, which occupies the same territory in the European warfare tradition, halfway between myth and history.

Whatever the reason for going to war, it is a surprising gamble in view of the uncertainty of the outcome and the enormous risks that flow from defeat. Why do successive generations of political leaders opt for war, given its disastrous history and its enormous cost in money, lives, property and human suffering?

Sometimes the motive is personal aggrandizement for the leader, and we can see the wars of Alexander the Great and Napoleon as examples of this ego-driven warfare. Sometimes the motive is indirect; a political leader wants to rally a nation behind him (or her) for electoral reasons and points to a foreign threat, real or imaginary. At least one British Prime Minister, Lord Palmerston, falls into this category.

Sometimes conflict is an integral part of a nation's culture; it certainly became so in ancient Greece, with complicated interactions among city-states striving for supremacy, and polarizing round a long-term power struggle between Athens and Sparta. Sometimes the prospect of large-scale economic gain, such as the mineral resources of the Middle East, is irresistible. Sometimes the conflict is motivated by the basic need to subsist. The Mycenaean states of ancient Greece were based on small pockets of fairly fertile lowland surrounded by dry and unproductive mountains. Poorly resourced, the Mycenaean elites resorted to warfare, raiding foreign cities, often on the other side of the Aegean, to supplement their resources. They were engaged in piracy, though no doubt glamorized it among themselves in the way Homer describes in the *Iliad*. The purely mercenary raids were given fake justifications in order to salve consciences; there is nothing like righteous indignation to fuel a war. In much the same way the invasion of Iraq was 'justified' by President Bush and Prime Minister Blair and their advisers in terms of military threat to the West – the notorious weapons of mass destruction – even though they must have known that the threat was non-existent. Sometimes wars are wars of faith and the motive is ideological: Islamic zeal in the eighth century, Christian extremism in the Middle Ages, the capitalist-communist polarization in the Cold War, the conflict between Western materialism and Islamic fundamentalism in the so-called War on Terror. And when ideology is involved, alarmingly the cost no longer matters.

There are many reasons for conflict. There are also many reasons for avoiding conflict. It goes almost without saying that hostility is unpleasant and makes life difficult. Probably all of us have encountered a hostile co-worker or neighbour, someone who opts for criticism, tension, opposition and confrontation, who 'picks a fight', rather than trying to be co-operative and friendly. Life is pleasanter and more enjoyable without conflict. Without it we can concentrate on life-enhancing activity. Conflict is also likely to generate casualties. Even the small-scale individual conflicts escalate to a point where someone gets hurt or property gets damaged. The large-scale armed conflicts that are the main focus of this book have caused horrific lists of casualties and unimaginably large-scale damage to cities, industries and infrastructures. Then there is the cost in cash. War is ultimately an impoverishing activity, often cripplingly so. The following selection of figures shows the scale of the losses, using America as an example.

Conflict	*Total number of deaths*	*Total cost in billions of US dollars (2000 equivalent)*
War of Independence	4,435	1
Korean War	33,651	263
Vietnam War	47,369	347
World War I	16,708	197
World War II	407,316	2,091
Civil War	558,052	44

Military conflicts do very obvious damage to people. The sample statistics just quoted show the scale of killing. They imply, though hide, an even higher scale of injuries and mutilations; in most battles, the number of wounded far exceeds the number killed. For some conflicts there are figures available for the number wounded, and the dead and wounded are lumped together as 'casualties'. But behind those casualties there are the countless numbers of people who are psychologically damaged by war. Soldiers are trained to fight, to put their lives at risk. There are men who are inherently tough, who can fight literally fearlessly, and they are able to inspire the lesser men around them. One such man was Legros, the heroic Frenchman who led the assault on the great gate at Hougoumont at the Battle of Waterloo. He fought without any thought for his own survival and had a kind of surplus of courage that spread to the men around him. In antiquity, this kind of charismatic courage was raised to an idealized level in the person of Achilles: not only the perfect Bronze Age warrior, but the model for warrior heroes for ever after. The battle really is to the strong.

But most men cannot match up to these standards, and we should in any case question whether it is really desirable for people to cut themselves so totally adrift from their other responsibilities as to throw their lives away on an officer's order. Should they not consider the responsibilities they have to look after their wives, siblings, children and parents when the war is over, to their potential contribution to society after and beyond the war? Should they not question the orders to commit atrocities? It was normal practice among Allied infantrymen during World War II to kill the crews of stopped or burning tanks as they bailed out. It was a particular cruelty of modern warfare that the order to kill was normally given, and normally obeyed. The command was given, and disarmed, demoralised, surrendering opponents were cold-bloodedly murdered; the men who did that were simply blindly obeying orders, as they had been trained to do.

The bravery of soldiers in battle is sometimes an illusion. Over the centuries, a great deal of coercion has been used to make men fight. Armies have usually operated different and more strenuous codes of law from those of the civilian community, together with different systems of punishment and different courts. A high level of coercion was used at the Battle of Waterloo; for instance by placing cavalry behind unwilling infantry battalions to make it impossible for them to run back, by ordering officers to flog their men forwards, by having infantrymen firing at cavalry who were faltering. This level of force created internal conflicts that often resulted in revenge killings. An officer who flogged his men forward risked getting a bullet in his back when he relaxed his guard; at the Battle of Saratoga, Colonel Breyman was shot by one of his own men, a grenadier he had struck with his cane. Similar things happened in the Burmese jungle in World War II; it was relatively common for an officer who bullied his men to be shot from behind during action, when a stray shot went unnoticed except by the victim.

Soldiers have frequently broken down under the stresses of battle. In the first two years of World War I, many men were branded as cowards and shot for desertion. Fear of the trenches and fear of the death penalty produced hysterical conversion symptoms; the anxiety was converted into disabling symptoms such as loss of sight or loss of the use of limbs. By 1916, the British and American army authorities were forced to recognize that it was not cowardice, but psychological breakdown, that was causing the soldiers to fall apart emotionally and run away. They called it 'shell shock', implying that it was caused by a single physical event, and began to treat the soldiers affected as patients. They were treated in special hospitals for the Not Yet Diagnosed, Nervous (NYDN).

Later wars have produced similar behaviour patterns. There are psychiatric casualties as well as physical injury casualties. The less damaged personnel are described as suffering from exhaustion, the more damaged as neuro-psychiatric cases. One British army psychiatrist estimated that, depending on the type of warfare, as many as thirty percent of battle casualties may be psychiatric. In World War II, men who broke down and were treated were often returned to battle, where a high proportion broke down again. Nor is it just the psychologically weak who are affected in this way. It seems that anyone who is exposed to the conditions of modern warfare for long enough will break down eventually. An American report on combat exhaustion in World War II concluded that 'there is no such thing as *getting used to combat* . . . Most men were ineffective after 180 days.' The psychological damage may be irreparable, seriously restricting the ex-combatants' prospects of leading useful civilian lives after the war is over.

The collateral damage to civilians caught up in wars is just as serious. Recently there was television coverage of the trial of a Khmer Rouge war criminal, a man who was allegedly responsible for killing 14,000 prisoners. One of the very few survivors tried to describe what had happened to him, but broke down in tears. He said his wife and child had been shot in front of him. It was decades after the event, but he sobbed and banged his head against a wall as he described it. War does that kind of damage to people on a scale that cannot be quantified, and those who take us to war never take it into account.

A major characteristic of conflict is that frequently one war generates another; there is a chain reaction effect. The Soviet invasion of Afghanistan led directly to a committed resistance by the Afghan people, and to the declaration of a jihad, or holy war, by Islamists from other countries who felt obliged to help their fellow Muslims eject the invading army. After the Soviet withdrawal from Afghanistan, this jihad was extended to target perceived oppressors of Islam elsewhere and directed towards America. This in turn led to 9/11. 9/11 led to the War on Terror, and that war provided the context for the US invasions of Afghanistan and Iraq. The effect is not unlike the way a fight between individual children develops. One boy pushes another boy, who pushes back harder. Then the first boy, who sees the response as disproportionate, punches the second boy – and so on. On a medium, and adult, scale we can see the same thing happening in the traditional Italian vendetta, in which one revenge killing follows another. With whole peoples, including nations armed to the teeth with the latest weapons technology, behaving in this tit-for-tat way, it should not be surprising that armed conflict is endemic.

Conflict is the most negative aspect of the human condition, the ultimate manifestation of humanity's dark side. Without it, so much more could be achieved. Conflict generates physical and psychological suffering, and armed conflict can cause death and destruction on a grand scale. To give one example, it is believed that in all 8.5 million people died as a result of World War I.

There are other, less obvious but no less disturbing, aspects of conflict. When political leaders, whether in archaic or modern societies, decide to wage war on another state or on an ethnic or religious minority within their own state, they frequently give false reasons. Wars are often 'justified' while the true reasons are concealed. This dishonesty about such a serious and momentous matter is in itself disturbing, but it can also make conflict resolution a great deal harder. If the aggressor has been dishonest about the reason for going to war in the first place, it is significantly harder to appease him and offer a satisfying peace treaty. There is in the world today a healthy disrespect for the declarations of politicians when they outline their reasons for waging war. With increased levels of education and a better quality of education, it is becoming much harder for politicians and their agents to get away with the sort of 'flannel' that surrounded World War I, such as massive censorship, misrepresentation and the unscrupulous propaganda tricks that were played on men to make them enlist. One of the most famous propaganda posters showed a little girl sitting on her father's knee, pointing at a book she is reading and asking her guilt-ridden father, 'Daddy, what did YOU do in the Great War?' It is unlikely that a bare-faced piece of emotional blackmail like that would work in the West these days.

Yet fairly sophisticated electorates, populations that are supposed to have the democratic power to get rid of their leaders, are being manipulated in a very similar way. Wars are still being waged for the wrong reasons, that is to say for reasons other than those stated. There is a strong suspicion that the War on Terror announced and launched by President Bush in 1991 has been eagerly underwritten and supported by other nations because their governments see it as a magnificent smoke-screen for gaining greater non-democratic control over their populations. By invoking fear of terrorism, the British Prime Minister was able to press for an extension of police powers, which the police had themselves long wanted. Police are now able to detain people for questioning for longer periods without bringing formal charges. Chief Police Officers asked for an extension of the maximum pre-charge detention on suspicion of terrorist activities from 14 days; Parliament agreed to extend that to 28 days, the police asked for three months and at the time of writing are trying to negotiate a compromise two months. In the same context, the police have asked for new powers to continue questioning suspects after charges have been brought. They have also asked for the creation of a new offence of not disclosing encryption keys for computers, which could clearly be used to invade the privacy of non-terrorists. They have asked for the admission of 'interception material' (meaning tapped phone calls) as evidence in criminal trials, and the extension of their stop and search powers on land out to a distance of twelve miles offshore. Individually, and within the context of the fight against the threat of terrorism, these measures sound reasonable and are hard to contest. Overall, and viewed as a package, they and the parallel developments in personal checks using the National Police Computer look like a massive and co-ordinated movement towards state control and loss of civil liberty.

With these and other anxieties in their minds, people are becoming increasingly sceptical when they hear the politicians' ringing rhetoric as they urge them into battle. 'Carthage must be destroyed!' Cato and other Romans once shouted as a slogan at every opportunity in the later stages of the Punic Wars. Churchill inspired a later generation of Britons with his speech, 'We shall fight them on the beaches.' Such things are becoming less and less possible, and it is perhaps time our politicians realized that their tactics have been understood, all too well.

It is impossible to cover every conflict in human history in a book of this length, and those included have been selected to show the range of conflicts, their origins, their immediate impacts and their long-term effects. There are obvious candidates for inclusion, such as the two great world wars in the twentieth century. Huge in scale and geographical reach, huge in their consequences, they could not possibly have been left out. Some less obvious conflicts have been included because they show the enormous complexity and the ramifications of strife. The Jacobite Risings that followed the deposition of King James II of England in 1688 are a good example of a conflict of great political, military and cultural complexity. They show how lies, deception and delusion can play key roles, and how the bias of human memory can with hindsight distort the character of the actual events: wars frequently acquire a mythic character as they unfold, and even more so after they are over.

I have not attempted to narrate every event in the conflicts included. Simply narrating World Wars I and II would fill at least three books of this length, so the narration is a sketch, to give an idea of the shape of the conflict. The same is true of individual battles within wars. Some are merely mentioned, while others are described in more detail. It is and always has been difficult to describe battles in a way that is useful to the reader. The 'General Staff' analysis of warfare of the past described battles in terms of type. There were about eight types of battle, such as battles of attrition, battles of envelopment, battles of breakthrough. But these are difficult to apply in any meaningful way to warfare across the centuries. The General Staff analysis would describe the Battle of

Cannae in 216 BC, the Battle of Ramillies in AD 1706 and the Battle of the Falaise Gap in 1944 as all the same, battles of encirclement of one army by another. But the weaponry involved, the cultural and political contexts and so on are so different that the phrase 'battle of encirclement' will not do any of them justice. I have therefore left out that kind of analysis.

Equally, the reader will not find here the rhetoric of battle history. The great ringing tones of patriotic battle pieces belong very much to a past culture, though they represent a long tradition of romantic, stirring, inspiring stories of derring-do. Moltke, the great nineteenth-century Chief of German General Staff and historian, argued that it was 'a duty of piety and patriotism not to destroy certain traditional accounts' if they could be used to inspire people. But ultimately these accounts are too partial, seeing the event from one side and not the other, and they are frequently distorted; it is better when writing the story of a battle or war not to take sides. Another reason for avoiding them is that they tend, and are intended, to inflame and spur hot-blooded young men to go off and do likewise. One message that I hope will emerge from this book is that, in nearly every case, people need to be discouraged from going to war.

There is one famous military historian who, when you read his accounts, seems to be very level-headed and objective, and that is Julius Caesar. Caesar's descriptions of his own battles are very clear-cut, but also very simplified. He mentions the names of only a handful of people, and nothing is revealed of their personalities. The emphasis is always on his role, the great invincible Caesar's role, as decision maker and charismatic war leader. In Caesar's descriptions, soldiers are robots who carry out the will of the leader. This presentation was an exaggeration designed to inflate the godlike importance of the general. But it was taken as literally true, and used as a model to emulate by later generations of military commanders. Maurice of Nassau and Gustavus Adolphus of Sweden believed that, given enough time and money, they could re-create armies of the type Caesar described. Inevitably this meant that they were overlooking a great deal. Classical scholars today have a much better grasp of the very varied inner lives of the Roman legions, each of which had its own culture and mindset. The legions were far more complicated, individual and capricious than Caesar makes out. Caesar's world is stereotyped, a world in which all soldiers are brave, all commanders are intelligent, all old men wise. His view of conflict is a significant falsification, but it has been extremely influential.

The study of conflict has rightly always been seen as a legitimate and worthwhile pursuit. Going to war is probably the largest-scale exercise of free will that any community makes. It is fascinating, and sometimes alarming, to discover how such a decision is reached, especially in sophisticated modern societies like ours. Who takes us to war? Why do they take us to war? Do they really know what they are doing and where this war is leading? These are big and important questions that we need to ask, and need to answer.

On the whole, this book deals with the grand sweep of conflicts, on wars rather than battles. Here and there, though, it is useful to move in to look at a particular battle in close-up, partly to show the style of fighting and decision-making, partly to show the culture and mores of the fighting forces, partly to show how – startlingly often – the outcome depends on chance factors such as the weather.

To give an example of this: if the Battle of Waterloo had taken place in a spell of dry weather, Napoleon would have engaged in battle earlier in the day, and very likely defeated Wellington's army before Blücher's army arrived to rescue it. As it was, Napoleon saw the wet and muddy battlefield as unsuitable ground on which to move his artillery, so he delayed for several hours in the hope that the ground would dry out somewhat, and the delay gave Blücher time to come to Wellington's aid. Exactly 400 years earlier, the battlefield at Agincourt in northern France was also wet and muddy. On that occasion the terrain again worked against the French and allowed a much smaller English army to win. The very wet ploughed field was an unsuitable surface for heavily armoured mounted knights to ride on; when they fell off their stumbling horses they were unable to get up again – and died where they fell.

Agincourt lives on in the English folk memory, partly through Shakespeare's *Henry V*, as a great battle nobly won, but the historical reality was muddy, bloody and gruesome. There is personal memory, there is collective memory, there is history, there is revisionist history. Above all there is the recurring contrast between the dream of conquest and glory on the one hand and the reality of destruction, death and suffering on the other.

I realized while researching this book that the amount of material available is overwhelming. Conflict is not only going on all the time somewhere in the world today: it has always been like this. It is as if the history of the human race is the history of conflict. It is a profoundly depressing thought that conflict may be an integral and inescapable part of the human condition.

I recently wrote a book called *The Attack on Troy* about the Trojan War which took place in 1250 BC. Writing any book has to be approached up a ramp of reading and thinking and once I started the research I was surprised how much literature there was and how much knowledge was available about this ancient war. The research led me through a vast amount of archaeology, of both the area round Troy and the homelands of the Mycenaean Greeks. It also led me back to the great ancient epic poem, the *Iliad*, which tells the story of part of the Trojan War. The detail in the poem turned out to be startlingly close to the story told by the archaeological evidence – but that really is another story. The *Iliad*, I discovered, once had a prequel, now lost, which was called the *Kypria*. This poem described the events leading up to the siege of Troy and it started with the wedding of Peleus and Thetis, the parents of the warrior-hero Achilles, probably the greatest warrior-hero of all time. All the gods except one attended the wedding as guests. Zeus left only one of the gods uninvited: she was the goddess Strife. The traditional explanation is that Zeus deliberately left her off the wedding list because he wanted the occasion to be one of unalloyed happiness, and Strife always made trouble. But I believe there is a deeper and darker explanation. Zeus did not invite Strife simply because there was no need.

Strife comes uninvited.

I
CONFLICTS OF THE ANCIENT WORLD

THE STRUGGLE FOR SUPREMACY IN THE EASTERN MEDITERRANEAN

THE BATTLE OF KADESH (CIRCA 1285 BC)

The Hittite Empire was a huge, sprawling confederation that covered most of what is now Turkey. Its capital, the magnificent fortified city of Hattusa, was close to its centre, a long way from its frontiers, and successive Hittite high kings had great difficulty in keeping control over the distant borders in the east and west.

When Suppiluliumas came to the Hittite throne in 1380 BC, he sent an army into northern Syria. At that time the Egyptians were unwilling to send warriors so far afield to defend Syria. The important trading city of Ugarit at the northern end of the Syrian coast was the extreme limit of Egypt's influence. Suppiluliumas persuaded the prince of Ugarit to switch his loyalty from Egypt to Hatti, the Hittite Empire. With a series of battles, the Hittites were able to extend their influence further south, past Kadesh.

At the time, the Egyptians were deeply involved in religious reform, so the Hittites were able to press further south, taking in the tribes of Canaan, who were ready to desert Egypt for Hatti. When the young pharaoh Tutankhamun died, his widow wrote a letter to Suppiluliumas asking him to send her one of his sons for her to marry. The Hittite king acknowledged that this was an enormous honour, implying as it did that the two powers, Egypt and Hatti, and their royal dynasties, were of an equal status. He was overwhelmed by the honour. But what might have turned into a major alliance by dynastic marriage came to nothing. The son set off for Egypt and was murdered on the way, probably by Ay, who was Tutankhamun's successor.

After a succession of pharaohs, Seti I ascended the Egyptian throne. He undertook an aggressive campaign to re-establish the dominance of Egypt on the northern frontier. He drove the desert tribes out of Palestine and established the area as one of Egyptian influence. Seti then sought to gain control of the kingdom of Amurru in Syria. He saw that the key to controlling the area was the Eleutheros Valley north of the Lebanon range; it was a vital line of communication between north-eastern Syria and the Mediterranean coast. The city of Kadesh, on the Orontes River, was in this area of high strategic importance. Seti led an army in battle against the Hittites at Kadesh – well before the time of the famous Battle of Kadesh. Egyptian images show Seti in his chariot attacking a fortification at Kadesh and Hittites showered with Egyptian arrows. Seti captured Kadesh, but both the city and the kingdom of Amurru returned to Hittite control shortly after he went back to Egypt. An agreement was reached between Egypt and Hatti, that Egypt would retain Canaan but not venture north to Kadesh and Amurru.

Seti's son and successor was not content with that agreement. This was Ramesses II, the most famous of the pharaohs. In the fourth year of his incredible 67-year reign, the young Ramesses journeyed northwards to attack Amurru, breaking his father's treaty. He was able to establish Egyptian control there fairly easily. The king of Amurru, Benteshina, agreed to be Ramesses' vassal.

Then Muwatallis, the Hittite king, decided on strong military action to turn the Egyptians back. Muwatallis was the high king of the Hittite Empire, a huge confederation of kingdoms that covered almost the whole of Anatolia, or modern Turkey. His neighbours were the Assyrian Empire to the east, the Egypt of the pharaohs to the south, and the Mycenaeans to the west. Along their borders, inevitably, there was friction, rivalry for territory.

The Egyptians had occupied what is now Israel and Lebanon and invaded what Seti had agreed was non-Egyptian territory, the kingdom of Amurru. Muwatallis decided to take an army south, to dislodge Ramesses from Amurru. He called on sixteen kingdoms in his empire to send contingents, and mustered a huge Hittite army to test the strength of Egypt's armies. Interestingly, there were contingents from kingdoms called Ilion, Dardania, Masa and Pedasa; these were adjacent to each other on the far north-western frontier of the Hittite Empire. Ilion was of course the kingdom of Troy. The land of the Dardanians lay immediately to the south-east of Troy, in the Scamander Valley, and Pedasa, with the port of Pedasos, was to the south. By the time of the Trojan War, a generation later, all of these small western kingdoms would have broken free of the empire.

Ramesses meanwhile grouped the huge, equally powerful, Egyptian army into four divisions, each 5,000 strong, the Amun Division, which Ramesses himself commanded, the Re Division, the Ptah Division and the Sutekh Division. The Ptah or Sutekh Divisions seem to have included contingents from Egyptian allies, so some of the warriors were Nubians and Canaanites; both of these divisions followed at a distance from the Amun and Re divisions. Ramesses was well-organised, but probably did not know where the Hittite army was. He seems to have decided to make a stand at Kadesh and do battle with the Hittite host there.

The social structure of Ramesses' army was similar, evidently, to that of the Hittites and Mycenaeans. The poorer citizens, armed with bows and slashing swords, served as infantrymen. It seems they acquired a special status through being warriors, rising above the status of scholars and priests in Egyptian society. The rich and aristocratic owned chariots and horses. The chariot corps represented the social and military elites of the period. The aristocrats in their chariots were also archers. Ramesses II himself was renowned as an archer, just like his father. In almost all the battle images of Ramesses he is shown drawing his bow and riding in his chariot.

The strength of the Hittite army lay in its huge chariot force. The chariots were lightly built of wood covered with hide and mounted on two six-spoked wheels. Each chariot carried three men, a driver, a warrior wielding a lance 2.5 metres (8 foot) long and an archer. The design concept was very similar to that of the Egyptian chariots; they were light, fast and the very latest in weapons technology. The nations with elites that could afford chariots became great powers – the Bronze Age equivalent of nuclear powers. The Egyptians had war chariots; the Hittites had war chariots; the Mycenaeans had war chariots.

The Hittite battle procedure was to send in a massive chariot force at the front, in effect to charge the enemy, then send in the infantry to finish off whatever was left. For the Battle of Kadesh, it was said in the Egyptian account that Muwatallis was able to muster 2,500 war chariots and two divisions of infantry, numbering 18,000 and 19,000; the numbers may have been exaggerated.

Ramesses took his huge army northwards through Gaza and Canaan, then on to the ford across the Orontes River near Shabtuna. It was there, on the hills above Kadesh, that the Amun and Re divisions made their camps. Probably Ramesses did not know where the Hittite host was, as the Egyptian account of the battle claims. He did in any case choose a good defensive site, perhaps suspecting that a battle was coming soon.

Egyptian soldiers caught two tribesmen near their camp and took them to Ramesses for questioning. They told him they were Hittite deserters and that Muwatallis was scared of meeting Ramesses in battle; he had fled northwards to Aleppo. Ramesses was pleased to hear this, felt he was in no danger, and divided his army. He took the Amun Division over the Orontes River to capture the city of Kadesh before Muwatallis could reappear. The Re Division followed about 2 km (1¼ miles) behind, and the remaining two divisions, Sutekh and Ptah, stayed on the south side of the river.

The Hittite deserters were in reality Hittite scouts, and they had told the pharaoh some daring lies. Muwatallis was not at Aleppo. He was gathering his huge army in the dense vegetation round Kadesh. When Egyptian scouts succeeded in capturing a Hittite warrior, they made him talk, and he revealed the true position of the Hittite army. It was just across the river. Now Ramesses was suddenly aware how dangerous his position was. He was on his own with only a quarter of his army, and about to be surrounded by Hittites. At night, he dispatched soldiers to summon the two divisions at the rear, Ptah and Re, to come to his aid.

The following morning, Muwatallis sent a chariot force across the river on the east side of Kadesh. The Re Division had just crossed the river and was hurrying to join the Amun Division. Muwatallis succeeded in ambushing and attacking the Re Division at a moment when it was completely unprepared. The remnants of the broken and panic-stricken Re Division ran for shelter in the Amun camp. The Hittite chariots followed the fleeing Egyptians, which added to the confusion in the camp. These chariots were crewed by men from Arzawa, Masa and Pidasa – all lands in the far west of the Hittite Empire. If Pidasa was the city of Pedasos (present-day Assos on the north-east coast of Turkey, opposite Lesbos) it was in the land of the Leleges, who lived right next to the Trojans, to the north, and the Dardanians, to the north-east.

Muwatallis sent in another 1,000 chariots and swiftly encircled the Pharaoh and his two divisions. Then he closed in. Soldiers unprepared for battle poured out of their tents. The Hittites began killing Egyptians on one side of the camp. Ramesses, in his tent at the centre was in extreme danger. Later, in an inscribed account, Ramesses reminisced dramatically, 'There was no high officer with me, no charioteer, no shield-bearer, my infantry and my chariotry scampering away; not one of them stood firm to fight.' It looked as though the Egyptian army was going to be massacred, and Ramesses with it.

Ramesses' luck changed because of the way Hittite soldiers were rewarded. There was no pay; they were there under a feudal obligation to Muwatallis. Their only possible reward was plunder in battle. The Hittite soldiers were tempted into the Egyptian tents to look for valuables, and stopped to rob the dead. As a result their attack lost momentum. In this way the Hittites lost their opportunity to capture or kill the pharaoh. They also lost an opportunity to disable or destroy all the unmanned chariots to stop the Egyptians from counterattacking.

During the delay, reinforcements arrived from the east. It was a small force, but enough to make a difference. The plunderers were seen off and Ramesses was saved. It is not clear who the saviours were, perhaps local Amurru troops loyal to Egypt. Ramesses and his bodyguards charged through the Hittite force surrounding his camp. Ramesses' account tells us, 'He mounted upon Victory in Thebes, his horse, and started forth quickly alone by himself, His Majesty being powerful, his heart stout, and none could stand before him.' He went on to strike the Hittite front along the river, and made his escape.

It is unclear why Muwatallis did not send in his infantry to support the chariotry. If he had followed through in this way, he might have routed the great army of Egypt and won the greatest victory of the ancient world. But for some reason he held back. When night fell, Muwatallis fell back into the city of Kadesh, accepting a stalemate.

The Egyptians left the field of battle and took home with them a version of events which gave Ramesses a decisive victory. In a poetic rendering of the battle, Muwatallis laid the capital of the Hittite Empire, the great fortress-city of Hattusa, at Ramesses' feet. This was pure fantasy. Even if Ramesses had won the battle, it was only a battle over a border dispute, over a town on the very edges of both their empires.

Muwatallis's brother Hattusilis was commander of the Hittites' army camp and chariot forces. It is thought that he conspired against his brother at the time of the battle with the ruler of Amurru, which was under the control of the Egyptians. But after the battle, the ruler of the Amurru, King Benteshina, switched his allegiance to the Hittites. This is a definite indication that, at the time and at the location, the Hittites were seen to be the victors of the Battle of Kadesh.

Aftermath

The Battle of Kadesh was remembered in ancient times as the battle that determined the future of the great empires. It marked the limits of Egypt's power, ensured that Egyptian influence never expanded any further north, and ensured the status of the Hittite Empire as an equal and balancing power. It was a landmark battle. The lesser nations of the region remained just that: Amurru in Syria, Canaan on the coast south of the Orontes, the Hurrians of Mitanni to the east.

The place where the battle took place was in a key position, where Europe, Asia and Africa met.

The Hittites let Ramesses and his army retreat peaceably; there was no pursuit, no rout. But it was understood that Kadesh was now in the Hittite sphere of influence. Muwatallis moved south to take another town, Kumidi, that had fallen under Egyptian control before turning north for home, leaving his brother to supervise the newly captured lands. Ramesses was powerless to stop any of this.

Muwatallis had successfully defined one border of his empire. But doing this was a diversion from a major development to the east. The state of Mitanni was turned into a vassal-state by the Assyria, so suddenly the Hittites were without a buffer-state between them and the Assyrians. Muwatallis did not in any case live long enough to enjoy his great victory over Ramesses. He was dead within the year and succeeded by his son Urhi-Teshub, known as Mursilis III (1285–78). The dead king's brother Hattusilis (who eventually became Hattusilis III) exploited his nephew's youth and inexperience, declaring war on him. They became locked in a power struggle and while that was going on, the kingdoms in the far west detached themselves from central Hittite control, gaining a measure of independence.

The most striking feature of the Battle of Kadesh is that it was so successfully presented as a victory by Ramesses II back in Egypt. In fact it would probably not have been safe for Ramesses to have admitted the extent of the disaster; he was a young, unproven pharaoh and not yet secure. The real battle was a fiasco as far as the Egyptians were concerned, yet the propaganda presentation made it a victory. It demonstrates how important the writing of history is; sometimes what is written about an event can be far more potent than the event itself.

THE TROJAN WAR (1250 BC)

During the reign of Mursilis III, the Hittite king, the dynastic power struggle left the kingdoms of the far west in Anatolia (the west coast of Turkey) to go their own way. Many of these kingdoms became independent states. Because they were no longer governed or guarded by the central power in Anatolia, they were vulnerable to attack and annexation by the Mycenaeans. The Mycenaeans were the Bronze Age people of Greece and the Aegean. The political structure seems to have been a reflection of the Hittite structure. There were many small kingdoms, often centring on fertile, food-producing plains and bounded by mountain barriers. The Peloponnese, the peninsula of southern Greece, was divided into six of these kingdoms - Elis, Achaea, Arcadia, Messenia, Laconia and Argolis – and there were about twelve more Mycenaean kingdoms in central and northern Greece. The Hittite high kings left enough documents for us to be sure that there was an overall high king based in Hattusa. Many of the documents are archive copies of important diplomatic letters. No such documents have survived from Mycenaean Greece, or at least none have been found. On the other hand, Homer, writing perhaps 500 years later, tells us that there was a high king called Agamemnon, who was able to rally warriors and ships from the whole confederation in exactly the same way that Muwatallis was in Anatolia a generation before.

The Trojan War should be regarded as a real historical event. The evidence for it comes not just from Homer's *Iliad* but from a much wider ancient Greek literary tradition, from surviving lists of slave women and their countries of origin, from finds of Mycenaean objects – even weapons – on the Turkish coast, from correspondence in the Hittite archives, and not least from archaeological evidence uncovered at Troy itself.

The weakening of the Hittite central power allowed the Mycenaean Greeks to gain control of islands and coastal towns along the south-west coast of Turkey, towns such as Ialysos, Knidos, Halikarnassos and Miletus. The northernmost of these colony towns seems to have been Apasa (Ephesus). The Trojan War consisted of a series of Mycenaean forays, raids and military expeditions to gain control of the coastal towns along the rest of the coast, which belonged to the non-aligned independent kingdoms of Wilusa (Homer's Ilios), Seha River Land, Appawiya and Arzawa-Mira. This phase in the conflict was described in the now-lost epic *Kypria.* Summaries and fragments of the epic survive, so we know the sequence of events. There was an early attack on Troy, in the extreme north next to the entrance to the Dardanelles, which the Trojans under Hector repulsed. After that there were attacks on each of the harbour towns along the coast to the south. Along the Gulf of Edremit, the harbour and near-coastal towns of Pedasos, Lyrnessos, Adramyttis and Thebe were sacked. The towns on the large neighbouring island of Lazpaz (Lesbos) were also sacked and taken over.

The military leaders of this rampage were Agamemnon, the Mycenaean high king, and Achilles, a wild and gifted young warrior. It was Achilles' idea to isolate and weaken Troy by attacking its neighbours and allies first, and this Great Foray had the desired effect of partially disabling at least four of the Trojan ally kingdoms, the lands of the Kilikes, Dardani, Leleges and the (three?) kingdoms of Lesbos.

The lost epic poem goes on to describe more attacks on coastal towns further to the south. The last of these was Colophon. Significantly, we know from archaeological evidence that beyond Colophon the Anatolian coast was already under Mycenaean control, so there was no need for Achilles to go any further. The epic poem also refers briefly to attacks on coastal towns to the north of Troy. The city of Abydos, well inside the Dardanelles, was one of them, and it represents one of the most important towns in the adjacent kingdom to the north of Troy.

Although the saga gives an impression of a wild rampage, overall it represents a systematic, and very time-consuming, campaign to bring the whole of the eastern coastline of Anatolia under Mycenaean control – and isolate Troy. The Trojan War was said by the ancient Greek poets to have taken ten years. The siege of Troy itself was probably much shorter, but it is easy to see that taking control of the whole coastline, involving capturing many towns, might well take ten years. In fact it probably took nearer fifty years and was not the work of a single military leader: not one Achilles, but several.

The ultimate prize, though, was Troy. Troy was at the entrance to the Dardanelles, in a good position to stop ships from passing through, and a key trading post. It had become a wealthy emporium, at the gateway to the Black Sea and, via the Black Sea, the Danube Valley. Getting control of Troy was the focus, the ultimate goal.

The Mycenaeans landed first on Tenedos, the closest island to Troy. Possibly, by landing on the south-west coast of Tenedos, the Mycenaeans hoped to conceal their presence from the Trojan lookouts. From there it was a short distance across to Besika Bay, where the ships were drawn up onto the beach and an encampment set up. A great many problems were encountered by Homer scholars who assumed that the bay used by the Greeks was the big Bay of Troy, now completely silted up, which in antiquity lay immediately to the north-west of Troy. Very little of Homer's descriptions of landscape and tactics make sense on that basis and this led many scholars to dismiss the *Iliad* as a work of fiction. But seeing the small Bay of Besika, about 7 km (4½ miles) to the south-west of Troy, as the site of the Greek camp makes a huge difference; suddenly all the topographical detail Homer describes, and the battle tactics, make perfect sense. To clinch it, archaeological traces of an unusual Mycenaean settlement and cemetery have been found on the north side of Besika Bay. The Greek camp was shielded from view by a low hill, so the Trojans could not see what the Greeks were doing there. It was possible for the Mycenaean warriors to march or drive their chariots out onto the Plain of Troy with little warning.

The Trojans and their allies mustered on a low hill called Thorn Hill. This was in effect the eastern side slope of the wide valley of the Scamander. Assembled on this rising ground in a long line from just outside the south gate of Troy and going on for perhaps 3 km (1¾ miles), halfway to the town of Thymbra, the allied contingents had a good view of the Mycenaeans' movements out on the Plain of Troy. Thorn Hill was directly opposite the valley leading to the Greek camp, and afforded plenty of space for the host of warriors, their tents, servants, armourers, surgeons and caterers. The River Scamander flowed across the plain in front of the site, giving the Thorn Hill encampment a significant defence. It would not have been possible for the Greeks to charge across the river and make a surprise attack on the allies' camp. The river was negotiable, but only slowly and with care. The Thorn Hill site was also close to the south gate of Troy, the Scaean Gate, if they were in desperate need of refuge, or if Hector and the other Trojan leaders needed to consult King Priam, who watched everything from his vantage point in the citadel.

The muster was organized so that the Trojans and their closest allies, their neighbours the Dardanians, were in the centre with the Lykians, Mysians, Phrygians and Maionians on their left flank and the Carians, Paionians, Leleges, Cauceones and Pelasgoi on their right flank. The Thracians, who arrived late, probably assembled at the north-western end of this impressive array of warriors, on the extreme end of the ridge, very close to the southern shore of the Bay of Troy.

Homer describes five battles, which followed much the same pattern: armed skirmishing with infantry and chariots on the Plain of Troy. After each battle or skirmish, the Mycenaeans withdrew to their camp and the Trojans withdrew to Thorn Hill. After the fifth attack, in which the Mycenaeans routed the Trojans, the victors broke into the city of Troy and rushed into the citadel. Achilles led the attack on the citadel, where he was killed by Paris, one of the many sons of Priam. It was at this moment of crisis that Aeneas, the ruler and military leader of the Dardanians, dissociated himself from the Trojans' fate and went home to Mount Ida. This could have been presented as epic cowardice and betrayal, but somehow the reputation of Aeneas has survived unscathed. The epic poems explain his behaviour as a response to omens. The reality may be that when he saw the Mycenaeans wheeling siege engines across the plain he knew the siege could only end in defeat for the Trojans. Aeneas took his Dardanian warriors back home so that they would live to fight another day. It is likely that other Trojan allies fell away at this point too, leaving the Trojans to suffer the humiliation of capture and slaughter alone.

The famous 'wooden horse' was almost certainly an ancient poet's misunderstanding of a Mycenaean siege engine, which may have been nicknamed a 'horse'. Images survive from the time of the Trojan War, showing large, roughly horse- or elephant-shaped siege engines. Each engine was a leather-covered cart with a short tower in front. Inside a team of men manoeuvred a heavy duty spear many metres long; this was used to prod the upper parts of the walls. The lower parts of the walls of Troy were made of stone, but the upper parts were made of mudbrick. The siege engines were used to poke holes in the upper walls. Once the walls were lowered, ladders could be thrown up to let the invaders in. It was a technique in use throughout the Middle East at that time and in later centuries.

The Mycenaeans captured and sacked Troy, killing its king, Priam, its crown prince, Hector, and all of Priam's other sons and, in their usual way, taking women as prizes. There is no epic poem tradition of 'what happened next' at Troy, beyond the bare fact that it was Aeneas, a third cousin of Hector's, who became king of Troy and king of Wilusa.

The epic poems concern themselves with what happened to the Greeks, and in particular the Greek leaders. The war exhausted the Mycenaean Greeks and although they had technically won the war by sacking Troy, they did not take the city over and turn it into a Greek colony. The whole enterprise had drained their resources, and while they were away from home (for far too long) their kingdoms were subverted by usurpers. It was only a matter of decades before the Mycenaean civilization collapsed. One Mycenaean centre after another, including Agamemnon's Mycenae, fell around the year 1200 BC.

Repercussions

The motives for the Trojan War were partly political and partly economic; the Mycenaeans wanted to control the eastern coast of the Aegean as well as the western coast, and they wanted to encroach on the Hittite sphere of influence while they could. They were also partly cultural. Military exploits and adventures were an integral part of the culture of the warrior elites. The acquisition of women was a secondary motive: something to take home for the weekend. Taking women as loot was a normal part of warfare. Some were used as sex slaves, others were used to swell the workforce in the textile industry.

The taking of Helen by Paris – if that actually happened - was probably just one of thousands of such abductions in the Bronze Age. But it is rather unlikely that getting Helen back was the real reason for waging a large-scale and protracted war. That looks like a romantic gloss added for poetic effect. One of the most sobering aspects about the Trojan War is that it was remembered by succeeding generations, right through to the present day, not because of what actually happened but because of what was written about what happened. The literary war –

the bards' version of the war – was, from at least as early as 700 BC, far more momentous and influential than the actual war. The young men of one generation after another have tried in some way or another to measure themselves against the Homeric ideal of heroism, of what it means to be a man. The character of Achilles in particular has remained the ultimate role model for young soldiers. Alexander the Great always slept with a copy of the *Iliad* under his pillow.

THE PERSIAN INVASION OF GREECE
(494–48 BC)

The main sources of information for this early conflict are the writings of Herodotus, who died in about 424 BC, and Thucydides, who wrote a history of the wars. There is also an account of the Second Persian invasion in the drama *Persae* by Aeschylus, who fought at the Battle of Marathon in the First Invasion and may have fought in the Second Invasion, too.

THE FIRST PERSIAN INVASION 490 BC

The Persian Empire had been created in a very short time by Cyrus the Great, a daring military strategist and skilled diplomatist. The Aegean coast of Anatolia was conquered for him by Haspagus, while Cyrus himself concentrated on taking Babylon in the east. Cyrus was succeeded by his son Cambyses, who was overthrown and replaced by Darius the Great. Darius reorganised the Persian Empire into twenty provinces and decided to enlarge it into south-east Europe.

He led his invasion army across the Bosporus and first took it northwards to the Danube Valley. But he fared badly in battle against the Scythians and the Imperial force would probably have been surrounded and massacred but for the Ionian Greek contingent (from south-western Anatolia), which held the Danube bridgehead while the Imperial force withdrew. This experience led the Ionians to decide that it was time to rebel against Persian rule. They sent an envoy from Miletus, their main city, across to Greece to ask the Greek city-states to give them armed support against the Persians. Sparta refused, but

Athens agreed, offering twenty ships; the town of Eretria on Euboea sent five ships.

Initially the Ionian revolt was successful. The Greeks marched into the city of Sartus, where the Persian provincial governor (satrap) had his headquarters, and destroyed it. Then the Persians retaliated. At the battle of Lade in 494 BC they destroyed the Greek fleet; then Miletus was destroyed and its inhabitants massacred or enslaved. Darius then launched a punitive strike against the Greek mainland states that had aided the Ionians, though the first fleet to cross the Aegean was seriously damaged in a storm off Mount Athos. A second fleet was sent under new commanders. Eretria was immediately captured and destroyed. Then the Persian fleet crossed from Euboea to the north coast of Attica, the Athenians' territory, landing on the Plain of Marathon.

THE BATTLE OF MARATHON 490 BC

From Marathon the road ran south to Athens. It was really the only road to Athens, as it skirted the slopes of Mount Pentelicus. The Persians arrived to find the Athenians blocking the road. In a fierce and desperate battle for survival, the Athenian warriors routed the Persians.

The Persians who fought in the battle and survived joined those who had not been assigned to it; they went by sea round the coast of Attica to Cape Sunium with the intention of reaching Athens from the south. But they found that the Athenian army had returned from Marathon and were manning the city's defences. The commanders of the Imperial fleet decided to withdraw and return to Anatolia. The Battle of Marathon had been a complete success in fending off a Persian attack on Athens.

THE SECOND PERSIAN INVASION 480 BC

During the ten years that followed, Darius the Great was succeeded as Persian King of Kings by his son Xerxes, who prepared a new invasion of Greece. He began with a diplomatic initiative, sending envoys to each of the city-states to persuade as many of them as possible to surrender without bloodshed.

He also prepared an ambitious plan to create a huge floating pontoon bridge across the Hellespont, the sea channel separating Asia Minor from Europe. The bridge, really a double bridge, deployed more than 600 ships. Remembering the earlier maritime disaster off Mount Athos, he also ordered the digging of a navigable canal across the isthmus of the narrow peninsula, so that his fleet would not need to sail round its tip.

Then Xerxes conscripted contingents from every province of the Persian Empire. This was the same technique for gathering a large army that had been used by the Hittite high king Muwatallis for the battle of Kadesh and by the Achaean (Mycenaean) king Agamemnon for the Trojan War. Xerxes' army was the biggest army that had until that time been gathered; probably more than 150,000 men, though Herodotus claimed it was more than a million. The army included well-trained fast cavalry armed with spears and bows. The fleet consisted of about 1,200 ships, some for transporting warriors and horses, some for carrying supplies. The horses had to be carried everywhere from battlefield to battlefield as they were not at this time fitted with horseshoes. Greece was an arid and mainly unproductive land, so provisions for the army had to be available from the sea.

From his headquarters at Sardes in Lydia, Xerxes sent envoys to all the Greek city states except Athens and Sparta, demanding their submission. Xerxes was planning to annexe the whole of Greece, and this was why he made such elaborate and expensive preparations – including negotiating agreements with Carthaginian and Phoenician cities in the Western Mediterranean by which they would attack the colonies of the Greeks there and so stifle Greek resources.

Finally, when all of his preparations were in place, early in 480 BC Xerxes led his great army across the Hellespont bridge into Thrace. There he boarded his fleet and made his way in three separate divisions south-westwards towards Thessaly.

The Greeks were well aware of the impending confrontation, and all the Greek city-states sent representatives to a Congress in the Temple of

Poseidon at the city of Corinth in 481 BC to discuss their strategy. The Athenians and Spartans led the way by forming a defensive alliance; a combined response gave them the best chance of success. Morale was given a severe blow when the oracle at Delphi predicted disaster for the Greeks and told them their only hope was a wooden wall. Most people assumed the oracle meant the timber palisade round the Athenian Acropolis, but Themistocles had a different interpretation; he thought the oracle meant that Greece would be saved by its wooden ships.

Different strategies for defence were favoured by different representatives, according to their location in Greece. The Spartan and other Peloponnesian delegates wanted the main defence installed at the Isthmus of Corinth, which was the only land route into the Peloponnese. The Athenians and the delegates from city-states in central Greece objected strongly to this proposal, as it left their states exposed to invasion by the Persian army. The defence of the Isthmus in any case ignored the possibility (probability) that the Persians would simply use their ships to land troops by sea on each side of the Isthmus or at any point on the long coastline of the Peloponnese. The defenders of the Isthmus could too easily be outflanked. The defence of Greece need to be the defence of the whole of Greece and therefore needed to be further north.

A force would be sent to engage the Persians in Thessaly and hold them there. The Greek numbers were low, so defending Greece in that way could only be done by blocking narrow passes. In response to a request from the Thessalonians, a force of 10,000 foot soldiers was sent. It was led by Evaenetus and Themistocles. They travelled by sea to Hallos and marched from there to the Vale of Tempe. When they got there, Evaenetus realised that there were too many passes for his force to man, so he retreated to the Isthmus of Corinth, in spite of the earlier debate.

The Council of Corinth then decided to try to defend the states of central Greece, west of the Euboea Channel. This was an area of narrow and defensible passes. The narrowness of the Euboea Channel would also make it difficult for the huge Persian fleet to operate there. The idea was for the land force to hold up the Persian army long enough to tempt the Persian fleet into the Euboea Channel, where the Greek fleet stood a chance of defeating it. If the army was impeded and the fleet defeated, the Persians might then give up the invasion plan and withdraw.

THE BATTLE OF THERMOPYLAE 480 BC

The Greeks planned to make their stand at the Pass of Thermopylae, supported by their fleet in the Malian Gulf. The Greek army of between 7,000 and 8,000 foot soldiers (hoplites and lightly armed troops) was commanded by Leonidas, a Spartan king. Some of the warriors were Boeotians, whose loyalty to the Greek cause was suspected. There was also the Spartan King's Bodyguard, the famous Three Hundred, though it is likely from the historical and archaeological evidence that there were 3,000 of them in reality. Themistocles was in command of the Greek fleet. The legendary account has it that this force consisted of a mere 300 triremes, but again it was probably much larger, and perhaps 3,000 strong. This substantial fleet was stationed in the bay just to the north of Euboea.

The Persian plan was to make a co-ordinated attack, with the Persian army arriving at Thermopylae at the same moment that their fleet arrived at the northern end of the Euboea Channel and, an unpleasant surprise for the Greeks, the simultaneous arrival of a Phoenician fleet at the southern end of the Channel, trapping the Greek fleet. That, at any rate, is what historians believe Xerxes intended. There was a storm at sea, in which the Persian fleet lost 400 warships and the Phoenician fleet was scattered. This left the Greek fleet unharmed.

The disorder of the Persian fleet gave the Greeks an obvious advantage, and Themistocles attacked with his ships. The sea battle that followed had no clear outcome, but showed that the Greeks ships were more mobile than the Persians. The following day the Persians took the initiative in a counter-offensive, but this too had no clear outcome. There was heavy destruction on both sides, but at least the Greek fleet had succeeded in stopping the Persians supporting their army at Thermopylae.

The pass at Thermopylae consisted of three narrow ravines, which in the ancient accounts are described as 'gates'. Leonidas decided to defend the central defile, which was only 4 metres (13 ft) wide. It could be held by only a few men against an army of any size. In order to prevent his small force in the central gate from being outflanked from the south, Leonidas positioned 1,000 troops to guard the next pass as a precaution – and waited for Xerxes' warriors to arrive.

When he reached the Malian Plain, Xerxes waited there for four days. Probably he was hoping to hear news that his fleet had crushed the Greek fleet in a great naval victory before going on to attack the Greek hoplites in the pass at Thermopylae. On the fifth day, Xerxes mounted his attack. He was repulsed. The Greek hoplites were well trained, well armed, well equipped. Under the closely confined conditions of the narrow pass, Xerxes' superior numbers counted for nothing. Xerxes sent in his troops again on the second day and he was repulsed in exactly the same way and realised that some other way would need to be found to break through. But he was running out of supplies, and the Persian navy was being held back by the Greek fleet.

Xerxes was given the solution by a man called Ephialtes, who told him about the existence of the pass that was guarded by the Phocian force. Xerxes sent his troops, called the Immortals, along this path, guided by Ephialtes. The Persians routed the Phocians, cleared the path and gained access to Leonidas' defile from the far end. Leonidas heard that he and his troops were in danger from behind and started to make a strategic withdrawal. He sent the contingents from central Greece south, keeping only a small force, a core of Spartans, Peloponnesian allies and some Theban troops. Some historians believe the contingents who moved away actually fled, ran away, but this is uncertain. Leonidas moved the small remaining force to a hillock east of the middle gate and prepared to make a final rearguard stand there. He sent a messenger with news of the disaster to Artemision, where the Greek fleet was waiting. By the time the messenger had reached the fleet, Leonidas and his Three Hundred were overrun by huge numbers of Persians. It is said that only the Thebans asked to be spared. Leonidas and those who remained were surrounded and massacred. When Themistocles heard the news from Thermopylae, he moved the Greek fleet south, round the coastline of Attica, withdrawing to the relative safety of the Saronic Gulf, the bay south of Athens. The Greek fleet was finally anchored off the island of Salamis. The fleet was safe, but the whole of Attica was now left wide open to the Persian invaders. The Persians occupied Boeotia, setting up their headquarters in the city of Thebes, preparing to move south. The Athenians saw that there was no hope of defending their city, so they evacuated the old, the women and children to the islands of Aegina and Salamis for safety; almost all the able-bodied men boarded the ships, ready to fight the next battle. A small garrison was left to defend the Acropolis.

The Spartans and the rest of the Peloponnesians set to work making a fortification across the narrow neck of land connecting the Peloponnese with the rest of Greece. This was the defensive work the Spartans had wanted from the start.

THE BATTLE OF SALAMIS 480 BC

The Persian army moved south into Attica and met little resistance. Soon all of Attica was under Persian control. But as long as the Greek fleet hovered in the bay just off the south coast of Attica the Persians could not be totally secure. Xerxes knew he would have to confront the Greeks at sea.

Themistocles himself wanted an early battle with the Persians, so that the fighting could be on their own, Greek, terms, but other Greek leaders did not agree. The Peloponnesians as always wanted to focus on defending the Isthmus. Themistocles nevertheless managed to get his way, simply because the Athenian contingent now made up over half the fleet. Themistocles was able to argue that if the fleet was not going to be used to defend Athens he would withdraw all the Athenians.

Themistocles was keen to wage a sea battle with the Persians in the narrow strip of water between Salamis and the mainland of Attica because he knew the Greek ships were far easier to manoeuvre than the Persian ships in the confined space. They also had the advantage of knowing the waters well. It was a location that favoured a Greek victory. Themistocles had his way.

The Greek fleet was poised between the north coast of the island of Salamis and the Attic coast just north-west of Piraeus. The Persian fleet took up its position in a line from Salamis to Piraeus, the ships facing north and three deep. Themistocles deliberately left the channel to the west, between Salamis and Megara, open in the hope of tempting Xerxes to divide his fleet and use the same tactic he had wanted to deploy in the Euboea Channel. Themistocles' trick worked. Xerxes did exactly as Themistocles hoped and sent a flotilla of Egyptian ships round Salamis to the south to seal the western channel.

The Greek fleet drew up in battle formation, facing the coast of Attica, the Athenians on the left wing, and the ships from Aegina on the right wing. The Persians were organizing themselves, with the Ionian ships on the left wing and the Phoenicians on the right, when the Greeks attacked, forcing the Persian ships in the front line back into the rows behind and causing major confusion. Then the Athenian flanking ships attacked the Phoenician ships, pushing them back into the middle of the Persian fleet and onto the Attic coast. This successful opening manoeuvre by the Greeks was followed by a complete encirclement of the centre of the Persian fleet. The Ionian ships withdrew and the battle was over.

Xerxes had suffered a resounding defeat, losing as many as 200 ships. He took the remains of his fleet back to Phaleron, then to the Hellespont. Xerxes was now in an impossible position. His fleet was disabled and he was unable to provision his huge land army without it. He had no choice but to withdraw his troops from Greece. Xerxes had made the fundamental mistake of assuming that his superior numbers would be invincible. It had led him to be lazy in his tactical thinking. He also underestimated the inspiriting power of independence as a cause worth fighting for. The Greeks had shown remarkable courage, energy and creativity in the war, simply because their survival as free nations depended on winning. They had to win or die. The victory at Salamis restored the morale of the Greeks, while the heroic last stand of Leonidas at Thermopylae became a defining legend in ancient Greece.

Xerxes had to return to Asia Minor to stop the widespread revolt that his defeat might inspire. He took the bulk of his army back across the Hellespont and sent his fleet across as well. In Thessaly, Thrace and Macedonia, he left some troops under the command of Mardonius and Artabazus, and these were a continuing threat to the Greeks and their future independence.

THE BATTLE OF PLATAEA 479 BC

The Persians tried to entice the Greeks into making a treaty with Persia, but they failed. Then Mardonius marched on Athens, with a view to menacing them into submission. The Athenians made an agreement with Sparta to launch an immediate offensive against Mardonius, not least because there was a possibility that Xerxes might send Mardonius massive reinforcements at any time; it was safer to defeat Mardonius before any reinforcements arrived.

The Spartans advanced to Corinth and across the Isthmus. Meanwhile Mardonius had reached Athens and set the city on fire. After that he withdrew to Boeotia, where there were extensive plains on which he could use his cavalry units to effect. Mardonius was choosing where he would fight the Greeks. He deployed his army on the Asopus Plain between Thebes and Plataea. While he waited for the Greeks, he had his men clear the trees from the plain; he was preparing his field of battle like a cricket square. Then he waited.

A Greek hoplite force numbering 35,000 and led by Pausanius appeared, and camped close to Plataea, overlooking the plain. Mardonius then foolishly attacked at once with his cavalry, but the hill slope was entirely unsuitable for cavalry. The Persians lost the battle and were forced to retreat. Some historians believe Mardonius deliberately sacrificed his cavalry in order to embolden the Greeks into going down onto the plain and so put themselves in a much more vulnerable situation.

Pausanius marched his troops onto the plain between Plataea and Asopus. The Greek warriors lined up facing them across the river. They stayed in these positions for eight days, each side waiting for the other to make a move. After a week Pausanius could no longer continue to wait because Persian raids in the hills behind him were threatening his food supplies, but it was Mardonius who made the first move, attacking with his cavalry.

The Persians outflanked the Greeks and separated them from their single source of water, a spring that lay behind the Spartan position. The Greeks were now in a difficult position. Mardonius seemed content to hold them down until they ran out of food and water. Pausanius proposed to withdraw the Spartans, letting them get back up into the hills to retake the main passes and secure the supplies of food and water. Meanwhile the allied troops at the centre of the Greek army would retreat south towards Plataea, and after that the Athenians would move south-eastwards to take up position as the new Greek centre.

It was a complex manoeuvre and several factors impeded it. To begin with, Pausanius was attempting to do all this under cover of darkness, which made co-ordination very difficult. It looks as if the Athenians may have refused to obey Pausanius' order to retreat, and that meant that they found themselves cut off from the rest of the army. There seems also to have been disagreement among the Spartans, which caused delays, and the manoeuvre was not completed until daylight.

Mardonius sent in the Persian cavalry to distract the Spartans until the Persian infantry could be sent in. He also sent the Boeotians to attack the exposed Athenians. The Greek cause for a while appeared to be lost, but Pausanius saw that the sheer numbers of Persians were causing confusion – on the Persian side – and launched a counter-attack. A violent and bloody battle followed, and it reached no conclusion until Mardonius himself was killed and his men fled.

The battle had come close to being a massacre of the Greek army, but as so often happens chance played a major part. The chance killing of the Persian commander was in this instance the decider. The Greeks were able to make huge capital out of the victory, going on to capture and destroy the Persian camp. They then laid siege to the Persian-occupied city of Thebes, which fell after twenty days. The Theban city leaders who had gone over to the Persian side were summarily executed. The rest of the Persian army was by this stage in full retreat, falling back to the Hellespont under the command of Artabazus.

SECOND IONIAN REVOLT 478 BC

The Greeks had word from their Ionian cousins asking for help in a second revolt against Persian rule. They asked, once again, for a Greek fleet to help them oust the Persians. The Greeks obliged, sending a fleet from Delos under the Spartan king Leotychidas. It called at the island of Samos, close to the Anatolian coast, and sailed on from there to Mycale, where the local Persian power base was. Leotychidas landed there and attacked the Persian position. He also attacked and destroyed the Persian fleet which was hauled up on the beach.

By destroying the sea power of the Persian Empire, the Greeks made themselves safe from any further invasion from Asia Minor. The Greeks had won so decisively, and against such overwhelming odds, that no successor of Xerxes would be so foolish as to try it again. It meant that for a very long time to come, Greeks would be masters of the Aegean Sea.

The Greeks moved north to take the town of Sestos and take control of the Hellespont, which the Persians regarded as their doorway into Greece. Xanthippus led the Athenians in the siege of Sestos, which fell early in 478 BC. There were still some Persian troops in Thrace, and the fighting did not end, finally, until the Peace of Callias in 448 BC.

THE PELOPONNESIAN WARS

(431–404 BC)

This was a protracted conflict fought by the city-state of Athens and its neighbours and allies against the Peloponnesian League, a confederation of southern Greek city states led by Sparta. It fed on the same tensions that had divided the states to the north and south of the Gulf of Corinth during the war against the Persian Empire.

What we know about these wars comes from two main sources. The most famous account is the *History of the Peloponnesian War* by the Athenian general and statesman Thucydides. This covers the wars until 411 BC and has been accepted by most subsequent historians as a true and honest account of what happened. In 424 BC, Thucydides was exiled for a military failure, and he wrote his history mainly during the period of exile that followed. Xenophon's *Hellenica* continues where Thucydides' account stops, though Xenophon was writing a memoir rather than a history, and his account is selective and less objective.

THE FIRST PELOPONNESIAN WAR, OR ARCHIDAMIAN WAR

The city-states of southern Greece were almost exclusively land powers. Sparta and its allies were able to muster big land armies that were almost invincible, thanks to the rigorous training of the Spartan troops. The Peloponnesian armies repeatedly invaded Attica, the state of which Athens was the capital. Meanwhile Athens, using its supremacy at sea, raided the coastal towns of the Peloponnese. The Athenian Empire was mainly based on the mainland peninsula of Attica, but its wealth came from the islands of the Aegean Sea, which were forced to pay tribute to Athens. This empire was naturally maintained by naval power. Because of their significantly different power bases, Athens and Sparta were not able to fight decisive battles, which led to the attenuation of the war.

The strategy adopted by Sparta in the Archidamian War, named after the king of Sparta, Archidamus II, was to invade the farmland round Athens and cut the city off from its resources. In fact Athens did not suffer greatly from this as it was able to maintain its access to the sea, and therefore imported supplies, by means of a strongly defended corridor leading from Athens to the port of Piraeus; it was called the Long Walls. When the Peloponnesian armies were in Attica, many of the farmers abandoned their farms and took shelter inside the Long Walls. This was not a major hardship as the Peloponnesian armies only stayed in Attica for three weeks at a time before returning home. This was in the old tradition of hoplite warfare, in which warriors expected to be released from duty to take part in the harvest. It was also not safe for the Spartan slaves to be left for too long unsupervised: they might get out of control.

The Athenians were guided by their general Pericles, who advised avoiding fighting an open battle with the highly trained Spartan hoplites. He recommended relying on the Athenian strength, naval power. The Athenian fleet went into the attack, winning a victory at Naupactus. But in 430 BC Athens was struck by an outbreak of plague, which wiped out 30,000 of its citizens, including Pericles and his sons. A quarter of the Athenian population died. This drastically reduced the Athenians' fighting power, and fear of catching plague made it difficult for Athens even to hire foreign mercenaries.

After the death of Pericles, the Athenians swung away from his strategy of avoiding direct confrontation. Instead they took the offensive. The rising figure in the Athens democracy at this time was Cleon, who was a hawk. The Athenian troops were led by a talented new general called Demosthenes, so this new strategy met with some success. Athens took the war into the next states to the west, Boeotia and Aetolia, and started establishing fortified military posts round the Peloponnese. One of these was on the island of Sphacteria, close to the town of Pylos in the south-west. Here the Athenians had a significant success.

The Spartan way of life and in particular its aggression in warfare depended on its slave class, who were called helots; these helots were expected to attend to food production while the citizens warriors were either in military training or fighting. Not surprisingly, during the war, many of these helots took the opportunity to run away. Many of them ran to Pylos, a good long distance from the city of Sparta, and they were attracted to the Athenian post on Sphacteria. The Spartans were afraid of a helot revolt anyway, and this group of helots was getting bolder because of the presence of the Athenians; the Spartans decided to take action.

Demosthenes succeeded in trapping a group of Spartan warriors on Sphacteria, but then found that they would not surrender to him. Though he was inexperienced in the field, Cleon rashly boasted to the Assembly in Athens that he would finish the stalemate, and then won a spectacular victory over the Spartans at the Battles of Pylos and Sphacteria in 425 BC. During these battles, the Athenians were able to capture up to 400 Spartan hoplites, which gave them bargaining power as well as victory.

Then the Spartan general Brasidas raised an army and seized an Athenian colony at Amphipolis, which controlled the nearby silver mines that financed the Athenian war effort. It was Thucydides' failure to prevent the Spartan seizure of Amphipolis – he arrived too late – that led to his exile. In a subsequent battle Brasidas was killed; then the Spartans and Athenians agreed to exchange hostages and sign a truce.

THE PEACE OF NICIAS

Both Brasidas and Cleon had been killed in the fighting. With the leading hawks on both sides dead, there was an opportunity to sign a truce. The Peace of Nicias lasted six years, but it was an uncertain and unsatisfactory peace, with continual skirmishing breaking out all round southern Greece. The Spartans themselves were not fighting, but their allies were keen to break the truce and rebel. Argos, a powerful state that had kept independent of Sparta, was encouraged and supported by Athens in creating a coalition of democratic states in the Peloponnese, including Elis in the north-west. Sparta tried to break this rebel coalition up, failed and as a result the leadership of King Agis of Sparta was called into question by the Spartans themselves.

This moment of Spartan weakness was seized upon by the Argives and their coalition allies. Together with a small Athenian force under Alcibiades, they moved to take the city of Tegea, north of the city of Sparta.

The Battle of Mantinea was the biggest land battle to be fought in the whole of the Peloponnesian Wars. The Spartans and Tegeans faced a coalition army composed of warriors from Argos, Athens, Mantinea and Arcadia. At first the coalition army was successful, but in the end the Spartan élite force overcame it and won a victory which saved the city of Sparta itself from defeat. Defeated, the coalition broke up and most of its members rejoined the Peloponnesian League. The victory at Mantinea was a very important one in pulling Sparta back from the brink of defeat and re-establishing its power throughout the Peloponnese.

THE SICILIAN EXPEDITION (415–413 BC)

After seventeen years of the Peloponnesian Wars, the Athenians had word from Sicily that one of their allies was under attack from the city-state of Syracuse. The Syracusans were ethnic Dorians, like the Spartans, while the Athenians and their allies in Sicily were ethnically Ionian. This ethnic contrast gave a particular point to the Athenian decision to go the aid of their distant allies. It was a huge mistake.

The expedition leader was the brilliant and volatile young Alcibiades, who urged the Athenians on into this new war. A vision of great additional wealth was conjured up; conquering all of Sicily would have brought Athens a huge new tranche of resources. There was a peculiar and unsettling incident shortly before the expedition was due to depart. The herms, the religious statues in the streets of Athens, were deliberately mutilated. Nobody knew who had committed this sacrilege, but suspicion fell on Alcibiades and he was formally accused. He asked to be put on trial at once, but the Athenians decided to send him to Sicily first. By the time he had arrived in Sicily, the Athenians had changed their minds and recalled him for trial. Suspecting, with justification, that his enemies had been plotting against him in Athens and that his conviction was a foregone conclusion, Alcibiades defected to Sparta. He told the Spartans that the Athenians intended to conquer not only Sicily but all of Italy, then use all of the new resources and additional manpower to conquer the Peloponnese.

Now Nicias was given command of the Sicilian expedition. He had over 100 ships, about 5,000 infantrymen and only thirty cavalry. Really, it was too small a force to succeed against the big and well-trained army of Syracuse, which was a large port, stoutly defended by walls. Even so, the early indications were that the Athenians might succeed. Several Sicilian cities joined the Athenians straight away. But Nicias did not pursue his advantage. He did not attack Syracuse straight away and by the close of the campaign season of 415 BC he had inflicted very little damage on Syracuse.

As winter came on, Ninias withdrew to gather allies for a spring offensive. But this long delay enabled the Syracusans to send to Sparta for reinforcements. The Spartan general Gylippus duly arrived with extra troops, raised even more extra troops from other Sicilian cities and went to relieve the siege of Syracuse. When he reached the city he took charge of the Syracusan force and routed the Athenians.

Demosthenes tried to persuade Nicias to retreat to Athens, but again Nicias delayed. Nicias eventually agreed to this, but then there was a bad omen, an eclipse of the moon, which made him delay longer. This delay proved costly, as it forced the Athenians to fight the Syracusans at sea in the Great Harbour of Syracuse. The Athenians were totally defeated in this great battle. Nicias and Demosthenes marched their surviving troops along the coast to the south, hoping to encounter allies and support, but the Syracusans sent their cavalry after them. The Athenians were all either killed or taken as slaves; the entire force was annihilated.

The Sicilian expedition was a total catastrophe for the Athenians, and a grim prelude to the final phase of the Peloponnesian Wars.

THE SECOND PELOPONNESIAN WAR

The Spartans had sent aid to Syracuse. Now they decided to pursue their advantage and take the war all the way back to Athens. Following the advice of Alcibiades, the Spartan army fortified Decelea, near Athens. This made it impossible for the Athenians to feed off their agricultural land and also stopped them receiving incoming supplies overland. Now Athens could only be fed from the sea, which was a great additional expense. The Spartans also crippled the Athenian economy by stopping mining activity at the nearby silver mines. This they achieved by freeing the 20,000 Athenian slaves who operated the mines. The Athenians' wealth ebbed away, forcing them to levy even higher tribute from subject territories; this in turn raised the political tension within the Athenian Empire, making open rebellion more likely. When news of the total Athenian defeat in Sicily arrived, it looked to everyone as if the end of the Athenian Empire was imminent.

Yet the Athenians managed to survive. One reason was that their enemies were slow to act. Another was that the Ionian states that mounted rebellions expected the Peloponnesian League to offer them protection. When that was not forthcoming, the rebel states decided to go back to Athens. Even the Persians, who were by this stage allies of the Spartans against Athens, were slow to provide funds and ships. Another problem was that although Spartan troops were well trained in warfare, their officers were not trained to negotiate; they were clumsy and politically inept.

The Athenians had cunningly put aside 100 ships to be used only in an emergency. Now the emergency was upon the city, and they functioned as the core of the Athenian fleet during the remainder of the war. In Athens itself there was a revolution, in which a group of 400 men seized power. At this point, with the change of regime, a negotiated peace with Sparta might have been achieved. Unfortunately the revived Athenian fleet, which was currently stationed at the island of Samos on the far side of the Aegean, would not accept it.

In 411 BC, the Athenian fleet fought the Battle of Syme against the

Spartans. In an extraordinary new development, the Athenian fleet appointed the unreliable Alcibiades as its commander, and continued to fight the war against Sparta in the name of Athens. The intransigence of the Athenian fleet led to the reversal of the regime change in Athens, where a democratic government was re-established within two years.

Alcibiades still carried enormous weight in Athens. He was a known and formally condemned traitor, but he was still a major player, a charismatic celebrity. It seemed that the Athenians could no more do without Alcibiades than Homer's Greeks in the Trojan War could do without the volatile Achilles. Alcibiades helped to re-establish democracy in Athens, by applying pressure from outside. He also persuaded the Athenian fleet to attack the Spartans at the Battle of Cyzicus (410 BC); the Spartan fleet was destroyed.

Following this turning point, the Athenians won a sequence of victories, and regained many of the lost territories of its empire. Alcibiades was largely responsible for these successes.

LYSANDER AND THE SURRENDER OF ATHENS (406–404 BC)

The Spartans had a talented general called Lysander. In 406 BC, he was responsible for winning a victory for the Spartans at the Battle of Notium. This was only a minor sea battle, but it meant the end of Alcibiades' career. The Athenians would not re-elect him as general after that and he went into self-imposed exile, perhaps sensing that it was dangerous for him to remain in Athens. After that the Athenians were victorious at the Battle of Arginusae; the Spartans under the command of Callicratidas lost seventy ships, while the Athenians lost twenty-five. Even so, because of the bad weather conditions during the battle, the Athenians were unable to rescue stranded crews or finish off the Spartans. These failures outraged the citizens of Athens, who in an act of supreme folly put on trial six of their greatest naval commanders – and executed them. It was a major self-inflicted injury. The navy was then demoralised and functioning without its most experienced commanders.

Lysander, the new Spartan general, was a great naval strategist. But he was also a very cunning diplomat. He had developed a good personal rapport with Cyrus, the son of the Persian king Darius II. In 405 BC Lysander took his fleet to the Hellespont, which was where Athens' supply of grain entered the Aegean Sea. The Athenian fleet had no choice but to follow. What followed was a straightforward battle for survival. The Battle of Aegospotami was an unqualified victory for Lysander and a total defeat for the Athenians, who had 168 of their ships destroyed; the Spartans captured up to 4,000 Athenian sailors, too. Just twelve Athenian ships escaped from the battle, and several of them sailed to Cyprus, taking with them General Conon, who was understandably keen not to face the Athenian assembly, which would certainly have condemned him to execution.

By 404 BC, Athens was faced with starvation after the long siege. What happened next would have seemed unthinkable a few decades earlier: Athens surrendered. Her allies quickly surrendered, too. Sparta then set about humiliating the Athenians. The great defensive walls were demolished. The city was stripped of its remaining ships and all of its overseas possessions. Thebes and Corinth wanted to see the city of Athens completely destroyed and all of its citizens enslaved. The Spartans showed a certain amount of magnanimity in victory and held back from this total destruction. They announced that Athens had done the Greeks a good service at a time when Greece was in danger and they would not destroy the city. Instead Athens was taken, in effect, as a Spartan colony; the city was to have the same friends and enemies as Sparta. The Spartans had their way, as neither Corinth nor Thebes was strong enough to disobey the will of Sparta.

The Spartans set up a reactionary regime in Athens, rule by Thirty Tyrants, but this was overthrown and democracy was restored by Thrasybulus in 403 BC.

Aftermath

The Peloponnesian Wars brought about sweeping changes in the world of ancient Greece. Athens had been by far the strongest city-state in mainland Greece or the Aegean basin before the wars began. At the end of the wars, Athens had been stripped of its power and status, and reduced virtually to a vassal-state, while Sparta was the strongest state in Greece. There were major economic consequences as well. Athens was devastated and never regained its pre-war economic buoyancy. There were long-term shifts in Greek society and mentalité; from that point on the conflict between Athens and Sparta made civil war a recurring civil war a commonplace and that warfare became an all-out struggle between city-states, with no holds barred – warfare complete with large-scale atrocities. Long-held religious and cultural taboos and chivalric customs were cast aside. Whole cities were destroyed. The Peloponnesian Wars marked the end of the golden age of Greece.

THE WARS OF ALEXANDER THE GREAT
(338–323 BC)

THE CONQUEROR

Alexander the Great (356–323 BC), who was Alexander III, King of Macedon, from 336 BC until his death, was one of the most successful military leaders of all time. He won every single battle he fought. Alexander's first task as a conqueror was to unify the many city-states of Greece. After achieving this, he went across into Asia Minor to conquer the Persian Empire and he gradually extended his own empire eastwards until it reached the Indus Valley. He would apparently have gone on, driven by a desire to reach the edge of the world to see the Great Outer Sea Aristotle had told him about, but he turned back, at the insistence of his own army. After a twelve-year campaign of almost constant fighting, Alexander died. It seems that, had he lived, he would have attempted to conquer Europe as well.

As a young man, Alexander helped his father win the decisive Battle of Chaeronea in 338 BC. This battle was fought against Athens and Thebes. It was the cavalry wing commanded by Alexander that wiped out the Theban elite corps, the Sacred Band of Thebes, that was regarded as invincible. After the battle, Philip of Macedon threw a great celebratory feast. Alexander was conspicuously missing from the celebration and it is believed that at the time he was tending the wounded and burying the dead – of both sides.

Following the assassination of Philip, the army proclaimed Alexander king. The city-states to the south which had reluctantly pledged loyalty to the dead king saw his replacement by a young and inexperienced new king this as an opportunity to revolt, possibly even regain their independence. But Alexander moved fast. The Thebans were startled to see the twenty-year-old Alexander at their gates with his army, and they submitted to him at once. When representatives of the Greek states assembled at the Isthmus of Corinth, they elected him as commander-in-chief of the Greeks in the struggle against Persia. This was a role previously bestowed on his father.

In 335 BC, Alexander attacked and subdued the Illyrians and Thracians in order to secure the lower Danube Valley and make his northern border safe. While he was very successfully engaged to the north, the Thebans and Athenians thought it was safe to mount new rebellions. As before, Alexander responded immediately. Athens relented, but Thebes resisted. But the resistance was futile. Alexander suppressed the Theban rebellion with great force and violence. Thebes itself was demolished, its territory was divided among its Boeotian neighbours, and all of the Thebans were sold into slavery. The only people in Thebes who were spared were the leaders of the pro-Macedon party, the priests – and the descendants of the poet Pindar. Pindar's house was the only building left standing. This detail is often recounted in an attempt to show how sensitive and cultured Alexander was. In fact he must be counted among the most ruthless, destructive and bloodthirsty military dictators of all time; he had no regard for the large number of entirely innocent people in Thebes who had had no role in opposing him. In just the same way that the Nazis occasionally made punitive examples of villages by destroying them, Alexander meted out a disproportionate and extreme punishment to Thebes in order to warn other cities that might think of rebelling. What happened to Thebes caused the Athenians to submit, so the technique of brutal intimidation worked.

THE INVASION OF THE PERSIAN EMPIRE

Alexander took 42,000 soldiers across the Hellespont, men from Macedon, Thrace, Paionia, Illyria and the southern states of Greece. He made a ceremonious visit to the site of Troy, where he offered libation to Athena and performed a ritual in which he and his companions raced naked round the mound that was believed to be the Tomb of Achilles. He was signalling to his troops that he was Achilles and that they were re-staging the Trojan War. Alexander saw his own life in these mythic terms, and persuaded to do so, too, which is perhaps why he was so successful.

At the Battle of Granicus, he won a major victory over the Persian army and accepted the surrender of the Persian provincial capital Sardis. Taking the treasury of Sardis as loot, Alexander followed the western Anatolian coast, taking town after town, just as the epic cycle poems said Achilles had done. He took Halicarnassus and other ports, then went inland to pursue the conquest of Asia Minor.

At the Battle of Issus in 333 BC, Alexander defeated the main Persian army commanded by Darius III. The Persian emperor was forced to flee from the field of battle, leaving behind his wife, mother, daughters and much of his treasure. Afterwards Darius offered Alexander a huge ransom to return his family and much of the conquered territory, and agree a peace treaty. Presumably Darius thought Alexander was a small-time opportunist who would not want to risk further battles with the Persian army. He misjudged his enemy. Alexander answered that he, Alexander, was now king of Persia and that he would decide for himself who possessed which territory.

Alexander moved from Asia Minor into the Levant, taking Tyre and Gaza after major sieges. He passed through Judaea but it seems he did not visit Jerusalem. His focus was on Egypt, where in 332–1 BC he was welcomed as a liberator. Presumably Alexander's reputation as a ruthless conqueror had preceded him; the Egyptians knew better than to resist and be destroyed. The priests of Amun declared that he was the son of Zeus, which is just what Alexander wanted to hear. From then on, he referred to Zeus-Ammon as his true father and had himself portrayed on coins with ram's horns growing from his forehead to reinforce this conception of himself. He was now more than a hero, he was a demi-god.

In Egypt, Alexander founded the city of Alexandria on the Nile Delta, a great city that would long outlast him. He then marched his army north-eastwards to Assyria (now northern Iraq). There he fought the Battle of Gaugamela in which he again defeated Darius. Darius's charioteer was killed and he once again fled from the battlefield. Alexander chased him as far as Arbela. Darius escaped over the mountains to Ecbatana (now Hamadan). Alexander let him go, and marched his army on to Babylon.

After Babylon, he marched to the city of Susa, capturing its treasury, then marched on to Persepolis. He allowed his soldiers to loot Persepolis. A fire broke out in the eastern palace of Xerxes, and it is thought that this was started as a deliberate act of revenge for the Persian firing of the Athenian Acropolis. The fire spread and engulfed the whole city. Persepolis was a great and beautiful city, a wonder of the ancient world, and what Alexander did to it was a large-scale act of vandalism.

Alexander then resumed his pursuit of Darius. Darius was finally brought down by an act of treachery. One of his kinsmen, Bessus, had him kidnapped and murdered, proclaiming himself Darius's successor. He took the name Artaxerxes V, withdrew to central Asia and organised a campaign of guerrilla warfare against Alexander. As far as Alexander was concerned, the war was over. He released his allies from obligatory military service in the campaign, although any individual soldiers who wanted to were free to enlist in the imperial army.

There were still pockets of resistance, and Alexander waged a three-year campaign to suppress Bessus and then Spitamenes, the provincial governor of Sogdiana. This campaign involved long marches through Media, Parthia, and what is now Afghanistan. Along the way he founded a series of new cities. It is the surest indication of Alexander's megalomania that he named all of these cities after himself, Alexandria. As with Darius, the enemy leaders were in the end betrayed by their own people.

THE INVASION OF INDIA

Alexander was free then to move forward to invade the Indian subcontinent. He called all the chieftains of the province of Gandhara (now northern Pakistan) to a meeting with him, at which they were invited to submit to his authority. Some complied, but others did not. The hill clans were particularly resistant, and Alexander dealt with them in his usual way. He led his army against the Kamboja clans who resisted, though he did not find it easy to take their strongholds. One clan, the Aspasios, fought back fiercely; in the fighting Alexander himself was wounded in the shoulder by a dart. But eventually the Aspasios were defeated and Alexander enslaved them – all 40,000 of them. Another people, the Assakenois, raised similarly strong resistance, confronting him with an army of 30,000 cavalry, 38,000 infantry and thirty elephants. They also manned fortresses such as Ora, Bazira and Massaga. Massaga was only taken after several days of fighting. Alexander was wounded again, this time in the ankle. The chief of Massaga was cut down in the battle, so the command of the army was taken over by his elderly mother, Cleophis. Inspired by her example, all the women of the area joined in the fighting; they realised they were fighting for sheer survival. Massaga only fell by treachery. Alexander once again showed his ruthless nature. He demolished the buildings and slaughtered the entire population. Then he went on to do the same at Ora. The Assakenian survivors headed for a high fortress named Aornos where, after a one-day siege, Alexander slaughtered them. He had promised these people their lives on surrender, but when they did surrender he executed them. Alexander piled atrocity on atrocity.

Then he crossed the River Indus and in 326 BC fought a large-scale battle, the Battle of Hydaspes, against Raja Puru, referred to in the Greek reports as Porus. Raja Puru ruled part of the Punjab. The raja was defeated, but Alexander was so impressed by his bravery in battle that he appointed him governor of his own kingdom. To the east of the kingdom of Raja Puru lay the Ganges and the powerful empire of Magadha. Alexander's army was exhausted by the long years of campaigning, and did not want to fight another battle against another huge Indian army. He was ordering them to cross the Ganges, and they had heard this was a river of prodigious size, a hundred fathoms deep, it was said. And they had heard that waiting for them on the other side would be a formidable army consisting of 80,000 horsemen, 200,000 infantry, 8,000 chariots and 6,000 elephants. It was too much to contemplate. At the Hyphasis River (now the Beas) Alexander's army mutinied. This was to be where Alexander's conquests would end, the eastern boundary of his enormous empire.

Instead, Alexander turned south, where he encountered the Malli tribes, the most warlike of all. He engaged them in battle and, as they retreated to their citadel, he was badly wounded by an arrow. Alexander's troops believed he was dead, and in their fury they took the citadel and massacred the Malli who had taken refuge there. The surviving Malli surrendered, and Alexander moved west into Carmania (now Iran), leaving some troops and provincial governors in India.

On his way back through the Middle East, Alexander died. It was on 11 June 323 BC that he died of unknown causes in Babylon, at the palace of Nebuchadrezzar. He was thirty-two. Before he died, he mumbled something about his successor, but it may have been a phrase meaning 'the stronger' or 'Craterus', the name of his most important army officer. The empire was to be ruled instead by Alexander's half-brother Philip Arridaeus (who was mentally ill) and Alexander's son, Alexander IV (who was a baby). Two regents were named: Perdiccas and Craterus (who was assassinated). This left Perdiccas in power, though he too was assassinated by his troops in 321 BC. The power struggle was eventually settled after the Battle of Ipsus in Phrygia in 301 BC, when the empire was divided into four. So, even the death of Alexander resulted in continuing conflict and violence.

Aftermath

Alexander's sprawling empire did not survive. It extended from the lower Danube in the north to Egypt in the south, from Greece in the west to the Indus Valley in the east. Given the communications systems of the time, it was simply too big. It was also too diverse culturally to remain a single entity. Within a few years it was divided into four, with India returning to self-government. By 270 BC, the remaining Hellenistic states had crystallized into three empires: the Antigonid Empire (Macedonia and Greece), the Ptolemaic Kingdom (Egypt and Palestine) and the Seleucid Empire (Persia and Mesopotamia).

Alexander's conquests marked the beginning of the Hellenistic age. The influence of Greek culture was spread over a very wide area, fusing with native Middle Eastern culture to produce something new. Alexander was tolerant and broad-minded about religious beliefs and practices, and some interesting hybrid religions emerged in the towns he founded in Central Asia. It is no accident that the first realistic portraits of the Buddha appeared at this time, looking rather like Greek statues of Apollo. Several Buddhist traditions were influenced by Greek tradition. The concept of the Boddhisatvas is similar to and probably based on the idea of Greek heroes; there are even variations on the Trojan War story in the east, which presumably originated in the Greek homelands.

Alexander's conquests also resulted in Greek becoming the common language throughout what was then thought of as the civilised world. This is why the standard version of Hebrew scriptures used by Jews in Egypt at the time of Jesus was written in Greek.

The narrative of Alexander's life and exploits became a kind of second Homer, which is what he intended. He not only carried a copy of the *Iliad* everywhere, he made a point of making a self-dedicatory visit to Troy at the very start of his imperial conquests in the east. He wanted to become Achilles. In this he was amazingly successful, as his personal myth has survived down to the present day, not only in history but in literary tradition.

Alexander was a major role model among the ruling class in ancient Rome. Julius Caesar wept at the sight of a statue of Alexander. Pompey rooted about in the cupboards of conquered nations to find the cloak of

Alexander. When he had found it, he wore the 260-year-old cloak as a 'costume of greatness'.

THE SLAVE REBELLION OF SPARTACUS
(73–71 BC)

Spartacus is the one and only Roman slave whose name most people know. Spartacus made that name famous by leading the biggest and most successful of the slave rebellions against the Roman Republic in the first century BC.

Spartacus, according to ancient historians, was originally from the province of Thrace, in the Eastern Empire, and he served as an auxiliary or a mercenary in the Roman army. His wife was also a Thracian and from the same tribe. Both were at some stage imprisoned and enslaved; Spartacus was very strong and so was sold as a gladiator. Although ancient historians can often report accurately, there are reasons to question some of this. The adjective 'Thracian' could mean a native of Thrace, but it could also mean a style of gladiatorial combat, which was fighting with a round shield and a short sword. In view of this, the reported phrase 'Spartacus the Thracian' is ambiguous and we cannot be certain where he came from. He could have come from Thrace, as the name was used by other men in the Black Sea region. There were kings of Pontus and Cimmerian Bosporus called Spartacus, and the father of King Seuthes I of the Odrysae was called Spardacus. This suggests that the Roman slave Spartacus, our Spartacus, really was from Thrace as he had a Thracian name. Spartacus is one of those fascinating and shadowy figures on the fringes of history who do great things yet somehow remain out of view. Most people do disappear from view, as we sometimes need to remind ourselves.

THE CAMP ON MOUNT VESUVIUS

Spartacus was trained in gladiatorial combat at the gladiatorial school of Lentulus Batiatus near Capua. In 73 BC, about seventy gladiators including

Spartacus seized the knives in the kitchens as well as a wagon loaded with weapons and made their escape. They went up into the caldera, the outer crater, of Mount Vesuvius above Pompeii, where they hid and made their base. There they were joined by other rural slaves who absconded from their masters, taking the number rapidly up to several hundred.

The band of runaway slaves subsisted by plundering the region. Spartacus, apparently by this time emerging as their leader, tried to hold them back from random pillaging. His main aim was to escape from Italy, it seems, and move out into the provinces; perhaps his ultimate aim was to return home – perhaps to Thrace. The greater the disturbance they made in the Pompeii area, the more likely it was that the Roman authorities would send an army to deal with them, so he may have felt that it was safer to steal only what they needed.

Spartacus' lieutenants or co-leaders were four gladiators, Crixtus, Gannicus, Oenamus and Castus, who came originally from Gaul and Germania, and a Jewish slave called David.

At that time there were huge numbers of slaves in Italy. That meant that a slave rebellion could completely destabilise the Roman polity. On the other hand the authorities saw slaves as incapable of organised behaviour and could never be a match for a trained legion. Because of this complacency, they took no immediate action against the slave revolt in the south. As it happened, all the legions and officers with battle experience were away, so when the Senate eventually decided to send a force to deal with Spartacus, they sent an inexperienced one.

The Senate sent Claudius Glaber with 3,000 troops to Vesuvius. They surrounded the gentler lower slopes on one side of Vesuvius to stop the rebels from escaping. Spartacus responded to this by having his men make ropes out of vines. Then, under cover of darkness, they used the ropes to climb down the precipitous slopes on the other side of the volcano. They came up behind the soldiers and took them by surprise. The soldiers had expected to suppress this revolt easily, and had not taken the trouble to fortify their camp or even post sentries. The surprise was total. Most of the soldiers were still asleep when the attack came; nearly all of them were slaughtered, including Claudius Glaber.

In the wake of this spectacular success, many more slaves ran away to join Spartacus. His army grew to an enormous size, estimated by some at 120,000.

The escape from Vesuvius shows Spartacus as a clever military tactician, and he may have learned some of this skill during his time as a Roman auxiliary soldier, which may have given him opportunities to observe legionaries in action. But, whatever skill and experience Spartacus had, most of his followers were unskilled former slave labourers with no military training or background at all. Spartacus tried to rectify this by giving them some training. While they were hiding in the caldera on Mount Vesuvius, then heavily veiled in forest, it was possible to have proper training sessions in combat without arousing any suspicion in the neighbouring towns. It was this training that enabled the slave army to overwhelm Claudius Glaber and his troops.

BATTLING AGAINST ROME

Spartacus knew that the massacre meant that the Senate would soon send a larger force, so he needed to prepare his ragged army for a proper battle. He delegated the training to his fellow gladiators, the seventy who had escaped with him. They were to train small groups of slaves, who would then be responsible for training further small groups. This cascade system enabled him to provide basic military training for the whole force in just a few weeks.

With that preparation, Spartacus' army was able to defeat two more legions that were sent to suppress the slave rebellion. After that, he settled on the southern coast for the winter, using the time to make weapons. By this stage, the rebel army had attracted large numbers of camp followers: women, children and older people who were attracted to the slave army for protection. It was now more than an army, it was an entire slave population.

In the spring, Spartacus marched them all northwards, towards Gaul. This was rash, as heading towards Gaul inevitably meant heading towards Rome. The Senate became alarmed at this development. A band of runaways in the far south of Italy was one thing. An army of more than 100,000 marching on Rome was quite another. The Senate sent two consuls, Gellius Publicola and Gnaeus Cornelius Lentulus Clodianus, against the slave army with a legion each. The slave leaders began to disagree about what to do next. Crixtus wanted to stay in Italy; Spartacus wanted to go to Gaul. There was no resolution, so Crixtus left Spartacus and took about 30,000 supporters with him.

Crixtus and his army were afterwards defeated by Publicola's legion, and Crixtus himself died in battle. Spartacus and his larger force succeeded in winning battles at Picenum in central Italy first against Lentulus, then against Publicola. After defeating the two consular armies, Spartacus moved northwards. Then he encountered another legion under the command of Gaius Cassius Longinus, who was the governor of Cisalpine Gaul, or Gaul this side (the Roman side) of the Alps. This confrontation with Longinus took pace at Mutina, the modern town of Modena, and Spartacus won yet again. It was an incredible achievement.

Spartacus had parted company from Crixtus because he had wanted to move the slave army into Gaul or maybe even Hispania, where he might have joined the rebellion led by Quintus Sertorius. Now he reconsidered. For some reason he changed his mind, and it turned out to be a fatal change of mind. If he had crossed the Alps into provinces where Roman control was less secure, he and the other slaves would have stood a better chance of surviving.

Some historians believe that some of the non-combatant camp followers, maybe 10,000 of them, decided to cross the Alps after Mutina, and return to their tribal homelands in what are now France, Switzerland and Germany. The rest of the army, led by Spartacus, turned back south. There he met two more Roman legions in battle, under the command of Marcus Licinius Crassus, known to be the wealthiest man in Rome. Spartacus defeated Crassus too.

By the end of 72 BC, Spartacus had reached the toe of Italy, where he made camp at Rhegium (Reggio Calabria), close to the Strait of Messina, the channel separating Sicily from Italy. Spartacus' plan was to move across to Sicily. He struck a deal with pirates from Cilicia to ferry his army across, but the deal fell through. Now Spartacus found himself trapped in the toe of the Italian boot. In the early part of 71 BC, the Senate sent a large force against Spartacus. Not one legion or two this time, but eight, under the command of Crassus. The rebellion in the province of Hispania collapsed when its leader, Quintus Sertorius, was assassinated, so the Senate was able to recall the great general Pompey from Hispania to join what was now a determined thrust to suppress the slave revolt. The Senate also recalled Marcus Lucullus and his troops from Macedonia for the same purpose.

Spartacus was confronted by the army of Crassus. In a pitched battle, Spartacus and his army were able to break through Crassus's lines and escape eastwards across towards Brundisium (modern Brindisi). But in Lucania, Spartacus met his match. His army was intercepted by an army under the command of Pompey. The slaves were routed in a battle at the River Silarus.

It is not known for certain what became of Spartacus. Probably, given the sort of man he was, Spartacus fought to the death in that final battle, but his body was never identified. It is just possible that he escaped, though he was never heard of again. After the battle, the legionaries descended on the slave army's camp, where they were surprised to find (and rescue) 3,000 unharmed Roman prisoners.

The Roman authorities liked to make an example of those who opposed them. They were later to parade the captured Gaulish hero Vercingetorix through the streets of Rome before executing him. They might have done something similar with Spartacus if they had found him. As it was, they took 6,600 of the surviving slaves, Spartacus's followers, and crucified them at intervals along the Appian Way, the road from Brundisium to Rome. Crassus, who arranged for this vicious and cold-blooded punishment, gave no orders for the crucified bodies to be taken down, so they were left there, rotting on their crosses for many years. The skeletons of the runaway slaves reminded Rome's slave population what would happen to them if they rebelled.

About 5,000 slaves managed to get away after the final battle and flee to the north. There they were destroyed by Pompey, who then claimed credit for ending the slave war. In Rome this was believed, and Pompey was hailed as a great hero, the saviour of the city, while Crassus gained little credit.

Aftermath

The struggle of Spartacus and his fellow slaves against oppression became an inspiration for the freedom fighters of the nineteenth and twentieth centuries. He was Karl Marx's hero. He was admired by Che Guevara. Spartacus is an ancient historical figure who has become a modern folk-hero. The very fact that little is known about him as a person means that almost any heroic quality can be projected on to him, and he has acquired an almost demi-god-like status, the great icon of the disempowered struggling against oppressive authority.

JULIUS CAESAR'S GALLIC WARS
(58–50 BC)

THE ORIGINS OF THE GALLIC WARS

Julius Caesar was born into a Roman patrician family. At the time of the Roman republic, power lay in the hands of the senators and the ladder to power for an ambitious young man like Caesar was well defined. He had to work his way from one promoted office to the next. The ultimate hope was to reach the office of consul or praetor, which carried what was known as imperium, the right to command an army. With an army, he might conquer new territories 'for Rome' and so be awarded a triumph. This accolade would be remembered for ever in statues, monuments and inscriptions; it was the route to immortality, and that was what Julius Caesar wanted.

Julius Caesar achieved his praetorship by 62 BC, and even at that stage he was seen by many senators as far too ambitious – a dangerous man, in fact. For that reason, after his praetorian command in Spain (61–60 BC) they withheld from him the expected honour of a triumph. They also tried hard to prevent him from becoming consul, but he achieved that office in 59 BC.

At the same time, another ambitious Roman, Gnaeus Pompeius, often known as Pompey the Great, was building his career by the military route. Pompey returned to Rome from a campaign that added three new provinces to the empire and, almost incredibly, doubled the income of the Roman treasury. Pompey had great support from the people of Rome. Because of the scale of Pompey's achievement, it had suddenly become necessary to have more than an ordinary triumph to become the most conspicuous person in Rome. Pompey had raised the stakes.

Because of this, during his time as consul Caesar pressed through a law that gave him a five-year command in Illyricum and Cisalpine Gaul. This was northern Italy and the Yugoslav coast of the Adriatic. The region was already within the empire but Caesar saw it as a springboard for conquering new territories to the east, in the Balkans, or across the Alps to the west and north-west (Gaul). While he controlled this area, the most important part of the Roman army would be under his command, the units positioned at the southern border of Germany.

In order to outshine Pompey and win overwhelming public acclaim in Rome, Caesar mounted one successful campaign after another: a Helvetic Campaign in 58 BC, a Belgic Campaign in 57 BC, a Venetic Campaign in 56 BC, a German Campaign in 55 BC and a British Campaign in 54 BC.

THE WARS

When Caesar took over Cisalpine Gaul, most of Gaul on the far side of the Alps (what is now France) was free of Roman control and occupied by a variety of Iron Age tribes. They were war-like and frequently fought among themselves, though they had shrines and sacred places at their boundaries, suggesting that they periodically met there in peace to worship. Many of the tribespeople were farmers, and their homesteads were scattered across a mainly rural landscape. But there were also some oppida, or towns, fortified with earthworks and palisades. Cenabum (modern Orléans), for instance, was the principal oppidum of the Carnutes tribe. Native Gallic tradesmen lived and worked there; Roman traders were also operating there. Although Gaul was politically independent of Rome, there were some strong economic ties. The Roman way of conquest was often to infiltrate kingdoms in this way, economically and culturally, so that they drifted easily towards a political takeover; often military intervention was not needed. Even the local religions were gradually subverted, with local Celtic gods and goddesses being given Roman names. It was more a matter of converting the gods than the worshippers.

When Caesar first arrived in Gaul, there were two dominant and rival tribes, the Aedui and the Sequani. The other tribes of Gaul supported either one or the other. The Sequani formed an alliance with some German tribes and with their help they were able to defeat the Aedui and their allies. The Sequani killed many of the Aedui nobles, took as hostages the sons of many of the leaders, and forced the Aedui never to conspire against the Sequani. The Sequani thus became the dominant tribe in Gaul.

Caesar heard about this and tried to turn these developments to his advantage by forming an alliance with the Aedui. In exchange for grain, Caesar supplied Roman soldiers for the Aedui army. Caesar was in this way able to infiltrate the Aedui army, embedding Roman values and philosophies among the tribes through the army. There were many revolts, but mainly small scale and the Roman army was able to deal with them. Caesar knew that if the tribes of Gaul decided to form a pan-Gallic alliance it would be much harder for him to conquer Gaul.

One leader, Celtillus of the Arverni tribe in the Lyon area, attempted to do this and make himself the king of free Gaul. This was said to be contrary to Gallic beliefs and that his life was forfeit for attempting it. When he was found murdered, though, it looked as if he had been killed with Roman weapons. Vercingetorix, the son and heir of Celtillus, blamed the Romans for the assassination and was very angry. Like his father, he recognized that if the Gauls wanted to retain their freedom they would all have to act together. We know what Vercingetorix looked like as there is a vivid portrait of him on a contemporary coin. It is a surprising face, lean and sensitive, and looking like the young John Gielgud, though with long tousled hair.

The Carnutes tribe was the first to respond to Vercingetorix. The most sacred shrine in Gaul was in the territory of the Carnutes, which was where the druids met. The Carnutes invited the other tribes to bring their battle standards there, in other words to swear an oath of mutual alliance against Rome. On an agreed day, the Carnutes warriors, led by Cotuatus and Conconnetodumnus, went into the *oppidum* of Cenabum, killed all the Romans who had settled there and stole their property. As news of this raid spread across Gaul and reached the Arverni, Vercingetorix called his extended family together and outlined his plan for a rebellion. As word of this spread, other members of the Arverni tribe made their support known, then other tribes as well: the Senones, Pictones, Cadurci, Turoni and Parisii among others. Vercingetorix moved his warriors towards the land of the Bituriges. These people were allies of the Aedui. When they knew Vercingetorix was on his way, they sent word to the Aedui to help them. The Aedui sent them Roman soldiers, cavalry and infantry, but when they reached the River Loire, a substantial river separating the two territories, they were too frightened to try to cross it. As a result the Bituriges abandoned their alliance with the Aedui and allied themselves with the Arverni instead.

Now that Vercingetorix was in control of the lands of the Bituriges, he led his army towards the Boii *oppidum* of Gorgobina (possibly modern Saint-Parize-le-Châtel), which Caesar had put under the protection of the Aedui. Caesar sent word that he was coming to the aid of Gorgobina. On his way to Gorgobina, he stopped at Vellaundunum, the oppidum of the Senones tribe, and laid siege to it. His reason was that he needed to leave a safe, unthreatened road behind him so that he would be able to get supplies without interruption; this potentially hostile *oppidum* needed to be pacified. The siege lasted three days. Then a deputation came out to discuss terms of surrender. Once this was agreed, Caesar continued on his march towards Gorgobina via Cenabum.

The Carnutes tribe heard belatedly about the Roman siege of Vellaundunum. They were starting to gather warriors to garrison and defend the Carnutes stronghold of Cenabum and were startled to find that Caesar was already camped outside the town. They decided that they would try to escape by way of a back entrance over a bridge under cover of darkness, but Caesar was expecting them to do exactly this. He stationed patrols to keep watch through the night. When the planned escape got under way, the Roman patrols set fire to the oppidum gates. Because the bridge was narrow, very few Carnutes escaped. The rest were bottled up inside the fortified town. Caesar's revenge for the massacre of Roman citizens at Cenabum was swift, violent and apt. He had the oppidum burnt to the ground, all the men put to the sword and all the women and children sold into slavery.

Vercingetorix had by now lost several *oppida* to the Romans – Cenabum, Vellaunodunum and Noviodunum – and he decided to call a council of war. At this council he proposed to invest as much effort as possible into severing the Romans' supplies of grain and fodder. He also proposed a scorched earth policy, burning all the settlements along the Romans' line of march. He wanted to preoccupy the Romans with the need to forage, because small foraging parties would be relatively easy to pick off. He also proposed burning down any *oppida* that the Romans might be able to capture. It was a savage and hugely self-sacrificing strategy, yet those at Vercingetorix's council agreed unanimously with it. The next day, twenty settlements in the lands of the Bituriges were ablaze, and the people of other tribes quickly followed suit. Suddenly the landscape of Gaul was on fire.

The Bituriges could not bear to set their *oppidum* at Avaricum (modern Bourges) on fire. They said that to them it was the most beautiful town in Gaul. They argued that it was fairly well defended by forest and marsh. They argued and pleaded, and won the pity and support of other tribal leaders. In the end Vercingetorix agreed to let them keep Avaricum and sent some troops to defend it. He himself set up camp about 26 km (16 miles) away.

Caesar arrived and set up camp close to Avaricum while he tried to negotiate with the Boii and Aedui for grain supplies. The Aedui were reluctant to supply the Romans. Although the Boii were willing, they could not supply enough. Meanwhile morale in Caesar's army was dropping, partly because of the cold and wet weather. There was apprehension on both sides. Then the Gauls began pouring out of the *oppidum*. The fighting started and went on all night. The Gauls had the advantage because they knew the landscape well and had very powerful warriors. But the following day saw a transformation. The Biturigian warriors thought they faced defeat and massacre. They decided to leave quietly the following night. But their wives refused to be abandoned as slaves for the Romans and sabotaged their escape plan. As the men prepared to leave, the women shouted to the Roman patrols. The men had to give up their plan.

Caesar too was apprehensive. The siege had to end soon, or Vercingetorix would arrive and charge the Roman force from behind. Then it started to rain heavily. He organised a surprise attack. The Gauls were taken completely off-guard. There were 40,000 people living or sheltering inside the *oppidum* at the time. Of these, only 800 managed to escape, and that was at the very beginning of the attack. Those trapped in the oppidum threw their weapons away in desperation and rushed in a mass to the far side of the *oppidum.* There some were killed by Roman troops as they were crammed together in the narrow gateways; others managed to get out through the gateways but were then killed by Roman cavalry.

Vercingetorix was worried that this new loss would lead to a break-up of the alliance, and called another council of war. Then he decided to build a fortified camp.

The next major confrontation between Romans and Gauls came at Gergovia (modern Gergovie in Puy-de-Dome, central France). Vercingetorix arrived at Gergovia well before Caesar and set up camp there. When Caesar arrived he saw that the mountainous terrain would make a frontal assault too risky; he decided on siege tactics, ordering a double trench to be dug with the intention of encircling Gergovia and starving the Gauls into submission. But Caesar was interrupted when his unreliable allies, the Aedui, arrived. He had to break off and engage them in combat. It was fierce fight, but he defeated them.

He saw that the siege he had set up was now in danger. His only chance of success was to lure Vercingetorix off the high ground. He used a legion as a decoy, but Vercingetorix understood what Caesar was trying to do and ignored the bait. The decoy legion was then too far away to pick up Caesar's signal to return for the main assault of the town's defences. These miscalculations led to serious Roman losses (700 dead and over 6,000 wounded) and the failure of the siege. Vercingetorix had won and Caesar had lost.

The treacherous behaviour of the Aedui showed that they were no longer Roman allies. Instead they went to Vercingetorix to agree a joint campaign, but the two Aedui commanders wanted supreme command of the joint army. Vercingetorix refused, there was an argument and a general Gaulish council was called to resolve the leadership issue. Vercingetorix finally won the vote unanimously: he was to be commander-in-chief.

After a battle in which the Gauls under Vercingetorix took a beating from the Romans, they marched to Alesia, the oppidum of the Mandubii tribe (September 52 BC). When the Roman army arrived there, Caesar ordered the building of siege works. The Gauls charged the Romans while they were starting this work, and fierce fighting followed. The Romans were losing, so Caesar sent in his German allies on horseback. They slaughtered the Gauls, and as the Gauls retreated, the Germans followed them all the way to the fort.

The Gauls were bottled up in the stronghold of Alesia, and running out of food. Vercingetorix sent out a relief party to get supplies, then called a council to decide what to do next. What he did not know was that the Aedui were on their way not only with supplies but with 8,000 cavalry and 240,000 infantry – a huge relief force. To Vercingetorix and the Gauls trapped at Alesia the situation looked desperate. Then there were great celebrations when the Aedui arrived, but because of Caesar's elaborate siege works the relief could not reach the trapped Gauls. The Gauls broke out and engaged the Romans for several hours until, once again, Caesar sent in his lethal Germans. Another problem for the Gauls was that Caesar had prepared traps hidden in the grass. The sun set on that day's battle. Then the Gauls tried the same thing again, and again with no conclusive result.

Both Romans and Gauls were running out of strength, and the Gauls in Alesia were close to despair. Then Caesar himself led an attack with fresh soldiers, and this left the Gauls seriously broken. When the relief party heard of this victory of Caesar's, they left, returning to their home villages. Vercingetorix summoned his last council. He told the council that he had been fighting for the freedom of Gaul, not for himself. He had to surrender. He would place himself at Caesar's mercy. And that is what he did.

Aftermath

The fall of Alesia and the capture of Vercingetorix in 52 BC marked the collapse of free Gaul. From that point on, Gaul was a Roman province, a conquered land. Vercingetorix was recognised at the time, and has been recognised ever since, as one of the greatest freedom fighters of all time. He was shown scant respect by Julius Caesar, who imprisoned him in Rome until 46 BC. Then he was brought out and paraded through the streets of Rome in Caesar's triumph. Vercingetorix was executed immediately afterwards in prison, probably by strangulation, the usual fate of conquered kings.

But the Gallic Wars made Vercingetorix an immortal Gallic hero. An imposing statue of him was eventually raised at Alesia (1865). On its base is an inscription, in French:

United Gaul
forming a single nation
animated by a single spirit
can defy the Universe.

The campaign in Gaul, along with his other campaigns, brought Julius Caesar the public acclaim he wanted, but the formal political position that should go with that was denied him because of Pompey's ascendancy in Rome. Caesar advanced his troops across the River Rubicon, towards Rome, and this was rightly taken as a gesture of hostility towards the Roman state and Pompey in particular. Pompey made an attempt to stop Caesar but failed and then fled to Egypt, leaving Caesar to enter Rome as dictator, and one of the greatest military commanders of all time. So the Gallic Wars generated two legendary heroes, one on each side.

Julius Caesar wrote his own account of the Gallic Wars, which became a classic of military history. It also represents one of the earliest military memoirs. Like any history, it is partial, full of bias. Caesar had every reason to focus every success on himself in order to inflate his own importance; the purpose of the book was self-promotion in the most literal sense. What he also did, in many places, was to paint the conquered people as savages, barbarians who needed the civilising benefits of conquest. So Caesar and other Roman historians, too, have left us with a strongly biased view of the cultures of Europe that the Romans destroyed. Here and there, though, the strength and courage of the conquered people shine through. Caesar was full of admiration for the way a Gaulish defender of a gate under siege attack went on fighting until he was killed, and then another brave Gaul would immediately take his place and fight hard until he too was killed, and then another and another. He did not remark on the enormous discipline and courage of the nameless Gauls his soldiers were mercilessly killing, but his admiration for them is implicit in the bare facts of his description.

THE STRUGGLE FOR POWER AFTER CAESAR'S DEATH
(44–30 BC)

THE ASSASSINATION OF JULIUS CAESAR

Julius Caesar was at the peak of his success in 45 BC, by far the most powerful figure in the Roman world. In every age there are some people who like to shower celebrities with excessive honours, and this is what happened to Julius Caesar. Others looked on in mounting alarm as they saw Caesar emerging as a dictator. In February 44 BC he declared himself dictator for life and it was this act that turned many senators against him. There were rumours that he wanted to be king. He said he was not interested in honours, which may be true, but he went on accepting them. Significantly, he took to wearing red boots, as had been worn by the kings of Alba Longa. His friend and support Antony offered him the diadem, a white linen band which was the Greek symbol of monarchy. Caesar refused it, but it remains unclear whether this was genuine modesty or just a crowd pleaser.

The plot to kill Julius Caesar before he could be offered the diadem a second time, and accept it, seems to have originated with Cassius. Cassius was aggrieved because he had not been given a command in the forthcoming war against Parthia. It was a small grievance, and scarcely justification for murder, but he approached his brother-in-law, Brutus, for support. Brutus was fanatical and ruthless. He had fought on Pompey's side at Pharsalia, like Cassius, and Caesar had pardoned both of them. Caesar had been more than generous to both men and they owed him a debt of gratitude. Perhaps that was one of the reasons why they hated him – an unbearable, humbling sense of obligation. Neither of them had any real reason to assassinate Julius Caesar, but Cassius's mild feeling of slight combined with Brutus's tendency to fanaticism were enough to do it. Sixty members of the Senate were persuaded that the only resolution to the problem was Caesar's assassination.

On 15 March 44 BC the assassins summoned a seemingly unsuspecting Caesar to a session of the Senate in the Hall of Pompey. There they surrounded him and stabbed him to death. The assassins were envious of Caesar's power and popularity and they convinced themselves that they were ridding Rome of a tyrant, or at least a prospective tyrant.

THE AFTERMATH OF THE ASSASSINATION

The assassination of Julius Caesar was followed by weeks of indecision on the part of the conspirators. This was because of a lack of forward planning or forethought. Surprisingly, they had thought little further ahead than getting rid of Caesar. They did rehearse their excuses for killing him, but that was as far ahead as the thinking went. They associated Caesar with the word 'king', which was a title the Romans equated with 'tyrant', and other excessive or oppressive labels. Their intention was to make the memory of Caesar odious.

In the aftermath of the assassination there was chaos in Rome. Those who had been involved in the assassination hid, fearing a reprisal massacre from Caesar's friends and supporters. They in turn went into hiding, fearing that the assassins would want to purge the pro-Caesar party. So both parties went into hiding in fear of a massacre from the other, and nobody came forward to govern Rome. Another problem was that the assassins had no idea how to reform the government. The Republic was an ideal, almost a fantasy, and the insubstantial men who carried out the murder were incapable of organising a coup that would yield a working republic. The senators thought that once Caesar was out of the way democracy would regenerate spontaneously.

There was a power vacuum which the assassins themselves might have filled, but they were reluctant to do this. By doing nothing, they allowed Mark Antony to take control. Another serious mistake the assassins made was in underestimating the eighteen-year-old Gaius Octavius, known as Octavian. Because he was, as they thought, of little political consequence in himself, the assassins added to Octavian's power by giving him their support. What the assassins had not reckoned on was that the strong memory of Julius Caesar's great charisma, his genius, would survive his death. As the ancient biographer Plutarch put it, 'The great genius which attended him through his lifetime remained as the avenger of his murder, pursuing through every land and sea all those who were concerned in it.' The Roman world was a world of superstition. It was widely believed in the ancient world that it was through ignoring omens that Caesar had met his death. The superstitions multiplied after his death. A comet appeared in the sky for seven nights after the assassination and the sun dimmed for the rest of that year, resulting in damp weather and a poor harvest. These signs were taken by ordinary people as indications of Caesar's divinity and of the general wrongness of his murder; they contributed to the assassins' failure. In effect everything that happened after the assassination helped to turn Caesar into a mythic figure and inclined ordinary people to support his surviving friends.

The avoidance of tyranny was something Julius Caesar was apparently himself interested in. One of Caesar's friends, Gaius Matius, commented, 'If Caesar with all his genius could not find a solution, who is to find one now?'

As the tension decreased and the general populace in Rome thought that things had been settled, Mark Antony called the Senate and asked if he could deliver Caesar's eulogy. The senators were reluctant to allow this, and only agreed on condition that he would neither glorify Caesar nor condemn the assassins. They did not know that Antony had in his possession Caesar's papers, including his will. In that will, Caesar ordered the creation of gardens for the poor people of Rome and left money for all the citizens of Rome. When Antony delivered his eulogy he revealed this information, which filled the people with affection for Caesar's memory, and enraged them against his murderers. A mob gathered and drove the conspirators out of the city.

The Senate had made a serious error in allowing Antony to tap the emotions of the mob in this way. Suddenly, Antony was controlling events. The Senate knew Antony was Caesar's friend, his most loyal general, and therefore dangerous, but they were unable to stop him. He was rewarded in effect for his daring. The Senate was filled with men who were conscious of their own inferiority, in fact so much so that they were incapable of steering Rome under these unusual circumstances.

Once the Senate realised Antony was taking control, they began to support Antony's great rival, Octavian. Octavian was also a friend of Caesar. In fact Caesar had left him three-quarters of his property and named him as his heir. Antony bridled at this, as he had expected to be honoured in this way himself in Caesar's will. There was an immediate rift between Octavian and Antony. Purely out of fear of Antony, the Senate curried favour with the young Octavian by advancing him ahead of his years. They overlooked his age to raise him to the rank of senator and then consul. They also officially recognised his status as Caesar's adoptive son, at the same time deifying Caesar. Octavian in this way became a very powerful individual indeed, one who could claim to be the son of a god.

In spite of this promotion and advancement, the Senate still thought of Octavian as a mere boy with no real power other than through themselves. They assumed that Octavian would be under their control. But Octavian was extremely intelligent and ambitious and he used the power that the Senate recklessly bestowed on him to seize control. Leaning on Caesar's name, he summoned all his father's legions and supporters and gained their support. Now he had both political and military power and became an unstoppable force. Octavian became a dictator, a tyrant, a king in all but name. It was ironic that Caesar had been murdered to stop him from doing this, even more ironic that the Senate had given Octavian power in order to stop Antony from doing it. The senators were a very inept group of men, failing to judge the people they were dealing with, failing to assess situations and failing to anticipate consequences. The very fact that the extremely astute Julius Caesar had hand picked Octavian to succeed him should have given the senators the clue they needed as to the sort of man Octavian was going to be.

Then the long power struggle between the supporters of Caesar, the uneasy alliance of Octavian and Mark Antony, and the assassins, who were also known as the 'liberators'. Brutus and Cassius had left Italy and taken control of the Eastern provinces from Greece to Syria. In Rome, the three main supporters of Caesar's cause, Octavian, Lepidus and Mark Antony, were in control of the western armies, and were in complete control of the Senate. They formed the second triumvirate (a three-man military dictatorship). Their first task was to avenge the death of Caesar. Octavian and Antony, the two strongest members of the triumvirate, left Lepidus in control in Italy while they took armies (a total of 28 legions) east to hunt down the assassins.

They tracked them down in northern Greece. Brutus and Cassius wanted to avoid a full-scale confrontation in a land battle. Instead they preferred to reach a strong defensive position for their armies and use their naval superiority to blockade Octavian's and Antony's supply route through the Aegean back to Italy. Brutus and Cassius had spent three months raiding cities in Greece to fill their war-chest. They commanded armies of 100,000 men in all. They were therefore fairly strong, certainly strong enough to seize and hold a good defensive position on high ground about 3 km (1¾ miles) west of the city of Philippi, with a defending marsh protecting them on the south side. They fortified their position with a rampart and ditch.

Antony and Octavian arrived shortly after this, bringing armies of about the same size as the Liberators'. The soldiers in the Liberators' armies who were expected to fight against Octavian were being put in a difficult position, and Brutus and Cassius knew this. Octavian was not actually known as Octavian at this time. Later he would be known, as he is to us today, as Augustus, but at the time of Philippi he was known by the name Gaius Julius Caesar. And with that name it was impossible to gloss over the fact that he was the son and heir of the great Julius. Many of the soldiers in the Liberators' armies had fought under Caesar and must have felt divided loyalties at this moment of confrontation. It may even have affected the outcome of the battle. Cassius tried very hard to compensate for it by working on the soldiers' loyalty. He made fine inspiring speeches. Among other things he said, 'Let it give no one any concern that he has been one of Caesar's soldiers. We were not his soldiers, but our country's.' Cassius also gave each soldier a gift of money.

The great Battle of Philippi in Macedonia in 42 BC consisted of two separate engagements on the plain west of the city of Philippi. On 3 October 42 BC, the four armies met, Brutus facing Octavian, Cassius facing Antony, and finally came to battle. Antony offered to do battle, but the Liberators were reluctant to leave their strong defensive positions. Antony tried an outflanking manoeuvre, making a causeway eastwards across the marsh to the south of Cassius. Cassius had believed the marsh to be impassable, and when he saw what Antony was doing he sent part of his army south into the marsh to build a cross rampart to obstruct Antony's right wing and stop him from encircling the hill. This move brought the two armies into general battle.

At the same time, to the north, Octavian's army goaded Brutus into fighting. Brutus's army rushed down towards Octavian's army before being ordered to attack. It proved successful because spontaneous; it was a surprise to both sides. Octavian's soldiers fled in disarray and were chased back to their camp, which Brutus's men captured. Brutus's men viciously stabbed and cut Octavian's couch to pieces, but could not find Octavian himself. Apparently he went and hid in a marsh.

On the southern side of the battlefield, the battle was going the other way. Antony stormed Cassius's fortification and easily captured his camp. When the battle ended, Cassius had lost 9,000 men. Octavian had lost twice that number. But the field of battle was huge and great clouds of dust had been sent up in the air during the battle, so it was impossible for anyone to be sure what had happened. Cassius believed he had been overwhelmingly defeated and ordered his freedman Pindarus to run him through with his sword. Brutus grieved over his friend's body, describing him as 'the last of the Romans'.

Brutus had done well to put Octavian and his army to flight, but looting by Brutus's army gave Octavian's army time to regroup. If Brutus had followed through he might have defeated Octavian's army outright, found and killed Octavian, and the course of history would have been very different. There would have been no Augustus, perhaps no Roman emperors at all.

On that same day reinforcements of troops and supplies for Octavian and Antony were intercepted at sea, so their strategic position became precarious. But the Liberators were also left seriously disadvantaged by the death of Cassius. It was Cassius who had the mind for strategy. Brutus was relatively inexperienced and, worse still, he could never win the same respect from his soldiers.

Over the next three weeks, Antony gradually moved his army to the south of Brutus's army and made a fort on a hill close to Cassius's former camp. Brutus had carelessly left the hill unguarded. Brutus wanted to remain on the higher ground, and wait for the fleet to wear the enemy out, but in the end his officers and men became impatient to give battle and they demanded the chance to fight. Brutus had to give in to them for fear that dwindling morale might result in soldiers changing sides, which would have been catastrophic.

On 23 October, the battle known as the Second Battle of Philippi commenced. Brutus's army went down the slope into the marsh and attacked Antony's army there. The solid lines of soldiers fought face to face, stabbing and slashing at each other with their swords. The slaughter was appalling. Brutus and his army were pushed back. Antony's troops pursued and routed them. Octavian managed to reach Brutus's camp before Brutus and therefore block his retreat. Brutus escaped into some hills nearby with four legions, but realized that he would have to surrender. He decided to commit suicide instead. His last words were, 'O wretched Virtue, you were but a name, and yet I worshipped you as real indeed; but now it seems you were but Fortune's slave.' The high-flown rhetoric was a long way from what Rome needed from its rulers. When Antony saw the body of his one-time friend he grieved and laid a purple cloak over it. Antony knew that Brutus had only agreed to join the conspiracy on condition that Antony himself would be left untouched.

The suicides of Cassius and Brutus during the Battle of Philippi brought this phase of the civil war to an end. The two leading conspirators were dead and Caesar's death was avenged. Many other young Roman aristocrats lost their lives during the battle or after it, some like Brutus committing suicide. Among them were Marcus Porcius Cato, the son of Cato the Younger, and Marcus Livius Drusus Claudianus, who was the father of Livia, later to become the wife of Augustus. The nobles who surrendered chose to surrender to Antony; Octavian already had a reputation for ruthlessness. The remnants of the Liberators' armies were rounded up and 14,000 of them enrolled in the triumvirate army. Some veterans decided to retire and set up a community at the nearby city of Philippi, which became a Roman colony. The triumvirate (the military dictatorship shared by Octavian, Lepidus and Antony) was then in full control of the Roman Republic. But then the power struggle among the three men became the main source of the conflict.

The Battle of Philippi was the high point of Mark Antony's career. He was the most celebrated general in the world and conspicuously the senior partner in the triumvirate. If anyone was predicting who would become emperor, they would certainly at that moment have guessed that it was going to be Antony.

One major source of tension in the triumvirate was the threat felt by Octavian from Caesarion, the son of Caesar and Cleopatra. Octavian held power because of his link with Julius Caesar through adoption. That guaranteed him popularity and loyalty among the legions. But Antony mischievously declared Caesarion to be Caesar's legitimate heir, and because of the blood relationship Octavian's position was seriously threatened. A propaganda war developed between Antony and Octavian.

Antony spent too long in the Eastern Mediterranean, famously dallying with the Egyptian queen, Cleopatra VII, while Octavian consolidated his position in the West. The triumvirate ended in 33 BC, when the Senate deprived Antony of his power and declared war on Cleopatra. The decision divided the Senate, a third of whom joined Antony's side. War broke out in 31 BC when Octavian's army captured the Greek city of Methone. The Battle of Actium in 31 BC was the decisive action between the forces of Octavian and Antony, which left Octavian the victor. The battle took place on 2 September 31 BC in the Ionian Sea, close to the Roman colony of Actium on the west coast of Greece.

Octavian's fleet was under the command of Marcus Vipsanius Agrippa. Antony's fleet was supplemented by the fleet of Cleopatra. It was on the morning of 2 September that the two fleets met. Antony was leading 220 warships through the narrow straits at the entrance to the Gulf of Ambracia towards the open sea when he met Agrippa's fleet outside. Antony's warships were massive quinqueremes, huge oared galleys with five banks of oars, armoured with bronze plates and fitted with deadly rams. The ships looked impressive and invincible, but in their present state they were seriously undermanned after an outbreak of malaria. Many of Antony's oarsmen had died before the battle started. This meant that the ships were underpowered and unable to do what they were specifically designed to do – ram other ships and cause them terminal damage. Antony did what he could to reduce the problem by concentrating his crews into a smaller number of ships and burning those he could not man.

Octavian's ships were mainly smaller, crewed by men who were better trained. His ships were lighter and therefore could manoeuvre much more easily than the big quinqueremes. Before the battle, one of Antony's senior officers, Delius, went over to Octavian with Antony's battle plan. Antony hoped to use his biggest ships to push Agrippa's northern wing back, so Agrippa kept his entire fleet safely out of range. After midday, Antony had to try another manoeuvre. He took his line of ships out, away from the protection of the shore, and engaged Agrippa.

Once she saw that the battle was going against Antony, Cleopatra took her fleet away, out towards the open sea. After that, Antony himself transferred to one of the smaller ships, took a flotilla with him to break through Octavian's lines and fled. It was, by the standards of any age, disgraceful behaviour by the commanders. The ships that were left behind were completely at Agrippa's mercy; they were captured or sunk. The Battle of Actium was such a disaster that Antony's army deserted in large numbers. Around nineteen legions of infantry and 12,000 cavalry deserted under cover of night. In spite of this, Antony was able to win a victory at Alexandria on 31 July 30 BC, but yet more soldiers deserted and he no longer had a large enough army to go on fighting. Antony fled again. There was a breakdown in communications and false information was given to Antony to the effect that Cleopatra had been captured by Octavian. Believing this report, he committed suicide. Then, on 12 August 30 BC, when Cleopatra heard about Antony's death, she too committed suicide. The remorseless Octavian then had Caesarion killed, which made him, Octavian, safe as the only son and heir of Julius Caesar.

Octavian's victory at Actium meant that he was then able to consolidate his power over Rome. Perhaps bearing in mind what happened to the divine Julius when he appeared to be heading for kingship, he adopted the title *princeps*, meaning 'first citizen' of Rome. He also accepted the title Augustus from the Senate. He also held, strictly within the law, a whole collection of offices that were granted to him for life by a weak Senate – offices such as tribune, censor and consul – without having to go through any election. Under these titles, he carefully preserved the outward appearance of a restored Republic, but the reality was really a termination of the Republic. He was emperor in all but name. With hindsight it became clear that the rule of Augustus was the beginning of the Roman Empire.

Consequences

The assassination of Julius Caesar was one of the most momentous events of Roman history. It not only marked the end of a remarkable individual military and political career, but generated a complicated conflict that took the history of Rome in unanticipated new directions. The chain of events that followed the assassination is a fascinating story in itself, but all the more so because no one knew, at the time, where on earth it might be leading, including the main protagonists. Even the ambitious and ruthless Octavian could have had no idea where destiny was taking him.

One of the most startling aspects of the assassination is that the Romans who killed Julius Caesar did not think at all about the consequences of their actions. By failing to set up a viable alternative government for Rome, the assassins made the establishment of a dictatorial monarchy *more* not less likely. Ironically, their action did not do away with a tyrant, it created one, and not only that but a string of tyrants, an hereditary tyranny. Julius Caesar might have been on his way to becoming a 'king' of some kind, but his assassination produced a dynasty of emperors, which was far worse.

The removal of Julius Caesar hastened the beginning of Octavian's reign. Octavian succeeded Julius Caesar, just as Caesar intended that he should. We can never know whether Julius Caesar was fully aware that the teenaged Octavian had the personal qualities necessary to turn him into the political giant that he became; either way, it was certainly an inspired nomination for a future ruler, I think unparalleled in history. Octavian learned some crucial lessons from Caesar. One of them was how to control the Senate, by neutralising it, giving it no power, and extorting decisions from it by military might.

The fallout in Egypt was also momentous. The surrender of Egypt and the death of Cleopatra meant the end of the Ptolemaic Kingdom of Egypt, and the end of the Hellenistic Age.

THE BATTLE OF THE TEUTOBURG FOREST

(AD 9)

The Romans had difficulty in maintaining a continuous hold over their huge empire. The famous networks of straight roads were an attempt to ensure that imperial troops could reach any trouble spots quickly and put down revolts. One such military expedition was led by Publius Quinctilius Varus, an aristocratic administrative official who was governor of Gaul and in that capacity he was assigned to set up the new Roman province of Germania in AD 7.

The enemy of Rome in this conflict was a man called Arminius, who had in his youth lived in Rome as a hostage. It was common for Rome to take provincial princes as hostages, to ensure the unswerving loyalty and good behaviour of their fathers. Arminius had been given a military education in Rome. When he returned to his homeland he became an adviser to Varus, who trusted him. In secret, Arminius worked hard to form an alliance of German tribes which traditionally been enemies. Arminius was able to persuade them to collaborate when they were outraged by Varus's intrusive administration. The tribes were the Cherusci, Marsi, Chatti and Bructeri. The measures they were incensed about were the normal impositions made by the Romans whenever they took over territories for incorporation into the empire – and the indignation and aggression they provoked were the normal responses, too.

Varus made his way from his summer camp somewhere to the west of the River Weser, perhaps near the modern city of Minden, to his winter headquarters near the Rhine. While travelling westwards across what is now Germany, he received reports of a local rebellion, reports that were concocted by Arminius in order to persuade Varus to make a detour. Varus fell for this deception, and decided to put down the imaginary revolt straight away. Arminius was with Varus on the journey, and probably guided him and his army directly to the ambush. Arminius then left Varus and his army on the pretext of enlisting the support of loyal German tribes who would support the Romans in putting down the revolt. Instead, he went off to join his own troops, who were apparently waiting for him in the neighbourhood. Arminius then went off to attack the Roman garrisons in the area, presumably to reduce the possibility of any reinforcements going to the aid of Varus' three legions when the trap was sprung.

The Roman accounts suggest that Varus and his troops must have been marching in a north-westerly direction somewhere to the east of Osnabruck. They camped in that area just before being attacked.

Varus was in command of three legions (XVII, VXIII and XIX), six cohorts of auxiliaries and three squadrons of cavalry. Although the force was large, many of the men had had little or no experience of fighting German tribesmen. The Romans were not marching in battle order, either, and the troops were separated from one another by large numbers of camp followers. Then they entered the Teutoburg Forest just to the north-east of Osnabruck. The road was narrow and muddy, which made the line straggle out; it was raining. Varus entered the forest blind, having failed to send any scouts ahead to check the terrain. The Roman army was now stretched out into a long attenuated line, perhaps as much as 20 km (12½ miles) long. It was by now extremely vulnerable to attack.

Then it was attacked.

Arminius knew the defensive tactics the Romans would use very well – they had been part of his education – and now he could use his knowledge to anticipate and forestall them. He had huge manpower at his disposal, and the attenuated Roman line made it easy to attack and pick off groups of soldiers. The Romans managed to organise a fortified camp for the night, and the next morning they broke out of the forest into open country near the modern town of Osterkappeln. Breaking out cost a great many lives, and so did the attempt to march through a second forested area.

Heavy rain prevented the Roman archers from using their bows, and their shields became waterlogged and heavy, so that they became impossible to carry. The Romans tried to escape by using a night march, but walked straight into a new trap prepared by Arminius at the foot of the Kalkriese Hill. At this point, the open sandy belt where the Romans could march fairly easily was narrowed off by the hill, and there was a gap of only 100 metres (330 ft) between the woods and the marshland. The road had been blocked by a trench. On the forest side an earth wall had been built along the side of the road. This provided the German tribesmen with cover; they could attack the Romans from behind the wall. The Romans attempted to storm the earth wall, but failed. One high-ranking officer, Numonius Vala, second in rank only to Varus, abandoned his troops to ride away with the cavalry, but he, too, was overtaken by German horsemen and killed.

After that the German tribesmen surged across the whole area, slaughtering Romans wherever they found them. Varus himself committed suicide when he saw his legions massacred around him; other officers did the same. It is believed that as many as 15,000 or 20,000 Roman soldiers died in this appalling and historic massacre. The Roman historian Tacitus said that many officers were sacrificed in pagan ceremonies, but this may be Roman propaganda; the Romans were always keen to paint their conquered European neighbours as barbarians. Some Roman officers at least were ransomed and the common soldiers appear to have become slaves.

The accounts written by the Romans all stress that the Roman defeat was total, that the Roman casualties were extremely severe and that the German tribes suffered very few losses. These aspects of the Roman version of the story can be believed. At Kalkriese, about 6,000 fragments of Roman equipment have been found and only one that is identifiably Germanic. Even if some of the German tribesmen were recycling pieces of Roman gear, the archaeology suggests that German losses were slight compare with Roman.

Following the German massacre of the three legions of Varus, German tribesmen swept across the Roman forts, garrisons and cities east of the

Rhine. The Roman garrison of one fortress, Aliso, managed to fight off the Germans for many weeks before breaking out under the command of Lucius Caeditius and reaching the River Rhine – and safety. That garrison included survivors of the Teutoburg Forest massacre.

Aftermath

When the Emperor Augustus heard about the massacre, he went into shock. He seems to have had a nervous breakdown. He banged his head against the walls of his palace, shouting, over and over again, 'Quinctilius Varus, give me back my legions!' The three destroyed legions were never resuscitated or re-formed afterwards; their legion numbers were never used again.

The massacre brought to an end a period of confident, successful and exuberant expansion of Roman interests and territories. With Emperor Augustus' nerve gone, his stepson Tiberius effectively took control of military matters and prepared to continue the war.

The German tribes profited from their plunder, developing economically and politically. They were still a long way from unification, which seems to have been what Arminius was trying to achieve. He was right to try. Faced with a big, highly organised and aggressive neighbour like Rome, the only survival strategy was confederation – to combine forces and form alliances. Arminius sent the severed head of Varus to Marbod, the powerful king of the Marcomanni tribe. Taking your enemy's severed head as a trophy was a common practice among the Iron Age tribes of Europe. Some chiefs displayed these heads on their walls, others mounted them in special niches in their sanctuaries. Arminius was keen to persuade Marbod to form an anti-Roman alliance with him, but Marbod declined. He sent the head to Rome as a gesture of his own continuing neutrality in the conflict. Even so, thanks to the impact of the massacre, the German tribes were able to trade with Rome, adopt those elements of Roman culture they chose – without suffering the full tyranny of Roman conquest.

But Tiberius was only biding his time. A plan was gradually prepared for the reconquest of Germania. After Augustus died and Tiberius became emperor, a large-scale raid was launched under the command of Tiberius' nephew Germanicus in AD 14. That was followed the next year by two campaigns involving a huge army of 70,000 men. The Romans succeeded in capturing Arminius' wife Thusnelda and visited the scene of the massacre. Tacitus says they found heaps of bleached bones and severed skulls nailed to trees; the Romans buried these horrifying remains. Archaeologists have indeed found at Kalkriese Hill burial pits containing remains that fit Tacitus' description.

After initial successes, Germanicus was defeated and fell back. He launched yet another huge invasion the following year, and this had no conclusive result. But, astonishingly, Germanicus managed to retrieve two of the three lost eagles, the battle standards so prized by the legions. One of Germanicus's officers, Lucius Stertinus, managed to get the Nineteenth Legion's eagle back from the Bructeri in AD 15. After the Battle of the River Weser in AD 16, the captured chief of the Marsi tribe told Germanicus where the second eagle was hidden. The third standard was not recovered until 41, when Publius Gabinius got it back from the Chauci tribe. The German tribes, for all their alleged barbarism, evidently knew a valuable trophy when they saw one. It is thought that the recovered eagles were ceremoniously deposited in the Temple of the Avenging Mars in Rome.

The military setbacks made Tiberius decide to stop any further campaigns against the Germans. He gave Germanicus a triumph and then redeployed him in Asia. Tiberius's large-scale German campaigns should not be regarded as mere retaliation, revenge for the Teutoburg Forest massacre. They were a resumption of the conquest. The fact that Tiberius was deploying as much as a third of the Roman army proves it.

In 50, the Chatti tribe invaded Roman territory, probably in Hesse. The Romans raised a force to defeat the Chatti, then found to their amazement and delight that they had liberated some of the survivors from Varus' legions, men who had been kept as slaves for forty years.

BOUDICCA'S REBELLION AGAINST ROME

(60–61)

BACKGROUND

Boudicca was the warrior queen of a British tribe called the Iceni, in the early years of the Roman occupation. Her tribal territory corresponded roughly with the modern county of Norfolk. She was an exceptional person in many ways. She was conspicuously intelligent, tall, with long red hair. She also had a harsh voice and a piercing glare. The ancient historian Dio Cassius described her in these terms: 'She was huge of frame, terrifying of aspect, and with a harsh voice. A great mass of bright red hair fell to her knees: she wore a twisted torc, [a decorative solid gold hoop worn round the neck] and a tunic of many colours, over which was a thick mantle, fastened by a brooch. Now she grasped a spear, to strike fear into all who watched her.'

Boudicca's husband was Prasutagus, the king of the Iceni from 47 until 60. When the Romans first invaded in 43, they were mainly concerned with gaining control of the south-east of England, then the fording-place across the Thames at London and the Home Counties. Prasutagus and his people were left alone while the Romans consolidated their position in southern England. The Iceni, like some other tribes, had voluntarily allied themselves to the Roman Empire. That made Prasutagus a client-king, governing his kingdom under Rome. The Iceni were keen to preserve what they could of their independence, though, and when the governor, Publius Ostorius Scapula, announced in 47 that they were to be disarmed they mounted a rebellion.

A civil war was being fought among the Iceni at this time, an intra-tribal struggle between King Anted and the factions of Aesu and Saenu, two rival aristocrats. Anted was king of the Iceni at the time of the Roman invasion and it was he who established the pro-Roman stance of the Iceni. The internal struggle erupted into an armed revolt against Rome in 47. The Iceni were generally treading a pro-Roman path, but also trying to maintain their autonomy under Rome. It was following the civil war that Prasutagus replaced Anted and became client-king of the Iceni.

King Prasutagus, whose palace and headquarters were at Thetford, was long-lived and wealthy. When he died, he left his kingdom jointly to the emperor, his widow Boudicca and his two daughters. At that time it was the normal practice for client kings to retain the partial independence of their kingdoms for their own lifetimes, and for those kingdoms to be left as legacies to Rome. The client-kingship was a transition to full incorporation into the empire. This technique had been used in other provinces of the empire on the European mainland. So Prasutagus's will was to that extent quite normal. The abnormal element was his wish to make his wife and daughters co-heirs. In Roman law, inheritance only occurred through the male line, so leaving the kingdom of the Iceni to three women was an illegal procedure as far as the Romans were concerned; they did not recognise it.

It was a classic case of culture clash. The two sides in the conflict were functioning within two different and conflicting sets of customs and traditions and by adhering to them causing one another offence.

When Prasutagus died, his attempt to leave his kingdom to his wife and daughters was ignored. The kingdom was annexed. Worse still, property and estates were confiscated, and nobles were treated with disrespect. The dead king had lived very well on the money that he had borrowed from Roman financiers. Now that Prasutagus was dead, the financiers decided to call in his debts. His subjects and probably his relatives became liable. There was little sensitivity in the way the debts were collected, either. No doubt the forthright Boudicca let the Roman officials know what she thought about the way she and her people were being treated. In response, she was subjected to a humiliating flogging and her daughters were raped.

THE REBELLION

In 61, the governor, now Gaius Suetonius Paulinus, led a military expedition to the Isle of Anglesey, off the coast of North Wales. The Romans saw the powerful British priests, the druids, as subversive elements, almost an alternative power to Rome in Britain. The Romans were determined to break the power of the druids, and that entailed a direct assault on the druid headquarters, on Anglesey. The high concentration of ancient megalithic monuments in the southern corner of the island may well have attracted the druids. In the same way, Stonehenge may have attracted a certain amount of religious cult activity at this time and this may explain the slighting of the ancient stone circle. Perhaps other megalithic sites suffered vandalism for the same reason. The druids' headquarters on Anglesey was seen by the Romans as an obvious place to attack.

The governor's absence with his army was an equally obvious moment to choose to stage a rebellion. The Iceni conspired with their neighbours to the south, the Trinovantes tribe, to join in a large-scale rebellion. Boudicca emerged as the natural leader of this rebellion. To the Romans a revolt led by a woman would have been unthinkable. The Iceni were inspired by the example of Arminius, who had organised an alliance that succeeded in driving the Romans out of Germany. A similar alliance in Britain could drive the Romans out of Britain. Boudicca herself was influenced by divination. She folded a hare into her tunic, and then released it; she made her decision according to which way the hare ran. She also appealed to Andraste, a local British goddess of victory.

It is probably not a coincidence that Boudicca's own name means 'victory'. As in the Roman world, abstractions like Victory and Fortune could be goddesses. The Roman goddess Fortune was sometimes portrayed on coins, looking remarkably like Britannia, who was probably unconsciously modelled on Fortune. The British goddess Victory was sometimes portrayed as a triple goddess, Frenzy, Battle Raven and Crow, whose sacred birds were allowed to feed on the impaled severed heads of slaughtered enemies. The goddess was invoked before the final battle by Boudicca under the name Andraste. She was not a different goddess, but Victory under a different name, and it was said that Boudicca sacrificed those she defeated in battle to Andraste. Historians have suggested that Boudicca may not have been the queen's personal name at all but a religious title, and that she was regarded as the personification of the goddess. That would go a long way towards explaining not only the fanatical devotion of her own tribespeople but the devotion of warriors from other tribes in the war alliance. It would explain their willingness to unite behind her and to offer her the leadership in battle; they might well have thought that to be led in battle by the goddess of Victory would be likely to lead them to success. The Romans had until that time found it quite easy to suppress the British tribes because of their lack of inter-tribal unity, their lack of collaboration.

Under Boudicca's inspiring leadership, the Iceni and the Trinovantes moved south through east Anglia towards what is now the town of Colchester, and was then the city of Camulodunum. The name 'Camulodunum' means 'Stronghold of Camulos', Camulos being one of the many Celtic gods of war. It had been the capital of the Trinovantes tribe, and was now taken over as a Roman colonia and garrison town. That in itself would have made Camulodunum a natural target for rebels. The Roman military veterans who had settled there treated the local Trinovantes badly. There was particular resentment over the new Temple to Claudius, which had been built at the Trinovantes' expense. Camulodunum and its temple were as natural a focus for resentment as the hated Bastille in the French Revolution.

The Roman settlers in Camulodunum sent for reinforcements from the procurator, but only 200 auxiliaries were available, insufficient to defend it. Boudicca and her angry army descended upon Camulodunum and sacked it. The cult of the Emperor Claudius seems to have blocked the construction of proper defences round the city. This may have been a result of the diversion of revenue away from defensive works and into temple building, or perhaps a failure of the Roman governor to see that an imperial cult centre might be seen as a military target. Either way, the failure to build adequate defences round the city was a fatal mistake. As Boudicca's army surged into Camulodunum, some of the citizens took refuge in the hated temple, and they were besieged in it for two days before being taken. Then the city was systematically destroyed. The Ninth Legion under Quintus Petillius Cerialis tried to relieve Camulodunum, but they too were routed. The infantrymen of the Ninth Legion were completely massacred and only the commander and some cavalry escaped alive.

News of this powerful and so far devastatingly effective rebellion reached Suetonius Paulinus, and he rushed his army back, south-eastwards along Watling Street towards Londinium (London). This was a new town, growing up beside the all-important wooden bridge over the Thames and the port developing immediately below the bridge. It was already developing as a town, mainly on the river terraces to the north of the river and becoming an important route centre. People wanting to travel from mainland Europe to Colchester crossed the Channel to Dover, then travelled along the Old Kent Road (or A2) to cross the Thames at the lowest bridging point, London Bridge. The Thames downstream from London Bridge was then considered too wide to bridge. The wooden Roman bridge was only a few metres from the modern bridge; some of its wooden piles have been found.

Suetonius Paulinus headed for Londinium, probably with the idea of attacking Boudicca's army there and saving the town. Perhaps while he was marching he heard more details about what the rebels had done not only to Camulodunum but to Quintus Petillius Cerialis and his troops. He decided that his force as it stood was too small to deal with such a fierce rebellion. He would not risk suffering the same fate as Quintus Petillius Cerialis; instead he sacrificed Londinium for the sake of the province. Londinium, then unwalled and virtually defenceless, was left to the rebel army. Many of the inhabitants had evacuated before the rebels arrived, but anyone still left there was slaughtered and then the town was destroyed.

Archaeologists have found a thick layer of burnt debris from this event. They also found, when the Jubilee Line was being built in 1998, evidence that Boudicca crossed the Thames. Buildings south of the Thames were burnt and destroyed in the same way as those burnt and destroyed by Boudicca in what is now the City of London. This shows that the attack must have taken some time, and was unopposed. Suetonius Paulinus really did totally abandon London, its buildings and its inhabitants to Boudicca.

Leaving Londinium in smoking ruins, the rebels next marched on Verulamium (St Albans), which was also destroyed. The scale of the destruction seems to have been unprecedented in Britain. Something approaching 80,000 people were killed in the three cities. The British tribesmen took no prisoners and had no interest in exchanging captives for ransoms. They were only interested, the Roman historian Tacitus tells us, in killing people.

THE ROMANS' RETALIATION: THE BATTLE OF WATLING STREET

Suetonius Paulinus set about mustering a force large enough and powerful enough to deal with Boudicca's army. He gathered the Fourteenth Legion, some detachments of the Twentieth Legion and whatever auxiliaries were available. Poenius Postumus, who was the prefect of the Second Legion, stationed in the West Country, refused to answer Suetonius Paulinus's call for aid and reinforcements. He evidently thought the rebel army was unstoppable and that confronting them would be virtual suicide. Suetonius Paulinus would have to manage without Poenius Postumus' Second Legion, but he was even so in command of 10,000 men.

Suetonius Paulinus and his army took up a position that has never been conclusively identified. It is known that it was somewhere along Watling Street, the major Roman road running north-westwards out of

Londinium, beginning with what is now the Edgware Road. The Roman position and the field of battle are thought by some historians to have been in the West Midlands, by other historians further south, perhaps in Northamptonshire. Specific locations that have been proposed include High Cross in Leicestershire, Mancetter, Kings Norton and Towcester. It is rather surprising that such a major event, which ought to have yielded huge numbers of artefacts, to say nothing of human remains, has vanished completely without trace or surviving local tradition and continues to be undetected by either history or archaeology.

The Roman army camped in a valley with a wood at the back of them. It was a substantial army, yet it was hopelessly outnumbered by the rebel army, which success had raised to 230,000, according to one ancient source. With her daughters at her side, Boudicca toured her assembled warriors in her chariot, shouting encouragement to them. Tacitus gives her a short speech, which may or may not be an accurate piece of reporting. The speech presents Boudicca not as a noblewoman avenging her lost wealth but as an ordinary person. She is fighting to avenge her loss of freedom, the beating of her body, the abused chastity of her daughters. Theirs was a just cause and the gods were on their side. The one Roman legion that had dared to face them had been annihilated. She was a woman and determined to win or die. If they as men wanted to live in slavery, then that was their choice.

The British host looked utterly chaotic and disorganised to the Romans, who must have watched with some trepidation at the huge numbers of warriors arriving. It was lucky for the Romans that the British host was chaotic. The British approach to warfare was very different from the Roman. British battle tactics involved trying to terrify and confuse the enemy. Their hair was dressed with lime to make spiky dreadlocks; their bodies were painted. They leapt around, gesticulating wildly, shouted, banged their weapons and blew trumpets. When one British army fought another, these preliminaries, which were the equivalent of name calling, were followed by individual champions challenging the champions of the opposite side to single combat. The champions would then ride forward in their chariots to fight duels. These heroes would later be praised in song. A melee would follow, in which the two sides rushed together in a general brawl. The style of fighting was really little changed since the days of the Trojan War.

This old-style British way of fighting was very different from the highly disciplined and cold-blooded style of the Roman army, which was far more effective. The Roman troops may have been alarmed at the huge assembly of British warriors, but also reassured by the high level of disorganization. The Britons gathered in informal groups round their various chieftains. They followed Boudicca, but not in any co-ordinated way. There was no battle plan. They relied on their huge numbers – and their anger – to overwhelm the Romans.

The huge numbers of British rebels in relation to the Roman numbers should have made the outcome of the battle that followed a foregone conclusion. But what should have been a British victory was a resounding defeat. The British may have had the gods on their side, but they did not have manoeuvrability, nor did they have skill or experience in fighting together in large numbers, nor did they have the communications system needed to deploy large forces effectively on the field of battle. Once battle was joined, as far as the British were concerned, it was a free-for-all – really one huge pub brawl. The Roman army, meanwhile, was highly disciplined and used to being given structured orders during battle. The valley floor site hemmed in by forest favoured the Romans, which is why they selected it. It was a confined field of battle, and it was only possible for Boudicca to confront the Roman army with a relatively small fraction of her total force at any one time.

The battle began with thousands of Britons charging at the Romans, who held them off with volleys of heavy javelins. The Romans then advanced in wedge formation to engage the second wave of Britons. The Britons then tried to retreat, but they were obstructed by their own families, who were installed in a ring of wagons on the battlefield edge. The Britons had thus made a confined battlefield even more confined. Many Britons were killed as they were caught between the advancing Roman wedge formation and their own wagons.

What could so easily have been an overwhelming British victory, a British equivalent of the Teutoburg Forest, turned into a total defeat. One report said that 80,000 Britons were killed in the Battle of Watling Street. What happened to Boudicca herself is a mystery. One Roman source says she fell ill and died, and was given a lavish burial; another says she fled from the battlefield and committed suicide by taking poison. There is what can only be described as an urban legend that the warrior queen lies buried underneath Platform 8 or 10 at King's Cross Station in London. This is untrue. It was mentioned in Lewis Spence's book on Boadicea, published in 1937, but is a hoax with no foundation in truth. Poenius Postumus, the Roman prefect who had refused to join Suetonius Paulinus, also committed suicide when he heard of the overwhelming Roman victory.

Aftermath

The surviving rebels dispersed, and the rebellion was over. Suetonius Paulinus organized punitive expeditions, but in Rome it was feared that these would probably provoke more rebellions. Suetonius Paulinus's actions were investigated by Nero's freedman Polyclitus and, as a result, Nero replaced him with a governor who was more conciliatory in manner and style, Publius Petronius Turpilianus.

The Boudicca rebellion was a failure. The territories of the Iceni and the Trinovantes remained under Roman control and Boudicca was dead. But in one way the rebellion came very close to success. Nero seriously contemplated abandoning Britain as a result of the actual outcome. Presumably if the Britons had won that major battle, Nero would have ordered a withdrawal. In that case, Britain would have returned to its pre-Roman British state in 61 rather than in the fifth century, when the Roman occupation finally did come to an end. If that had happened, then many more of the pre-Roman, Iron Age customs and practices of the British people would have been likely to survive.

One of the reasons the Roman historians recorded this particular rebellion in detail was the person of Boudicca. The Romans were astonished to see a woman leading an army, indeed taking any prominent role in public life. Such things were almost unheard of in the Roman world. The Romans knew of three queens, two in Britain, Cartimandua and Boudicca, and one in Egypt. Because the Roman historians were so struck by the incongruity of women as war leaders or heads of state, we have been left a very striking, vivid and enduring image of Boudicca. Boudicca was forgotten for many centuries, making no appearance in Bede or Geoffrey of Monmouth's *History of the Kings of Britain.* It was in the Renaissance, when the works of Tacitus were rediscovered, that Boudicca took on a new lease of life and she was included in Raphael Holinshed's *Chronicles* (1577).

Then, in the nineteenth century, she became a British national heroine, partly because she was seen to be Queen Victoria's namesake, though it is very hard to see how the Victorians could have seen the prim little modern queen as a modern counterpart to Boudicca. Nevertheless, a huge bronze statue of Boudicca in her war chariot was made in 1905 and mounted next to the Houses of Parliament. With some irony, she had by this stage become associated with the British Empire, which was modelled on the Roman Empire, when it was the Roman Empire that she had so strenuously resisted; the mythic queen was also shown vigorously *defending* the city the historical queen had actually *destroyed.*

By this stage, Boudicca had become a national icon with characteristics and dynamics that were quite different from those of the historical figure. She became a fiction, and naturally enough has featured as the heroine of several novels and two films. The age of women's liberation also saw Boudicca taken up as an icon of female emancipation and self-empowerment; the idea of one woman taking on the might of the Roman Empire had and still has enormous mythic power.

THE FALL OF MASADA
(74)

Masada, between Sodom and Ein Gedi, is an impressive natural desert fortress surrounded by steep cliffs up to 400 metres (1,300 ft) high. It stands on top of an isolated mountain on the edge of the Judaean Desert and the Dead Sea valley. It totters on the western rim of the Rift Valley occupied by the Dead Sea – a very wild place. The plateau summit is level and about 550 metres (1,800 ft) long. It was Herod the Great who fortified this rocky mountain top (37–31 BC) as a royal citadel, a refuge for himself in the event of a revolt. The summit plateau was fitted with a boundary wall 1,300 metres (4,300 ft) long and 3.6 metres (12 ft) thick and punctuated with towers. Inside were storehouses, a palace, an armoury, a barracks and cisterns that filled with rain water. Access from the plain below was difficult and steep, along three winding paths that led up to fortified gates.

Masada occupies a special place in Jewish history, where it is portrayed as the last outpost of the Zealots during the Jewish Revolt. It was the scene of what has been described as 'the most dramatic and symbolic act in Jewish history, where rebels chose mass suicide rather than submit to Roman capture.'

A hundred years after the fortress was built, in AD 66, an obscure band of Jewish extremist rebels, the Sicarii, captured Masada from the Roman troops stationed there. The documentation is scanty, but it appears that the Sicarii were an offshoot of the Zealots, who bore the brunt of the rebellion against Rome, specifically opposing the Roman rule of Judaea. The Sicarii at Masada were led by Eleazar ben Simon. In 70 they were joined by more Sicarii, along with their families, who were thrown out of Jerusalem by other Jews with whom they were in conflict. These events happened just before the Destruction of Jerusalem. While the

Sicarii occupied Masada they adapted some of Herod's buildings. One was turned into a synagogue which faced Jerusalem.

In 72, Lucius Flavius Silva, the Roman governor of Judaea, marched his troops to Masada. He and the Tenth Legion laid siege to the fortress. At first they tried in vain to break through the perimeter wall. Then, against the western face of the plateau, they created a huge ramp 114 metres (375 ft) high out of stones and beaten earth. The ramp was investigated by geologists in the 1990s and it was found that it mostly consisted of a natural spur of rock and that it only required a rubble layer 9 metres (30 ft) thick built on top of it to reach the fortress's defences. So, what has often been described as a triumph of Roman engineering was actually a much smaller-scale project.

It is not known whether the Sicarii made any attempts to counter-attack their Roman besiegers, but during the two or three month period of the siege they did apparently break out and attack a nearby Jewish settlement, Ein-Gedi, where they slaughtered 700 people. The historian Josephus mentions this incident.

The ramp was finished in early 73, and the Romans were able to reach and breach the fortress wall with a battering ram on 16 April.

When the Roman troops went inside the fortress they saw a startling scene. Nearly all the buildings were on fire and the 936 inhabitants had committed suicide rather than face execution or enslavement at the hands of the Romans. Jewish teaching forbids suicide, and Josephus explained that the defenders had drawn lots and killed one another, down to the last man, who was the only one actually to kill himself. Josephus also reported that they set fire to all the buildings except the store rooms, leaving these intact to show the Romans that they still had the means to live if they had chosen – but they had chosen to die. Archaeological excavation suggests that this was not true; they burnt the storerooms too. Josephus was told the story of the siege of Masada by two women who had survived the mass suicide by hiding in a cistern with five children.

The fall of Masada is an epic story that still grips us with its sweep and power, with its image of a small community of embattled 'believers' (whatever that may mean) besieged and doomed, heroic and uncompromising. Stories like this one become deeply embedded in national myth. They engender zeal; they inspire the young; they encourage stubbornness and the refusal to compromise; they also fuel conflict. The reality was probably much more complex than the myth, and we should not forget Ein-Gedi.

THE JEWISH REVOLT
(132)

The Jewish, or Bar Kokhba, Revolt was another in a long series of rebellions against the Roman Empire. This large-scale revolt took place at a time of high hopes and expectations – the Jews thought they would achieve the founding of a homeland and a Holy Temple – but ended in wretchedness, failure and slavery.

When Hadrian became emperor in 118 he at first supported the aspirations of the Jews. He let them return to Jerusalem and gave them permission to rebuild the temple there. Expectations and excitement rose as the preparations got under way to rebuild the temple. Then Hadrian changed his mind and instructed that the temple must be built on a different site. At the same time he started deporting Jews to North Africa.

The Jews were incensed at this unexpected breach of trust. They were ready to rebel, but Rabbi Joshua ben Hananiah persuaded them to quieten down. After that the Jews began secret preparations for rebellion, in case the opportunity arose later. They set up refuges or hideouts in caves. They also organised guerrilla units and in 123 they started springing surprise attacks on the Romans. This only made the situation worse, as Hadrian ordered in an extra legion, the Sixth Legion, to go to Judaea to deal with the terrorists.

Hadrian disliked Judaism because he saw it as the root of rebellion. To stamp out any further possibility of rebellion in Palestine, he decided, he must stamp out Judaism. He prohibited one Jewish practice after another. He tried to forbid the Jews from practising circumcision. He prohibited the Torah law and the use of the Hebrew calendar. The sacred scroll was burnt on the Temple Mount. He had Jewish scholars executed. He also appointed a harsh new governor for Judaea, Tinneius

Rufus. In 132 Hadrian ordered the building of a new city at Jerusalem, to be called Aelia Capitolina, and with a Temple of Jupiter standing on the site of the Jewish Temple. He installed two statues, one of Jupiter and one of himself. This was a major affront to the Jews, to whom the site was sacred. The problem was that in crushing Judaism in this relentless way, Hadrian was actually provoking rebellion, not averting it.

While Hadrian was in the area, the Jews remained quiet and acquiescent, but as soon as he left, in 132, they launched their large-scale rebellion. They took over towns, fortified them, fitting them with walls and underground passages. The Jewish guru Rabbi Akiva persuaded the Sanhedrin to support the imminent rebellion. He regarded the chosen commander, Shimon bar-Kokhba, as the Jewish Messiah. He took the star prophecy verse from Chapter 24 of the Book of Numbers as support for this view: 'There shall come a star out of Jacob.' The name bar-Kokhba means 'son of a star' in Aramaic. It was stretching a point, to say the least, to read the star prophecy as an indication that Shimon was the Messiah. Even so, Shimon bar-Kokhba, who was now not merely the rebellion's leader but perhaps the Jewish Messiah, organized the capture of fifty strongholds in Palestine and almost a thousand villages and towns. Jerusalem was one of them. In the Judaean Desert, archaeologists have found a collection of papyrus documents containing bar-Kokhba's orders.

The rebellion gained momentum, with Jews joining from other countries, and even some gentiles too.

Hadrian sent the governor of Syria, Publius Marcellus, to assist in the suppression of the rebellion. Such was the strength and determination of the Jewish rebels at this point that they were able to overcome the joint forces of the Syrian and Judaean governors. The rebels took control of the coast and engaged in sea battles against the Romans.

At this point the rebellion appeared to have succeeded. The rebels and not the Romans were in control of Palestine. The Jews organized the minting of new coins with slogans on them such as 'The Freedom of Israel' on them. The coins were well-struck in large quantities with fine designs on them and the date, 'Year One of the Redemption of Israel.'

For the next two and a half years a sovereign Jewish state was restored. The state administration was headed by Shimon bar-Kokhba, who adopted the title Nasi Israel, Prince of Israel. Presumably he and his advisers were careful to avoid the title King of the Jews. The Era of the Redemption of Israel was proclaimed. Rabbi Akiva, who had named Shimon Bar-Kokhba the Messiah, presided over the Sanhedrin, the Jewish High Court. Jewish religious observances were reinstated, including sacrifices on the altar.

THE ROMAN RECONQUEST

The power and effectiveness of the Jewish rebellion took the Romans by surprise. Hadrian organized a much larger force to quell the revolt. What was involved now was nothing short of a reconquest of Palestine.

Then Hadrian sent in major reinforcements to crush the three-year revolt. He sent Sextus Julius Severus, a general from Britain, and Hadrianus Quintus Lollius Urbicus, the former governor of the province of Germania, along with many extra troops. By now there were as many as twelve legions in Palestine. But the number of Jewish rebels was also very great. Sextus Julius Severus was an experienced and skilful general and he decided to avoid engaging in open battle with the rebels. Instead he laid siege to the rebel fortresses, depriving them of food supplies, weakening the rebel forces inside. Only then did he risk open warfare.

Once the Romans had retaken Jerusalem, Shimon bar-Kokhba and the remnants of his forces retreated to a refuge, the fortress of Betha, which itself came under siege. In the end, the Romans demolished all the fortresses settlements occupied by the rebels – a huge undertaking. The Romans suffered heavy casualties in the fighting and for once Hadrian refrained from sending to the Senate his customary message, 'I and my army are well.' It would not have been true. Among the Roman losses was an entire legion, the Twenty-Second, which was wiped out by the rebels.

The last and decisive battle of the revolt took place in Bethar, which was bar-Kokhba's headquarters. This provided accommodation for the

Sanhedrin, the Jewish High Court, and the leader, who was called the Nasi. Bethar was a crucial stronghold because it was strategically positioned on a ridge overlooking two major road routes. In addition, thousands of refugees had converged on Bethar during the course of the revolt. Hadrian's army laid siege to Bethar in 135, and on the day when the Jews commemorated the destruction of the first and second Temples the walls of Bethar fell. There was fierce fighting in Bethar as the Romans went in to destroy the rebel resistance. Every Jew in Bethar was slaughtered. The Jerusalem Talmud says that the numbers killed at Bethar were enormous, that the Romans 'went on killing until their horses were submerged in blood to the nostrils.' As an additional punishment, the Romans did not allow the dead to be buried for six days.

After this decisive battle, there were only a few minor skirmishes in the Judaean Desert, where some rebels made a last stand in their caves. In the Jewish Revolt as a whole, it is said that more than half a million Jews were killed.

Aftermath

The Roman suppression of the Jewish Revolt was a human disaster. It caused enormous religious, cultural and demographic damage. Judaea lost its independence totally. Jews were sold into slavery, many of them transported to Egypt. The destroyed settlements were in many cases not rebuilt. Hadrian went ahead with his plan to convert Jerusalem into a pagan city named Aelia Capitolina, from which Jews were excluded. Even the identity of Judaea was taken away. The one-time kingdom and now province of Judaea was henceforth to be called Syria Palestina. Hadrian deliberately named the province after the enemies of the Israelites, the Philistines.

Hadrian launched a continuing persecution of Jews, and in particular against Jewish religious observances, that lasted for the rest of his reign. Some Jews, such as Rabbi Akiva, were martyred for continuing with their customary observances.

At the time the rebellion broke out, Christianity was still a sect within Judasim, and religious historians believe that the claim that bar-Kokhba was the Messiah alienated many Christians, who believed that Jesus was the Messiah. This conflict widened the split between Jews and Christians, and made the launching of Christianity as a separate religion more likely.

The massive destruction of the Jewish way of life in Palestine has led some scholars to date the start of the Jewish diaspora (dispersal) from the revolt. Most of the Jews were killed, exiled or sold into slavery as the revolt ended. Judaea would never become a Jewish religious centre again until the modern era.

There were major shifts in Jewish religious thought. Messiahs had been claimed repeatedly, but now the concept of the Messiah became more abstract and spiritual than political. The approach became more cautious. In the Talmud, for instance, Shimon bar-Kokhba is referred to as 'ben-Kusiba', a derogatory term expressing the idea that he was a false Messiah. The ambivalent position that the rabbis adopted towards Messianism from then on was a response to the traumatic failure of this Messianic rising. Later on, the Jewish Revolt became a symbol of national resistance, and of a great persecution that was in its way the forerunner of the Holocaust.

2

MEDIEVAL CONFLICTS

THE BIRTH OF ISLAM

616–632

The prophet Mohammed, who was born in 567 or 569, spent his early life as a caravan conductor, though he was drawn to a very different sort of existence, the life of religious contemplation. After his marriage to Khadija, a wealthy forty-year-old widow who was fifteen years older than him, he seems to have become part owner of a shop selling farm produce and he began to acquire a reputation for practical wisdom.

At the time when Mohammed decided that he was to become the legislator or mouthpiece of God, northern Arabia had fallen under the influence of the Byzantine Empire, a Christianising influence. Southern Arabia had fallen under a number of successive influences – Jewish, Abyssinian and Persian. It was in this melting pot of spiritual influences that Mohammed had his revelation.

Mohammed's claim to be the mouthpiece of God was a claim to authority, to a definitive expression of faith, but he was very cautious about the way he expressed his claim. For three years he and his followers formed a secret society, and that was preceded by a period of preparation which involved a revelation on Mount Hirah near Mecca. The earliest of these revelations took the form of pages of text that were to be revealed only to his nearest relatives, and these solemn divine utterances were in the form of rhymes. The prophet would speak in a trance while followers wrote down his utterances. The revelations would eventually make up the Koran.

Thus far, the evolution of Islam as a distinct faith caused no conflict. This was largely because it was happening mainly in private, within the family. By the time Mohammed made his first appearance as a public preacher in Mecca in 616, he was already the head of a united community of followers. The new religion was already fledged. It was now, when Mohammed's new faith was public, that the conflict began. As he became more successful, some of his followers were persecuted, and he found a refuge for them in Axum in Abyssinia, where the Abyssinian king took their side, evidently thinking mistakenly that they were persecuted Christians. This support from outside infuriated the Meccan leaders, who blockaded Mohammed in one quarter of the city.

Mohammed showed a conciliatory side to his nature at this point. He had a revelation which showed that the Meccan goddesses should be recognized as well as Allah. Later on, though, he would renounce this revelation as a fabrication of the Devil.

Then both Abu Talib, Mohammed's uncle and guardian, and his wife Khadija died. This left Mohammed unprotected in an increasingly hostile Mecca. He fled to the oasis of Taif, from where he negotiated with various wealthy Meccan citizens for protection. Mohammed was glad to be invited to go instead to the city of Medina (then named Yathrib) as dictator. The citizens there suffered from feuding and wanted an impartial and wise outsider to go and act as arbitrator. Mohammed accordingly went into exile or hejira (flight); the date, 16 July 622, is taken as the beginning of the Islamic era.

The Meccan authorities were alarmed at the prospect of a hostile regime in control in Medina, which lay on a major caravan route, and plans were laid to have Mohammed killed. The Prophet, as he came to be known, took refuge in a cave, delaying his arrival at Medina until September 622. From then on the power of Mohammed and the power of Islam grew. He bound his followers to himself and one another by a range of ties including brotherhoods. He seems to have courted an alliance with the Jews, but the difference in beliefs was too great. Islam began to develop its own customs and practices, so that it became a distinct and recognisable culture. The prohibition on wine, which was introduced in 625, was a response to the drunken behaviour of one of the followers. The new religion spread quickly, not least because proof of conversion was reduced to the simplest threshold, the expression of belief in Allah and Mohammed.

Mohammed and his followers needed a source of income, and this became a further cause of conflict. Attacking caravans was their only option. From this point onwards, the culture of Islam became aggressive and war-like. Mohammed gave his followers permission to go to war to fight the enemies of Islam, and a state of war son developed. The Meccans were defeated at the Battle of Badr in 624 and three years later Mohammed repelled an attempt by the Meccans to take Medina. In 629 Mecca itself fell to Mohammed and within the year the whole of Arabia was under his control.

Aftermath

The Middle East had for a long time been a battleground of competing ideas, religions, dynasties and empires. The creation of Islam introduced a dynamic new force, and it was one that swept like a bush-fire through the entire region and outwards in all directions. As a socio-political force, it was sometimes positive, sometimes negative. When areas under Byzantine rule were conquered by Muslim invaders, the inhabitants frequently felt it as a liberation from oppression. But the spread of Islam by the sword was also to cause a great deal of bloodshed during the centuries to come.

ISLAMIC EXPANSION

632–1025

Mohammed's political successors were called caliphs. The caliph was often referred to as Amir al-Mu'minin, the Commander of the Faithful, and he was the acknowledged Muslim leader. The first four caliphs after the death of the prophet Mohammed in 632 were Abu Bakr, Umar ibn al-Khattab, Uthman ibn Affan and Ali ibn Abi Talib. They were known as the Rashidun, or Rightly Guided, caliphs, because of their conscientious adherence to the Koran. After them, the title caliph was claimed by successive dynasties, the Umayyads, the Abbasids and the Ottomans. The caliphs were quickly to become emperors in all but name, political leaders of a huge and expanding Muslim Empire. The phenomenal spread of Islam under the caliphs was achieved by means of a series of interconnected and aggressively pursued wars that began on Mohammed's death and went on until the start of the Crusades.

It is hard to be sure of the detail, because religious zeal (on every side) has tended to colour the history of events in the Middle East. Later Muslim writings, for instance, tell us about the Battle of Tabouk, which is supposed to have taken place in October 630 in the north-west of what is today Saudi Arabia. Mohammed and Emperor Heraclius themselves are supposed to have taken part in the battle, on opposing sides. But Greek sources make no mention of such a battle, and that suggests that it may not have happened. The initial Muslim conquests took place under the Rashidun and Umayyad caliphs, when the eastern borders of the Byzantine Empire were eroded. The Byzantine Empire, under its emperor Heraclius, had just emerged exhausted from the Roman-Persian Wars; that was why the Byzantines were unable to make any effective resistance to the advance of the Arabs. The first wars after the prophet Mohammed's death were the Ridda wars. These were skirmishes with the Arab client states which blew up into a full-blown war, which ended with the Arab conquest of the Lavant and Persia under two Rashidun generals, al-Walid and al-'As.

The first phase of the Byzantine Arab Wars (634–717) had the Second Arab Siege of Constantinople as its climax. This marked the end of the expansion of the Arab Empire into Asia Minor.

The Arab conquest of Syria (634–638) was made easier by the indisposition of the Emperor Heraclius, who was too ill at the time to lead his armies into battle. As a result, the Rashidun caliphate army led by General Khalid ibn al-Walid was able to conquer both Syria and Palestine in 634. The conquest was enthusiastically welcomed by Jews and Christians in Syria, because they had been oppressed by Byzantine rule in terms of both taxation and persecution. Heraclius mounted a campaign to regain Syria, but in the Battle of Yarmouk in 636 he was defeated. Once back in Constantinople, Heraclius prepared his army to defend Egypt.

In February 638, the Arabs took Jerusalem, which was surrendered by Patriarch Sophronius, the city's chief magistrate. Once again the local people welcomed the conquerors as they entered the city, led by the Caliph Umar on a white camel. He was wearing worn and filthy robes and his army too was filthy, but their discipline was perfect. Umar rode straight to the Temple Mount, the spot where his friend, the prophet Mohammed, was said to have ascended to Heaven. The patriarch was in tears at this scene, remembering the words of his own prophet, Daniel; he murmured, 'Behold the abomination of desolation', sensing that the Jews were about to lose the holiest of *their* holy places.

By the time of the Emperor Heraclius' death, he had lost much of the Roman province of Egypt to the caliphate, and with it much of his wheat supply. General Amr ibn al-'As moved into Egypt from Palestine with 4,000 Arab warriors in December 639. Using their navy, the Byzantines temporarily won back Alexandria in 645 but lost it again after the Battle of Nikiou in 646. The local Christian Copts welcomed the Arabs in. Cyprus fell to the Arabs in 643 and in 644 Caliph Umar died, to be succeeded by Caliph Uthman. In 647 the Arab army moved west to take Tripolitania and returned to Egypt loaded with booty.

There was a civil war within the Arab Empire, after which the Umayyad caliphs came to power. Under their leadership, the rest of North Africa fell to the Islamic conquest. The Arabs were able to reach Visigothic Spain by using the Strait of Gibraltar.

At that time, the Byzantine navy was still the main naval power in Europe and the Middle East. The Byzantine emperor commanded a powerful navy of 300 biremes fitted with battering rams. There was a great sea-battle off the coast of Lycia in western Anatolia in 655, and in that battle 500 Byzantine ships were destroyed, yet even after that huge loss Byzantium went on being the dominant sea power. The Arab forces systematically whittled away that power, neutralizing one Byzantine naval base after another. They took the major port of Rhodes, off the south-west coast of Anatolia, in 655. They did not destroy the Colossus of Rhodes, the huge statue of Helios at the harbour entrance in 280 BC, as that had fallen down in an earthquake in 226 BC, and the broken pieces of bronze were left on the waterfront. The Arabs sold these to a trader from Edessa for scrap, which meant that the Colossus could never be re-erected. They were taken away on the backs of 900 camels.

Caliph Muawiyah then consolidated both the eastern part of the Islamic Empire, from the Nile right across to the Aral Sea, and the western part, from the Nile right across North Africa to Morocco. The empire reached the Atlantic Ocean in the west (682) and the Sahara in the south. There, for the moment, the expansion paused, partly because of another Muslim civil war following the death of Muawiyah in 690. There were to be four caliphs in the following five years; then Caliph Abd al-Malik succeeded.

Meanwhile the Byzantines kept trying to hold the Arab conquest at bay. The so-called 'Saracen Wars' of Emperor Justinian II, who was the last of the Heraclian dynasty, were chaotic. Justinian was deposed in 695; the Byzantines lost Carthage to the Arabs in 698; then Justinian returned to power for six more years, but this second reign was marked by yet more losses to the Arabs, who seemed to be unstoppable.

In the 670s the Umayyad Caliph Muawiyah had laid siege to Constantinople when it was the headquarters of Constantine IV. On that occasion the magnificent walls of the city proved to be impenetrable and the Arabs had blockaded the city, but in the end winter forced the Arabs to withdraw. Among those killed in the siege of Constantinople was Mohammed's standard bearer, Eyup. He was Mohammed's last surviving associate. Before the siege a Syrian Christian refugee called Callinicus of Heliopolis had invented a startling new weapon for the Byzantines. It was Greek fire. This was a spectacular flame-thrower that was capable of destroying ships. In 677, at the Battle of Syllaeum in the Sea of Marmara, the Byzantine fleet used Greek fire against the Arab navy and defeated it; the siege of Constantinople was lifted and the Arab expansion into Europe was brought to a standstill for thirty years.

There was a second Arab Siege of Constantinople in 717–18. Once again a land force was blocked by the massive city walls and the naval force was overwhelmed by the use of Greek fire. This siege brought the initial conflict to a close.

LATER CONFLICTS

The Arab expansionist strategy was revived but with less energy and less success after the siege of Constantinople in 718. The process went on for three hundred years, but at a slower pace. The Arabs tried to take Anatolia, but failed at least until the Seljuks arrived.

The Byzantine-Arab Wars had a major effect on the Byzantine Empire, not just because of the loss of territories and the absorption of military expenditure, but because of the religious unrest it stirred up. In 726 the Wars of the Icons started. An edict of Leo the Isaurian said that the crucifix, until then usually complete with the depiction of the martyred body of Christ, was to be replaced by a cross without Christ. This set off a great controversy. It seems that Leo saw the continued success of the Muslims as evidence that God was displeased with Byzantium. The eruption of the island of Thera reinforced this view.

God was displeased – Leo decided - with the Byzantines' excessive dependence on religious icons. Leo arrived at this conclusion because he was aware that the Muslims had placed a ban on representation in religious art; depictions amounted to idolatry. Leo was so certain that his analysis of the situation was correct that he did not see any need to consult other churchmen. He was taken by surprise when he encountered intense popular opposition. In 732 Leo took the extraordinary step of ordering a fleet to be sent to arrest Pope Gregory III, who had defied his edict. The ships were lost in the Adriatic, and Leo's superstitious mind might have interpreted this as a divine intervention, at the very least an intimation that he was wrong.

But the rights and wrongs of the icon argument are not the point. The point is that a major spiritual and political conflict was generated, one that seriously weakened the Byzantine culture. It also brought about a schism (rift) between the Patriarch of Constantinople and the Bishop of Rome and thus further separated the two parts of the former Roman Empire.

Between 750 and 770, Emperor Constantine waged campaigns to try to get back some of the territories that had been lost to the Arabs.

The Byzantine Empire was divided by occasional civil wars, and these were often encouraged by the Arabs. Caliph Al-Ma'mun supported an Arab invasion of Anatolia led by Thomas the Slav. Within a very short time, most of Anatolia had been taken by the Arabs. Thomas even succeeded in capturing the town of Thessalonica, but lost it to the Byzantines shortly afterwards. He tried to lay siege to Constantinople in 821, but was defeated (once again) by the city's massive walls.

The Arabs conquered Crete in 824 and then Sicily, starting with Palermo in 831 and taking Messina in 842. Then the tables were turned. From 867 the Byzantine Empire was led by stronger and more unified leaders. The Muslim Abbasid Empire conversely had fragmented into many factions and was weaker. Basil I gave the Byzantine Empire new vigour, turning it once more into a major regional power that was the strongest in Europe. There was also a new approach to church matters which made for much better relations with Rome. Then Basil was able to form an alliance with the Holy Roman Emperor Louis II, the nominal head of the largely fictitious Western Empire, to strengthen the European stand against the Arabs.

In 871 Louis II captured the Italian town of Bari, which had been captured by the Arabs, and successfully cleared the Adriatic Sea of Arab pirates. But there were major reverses too. Syracuse in Sicily fell under Arab control again in 878, then the Sicilian fortress of Taormina in 902. Sicily then stayed under Arab control until the Norman invasion in 1071. On the other hand, the Byzantines regained much of Calabria in Italy in 880 and Crete in 960.

The Byzantine emperor Basil II struck out against the Arabs in a major new campaign in 995. He made great progress in Syria, which he reclaimed for the Byzantine Empire, but did not have enough military strength to continue south and reclaim Jerusalem. By 1025, the reclaimed territories of the Byzantine Empire stretched from the toe of Italy and the Adriatic in the west to the Danube and the Crimean Peninsula in the north, and to Mesopotamia in the east. The Byzantine Empire had reached a zenith.

Aftermath

The close of this phase in the conflict did not come with peace, reconciliation or resolution. It came with diversions and new threats from elsewhere. The Byzantine emperors had to deal with threats from the Seljuk Turks, rather than with the Arabs. The Arabs meanwhile had to deal with the Crusades and then later with invasions by Mongol hordes. As so often in history, the conflict was not resolved. It simply spawned new conflicts.

These very long drawn out wars had major effects on the Arab states and the Byzantine Empire. The Byzantine Empire suffered huge losses of territory, while the Arabs gained control over large areas in the Middle East and Africa. There were huge indirect effects on Europe. The Byzantines were continually preoccupied, for hundreds of years, with fending off Arab invasions on their eastern frontier. This distracted them from expanding to the west. Without the aggressive expansion of the Muslim Empire, Europe would almost certainly have been overwhelmed by a similarly aggressive expansion of the Byzantine Empire. The fact that Europe was left untouched during this period meant that the feudal Christian states of medieval Europe were able to evolve.

The schism between Constantinople and Rome over the icons had the effect of isolating the Papacy and throwing it into the arms of the Franks. In other words, what began as Mohammed's religious mission led, through a complex and unpredictable chain reaction, to the career of Charlemagne and the rise of the Frankish Empire. The Byzantine emperors were irritated by the emergence of another empire in the West. The Byzantine emperor Basil sent an angry letter to Charlemagne reprimanding him for adopting the title emperor: the Frankish ruler, he raged, should remember that he was *only a king*.

VIKING RAIDS AGAINST ENGLAND
(793–1066)

Raiding by Scandinavian pirates at various places round the coasts of Britain started near the end of the eighth century. To begin with, these were hit-and-run attacks, often on vulnerable monastic sites. These were particularly attractive because they were often repositories of rich objects, they were undefended and the inmates were unarmed, and they were often in remote locations and therefore a long way from help. The Vikings, as they were called, did not stay, at least during the first few decades.

In 793, Alcuin of York wrote to Higbald, Bishop of Lindisfarne, and also to Ethelred, King of Northumbria. He lamented the Vikings' attack without warning on the monastery of Lindisfarne off the Northumbrian coast. These Vikings were probably Norwegians who had sailed directly across the North Sea. Lindisfarne was not destroyed in that raid, but over the next few decades many monasteries in the north of Britain were destroyed and along with them any record that might have been made of the raids. There are no surviving documents recounting raids in Scotland, though there must have been many.

In 802, the monastery on Iona was burnt and there was another raid four years later in which nearly seventy monks were slaughtered. The survivors left Iona – it was too dangerous a place to stay – and fled to Kells in County Meath. They took with them a remarkable illuminated book of Gospels. It was probably written and illuminated on Iona, though it is known as the Book of Kells. Some monasteries in northern England and Scotland disappeared from the historical record. Lindisfarne, like Iona, was too isolated and too vulnerable and was given up. The monks of Lindisfarne went on a peregrination of northern England, carrying with them their greatest treasure, the body of St Cuthbert. Eventually they made their home at Durham, where the saint was given his final resting place.

Given the lack of documentation it is hard to be sure what impact the Vikings had on Scotland. In Orkney and Shetland, Caithness and Sutherland, the dense scatter of Scandinavian place names tells us that there was heavy colonization of these areas. There is also substantial archaeological evidence on Orkney of the presence of a Viking elite. It is probable that the presence of Norwegians in the north of Scotland and the islands was a major factor in the disappearance of the kingdom of the Picts. In the eighth century the kingdom of the Picts was one of the most important in Britain – it was certainly one of the biggest. By 1000, the Picts and their kingdom had vanished. Instead there was a kingdom called Scotland, controlled by people called Scots. These Scots were the descendants of Irish immigrants who had arrived in the fifth century.

In England the raids were spasmodic until the 840s. But from 850 onwards Viking armies started overwintering in England. This was an indication of growing self-confidence and something of a declaration of intent. It would not be long before they were staying for good. Indeed, in the 860s the Vikings started assembling bigger armies, and that can only have been with the intention of conquering at least parts of Britain for colonisation. It is possible to portray the decades of pirate raids as patternless and opportunistic robbery. It is also possible, given what happened next, to see them as part of a learning process, a series of geography field trips or reconnaissance expeditions to find out which areas would be rewarding for food production and settlement – and which areas would be ripe for extortion.

In 865, the Vikings applied pressure on the East Angles to supply contingents for an army. In the following year that army successfully captured York and in 867 conquered the southern part of Northumbria. The Vikings left little in the way of documentation, so there are only the Anglo-Saxon Chronicle and a certain amount of folk memory to go on. One later tradition had it that there were two principal Viking leaders,

Ragnar Hairy-Breeks and his son Ivarr the Boneless, and they were responsible for killing King Aella of Northumbria in 867 and King Edmund of the East Angles in 869. They were also credited with destroying Dumbarton, the ancient fortress-capital of the old British kings of Strathclyde. The Annals of Ulster list Ivarr's death as occurring 873, but they also describe him as 'king of the Northmen in the whole of Ireland and Britain.' It is difficult to know what to make of that, as the Northmen, or Vikings, or Danes as they were variously described did not have control over the whole of the British Isles. But perhaps what is meant is that Ivarr had the overall governance of and responsibility for all the various Viking settlements and colonies in the British Isles, even though they were not continuous.

On the other hand perhaps we have to be sceptical of this information in the Ulster Annals. Other sources suggest that the Viking leader was Halfdan, who may have been Ivarr's brother. Halfdan led the Viking army in a conquest of the kingdom of Mercia (the English Midlands) in 874. He also organised the apportionment of land among his fellow Vikings in Northumbria in 876. In 878 he moved south and forced most of the kingdom of Wessex (central southern England) to submit. The overall picture that is building here is that the Vikings had control over very large areas in the British Isles as a whole and had conquered almost all of England.

By 900, the Vikings were definitely staying. There were Viking settlements in various parts of Britain, from East Anglia in the south to Shetland in the north, and the Vikings had gained control over large continuous areas.

KING ALFRED THE GREAT

The struggle for control between the existing population of Britain and Ireland on the one hand and the incoming Scandinavian population on the other was reaching a climax. A kind of last stand was made by the King of Wessex, Alfred. Alfred had no reason to expect to become the king of Wessex as he had three older brothers, Ethelbald, Ethelbert and

Ethelred. But the two eldest brothers, reigning and dying in quick succession, left him as second in the kingdom when his brother Ethelred came to the throne in 866. Then Alfred's public life began. In 868, he fought alongside his brother to try to keep the Danes out of Mercia, the kingdom immediately to the north of Wessex, but without success. Wessex itself was left alone for two years because the West Saxons offered the Danes money not to attack. But when that period expired, the Danes came to Wessex, 871 was Alfred's 'year of battles'. He fought against the invaders nine times. There was a serious defeat for the West Saxons at the Battle of Reading on 5 January 871, but Alfred is credited with a great victory over the Danes at the Battle of Ashdown on 9 January. In April, Ethelred died. Alfred succeeded to the Wessex throne, apparently because he had been formally named the heir, because he was an adult and because he had battle experience; so Ethelred's two sons were overlooked.

A new Danish leader, Guthrum, succeeded in attacking Alfred's major port of Wareham in Dorset and then moved west to take Exeter in Devon. Alfred managed to bottle them up there and force them to submit and withdraw. Then, during the Christmas feast in January 878, they took Alfred and his court by surprise when they attacked his stronghold at Chippenham. This was a devastating attack, in which many of Alfred's men were killed. A small band, led by Alfred, escaped and made their way to Athelney, an island in a marsh, where he found refuge and made his temporary headquarters. From there, Alfred mustered his army for the Battle of Edington, which was a decisive West Saxon victory. The Danes conceded. Guthrum and many of his followers agreed to convert to Christianity. By the Treaty of Wedmore, the south-west of England was to remain Saxon, while the north-east was to remain in the hands of the Danes. By the following year, 879, the two large southern English kingdoms of Wessex and Mercia had been cleared of Danes.

There was a lull lasting a few years, while the Danes were active on the European mainland. The Viking winter quarters for 886-87 were in Paris, and this gave Alfred time to prepare for war. Alfred built forts, built a navy and designed a defence strategy. When the Vikings returned from France in the 890s, the kingdom of Wessex was in a position to put up a strong defence. In 892, after setbacks across the Channel, a large number of Danes crossed to Kent, establishing themselves at Appledore and Milton. The warriors brought their families with them, making it clear that they meant to settle and colonise Kent. Alfred and his son Edward led an army to thwart this attempt at conquest. This was successful, but while Alfred and his son were occupied in Kent (and Essex) Danes from east Anglia and Northumbria were able to lay siege to Exeter. Alfred raced west to save Exeter. The 'Kentish' Danes under Haesten marched up the Thames Valley, apparently trying to reach either the West Country or Mercia, but their progress was blocked by a large army under the military leaders of Mercia, Somerset and Wiltshire; they were diverted across to the Welsh borders.

By 895, the Danes were ensconcing themselves in the Thames Estuary and the Lea valley. Alfred managed to bottle the Danish fleet in the estuary, and the Danes had to escape on foot to the north-west. The following year, they gave up trying to conquer southern England, retreating to the north. This marked the successful conclusion of Alfred's long and costly campaign to keep the Danes out of southern and central England. When Alfred died in 899, he was the king of the only surviving independent English kingdom. All the others had fallen to Scandinavian control.

Alfred was an incredibly forward-looking monarch. He even had a propaganda machine in the form of Bishop Asser who, probably under Alfred's direction, wrote a biography of the king, using the *Life of Charlemagne* by Einhard as a model. This is how, over 1,000 years on, we know so much more about Alfred than we do about other kings of that time. It was also Alfred who ordered the compilation of the Anglo-Saxon Chronicle, which was initially retrospective, going back to the initial Anglo-Saxon colonization at the end of the fifth century, and then added to as events occurred right up until the twelfth century.

ENGLAND AFTER ALFRED

King Alfred was succeeded by his son, Edward the Elder (899–924) and then by his grandson Athelstan (924–939). Alfred's self-publicity has blinded later generations to the huge achievements of his successors. Edward led several military expeditions against the Danes, winning back large areas of southern England from them, and annexed Mercia into his kingdom. He was given significant military aid by his sister Aethelflaed, who had married the king of Mercia and now, as his widow, fought on to rescue her dead husband's kingdom from the Danes.

Edward built a castle at Bakewell in Derbyshire and it was there, at the northern frontier of his enlarged kingdom, an embryonic England, that he was chosen as 'father and lord' by the king of the Scots, the king of Strathclyde and the people of Northumbria. The strange title 'father and lord' seems to have no parallels, but it sounds as though it was a revival of the idea of 'bretwalda', which was used by the first few generations of Anglo-Saxon colonists. When the first generation of colonists had to fight the native Britons, they appointed their most senior king, Aelle, King of the South Saxons, as their bretwalda. The title meant something like commander-in-chief or over-king. The Anglo-Saxons adopted this title to parallel the British titles 'gwledig' or 'pendragon', which were sometimes rendered into Latin as 'dux bellorum', meaning leader of battles. So the implication is that the kings in the north of Britain were ready to acknowledge King Edward of Wessex as their commander-in-chief and over-king. They may well have been driven to do this because some serious military co-ordination was clearly needed to combat the threat of invasion by the Vikings based in Dublin.

Athelstan was to receive a similar submission at Eamont in Cumbria from the kings of the north in 927. Then the Welsh kings joined in as well. King Hywel Dda (Hywel the Good) was a close ally and a great Anglophile; he gave one of his sons an English name, Edwin, and drafted a code of laws based on the English model.

This gradual federal aggregation of small kingdoms under the protective umbrella of a Wessex over-king was a defensive manoeuvre against the Vikings. The threat was so serious that isolated small kingdoms could not survive. The thought was 'safety in numbers'. The threat from the Vikings was, ultimately, what forged England into a nation.

Athelstan's great military triumph was at the Battle of Brunanburh in the north of England. Olaf Guthfrithson led his Viking army in an invasion of the kingdom of Northumbria in 937. Olaf was supported by troops supplied by the kings of Scotland and Strathclyde. The battle was a huge setback for the Viking cause; in it, seven of Olaf's earls, five kings and the heir of King Constantine of Scotland were killed. In Britain, Athelstan's reputation was, as it still is, overshadowed by that of Alfred, but on the mainland of Europe he had enormous prestige. Even so, Athelstan's great victory at Brunanburh did not end the Viking threat. The last Viking king of York, Eric Bloodaxe, was not ejected from Northumbria until 954, which was fifteen years after Athelstan's death.

DANEGELD

After that there was a generation of peace in Britain. King Edgar, ruler of England from 959 to 975, was able to rule 'without battle'. He set out laws 'for all the nations, whether Englishmen, Danes or Britons.' This was a relaxed and enlightened acknowledgement that England was multi-ethnic.

During the long reign of Ethelred the Ill-Advised (978-1016), Denmark was emerging as a powerful European neighbour. Denmark was recently converted to Christianity and recently unified under King Harald Bluetooth. The emergence of Denmark as a major European power marked the dawn of a new Viking age, very different in character from the first Viking Age. There were seaborne raids as before, but on a larger scale. This time instead of being run by bands of pirates, they were organized by royal sponsors. This time, instead of robbery, the object was extortion, protection money.

When the Danes crossed the North Sea to visit England in 991, they were given a large quantity of silver – 4,500 kg (9,900 lb) – to return home again. By 1012, these blackmail payments to the Danes, known as

Danegeld, had risen to 22,000 kg (48,500 lb). England was a rich country, which is what had attracted the Danes in the first place. But the necessity of raising these huge sums in Danegeld meant that the taxation system, the means for collecting all this money, had to be sophisticated and efficient. So the Viking raids had the effect of stimulating an economic and financial system that was even more advanced, more highly organised, than before.

THE VIKING CONQUEST OF ENGLAND

By the early years of the eleventh century, the process of infiltration was complete. England had a Viking king. The King of Denmark, Sven Forkbeard, forced Ethelred into exile and became king of England, too. Then, in 1013, the extortion of Danegeld came to a halt. Sven's son and successor, Cnut (or Canute) became King of England in 1016 and by 1027 he was able to boast that he was King of England, Denmark, Norway and parts of Sweden. It was a Viking Empire.

Cnut attempted a reconciliation with the English by way a marriage with Emma, Ethelred's widow and daughter of the Duke of Normandy. Emma bore a son by Cnut, Harthacnut. But she also had a son by Ethelred, who was to succeed Harthacnut as Edward the Confessor. When Edward the Confessor died without an heir, Emma's great-nephew, Duke William of Normandy, laid claim to the English throne. And he, as it happened, was a descendant of a Viking settler in northern France. So it came about that in 1066, one of the most momentous years in English history, there were two separate and almost simultaneous invasions, both ultimately Scandinavian in origin. The attack in the north of England was mounted by Harald Hardrada, King of Norway, who landed on 20 September. The better-known invasion in the south of England was staged by William, Duke of Normandy, who was a descendant of Rollo the Viking. He landed at Pevensey just a week later, on 28 September.

THE CRUSADES
(1096–1291)

The crusades were military expeditions mounted in the name of Christianity to 'liberate' the region known to the crusaders as the Holy Land. This was not a country but a region corresponding to modern Israel, Jordan, Lebanon and Syria. The crusades were seen in Western Europe as a highly idealistic adventure and the men taking part were seen as representing knightly perfection and chivalry. They were obliged to swear an oath to the pope or one of his legates in a ceremony in which they were presented with a crucifix; this ceremony was known as 'taking the Cross'.

By the time of the crusades there was a long-established tradition of pilgrimage from Western Europe to the Holy Land, and to Jerusalem, the city where Jesus was crucified, in particular. For several centuries, those who could afford to do so, made the attempt to visit the Holy Sepulchre, the tomb of Christ, before they died.

In 1071, the Seljuk Turks, after conquering Syria and Palestine, captured Jerusalem. On top of this, the Turks started molesting and persecuting Christians who were making pilgrimages to Jerusalem. The idea of mounting a crusade to free Jerusalem and the pilgrimage route to the city was discussed for a long time.

THE FIRST CRUSADE (1097–99)

The crusade was publicly announced by Pope Urban II at the Synod (church council) of Clermont in 1095. During a sermon delivered in a field outside Clermont Ferrand on 27 November 1095, Pope Urban outlined his plan for a mission to rescue Jerusalem and called on his congregation to join the crusade. The response was very positive, and

Urban instructed his bishops to return home to their sees and muster support there for the crusade. Each group of crusaders would be responsible to its own local leader, and be self-financing. The groups would then assemble in August 1096 and set off for Constantinople. There they would join the huge army of the Byzantine Empire, drive the Seljuk Turks out of Anatolia and push south through Syria to Jerusalem.

Four large armies of crusaders duly assembled and made their separate ways to Constantinople. The first to arrive, in December 1096, was the group from Lorraine, northern France and Germany, led by Godfrey de Bouillon. The second to arrive was a contingent of Normans from southern Italy, led by Duke Bohemond of Otranto and Count Tancred. A third group arrived from southern France under Count Raymond of Toulouse. The fourth consisted of Frenchmen, Normans and Englishmen under the command of Duke Hugh de Vermandois, Robert Curthose of Normandy and Stephen of Blois; they arrived in May 1097.

Once in Constantinople, the crusader leaders were pressed by the Emperor Alexius I to agree to hand over any former Byzantine territories to him. They were unhappy about this and deeply suspicious of Alexius' opportunistic motives in joining the crusade. Crossing into Anatolia, the crusaders headed for Nicaea, which was the Anatolian Turks' capital. Alexius persuaded the garrison there to surrender to him personally rather than to the crusaders, which further reinforced the Western crusader leaders' suspicions about the Byzantine emperor.

Then the crusader armies split up, different groups taking the cities of Tarsus, Antioch and (across the Euphrates) Edessa. Most of the crusaders' targets yielded easily against their huge forces, but Antioch held out under siege for seven months, finally surrendering just before a huge Turkish arrived to relieve it. After Antioch, the crusaders rested before going on to Jerusalem. They arrived in sight of Jerusalem on 7 June 1099, to find the city firmly under 'Saracen' (Muslim) control with an Egyptian garrison. Another crusader arm arrived from Genoa with the siege engines that were needed to attack the walled city. Now well-prepared, the crusaders attacked Jerusalem and took it fairly easily on 15 July.

Then came the first great and terrible atrocity of the crusades, which remains a stain on medieval Christianity. The crusaders closed the gates of Jerusalem and massacred every single non-crusader in the city – every man, woman and child. The justification given was that the blood of the infidels (non-believers) would purify the Holy City.

Then the crusader leaders met and elected Godfrey de Bouillon King of Jerusalem, though he modestly declined the title 'king'. Shortly afterwards the main body of the crusader armies left for the journey home, leaving Godfrey with a small force to keep the city. In the wake of the First Crusade, several new states were formed, the principality of Antioch, the counties of Edessa and Tripoli and the largest of the states, the kingdom of Jerusalem. Godfrey died within the year and was succeeded by his brother Baldwin I, who accepted the kingly title that Godfrey had been too modest to accept.

News of the success of the First Crusade spread across Europe, inspiring many to imitate it. Three groups of crusaders passed through Constantinople, but all three met with disaster in Anatolia. The First Crusade had not created a stable political landscape in the Middle East by any means. The new kings of Jerusalem were in a continual state of war, defending the territory against repeated Saracen attack. The Muslim world united under the leadership of Zangi, the ruler of Mosul, and in 1144 Zangi led his army against Edessa and recaptured it.

THE SECOND CRUSADE (1147–1149)

In 1145, the Pope declared a Second Crusade in direct response to the loss of Edessa. The crusade attracted many recruits, including the king of France, Louis VII, and the Holy Roman emperor, Conrad III. Conrad set off from Nuremberg in May 1147 and Louis followed a month afterwards accompanied by his wife, Eleanor of Aquitaine. The German army reached Constantinople, where Conrad was given some good advice by the Byzantine emperor, Manuel I. Manuel told Conrad to take the coast road round Anatolia and send home the non-combatant pilgrims in his party. Conrad ignored Manuel's advice, taking the entire party by the inland route, where they ran out of food and water and were caught by the Turks. In October 1147, at Dorylaeum, they were massacred; Conrad was one of the few people to escape alive.

The remnants of the German army joined the French army at Nicaea and followed them round the Anatolian coast. The French army lacked discipline and, after engaging with the Turks, Louis decided to split his army, taking his court and his cavalry by sea to Antioch. The rump of his army also divided; then they were attacked by Turks. Only half of the original French contingent reached Antioch.

The problems were by no means over. In Antioch, Louis was met by Prince Raymond, who was Eleanor of Aquitaine's uncle although he was only a few years older than her. Raymond proposed a joint expedition to relieve Edessa. For what seem to have been personal rather than strategic reasons, Louis was determined to go south, straight to Jerusalem. He had the idea that the relationship between his wife and Raymond was incestuous, and wanted to get her away from Raymond as quickly as possible. Louis virtually abducted Eleanor and set off for the Holy Land. They arrived there in May 1148, joining Conrad who had got there a month earlier.

Once they had rested, Louis and Conrad had a meeting with Baldwin, King of Jerusalem, at which they agreed to go off and attack Damascus. It turned out to be a disastrous mistake. Their huge army went to Damascus and was obliged to withdraw five days later after sustaining terrible losses (July 1148). The crusader leaders then quarrelled, separated and went home.

THE THIRD CRUSADE (1189–1192)

In the wake of the disastrous Second Crusade, the Muslims were in a position to regroup and resolved their differences with one another. Zangi's successor Nur greatly expanded the Muslim territory, creating a major Middle Eastern power. His success reached a zenith in 1169, when his forces, under the command of the brilliant warrior Saladin, conquered Egypt. When Nur died, Saladin became his successor.

Saladin was keen to rid the region of the crusader presence and invaded the Kingdom of Jerusalem in 1187. At the Battle of Hattin in Galilee, he overwhelmingly defeated the crusader army, after which he took many of the finely built crusader castles. The city of Jerusalem itself surrendered to Saladin on 2 October. Now, of the major cities in the region, only Tyre was still in crusader hands.

The news of Saladin's successes reached western Europe and on 29 October 1187 Pope Gregory VIII formally announced a Third Crusade. In spite of the appalling losses and mistakes of the Second Crusade, there was once again great enthusiasm for another. The three most powerful monarchs in Europe took the Cross: Holy Roman Emperor Frederick I, King of France Philip II and King of England Richard I. The German army, 30,000 strong, departed for Constantinople in the spring of 1189. The following year they continued into Anatolia, fending off several attacks by Turks. Frederick himself was accidentally drowned in a river and after that the army was gradually diluted by losses to disease and starvation, and men deciding to return home. Only 1,000 people arrived in Acre.

King Richard and King Philip set off a year after Frederick, travelling by way of Sicily and spending much of their time quarrelling. In the end they parted company, Philip sailing direct to Acre, Richard stopping at Cyprus. There the English king quarrelled with the local ruler and then, in May 1191, took the island from him; it was more or less by accident, but the result was that the crusaders then had a useful base from which to attack the Holy Land. Then Richard continued to Acre, where he took charge of the major siege already under way. He forced a surrender. One of the terms of the surrender was the payment of a ransom, but that was not forthcoming. Because the terms of the surrender were not met in full, Richard responded by ordering the massacre of the town's inhabitants: 2,000 Muslims, men, women and children. It was another major war crime, to match the earlier massacre at Jerusalem.

After taking Acre, Richard marched his troops south, with his fleet accompanying them along the coast. He was attacked by Saladin's army, but won a victory at the Battle of Arsouf (1191). In open battle, Richard was able to fight and beat Saladin, but he could not cope with Saladin's scorched earth policy. The crusader army was running out of food, which prevented it from taking Jerusalem.

Saladin himself descended on Jaffa in July 1192. He had almost taken it, when Richard arrived there by sea. A battle ensued in which the two sides were very evenly matched; in the end the victory went to Richard, now known as Richard the Lionheart. Richard made a treaty with Saladin and finally left the Holy Land in October 1192.

THE FOURTH CRUSADE (1202–1204)

In 1199, Pope Innocent III issued another call to arms. Christian knights from all over Europe were to get Jerusalem back from the Saracens. This Fourth Crusade was led by Count Theobald III of Champagne, supported by Count Baldwin of Flanders and Count Louis de Blois. This time the crusaders were to assemble at Venice, and the Venetians would transport the estimated 25,000 men to the Holy Land by way of Egypt. The city of Venice was expecting to do well out of this expedition; it was to have 85,000 marks and half of any conquests the crusaders made.

There was a change of plan. Instead of landing in Egypt and then travelling north overland to Jerusalem the crusader army would be landed in Constantinople, crossing Anatolia on foot – the now-traditional route.

A problem at the outset was that once the crusader army had assembled at Venice, the 85,000 marks had not been raised. The Venetians agreed to go ahead on condition that the crusaders captured the city of Zara on the Adriatic coast and handed that over to Venice. This was another problem, as Zara was a possession of the king of Hungary, and he was not only a Christian but a crusader. The Pope heard about the immoral project and threatened everybody concerned with excommunication. This was not a sufficient deterrent, and Zara was taken on 24 November 1202. The Pope's excommunication duly came into effect. Then he relented, stipulating that no further Christian possessions should be attacked. The angry Pope must later have regretted this weak decision. He and many Christians throughout Europe must have been astonished by what happened next.

In June 1203, the crusaders arrived in the Bosporus off Constantinople aboard their Venetian transports. They went ashore and made camp. Then in a combined sea and land attack, Constantinople itself was captured. The crusaders demanded payment of 200,000 marks and withdrew to await their money. It was an act of sheer piracy. In January 1204 some of the Byzantine noblemen objected to the huge charge and this led to a short but violent siege (April 1204). At the end of this the crusaders and Venetians recaptured Constantinople and sacked it with unprecedented violence. In the wake of this new atrocity, the Venetians set up a Latin Empire of Constantinople, which lasted for sixty years, did nothing to defend Christianity in the Middle East and did a great deal to undermine it. Constantinople had been a bulwark of Christianity in the East, and now the crusaders had ravaged it.

THE FIFTH CRUSADE (1218–1221)

After this catastrophic expedition, eleven years went by before Pope Innocent III decided to make another attempt. This time the crusaders were led by King Andrew of Hungary and they assembled at the port of Split in the Adriatic. Once again there was enormous support for the crusade, more than expected, and there was insufficient transport for everyone; many had to return home. When they arrived at Acre, there were not enough of them to be useful in a major attack, so they were deployed in a variety of minor assignments, such as attacking a Saracen camp.

When more contingents arrived, though notably not from France, King Andrew decided that he had had enough and went home (January 1218). King John of Jerusalem took over the command of the crusade and decided to mount an expedition against the Egyptian fort of Damietta at one of the two major mouths of the Nile. This entailed a three-month siege, after which the fortress fell; Damietta itself withstood siege for a year and a half, falling to the crusaders in November 1219. After long delays, the 46,000 crusaders were ordered to march on Cairo. The Nile rose unexpectedly and the crusaders were forced to withdraw, losing everything they had gained. The Fifth Crusade broke up in defeat and disillusionment.

THE SIXTH CRUSADE (1228–1229)

Holy Roman Emperor Frederick II had for various domestic reasons failed to support the Fifth Crusade as he had solemnly sworn to do. He married the thirteen-year-old daughter of King John of Jerusalem and then breathtakingly declared himself King of Jerusalem, as if somehow forgetting that his father-in-law was still alive; it was a strange situation. The Pope was by now very frustrated by Frederick's failure to fulfil his vow to go to the Holy Land. Eventually, in August 1227, Frederick did indeed set sail for the Holy Land, but within a few days he ordered his fleet to return to port; he was indisposed. The Pope was furious with Frederick and excommunicated him.

In June 1228, Frederick II set sail again, this time reaching his destination, Acre. Most of the crusaders refused to obey his orders as he not only had been excommunicated, he still was. Nevertheless, Frederick was a good negotiator and he managed to persuade the Saracens to restore to the Christians the principal holy Christian sites, Bethlehem, Nazareth and Jerusalem. He also negotiated a travel corridor to enable pilgrims to reach Jerusalem from the coast and a ten-year peace.

It was an extraordinary *volte-face.* Frederick had started out looking like a total disaster. Then within a short time he had achieved more than any of the earlier crusades had achieved, by diplomacy. It was an entirely new kind of crusade and a personal triumph for the Holy Roman Emperor.

Frederick completed his own personal pilgrimage to Jerusalem, where he crowned himself king on 18 February 1229. In spite of all of this, he was still excommunicated and shunned by both clergy and the heads of the Western states. In a piece of personal opportunism of his own, the Pope went a step further and declared a crusade against Frederick; Frederick's lands in southern Italy were forfeit and the Pope sent papal troops to occupy them. This time Frederick moved swiftly. He left the Holy Land, reached Italy in May 1229, threw out the papal troops and reclaimed his lands. His negotiating skills stood him in good stead, as within three months he had made his peace with the Pope.

THE SEVENTH CRUSADE (1248–1254)

Almost twenty years went by before the next crusade. This one was organized and financed by the French king, Louis IX, and it was a response to the Saracen recapture of Jerusalem in 1244. Louis spent four years planning and preparing, and the expedition set sail in August 1248. The crusader army landed at Cyprus, where it overwintered and made further preparations. The plan was to land in Egypt, establish a base there and then march across Sinai towards Jerusalem.

The landing in Egypt on 5 June 1249 was extremely successful, and Damietta was captured the next day. But the next move, the attack on Mansurah, was a catastrophe for King Louis and his crusader army. The crusader army found itself on one bank of a branch of the Nile Delta, with the Saracens on the opposite bank. The crusaders tried to build a causeway across, but they were bombarded with Greek fire. Eventually a cavalry force succeeded in fording the river and getting inside the town of Mansurah, but that was wiped out in the maze of alleys. Louis was forced to order a retreat, and then was captured. The Saracens demanded a colossal ransom, which was paid at once. Damietta was handed back to the Egyptians and the crusaders departed in total defeat.

Most of the crusaders then returned home, but Louis himself went to the Holy Land, where he spent four years organising the defences of the Kingdom of Jerusalem before returning to France in 1254.

THE EIGHTH CRUSADE (1270)

The final crusade was also organized by Louis IX. By now there was general disillusionment with the crusades, and Louis was unable to inspire his nobles. It is not clear why, but at the last moment, Louis decided to turn his expedition against Tunis instead of Egypt. Tunis was a well-defended city, and the crusaders were repulsed. Disease, too, took its toll among the crusaders. Louis himself died there on 25 August 1270. As he lay dying he is said to have whispered, 'Jerusalem, Jerusalem'.

Aftermath

The Saracens (Easterners) took the crusader cities and castles one by one, until the crusader states themselves collapsed. In the end, only one crusader city remained – Acre – and that too fell on 18 May 1291, marking the end of the crusades. The crusaders themselves retreated to Cyprus, and then later to Rhodes. The main material legacy of the crusades is the great crusader castle, Krak des Chevaliers, which has survived both Saracens and earthquakes in a remarkable state of preservation. For the rest, it is little more than a grand chivalric fantasy in the minds of popes and kings, and a huge amount of blood futilely shed in a cause that could not be won. The main intellectual or spiritual legacy is the idea of a war justified by religious faith – and a very dangerous idea that has proved to be.

PEASANTS' REVOLTS IN EUROPE

(1320–)

In the late medieval ages, there were several major peasants' revolts in different parts of Europe. The first of these revolts broke out in Flanders in 1323, when it began as a series of small and scattered rural riots but escalated in the hands of rebel leaders in the towns into a full-scale rebellion. It was serious enough to dominate Flemish politics for five years. The rising in Flanders broke out for two reasons: overburdensome taxation and the pro-French policies of the head of state, Count Louis I. In the end the French king intervened and at the Battle of Cassel in August 1328 the rebellion was decisively stamped out.

Just thirty years after the ending of the Flemish revolt, another peasants revolt broke out in northern France, centring on the valley of the River Oise. This revolt was known as the Jacquerie, after the nickname of its leader, Guillaume Cale, who was generally known as Jacques Bonhomme (the equivalent in English of 'Jim Goodfellow'). Later in French history, any peasant rising was referred to as a Jacquerie. The French king, John II, was captured by the English at the Battle of Poitiers in 1356 and kept confined in England. This left France without a king. During the king's captivity power was shared among the States General, the king of Navarre and the dauphin, Charles V, but the States General were divided and the two royal rulers quarrelled and created further disunity. This left the nobles and the clergy free to exploit the peasants by forcing them to pay higher taxes. This was particularly hard for the peasants to accept as they, the peasants, already held that it was the corruption of the French nobility that had led to France's defeat at the Battle of Poitiers.

In the background, there were other problems, too, such as the food crisis and consequent famine in 1315 and uncontrolled groups of bandits who were looting and plundering northern France during the period of anarchy; among the bandits were companies of unemployed mercenaries. There was also the possibility of another English invasion. The peasants had no respect for a government that was consistently failing to protect them from depredation. It was a time of unstable government with an absent king and an uncertain future.

The tensions and frustration erupted in 1358 in a series of violent rebellions in various places in France. A chronicler of the time, Jean le Bel, described the scale of the violence. He said that in one place, peasants 'killed a knight, put him on a spit and roasted him with his wife and children watching. After ten or twelve of them raped the lady, they wished to force feed them the roasted flesh of their father and husband and then made them die a miserable death.' Other chroniclers record similar atrocities in other places.

There seems to have been no central or even local organization to the French peasants' revolt. Jean le Bel speculated that tax collectors spread the word about the rebellion from village to village, encouraging people to join in with a view to upsetting the nobility. When they were asked why they were rebelling, the peasants said that they were just doing what they saw other people doing, which is all too easy to believe. There also seems to have been an idea in the air that the nobility might be destroyed. Froissart, another chronicler, reports that the peasants caused serious damage to more than 150 castles and mansions, sadistically murdering the noble families who lived in them.

In July 1358, Paris surrendered to the dauphin. Paris was under the control of Etienne Marcel, who had joined the rebellion, and now he paid the price by losing both his city and his life. His wealthy associates deserted him and his cause. The rebellion was put down by Charles the Bad of Navarre, commanding a force of French noblemen. Charles the Bad invited Guillaume Cale, the rebel leader, to negotiate a truce on 10 July. When he arrived at the town of Mello for the negotiation he was seized and beheaded. Cale's army, 20,000 strong, was routed by cavalry divisions at the Battle of Mello. This decisive defeat was followed by a campaign through the Beauvais area. Soldiers toured the villages, rounding up peasants at random and hanging them.

In England, a similar rebellion broke out in 1381. This Peasants' Revolt was also known as the Great Rising. The trigger for this rebellion was the imposition of the poll tax, which was the third since 1377. The government's excuse for imposing this arbitrary and unfair tax – everyone paid the same, regardless of wealth – was the need to finance military adventures in France. The 1377 tax had been one groat; but by 1381 the tax was three times higher. As in France, there was also dissatisfaction with a virtually kingless and corrupt aristocracy that was mismanaging the country. There was a king of England, Richard II, but he was only fourteen years old and inexperienced. The real political power was therefore in the hands of unscrupulous aristocrats like John of Gaunt, who was the regent, Sir Robert Hales, who was Lord Treasurer, and churchmen like Simon of Sudbury, who was Chancellor and Archbishop of Canterbury. These men were seen by the ordinary people of England as corrupt, ruthless, self-seeking tyrants who were exploiting the young king's weakness. The Peasants' Revolt was an expression of their hatred for these officials. It was Sir Robert Hales who was responsible for the Poll Tax.

Another cause of the rebellion was the 1351 Statute of Labourers. After the Black Death had greatly reduced the labour force, the surviving labourers were able to demand higher wages. The statute fixed wages and restricted the mobility of labourers, to block these demands. Naturally there was widespread discontent among the labourers at this manoeuvre to make their lives even harder.

The rebellion broke out in the village of Brentwood in Essex. John Bampton, accompanied by two guards, arrived in the village to demand that the villagers pay their tax. The villagers replied that they had already paid and would not pay any more. Bampton tried to arrest some of the villagers and in response about 100 villagers led by Thomas Baker drove him out of Brentwood. Bampton reported the incident back in London, and soldiers were sent. Baker and his men drove them back, too, beheading six of the company and forcing the man in charge of the detachment to swear never to return.

The incident shows the strength of feeling among the ordinary people of England, and the violence of the rebellion. The discontent and the violence quickly spread round South-East England. Soon the counties of Essex and Kent were in full-scale rebellion and converged on London in arms. One of the leaders, who headed the contingent from Kent, was Walter (Wat) Tyler. He was the most outspoken of the leaders, and emerged as the leader of the rebellion as a whole. When the rebels arrived at Blackheath on the outskirts of London on 12 June 1381, a rebel priest called John Ball preached an inspirational sermon to them. He asked the memorable question, 'When Adam delved and Eve span, who was then the gentleman?' This took the rebellion to a more profound level, bringing in the idea of the fundamental equality of people; class and privilege were man-made, not God-given. Encouraged by Ball's sermon, the next day the rebels crossed London Bridge from Southwark into the City of London.

At the same time, in what was evidently a well co-ordinated move, the Men of Essex gathered with their leader Jack Straw at Great Baddow and marched towards London. They arrived at Stepney. The rebels were extremely well-controlled at this stage, and they attacked only carefully selected properties associated, for example, with John of Gaunt. On 14 June they were met by the young king, to whom they presented a set of demands, including the dismissal of his most unpopular officials and the abolition of serfdom. There was one demand that has intrigued historians: 'that there should be no law within the realm save the law of Winchester.' Some think this means the statutes of the Charter of Winchester of 1251, while others think it refers back to the golden age of King Alfred the Great, who had his capital at Winchester.

While this meeting was taking place, other rebels managed to get into the Tower of London, where several of the iconic hate-figures were hiding. The rebels found Simon of Sudbury there, dragged him out onto Tower Hill and sadistically hacked off his head. Sir Robert Hales was also murdered. The Savoy Palace of John of Gaunt was destroyed.

The next day, the king agreed to meet the rebels at Smithfield. The king was prepared to agree to reform the status of serfs. Obviously the question of dismissing Sudbury and Hales did not arise as the rebels had killed them. Wat Tyler mishandled the meeting when he rode forward to speak to the king. He dismounted, called for a drink and generally behaved rudely and belligerently, even drawing his dagger. At this, the Mayor of London William Walworth drew his sword and gave Tyler a mortal wound in the throat. Ralph de Standish, a squire, ran his sword through Tyler's stomach. Tyler withdrew to a nearby house, dying. The rebels were in uproar. The king shouted to them, 'You shall have no captain but me!' which was cleverly ambiguous, but it impressed and steadied the rebels. He promised them all was well and that he agreed to their demands. They were to go to St John's Fields, where Tyler would rejoin them. They did, but by then Tyler was dead and the king's promise was not honoured.

The ruling class quickly re-asserted itself. A militia 7,000 strong was mustered and most of the leaders of the rebellion were captured and executed. Jack Straw betrayed many of his associates under torture, but was still executed. Once the rebellion was extinguished, the tax was levied again.

In spite of its name, the English Peasants' Revolt was not merely a revolt of the peasant or serf class. Many of those who were involved were members of an emerging lower middle class. The conspicuous participation of the priest John Ball was also significant. The revolt was an embryonic English Revolution. Perhaps it was premature, perhaps it was inadequately planned or resourced, but it represents the first attempt at the creation of a more egalitarian society with a more accountable ruling elite. It is interesting to speculate whether things might have turned out differently if Tyler had behaved with more diplomacy at Smithfield.

In 1515 a peasant revolt broke out in Slovenia. In this rebellion, the peasants were successful in capturing most of the castles in Slovenia. However, the Slovenian revolt was decisively put down at the Battle of Celje.

In 1524–25, the German Peasants' War broke out in the Holy Roman Empire. This, like the English Peasants' Revolt, was much more than just a revolt by peasants. It consisted of a series of revolts, with economic, social and religious motives, and it involved noblemen and townspeople as well as the rural peasants. It erupted mainly in the centre and south of what is now Germany and affected parts of Switzerland and Austria, too. It was a large-scale revolt, involving as many as 300,000 rebels, and must be regarded as the biggest and most significant popular rising until the French Revolution of 1789.

A major element in the German Peasants' War was the Reformation, the Protestant rebellion against the Roman Catholic Church. People were rebelling against the religious, economic and political hold that the Catholic Church held over their lives. There were also deep-seated social grievances. Germany was divided into several classes: princes, lesser nobles, churchmen, patricians, burghers, plebeians and peasants. The princes lived by levying taxes on the lower classes, the lesser nobles and churchmen paid no taxes and the burghers in the towns were often exempted from taxes, too; the result was that a heavy burden of taxation fell on the peasants, who were least able to pay them. The princes also introduced Roman Civil Law, which converted all land to private ownership. This removed the old feudal structure of land held in trust between lords and peasants, entailing obligations on the part of the lords as well as rights, and rights as well as obligations on the part of the peasants. Under the new arrangement, all land became the property of the princes and the peasants were turned into serfs.

There were occasional isolated rebellions against this situation, but they were easily suppressed. There were many structured complaints that were presented by the lower classes, but they brought no improvement. With Luther's proposals for a reformed church, people saw opportunities for change; the burghers, for instance, saw the focus of Luther's Church on the towns as a platform for increasing their power. The princes saw Luther's separation from the Catholic Church as an opportunity to gain autonomy from the Holy Roman Emperor Charles V as well as freedom from Rome. The plebeians were stirred by revolutionary preachers such as Thomas Muntzer, who offered the possibility of breaking up the old social structure. Peasants and plebeians wrote down lists of grievances. The definitive one was the Twelve Articles of the Black Forest. This gave a focus to the widespread unrest that finally erupted in Swabia in 1524.

The movement disintegrated as the burghers and nobles gave in to the armies of the princes. The old order was re-established often even more harshly than before under the overlordship of Charles V, actively implemented by his younger brother Ferdinand. Martin Luther let the rebels down. He had been condemned as a heretic in 1521 and directly accused of encouraging strife. Now he rejected the rebels' demands, and supported the German rulers' right to put down the rebellion. Luther's one-time disciple, Thomas Muntzer, held firm and went on being a radical agitator. The Protestants were by no means united; there were many differences of opinion on matters of doctrine and practice. Luther, for example, believed in the practice of infant baptism, whereas the Anabaptists were opposed to it. There were fierce quarrels. In one of them, Luther had some 'prophets' he regarded as heretics banned from their own churches; some of these were driven to celebrate the sacrament in private houses instead. Muntzer's crusade against the secular authorities had its inevitable outcome in 1525. At Frankenhausen on 15 May, the rebel forces were completely defeated; in the aftermath, several of the rebel leaders, including Muntzer, were executed. The German Peasants' War was over.

More than 100 years later, a Swiss Peasant War broke out. This was triggered by a devaluation of money (December 1652), which led to a tax revolt that spread across much of the Old Swiss Confederacy. The devaluation was caused by the replacement of silver coins with copper. But there were also socio-political problems that had been developing for a long time. Since the fifteenth century, political power in the city cantons such as Berne had become more and more concentrated in the hands of a small number of families in the cities. They came to regard the public offices they held as hereditary, and had become increasingly aristocratic and absolutist in style. This concentrated power in the city and, within the city, in a the hands of a small elite. The people living in the countryside outside the cities felt increasingly excluded, alienated and frustrated, as they were subjected to decrees to which they had not consented – and gradually lost their customary freedoms.

Because of their financial difficulties, partly created by mortgages taken out during an earlier boom period, the rural peasants wanted tax relief from their 'rulers', the city councils of their canton capitals, towns such as Berne and Lucerne. The demands were rejected, so the peasants threatened to blockade the cities. They joined forces under a treaty to form the League of Huttwil, which assumed full autonomy from the city authorities with its own political and military sovereignty.

Berne and Lucerne were put under siege and this yielded a peace agreement, negotiated by the elected leader of the peasants, Niklaus Leuenberger. After this Peace on the Murifeld (the field near Berne where the peasant army was headquartered), the peasant armies withdrew. Then the federal council of the Old Swiss Confederacy sent an army from Zurich to stamp out the rebellion, in effect after it had already ended. In the Battle of Wohlenschwil, the peasant army was easily defeated; it lacked equipment, especially artillery. After the battle a Peace of Mellingen was signed, in which the peasant leaders agreed under duress to abolish the Huttwil League. An amnesty was declared, and all the rebels were allowed to return home – except their leaders. Then the city authorities took their vindictive revenge. The Peace of Murifeld was declared invalid, and many of the rebel leaders were captured and tortured. Niklaus Leuenberger went into hiding but was betrayed by a neighbour, then beheaded and quartered in Berne on 6 September 1653. The retribution was harshest in Berne, which had not agreed to the amnesty; twenty-three death sentences were carried out and many other executions were carried out in courts-martial by the army.

The absolutist city authorities had won the conflict, but the experience had demonstrated that the cities were dependent on their rural populations. The rebellion had been put down, but only with difficulty, demonstrating the raw strength of the rural areas. The peasants were after all not to be taken for granted. Although initially it looked as if the Peasants' War had been lost, with military defeat and the execution of their leaders, in the end, the reforms the peasants demanded were brought about. The absolutist trends that had been developing in Switzerland were halted and the authorities started to treat the lower classes with more circumspection. District sheriffs were instructed to behave in a less pompous and authoritarian way. In the eighteenth century, the Swiss could boast a relatively low tax burden compared with other European states, and this was explicitly because of the government's fear of rebellion.

But there was also a clampdown on symbols of resistance, like the rebel flags or the weapons the rebels used, especially the nailed clubs they favoured. These weapons were outlawed, confiscated, destroyed. Pilgrimage to the places where the rebel leaders had been executed were forbidden; flouting this law carried the death penalty. The authorities even tried to ban pictures of the rebel leaders. But the folk memory of such events cannot be expunged by these means. By the nineteenth century, the Swiss were writing and depicting the events freely. One drawing, created in 1840 by Martin Disteli, shows one of the peasant leaders, Christian Schybi, undergoing torture in a dungeon at Sursee. The tied and spread-eagled Schybi is deliberately shown as Christ-like. By then the Peasants War was being given a new lease of life. It was seen as a precursor to a later freedom struggle by which Switzerland became a federal state (1848).

Aftermath

The Jacquerie was a violent rebellion suppressed with even greater violence. It was so totally suppressed that the lot of the peasant class in France was not in any way advanced. The lower (and middle) classes in France had to wait for the even greater excesses of the French Revolution for the 'old regime' to be brought to an end.

Wat Tyler's Rebellion in England was also suppressed, but it resulted in some reforms. It marked the beginning of the end of serfdom, with a softening of the feudal system and increased rights for the peasants. The

The Swiss Peasants War was suppressed, but the main demand was met, and the Swiss peasants were taxed more lightly for many decades afterwards. The war also brought about a change in attitude by the authorities, who treated the lower orders more carefully and considerately. The Swiss peasants were well organised and, unlike the other peasant risings in Europe, they formed proper armies against their rulers' militias. This was a major new development; whether this was learnt from earlier failures with disorganised small-scale revolts in Switzerland, or learnt from the New Model Army created to deal with Charles I in England, is not clear.

The Swiss peasants' goals went some distance beyond mere restoration of old customary rights, and in this marked a very significant forward movement from the earlier rebellions. The Huttwil League explicitly and radically denied that the existing authorities had an indisputable right to rule. That rule could, if abused, be challenged. This was an inherently seventeenth century political view, one that underlay the English Civil Wars.

THE HUNDRED YEARS' WAR

(1337–1453)

This conflict between England and France dragged on for 116 years. It was fought mainly over claims by the kings of England to the throne of France, which were hotly disputed by the French kings. It was not a continuous war; within it there were two long intervals of peace and several shorter ones. Naturally the phrase 'Hundred Years' War' was not used at the time, as no one knew how long it was going to last; the phrase was devised by later historians.

BACKGROUND, ORIGINS

The Hundred Years' War had its roots as much as 400 years earlier, in 911. It was then that Charles the Simple let Rollo the Viking settle in a region of his kingdom that was later to be called Normandy. In 1066, the elite of Normandy was led by William Duke of Normandy (the great-great-great-grandson of Rollo) in a conquest of England. William supplanted the Anglo-Saxon king of England, Harold, making himself king instead. The claim by subsequent kings of England that they had dual kingship was weakened by the fact that, as landholders in Normandy, the Norman leaders were vassals (in effect tenants) to the King of France. That remained true even when the Norman leaders became kings in England.

The Angevin kings of England – Henry II was the first of these – controlled huge tracts of land including Normandy, Maine, Anjou, Touraine, Gascony and Aquitaine as well as England. The area was large enough to be referred to as the Angevin Empire. The king of England may at this stage have ruled directly over a larger area of France than the French king, but he was still a vassal of the French king. This vassalage was seen by the Angevin kings as an irksome technicality and it generated continual conflict.

The French tried to clear this anomaly up, and partially succeeded, in three wars (in 1214, 1242 and 1324) in which the king of England's control of French territory was greatly reduced. By 1324, the English king was only in control of a small area of Gascony, and Normandy itself had been lost. In the early fourteenth century, French was still the official language in England. There was also a nostalgia among the English aristocracy for a time when grandparents had been in control of large tracts of continental Europe, tracts that they thought of as their homelands. This nostalgia drove a desire in England to regain the lost possessions across the Channel.

Meanwhile, in France, there were dynastic developments. For several centuries the firstborn sons of the Capetian dynasty had followed one another without a break. Then in 1314, Philip IV died leaving four children, three male heirs and a daughter named Joan. The three male heirs ruled consecutively in quick succession after Philip IV's death: Louis X (1314–16), Philip V (1316–22) and Charles IV (1322–28). Philip V used the rumour that his sister Joan was not his father's daughter in order to ensure that she would be excluded from the succession; he successfully bypassed her in this way. A curious by-product of this ruse was that a precedent was then established (or willingly perceived in France) that a woman could not inherit the French throne. When Philip V died in 1322, his own (legitimate) daughters were accordingly set aside in favour of Philip IV's third son, Charles, who succeeded as Charles IV.

In 1324, a brief War of Saint-Sardos was fought in Gascony, between the forces of Charles IV of France and Edward II of England. The English forces, under the command of Edmund of Woodstock, Earl of Kent, were obliged to surrender after the English stronghold of La Reole was bombarded for a month. This war ended in total defeat for the English, with only a narrow coastal strip and the town of Bordeaux still in English hands. The recovery of the lost lands of Aquitaine then became a major focus for the English. The disastrous war also made Edward deeply unpopular among the English aristocracy, and was one of several factors in bringing about his deposition and murder in 1327, leading to the accession of Edward III.

The following year Charles IV died, leaving a daughter (who would be disqualified for being female) and an unborn child who would also turn out to be a girl and also disqualified. This brought the Capetian dynasty to an end and there was a crisis regarding the succession to the French throne.

Charles IV's sister Isabella had been the intelligent but perfidious wife of Edward II, and incidentally also at least partly responsible for Edward's murder. She was now effectively regent, together with her lover Roger Mortimer, for the young Edward III. Edward III, as Charles IV's nephew, was the closest living male relative of the dead French king, and the only surviving male descendant of the senior line of the Capetian dynasty. By *English* feudal law, this made Edward III the legitimate heir to the French throne; in fact by *English* law he had become king *de facto* at the moment of Charles IV's death.

In France the situation was seen differently. The French nobles could not stomach the prospect of a foreigner becoming king of France, especially a foreigner who was already king of England. They argued, on the basis of their interpretation of ancient Salic Law, that the inheritance of the throne could not pass to a woman or through a woman – in other words, the succession could not pass through Isabella. According to that view, the most senior male of the Capetian dynasty was Philip of Valois, and he was regarded by the French as the legitimate heir. He became regent, and the moment Charles IV's widow gave birth to her second daughter he was declared king as Philip VI.

Joan of Navarre had a strong legal claim to the French throne, but lacked the power to enforce it. She was Louis X's daughter. In the kingdom of Navarre there was no tradition excluding female succession, so she had been allowed to inherit the crown of that kingdom. Joan and her husband Philip of Evreux produced a son, Charles II of Navarre, in

1332. He was regarded by the French as Philip IV's male heir in primogeniture.

After Philip VI's accession, England was still in control of Gascony, but held it as a fief from the French crown rather than owning it outright. A fief was a property granted by a lord in return for allegiance; this allegiance was usually interpreted as loyal and obedient military service. The English king therefore owed the French king homage, perhaps even military service for it if required. This inevitably became a source of friction. As Edward III's lord (in respect of Gascony), Philip VI demanded Edward's recognition of him as sovereign. Edward in turn wanted the lands lost by his father returned to him. After a long delay, in 1331 Edward accepted Philip as king of France and thereby gave up his claim to the French throne. In effect the deal was that Edward could keep Gascony if he abandoned his claim to the French throne.

That should have been the end of the matter, and it could have been but for the treachery of the French king. In 1333, Edward III launched into a war with Scotland. Philip saw this as an opportunity for him to reclaim Gascony for himself. However, the Scottish war was quickly won, with King David II of Scotland fleeing to safety in France. In 1336, Philip planned to restore David to his Scottish throne – and seize Gascony.

THE FIRST PHASE OF THE WAR (1337–60)

Hostilities began with French raids on settlements along the south coast of England and Philip's seizure of Gascony. Philip defended his action in Gascony by saying that Edward had broken his oath in failing to attend to the needs and demands of his lord. He was in effect reneguing on the deal he had struck with Edward. Edward retaliated by withdrawing from his part of the deal, which was to renounce his claim to the French throne; Edward now re-stated his claim, declaring that he was the rightful heir to the French throne. The bishop of Lincoln arrived in Paris to declare the defiance of the king of England and France. It was a formal declaration of war.

The war looked set to be very one-sided. The population of France was four times larger than that of England, and its army of knights was the largest in Europe. To compensate, Edward II attempted an alliance with the Low Countries and Flanders, but when nothing was achieved by this route the alliance collapsed. The cost of maintaining an army in France bankrupted the English treasury, which damaged Edward's reputation. Some towns on the Channel coast of England were repeatedly attacked by the French, and there was widespread fear that the French would mount an invasion; certainly French sea power was sufficient to make this viable. French dominance at sea was having a major impact on the English economy as the exporting of wool across to Flanders was obstructed; the wine trade from Gascony was similarly disrupted by French interference.

But there was a major reversal of fortunes in 1340. The French fleet tried to stop the English army from landing and during the Battle of Sluys that followed almost the entire French fleet was destroyed. It was a crucial battle. From this point on, English shipping dominated the English Channel – for the remainder of the war – and there was no further danger of a French invasion.

In 1341, a conflict within the larger conflict began. This was over the succession to the Duchy of Brittany. Edward III supported John of Montfort while Philip VI supported Charles of Blois. Over the next few years the city of Vannes changed hands several times as the struggle moved backwards and forwards across Brittany.

Edward III launched a major invasion of France, capturing Caen in a single day, which startled the French who had expected the city to withstand siege for much longer. Philip mustered a substantial army to stop Edward, who evaded a head-on confrontation by marching north-east towards the Low Countries, pillaging as he went rather than trying to take and occupy territory. Eventually he was unable to avoid facing Philip in battle and had to position his army ready to fight. Philip's army attacked – and was catastrophically defeated. This was the great Battle of Crécy, where the skill of the English longbowmen played a major part in the outcome.

Edward was then able to continue northwards without opposition.

He laid siege to Calais, which he took in 1347. This port, facing England on the French side of the Straits of Dover, was to become a major strategic asset. It gave the English a safe military base in France with the shortest possible supply line to England. It was a good year for Edward III as, at the Battle of Neville's Cross, the English defeated the Scots and this led to the capture of David II of Scotland.

The Black Death pandemic put a stop to military campaigns from 1348 until 1356, which gave the English treasury time to recover. After this breathing space, Edward III's son, Edward Prince of Wales (nicknamed the Black Prince) launched an attack on France from Gascony. At the Battle of Poitiers, the Black Prince and his army won a great victory, thanks to the skill of the English longbowmen. The victory was made complete by the capture of the French king, John II. John agreed a truce with the English king and was taken back to England, where he was held prisoner until a suitable ransom could be agreed; while he was away the government of France gradually fell apart. The Second Treaty of London was signed. Through this treaty Aquitaine was handed over to England and the French king was allowed to return home.

When he arrived, John found that his kingdom had descended into anarchy, with brigands rampaging round the countryside and the peasants rising in rebellion. Edward III decided to seize the opportunity to invade France; he hoped that amid the chaos he could seize the French throne. It was a strangely unsatisfactory venture. Edward's army was able to move around France unopposed – no French army came to meet him in battle – yet he was unable to take Rheims or Paris out of the hands of the Dauphin, who would later become Charles V. In 1360, Edward signed the Treaty of Bretigny. He now had in his possession Calais, Ponthieu, Brittany and Aquitaine. He also had as allies half of France's vassal states. Edward had made great capital out of John's period of absence and the resulting disunity. He had not won the French throne, to which he was entitled, yet the treaty made him renounce his claim – at least on paper. Meanwhile he had won back for England many of the lost possessions.

THE FIRST PEACE (1360–69)

King John's son, the Duke of Anjou, was sent to England as a hostage on his father's behalf. When Anjou escaped in 1362, King John of France was honourable enough to surrender himself up to captivity in England. He was housed in considerable style, and died in England two years later. Then the dauphin succeeded him as Charles V.

Edward III had not really let go of his claim to the French throne, so the Bretigny Treaty had no substance. Charles V, for his part, made every effort to reclaim the territory allocated to England in the treaty. Charles said Edward III had not met the terms of the treaty and declared war.

FRENCH ASCENDANCY (1369–89)

During the reign of Charles V, the English were pushed gradually back. There was a lack of leadership on the English side, because the Black Prince was conducting a war in Spain from 1366 onwards and his father, Edward III, was now too old to lead an army into battle. Pedro of Castile was linked to the English royal family through his two daughters, Constance and Isabella, who were married to the brothers of the Black Prince, John of Gaunt and Edmund of Langley. Pedro was deposed in 1370 with the help of the French. War broke out between Castile and France on the one side and England and Portugal on the other. This weakened the English significantly, as they lost their leading generals in the war.

Then came a severe blow to the English. The Black Prince died in 1376, a few months before his father Edward III in 1377. The English throne was then occupied by the under-aged Richard II. The threat to England from Scotland meant that the English needed to agree a peace with France, and a truce was called in 1389.

THE SECOND PEACE (1389–1415)

After the deposition of Richard II and his replacement by Henry IV, a new campaign in France was planned but Henry IV did not live long enough to carry it through. At the same time Charles VI of France was becoming insane and a power struggle began between his brother, Louis of Orleans, and his cousin, John the Fearless. Louis was assassinated and then the Armagnac family took his place in opposing John the Fearless. During this descent into civil war, both sides in the French power struggle tried to enlist the help of the English.

But England, too, was weakened by internal strife. There were rebellions in Wales and Ireland, a new border war with the Scots and two civil wars. The Scots invaded northern England in 1402, and were defeated at the Battle of Homildon Hill. The disputed spoils from this action led to a violent struggle between Henry IV and the Earl of Northumberland, which ended in the virtual destruction of the earl's (Percy) family. England was also weakened by piracy; the raiders came from France and Scandinavia. As well as robbery and damage, there was considerable dislocation of trade.

ENGLISH ASCENDANCY: HENRY V (1415–29)

This was the final phase of the Hundred Years' War and the best-known. This was the time of the most charismatic king of England, Henry V, and the most famous battle of all, Agincourt.

The plans for this campaign had been under preparation in the time of Henry IV, but it was not until the reign of his son that they would come to fruition. The Armagnac faction in France offered Henry V the Bretigny deal in return for his military support. However, he turned them down. Instead, he bullishly demanded a return to the borders as they were in the time of Henry II. To press his territorial claim, he set sail for France on 1 August with an army of 12,000 soldiers. He laid siege to the town of Harfleur and took it. He was tempted to march on Paris at once, but instead made an expedition across the north of France. Henry marched his dysentery-reduced army across Normandy, hoping to reach Calais without having to do battle with the French. A huge French army, perhaps three times larger than Henry's, had been mustered by the French king while the Harfleur siege had been going on. It mirrored the

English army's advance along the valley of the Somme, the two armies separated by the river. Then at Agincourt the French army barred the way. Faced with such overwhelming odds, the English should have lost this battle, yet they won and the battle immediately acquired a unique status in English history.

The battlefield had recently been ploughed and was muddy after rain. It was very unfavourable terrain for the heavily armoured and heavily equipped French knights, some of whom drowned in the mud when they fell into it and were unable to get up again. The ground conditions played a large part in giving the English victory.

Before the battle the French were understandably confident of defeating the much smaller English army. They even cast lots for the king and nobles, who were worth a great deal in ransom money. The English were astonished at the 'innumerable hateful French' but prepared their ground in a highly organised way under Henry V's exceptional leadership. He ordered wedges of archers to be interspersed among the lines of infantry, with lines of stakes in front of them to protect them from cavalry charges. For some reason the French were reluctant to attack. Those present wondered if the French were waiting for the English to break their battle order. In the end, knowing how short of food his army was, Henry V ordered his men forward. Then the French, too, moved forward. The flanking French cavalry on each side charged the English archers, and they were stopped and pierced either by arrows or stakes. When the English archers had run out of arrows, they picked up axes and swords from the men lying wounded or dead on the ground and used those to beat off the enemy. The battle was so violent and the odds were so against the English that the English took no prisoners. Every French combatant was struck down, regardless of rank.

Soon the French dead and wounded lay piled up in heaps in front of the English lines. English soldiers climbed up on top of the heaps and killed those still living underneath their feet. After about three hours the French fell back. The English began to sort out the heaps of French soldiers and separate the living from the dead, but were interrupted by shouts that the French were charging back at them in huge numbers.

For their own safety, the English had no alternative but to kill their prisoners. They killed all of them except for a few who were clearly, too, important to kill, such as the Dukes of Orléans and Bourbon.

Not long after that the French finally withdrew. In spite of the huge apparent advantage the French had at the start of the Battle of Agincourt, the French defeat was total and catastrophic, with many of the Armagnac leaders left dead on the field of battle.

After this major victory, Henry V was able to go on to take Caen in 1417 and Rouen in 1419, bringing most of Normandy under English control. He made an alliance with the Duchy of Burgundy, which had taken Paris. In 1420, Henry met Charles VI. They signed the Treaty of Troyes, which arranged the marriage of Charles VI's daughter Catherine with Henry, and the inheritance of the French throne by Henry's heirs. The dauphin was declared illegitimate.

Henry's triumph was short-lived. A Scottish army arrived in France under the Earl of Buchan. In 1421, at the Battle of Bauge, the Scots killed the English commander, the Duke of Clarence, and most of the other English leaders. The French were delighted, in spite of the recent treaty, and instantly made Buchan High Constable of France. Shortly after this, Henry V died of dysentery and Charles VI died not long afterwards. Henry's son, the infant Henry VI, was crowned King of England and France. In spite of this, the Armagnacs backed Charles's son and the war continued.

JOAN OF ARC AND FRENCH VICTORY (1428–53)

By 1428, the English were once again ready to renew the war with France, laying siege to the city of Orléans. They attempted this with too small an army to be effective, and if the forces available to the French had been mustered the siege could easily have been broken, but the French held back. In 1429, a peasant girl from Lorraine, Joan of Arc, persuaded the dauphin to let her go and drive out the English. She had heard the voices of saints telling her to do this. She raised French morale and as a result the French attacked the English, who in turn lifted the siege.

Not long after this a large French army managed to break through English archers with heavy cavalry at the Battle of Patay. An English army of 3,000 commanded by the Earl of Shrewsbury was defeated. This was the first big victory of the wars for the French, and it enabled the dauphin to march to Rheims to be crowned as Charles VII.

Joan was captured by the Burgundians in 1430, and later sold to the English, who executed her. Charles VII did nothing to save her. The three-cornered relationship between France, England and Burgundy was complex. In 1435, Burgundy changed sides, switching allegiance from England to France, while remaining unreliable; Burgundy's main focus was on expanding its territories in the Low Countries and this left little time for intervention in France. The long truces gave Charles time to reorganise and modernise both the French army and the government; there was a move towards centralisation.

The English continued to be successful, with the army under the brilliant command of the Earl of Shrewsbury. But in 1449 the French regained Rouen and in 1450 they defeated the English as they attempted to relieve Caen. Then the French retook Cherbourg and, in 1451, Bayonne and Bordeaux. Shrewsbury made an attempt to retake Gascony, but he was defeated at the Battle of Castillon in 1453, which was the last battle of this incredibly long, impoverishing and enervating war.

Significance

The Hundred Years' War was a time of progress in both weapons technology and military tactics. It was also a period of societal and political development, especially in France. England was already a modern state, with a central authority invested in Parliament. It had also revolutionised its military recruitment system, using a paid professional army rather than one functioning on feudal obligation.

At the outset, there was a general belief that heavy cavalry (heavily armoured and heavily equipped knights on horseback) was the most powerful unit in an army. Experience in several battles showed that this was not so. The spectacular success of the English longbow set up in fixed positions gave the English several important victories, such as

Crécy and Agincourt. The English also learnt (from fighting the Scots) how effective it could be to use lightly armoured mounted soldiers who could ride quickly to any point in the battlefield, then dismount and fight on foot. At Agincourt, the sheer weight of their armour immobilised the French knights when they dismounted or fell or were pulled off their horses; once they were off their horses, they were dead men. After the war ended, the concept of heavy cavalry faded.

Another important lesson learned was that armies needed to reflect the territories they were to occupy. The English, even when they being successful, found it very hard to occupy such a huge country. They needed to commit far greater numbers of troops in order to station garrisons in the towns they intended to keep. They also needed larger forces to lay siege to substantial towns and cities. Salisbury was trying to besiege Orléans with only 5,000 men, which was not nearly enough. The siege of Orléans was lifted relatively easily with the injection of Joan of Arc's charisma, and by a chance cannon shot that killed Salisbury.

An important by-product of the war was the shaping of a sense of national identity in both England and France. Although at the centre of the war was a dynastic conflict between French and English dynasties, ordinary people on both sides of the Channel became deeply committed, identifying closely with their national causes. In England there was not only a fear that the French would invade; there was a widespread assumption that when they arrived the French – horror of horrors – would make everybody in England *speak French.* There was a powerful retaliatory movement in England to remove French as the official formal language, the tongue of the ruling class and of commerce, and replace it with vernacular English. France itself moved some distance from being a feudal monarchy towards becoming a centralized state.

In England, the war raised questions about the limits of a king's authority. There was a gap in the succession when Edward III died and his son was still a minor. It was not a coincidence that this gap was chosen as the time for a major peasant rising, a protest in part about the levying of high war taxation. In France, too, at moments of royal weakness, the lower orders attempted to wrest power from the king.

This was very apparent during the captivity in England of King John II. The Estates General tried to make the French monarchy accept a sort of social contract called the Great Ordinance, which proposed some major constitutional changes and the sort of participation in national government provided for in the English Parliament.

The English monarchs meanwhile went on making claims to the French throne, even if only on paper in the lists of grandiose titles they compiled for themselves. They went on styling themselves 'King of France' until the Act of Union of 1801; it was only after that that the title was dropped. As in many other conflicts, the original cause, the original grievance, was frequently forgotten in the heat of battle and the hatreds of the moment. Wars frequently generate their own momentum. As in a nuclear reaction, they feed on their own energy.

THE FALL OF CONSTANTINOPLE

(1453)

The Byzantine Empire had existed for over 1,000 years. It had its origins in the Roman Empire. Even in the hey-day of ancient Rome, the empire was considered too large and sprawling to be managed easily as a single entity and had for convenience been administered in two halves, the Eastern and Western Empires. When the Roman Empire imploded, the Western Empire really ceased to exist but the Eastern Empire continued in the form of the Byzantine Empire.

The capital city of this powerful eastern empire was the equally powerful city of Byzantium, also known as Constantinople, and today known as Istanbul. In the 1,000 years of its time as capital of the Byzantine Empire, Constantinople was besieged many times, partly for its wealth, and partly because of its strategic position commanding the commercial sea traffic passing between the Black Sea and the Aegean Sea, and the land traffic passing between Europe and Asia Minor. Even though it was besieged repeatedly, it was captured only once, and that was during the Fourth Crusade of 1204. That led to the creation of a brief and unstable Latin state.

The Byzantine Empire disintegrated, forming several successor states such as Trebizond, Nicaea and Epirus. The Nicaeans reconquered the short-lived Latin state in 1261. During the next 200 years, a weakened Byzantine Empire experienced attacks from various neighbours, including the Serbians, Bulgarians and Ottoman Turks. By 1453, the Byzantine Empire comprised not much more than Constantinople itself, which was not unlike the twentieth century city-state of Singapore. There were also some outlying possessions, such as the Peloponnese, centred on the beautiful fortress city of Mystras near Sparta, and

Trebizond, which functioned as a virtually separate mini-empire on the Black Sea coast.

The Ottoman Turks were expanding their empire and absorbed and digested parts of the former Byzantine Empire. Thessaloniki was taken by the Ottomans in 1430. Then the city-state of Constantinople was very isolated; by 1453 only a few Aegean islands and some islands in the Propontis (the old name for the Sea of Marmara, the body of water linking the Aegean to the Black Sea) remained under Byzantine control. It was almost as if the city of Constantinople was waiting for the *coup de grace.*

When Sultan Mehmed (or Mohammed) II succeed to the Ottoman throne in 1451, he was perceived to be a weak and incapable ruler who was going to be no threat to Constantinople or other Christian possessions in the Aegean or Balkan region. This view was confirmed by the new sultan's friendly promise to respect the integrity of Byzantine territory. But then he began to send signals that his intentions were far from friendly. In 1452, he built a castle on the European side of the Bosporus, just outside the walls of Constantinople, and that was a clear threat to Constantinople and its control over traffic through the Bosporus. What was particularly noticeable about the new fortress was that it was positioned so that it would be able to block the arrival of any military aid for Constantinople from Genoese colonies on the Black Sea coast. Mehmed called the new castle Rumeli, which was the name given to the European part of the Ottoman Empire. The Turkish name for the fortress (Boğazkesen) has a sinister double meaning – 'strait-blocker' and 'throat-slitter'. The stronghold's Greek name (Laimaokopia) has the same double meaning.

The threat to Constantinople was very plain. Emperor Constantine XI appealed to the countries of Western Europe for help. But he was ignored. This was because of another conflict, between the Roman Catholic and Orthodox Churches. The Christian countries of Western Europe fell within the Catholic Church, while those of the East were within the Orthodox Church. In 1054, the two churches had excommunicated one another. Since then, the Catholic Church had been trying to recapture the Orthodox Church. A reunion had been attempted in 1274, and after that some Byzantine emperors had been received into the Catholic Church. In 1439, a Bull of Union was proclaimed in Florence, but in subsequent years the diehards in Constantinople had fought against the union of the two churches. In the backwash from this conflict, the Catholic countries of the West did not feel any great sense of duty to protect Constantinople.

When the Rumeli fortress was completed in the summer of 1452, Emperor Constantine wrote to Pope Nicholas V, begging for help and promising to implement the Union. The Pope was keen to help, but he was powerless to instruct or even influence the kings and princes of the West in the matter. Western Europe was in any case riven by its own debilitating conflicts at this time. England and France were in a weak economic state as a result of the Hundred Years' War. Spain was preoccupied with the closing stages of the Reconquest, its struggle to claim territory back from the Moors. Each country had its own internal problems, its own conflicts to deal with, and they all took priority over defending Constantinople.

The result was that there was no Crusade to defend Constantinople as there had been to defend Jerusalem. There was no co-ordinated Western defence of Constantinople against the threat from Turkey. There were some chivalrous individuals who decided that they would go, on their own account, to defend the city against the Ottomans. One was Giovanni Giustiniani. He was a highly experienced professional soldier from Genoa, and he arrived at Constantinople in January 1453 with 700 armed men – his own army, in fact. He was expert at defending the walls of cities, and the emperor instantly gave him responsibility for the overall command of the defence of the walls of Constantinople.

The captains of Venetian ships that happened to be in the harbour at Constantinople also offered their services in the defence of the city, even though this went against the current direct instructions from Venice. Back in Venice the debate continued about the nature of the help the Venetian Republic would offer. The senate decided in the end to send a fleet, but by the time it set sail in late April it was too late to be of any help to the stricken city; by the time the Venetian fleet arrived the fate of Constantinople had been sealed. The Pope himself sent three ships with provisions; they set sail at the end of March. With no concerted European will to save it, the defence of Constantinople was therefore a lost cause before it began. The army defending it was 7,000 strong, whereas the Ottoman army, when it arrived, totalled a formidable 100,000 men. Constantinople had magnificent defensive walls that had been built 1,000 years before, but they were very long and therefore difficult to man effectively. The Theodosian walls on the landward side were 5.5 km (3½ miles) long; the sea walls along the Golden Horn were 7 km (9⅓ miles) long; the sea walls along the Sea of Marmara were 7.5 km (9⅔ miles) long. The total of 20 km (12½ miles) of walls was far too long for a mere 7,000 men to defend, even though they were at the time the strongest fortifications in the world. They had also been recently repaired. The defenders were fairly well-equipped, thought the fleet was only modest in size, a mere 26 ships compared with the Ottoman fleet of perhaps 100-400 ships. The defensive force was overwhelmingly outnumbered by the sheer size of the Ottoman army, outnumbered by about 14 to 1.

The Ottoman attack was helped also by the quality of the cannon they had. The Ottomans were using the latest weapons technology, supplied by a Hungarian master founder called Orban, who sold Sultan Mehmet cannon that were guaranteed powerful enough to smash down the strongest fortifications ever built. Orban offered his advanced cannon to the Sultan and was given everything he needed. He built what was at that time probably the biggest gun ever made, 8.3 metres (27 ft) long and able to fire a cannonball weighing 1544 kg (1,200 lb) a distance of a mile. The problem with it was that it took three hours to reload, and there were very few cannonballs of the right gauge. It was even so a major engineering feat, one that struck awe into both sides in this epic struggle. The big foundry where the artillery for the attack was located was 240 km (150 miles) from Constantinople, so then there was a major logistical problem in transporting it. Orban's gigantic cannon was shepherded towards Constantinople by a team of ninety oxen and 400 men.

Sultan Mehmed's strategy was to attack the Theodosian Walls first. These were the fortifications that were designed to protect the city from a land attack. His army set up camp outside the city on 2 April 1453 and he himself arrived three days later, ready to launch the historic attack. The defenders manned the walls. Because there were not enough men to defend all the walls, it was only the outermost walls that were manned. Constantine and his troops guarded the middle section of the walls, the Mesoteichon. This section, which was crossed by the River Lycus, was considered the most vulnerable point and the emperor assumed the Ottomans would focus their attack there. Giusiniani was stationed to the north of Constantine, by the Charisian Gate, though later he moved to defend the centre. Minotto and some Venetian troops positioned themselves in the Blachernae Palace. To the emperor's left, on the south side, were the Genoese troops and Theophilus Palaeologus guarding the Pegae Gate. The stretch of walls between there and the Golden Gate was defended by troops under Filippo Contarini. The southernmost stretch of the Theodosian Wall was defended by troops under Demetrius Cantacuzenus. The other walls were very sparsely manned. The Byzantines had cannon, smaller in size than the Ottoman artillery, but even so their recoil did a considerable amount of damage to the walls.

The European troops of the Ottoman army were stretched out along the entire length of the walls under the command of Karadja Pasha. The Turkish troops were stationed along the Sea of Marmara. The sultan had his red and gold tent erected near the Mesoteichon, where the guns and his elite troops were assembled. Other troops were spread out behind the front lines and also to the north of the Golden Horn.

As the siege of Constantinople started, Mehmed sent some of his troops off to put the remaining Byzantine strongholds in the area out of action. This was to ensure the isolation of the city. Then the long, slow barrage began. For weeks the massive cannon was fired at the walls. It had little effect, partly because it was very difficult to aim accurately, partly because it took so long to reload. In fact there were long enough gaps between hits to enable the Byzantine defenders to repair the wall after each shot.

The Ottoman fleet commanded by Baltoghlu was to have entered the Golden Horn Harbour, but could not because of the huge iron chain the Byzantines had slung across its entrance. In spite of this, on 20 April a flotilla of four Byzantine ships succeeded in slipping into the Golden Horn after some heavy fighting. This escapade boosted the morale of the defenders and discomposed the Sultan. In order to get round the chain, he ordered a road to be constructed of greased logs across the neck of land on the north side of the Horn, and had seventy-two ships hauled across by oxen on 22 April. This manoeuvre was a threat to the city's supply line to the Genoese ships. On the night of 28 April, the Byzantines tried to destroy the Ottoman ships in the Golden Horn with the use of fire ships. The Ottomans had been warned beforehand, and were able to take avoiding action, forcing the Christians to retreat. After that, the defenders had to divert some of their troops to defend the Golden Horn, which weakened the defences of the walls accordingly.

By this time the Ottoman forces had made several fierce direct attacks on the land wall, but each time they had been forced back with heavy losses. It began to look as if, as in the past, the walls of Constantinople were impregnable. The Ottomans resorted to more radical methods to break through the fortifications. In the second half of May, they started digging tunnels under the walls in order to undermine them. Many of the sappers were Serbians, under the command of Zaganos Pasha. But the Byzantines counterattacked. They employed a Scottish engineer by the name of Johannes Grant who had countertunnels dug. These allowed Byzantines to reach the Turkish workers and kill them using Greek fire. On 23 May, Byzantine soldiers captured two Turkish officers and tortured them until they revealed where all the Turkish tunnels were. The Byzantines were then able to destroy all the tunnels.

Mehmed tried to persuade the Byzantines to surrender. He would lift the siege if they would hand over their city. The Byzantines declined this offer. Mehmed knew that he could eventually overpower the city by sheer force of numbers; the defenders would be worn out long before he ran out of soldiers. In council with his senior officers, Mehmed met resistance. One vizier, Halil Pasha, had always disapproved of the scheme to conquer Constantinople; now he pressed Mehmed to abandon the project. Halil was overruled by Zaganos Pasha, who advised immediate attack. This was the advice Mehmed wanted to hear and he took it. Mehmed suspected Halil of being in the pay of the Byzantines, and had him put to death later in the year.

The moon was the symbol of Constantinople. On 22 May 1453, the rising moon was seen to be eclipsed. It was seen as an omen; the city itself would be eclipsed. Four days afterwards the city was engulfed in a dense fog, which was unknown in May. As the fog lifted in the evening a strange light was seen playing over the dome of Hagia Sophia. The superstitious defenders saw this as indicating that the Holy Spirit was abandoning the Cathedral.

THE FINAL ASSAULT

As the Ottoman army prepared for the final assault that would take the city on 28 May, large religious processions were held inside the city. That evening a last solemn Christian service was held inside the Hagia Sophia. The emperor and members of both Latin and Greek Churches took part. There was a general awareness that the end had come.

At midnight, that end began. The Ottomans sent in their auxiliaries first. These were poorly trained and not very effective fighters, but the idea was that they would kill as many of the defenders as they could – and confuse the rest. The second assault consisted largely of Turks, who attacked the north-west side of the city, focussing on a section the wall that was already damaged. They managed to break through, as the Crusaders had in 1204, but were swiftly pushed back again.

Both the first and second attacks were repulsed. For a time the defenders were able to hold off the third assault, by the Janissaries, the Sultan's elite warriors. In this attack Giustiniani was badly wounded and had to be carried from the ramparts. The sight of this seriously disheartened the defenders. Giustiniani was ferried to Chios, where he died of his wounds a few days afterwards.

Giustiniani's demoralised troops fell back into the city and towards the harbour. Then Constantine and his soldiers were left isolated, though they kept holding off the attack for a time. It is thought that, perhaps inadvertently, perhaps through treachery, one of the gates in the wall, the Kerkoporta Gate had been left unlocked. The Ottoman troops discovered this and poured through. At the same moment, the defenders on the walls were being overwhelmed. The defence of Constantinople collapsed.

Emperor Constantine threw aside his purple regalia, led a final charge against the swarming Ottomans, and died in the streets fighting alongside his soldiers. His ultimate fate is not known for certain. One folk tale turned him into a 'sleeping king' hero of the same type as King Arthur. As the Ottomans descended on him, it was said, Constantine was rescued by an angel who turned him to marble and put him in a cave underneath the Golden Gate. There he waits to be brought back to life again. Such was the mythic power of this great event.

The Ottoman army converged on the huge square in front of the Hagia Sophia. Inside the cathedral, a great crowd of civilians had taken refuge, hoping that the Ottomans would respect their right of sanctuary. When the Ottomans broke down the doors, they sorted the people they found inside into different groups according to the prices they would fetch as slaves. Old people and small children were killed out of hand as commercially worthless.

The Byzantine historian George Sphrantzes saw Constantinople fall. He later wrote what happened on the third day after the conquest.

> *On the third day after the fall of our city, the sultan celebrated his victory with a great, joyful triumph. He issued a proclamation: the citizens of all ages who had managed to escape detection were to leave their hiding places throughout the city and come out into the open, as they were to remain free and no question would be asked. He further declared the restoration of houses and property to those who had abandoned our city before the siege; if they returned home, they would be treated according to their rank and religion, as if nothing had changed.*

In fact, by 1453, the city was already in a state of serious decline. The territorial contraction of the empire and its economic decline had left it in a very poor state. It had lost many of its people. In fact, behind the magnificent walled fortifications, behind the glamour of its name,

Constantinople was a poor settlement. It was a series of walled villages separated from one another by huge fields, though surrounded overall by the wonderful fifth century Theodosian Walls. The mayors of these villages surrendered to Mehmed and they became the administrators of a self-governing community.

What mattered most to Mehmed was that he had conquered Constantinople. That made him the successor to the Roman emperors. He styled himself 'Kayzer-I Rum', the Roman Caesar, but he became known simply as 'the Conqueror'. Hagia Sophia was transformed into a mosque. Many of the Greeks who had been living in Constantinople fled to the West, taking with them books and knowledge that were to energize the Renaissance. The migration of Greeks (and their stored knowledge) began as early as the twelfth century, but the Fall of Constantinople pushed another wave of migrants westwards. Once Constantinople had fallen, there was little hope for the remainder of the Byzantine Empire. In 1460, the fortress of Mystras in the Peloponnese fell; in 1461 Trebizond fell, too.

Consequences and significance

The final flicker of the Roman Empire had gone out; a Christian power had been supplanted by a Muslim power. The fall of Constantinople was much more than a great spectacle: it was a landmark of world history. Some say it marked the end of the Middle Ages.

The fall of Constantinople accelerated the exodus of Greek scholars to western Europe, where they would be a driving force in the Renaissance. The addition of Constantinople to the Ottoman Empire had the effect of giving it more political and commercial stability.

There were other far-reaching effects, too. The fall of Constantinople severed the main overland trade route from Europe into Asia. This had serious implications for European commerce. The result was that governments in Western Europe began to look for alternative routes to Asia – by sea. That led to the great voyages of discovery, the circumnavigation of Africa and the Columbus voyage west across the Atlantic.

THE WARS OF THE ROSES
(1455–1485)

The Wars of the Roses, a saga of two rival dynasties struggling for the English throne, had their ultimate origins in the unsatisfactory reign of Richard II. The trouble began in 1399, when the powerful Duke of Lancaster, John of Gaunt, died. John of Gaunt's son and heir had expected to inherit his father's property, but the land was confiscated by King Richard II. The disinherited son, Henry Bolingbroke, raised an army to try to retrieve it; when the king gave in, Bolingbroke seized the throne for himself. Henry Bolingbroke's 'Lancastrian' branch of the Plantagenet family had a poor claim to the throne. Yet Bolingbroke was able to establish himself, by *force majeure*, as King Henry IV after forcing the abdication of Richard II and then arranging his murder. Henry IV, the founder of the dynasty of the House of Lancaster, was a straightforward usurper.

The third in the line of Lancastrian kings, descended from Edward III, was mentally unstable, weak and incompetent; the combination of personal weakness and dynastic weakness led to a major challenge for the throne from the Yorkist line of the Plantagenets, also descended from Edward III. Gradually escalating tension between the two Plantagenet houses led to war, and that eventually led to seizure of the throne by the Yorkists in 1461.

KING HENRY VI

Henry VI inherited the throne as a boy, so the kingdom was for many years ruled by regents, which was unsatisfactory. When Henry came of age in 1437 the situation became worse as he turned out to be ineffectual. He was more concerned with the morals of his courtiers than affairs of state. Meanwhile, his courtiers and their factions manoeuvred for power and influence. The general management of the economy declined, prosperity declined and French pirates were able to raid the towns along the Channel coast with impunity.

One faction striving to seize power from the king was led by Richard Plantagenet, Duke of York. Like Henry VI, he was a descendant of Edward III, but he had a slightly stronger claim to the throne than Henry. The king himself was represented by, or rather controlled by, a faction led by his wife. She was Margaret of Anjou, a highly political and aggressive personality. She acted together with William de la Pole, Duke of Suffolk, and Edmund Beaufort, Duke of Somerset. The queen's party was easily able to control Henry VI and so represented the Lancastrian cause. So, from early on, the power struggle polarised into a duel between the Houses of York and Lancaster.

There was general popular discontent over the failure of the English army to succeed in the Hundred Years War (with France), and also with the corruption of the royal court. This popular feeling found expression in a rebellion in 1450 – the Peasants' Revolt led by Jack Cade. Although it was called a peasants' revolt, implying a power base among farm labourers, this rebellion had quite a lot of support from both working and merchant classes in London. There were in fact many interest groups who needed a stable and responsible government in order to prosper. The rebellion was put down relatively quickly, but it seriously weakened the controlling queen's party and strengthened the party of the Duke of York. After the rebellion, the Duke of York, who was the Yorkist contender for the throne, became Henry VI's chief minister and therefore effectively head of government in England. In the same year, the Duke of Suffolk was murdered, and the Duke of York forced Henry VI to acknowledge his own claim to the throne and name him as his heir.

In 1453, Henry VI had an episode of insanity. Given his personal inadequacies and the extraordinary and unusual pressures on him, it was hardly surprising. It is thought by modern medics that he was suffering from what is now called catatonic schizophrenia. Whatever the specific nature of his mental illness, it became clear to everybody that he was unfit to rule and that there would need to be a regency. Naturally, as the king's chief minister, Richard Duke of York declared himself Lord Protector and governed England. As he did so, he worked towards the progressive limitation of Queen Margaret's power.

But in 1453, York had a serious setback himself. Margaret of Anjou gave birth to a son, who automatically acquired the status of Heir Apparent, displacing the Duke of York as Henry VI's heir, though York remained protector. After fifteen months, Henry VI regained his sanity, and Margaret of Anjou obliged the Duke of York to relinquish his role as Lord Protector. She even managed to persuade Henry VI to dismiss York from all of his other offices, too. She was angry at the way York had tried to reduce her power during the period of her husband's madness, and now she exacted her revenge, moving to reduce York's land holdings and gathering an alliance of lords against him. By 1454, she had succeeded in having him cut out of the royal council. It was under this extreme provocation that the Duke of York resorted to fighting in order to re-establish himself.

THE FIRST BATTLE OF ST ALBANS

Now as it seemed fighting for his very survival, the Duke of York gathered a small army and marched south from his estates in the North of England to try to re-establish his position. On 22 May 1455, he was confronted at St Albans, just north of London, by an army of Queen Margaret's supporters. This confrontation is called the Battle of St Albans, though it was in reality little more than a skirmish. It was a landmark nevertheless, in that it was the moment when all the tensions and political manoeuvrings of the previous years erupted into open warfare. This was the beginning of the Wars of the Roses.

The Duke of Somerset was killed, which left Queen Margaret as the head of the defeated Lancastrian party. In an extraordinary reversal of fortune, the Duke of York once again shot to the top of the political hierarchy and resumed his position as protector – however, this would only be for a short time.

Henry VI himself had no role to play; he was a mere pawn in the game, his presence giving some sort of legitimacy to whichever side had him in its possession. For the next four years there was virtually no government in England. The big political players were busily gathering supporters and arming themselves for large-scale warfare, which was evidently now the only way to resolve the problem. The general anarchy led to rioting in the London streets; French fleets ravaging English shipping in the Channel and raiding south coast towns played havoc with the previously lucrative wool trade with Holland, which had come to a complete stop.

In the late summer of 1459, Margaret of Anjou and her army moved to the North. The Yorkist leaders, finding that they had traitors among their supporters, were obliged to flee overseas.

THE BATTLE OF NORTHAMPTON

It was in June 1460 that the remarkable power of the Duke of York's strongest supporter made itself felt. He was Richard Neville, Earl of Warwick, and such was his power that he became known as Warwick the Kingmaker. Warwick and the Duke of York's second son, Edward, Earl of March, sailed a small army across the Channel, landing at Sandwich in Kent. This army was welcomed by the people of Kent, the Archbishop of Canterbury and the City of London. With this injection of support and encouragement, Warwick's army was able to march north to Northampton, where it succeeded in routing Queen Margaret's army on 10 July 1460. The battle was fought on the sloping valley side leading down to the bridge over the River Nene. So many men were cut to pieces during the battle that the river literally ran red with blood.

The outcome of the Battle of Northampton was so overwhelming as to be decisive. Not only did the Yorkists win it, they captured the king, Henry VI, as well. With the king now fully in his power, York returned to London, locked the king in the Tower and asserted his own claim to the throne, which in terms of genealogy was stronger than that of the king. A reasonable compromise was agreed, by which Henry was to be allowed to continue as king for the remainder of his life, but on his death the throne would pass to York and his heirs. Seeing how badly things were going for the Lancastrian cause, the queen fled to Wales for safety, while the Yorkists set up a government and called a parliament.

Then, in October, Richard, Duke of York, pushed home his advantage. He would after all not wait for the death of Henry before taking the throne for himself. He demanded that Parliament should formally depose the king and make him, Richard, king at once. Parliament was stunned to be asked to do anything so radical; the demand was refused, though it was agreed to acknowledge Richard as Henry's heir. This meant disinheriting Prince Edward, who was Henry VI's son, the Heir Apparent.

In the West, the disinherited Prince Edward and his mother, Queen Margaret, naturally responded by raising an army to defend their family's rights. This led to a remarkable three-month-long armed struggle, a phase of continual fighting that lasted from December 1460 until March 1461.

THE BATTLE OF WAKEFIELD (1460)

The Battle of Wakefield (30 December 1460) was one action in this binge of fighting. It was the largest and bloodiest battle so far fought in England. Many of the key players on both sides died in the battle, including the Duke of York and his eldest son Edmund – two men who had up to the day of the battle seemed set fair to become the next two kings of England; now they were both dead. One significant result of the Battle of Wakefield was that the Yorkist claim to the throne now came from Richard Plantagenet's eldest son Edward. But it was Richard Neville, Earl of Warwick, who now became the real leader of the Yorkists.

In frustration, Queen Margaret took her army east and ravaged the farmland that supported the Yorkist cause.

THE SECOND BATTLE OF ST ALBANS (1461)

Warwick hastily gathered an army to fight a holding battle at St Albans on 17 February – this was the Second Battle of St Albans – and he lost. Warwick himself managed to escape from the battlefield alive and with some of his army still intact. Warwick had perhaps unwisely forced King Henry to take a place in the battle line, presumably to reduce the ferocity of the Lancastrian attack and demoralize the Lancastrian host, however the result was that Queen Margaret's army was able to rescue Henry immediately.

THE BATTLE OF MORTIMER'S CROSS (1461)

London was in a panic, as there was an expectation that Queen Margaret and all her supporters would descend on the capital with a vengeance and create mayhem there. Margaret of Anjou had a reputation as a fearsome pillager. But for some reason Queen Margaret hesitated. She did not drive into London, attempt to retake it and depose Edward.

Then Edward was able to win a victory for the Yorkists at Mortimer's Cross. On the strength of this, he was able to march unopposed into London and claim the throne of England as Edward IV – a spectacular success. So, instead of Queen Margaret, it was the Earl of Warwick and Edward, Earl of March, the dead duke's eldest surviving son and heir, who entered London.

It was on 4 March 1461 that the nineteen-year-old Edward of York was proclaimed King Edward IV. There was enthusiastic support for this proclamation in London itself and also among the lords of southern England generally. This was because of Queen Margaret's reputation for savagery; there were rumours that in her anger she would pillage all of England if she could. With this massive level of support in the South, the new king was able to set off for the North in pursuit of the Lancastrian army.

THE BATTLE OF TOWTON (1461)

On 29 March 1461, the two huge armies met near Towton. It is thought that in all there were about 35,000 soldiers on the field of battle, which was of the bloodiest of the Wars of the Roses. The soldiers of the two sides hacked at each other, inflicting terrible injuries. Edward IV had rather fewer men than Queen Margaret, but he led his troops brilliantly and with great ferocity. Eventually they broke the Lancastrian line. In the rout that followed thousands of soldiers died. The death toll in the Battle of Towton is believed to have reached 10,000. Totally defeated, Queen Margaret, the ex-king Henry and their son fled to safety in Scotland.

With help from the Scots, the Lancastrians continued to resist the Yorkist coup in the North of England for the next three years. Eventually, and perhaps inevitably, in 1465 the deposed king was captured by Edward IV's men and confined in the Tower of London. The Lancastrian cause now seemed completely lost, but then there was glimmer of hope as a quarrel erupted between Edward IV and Warwick in the wake of the king's marriage to Elizabeth Woodville (1464), a rift that eventually erupted into a rebellion.

For several years Edward IV consolidated his position and peace, order and prosperity returned. But the Wars of the Roses were not quite over. Warwick and the king's younger brother, George Duke of Clarence, had been the most reliable and committed supporters of the Yorkist cause, but once the fighting for the throne was over they found themselves pushed out of government and influence – out of the limelight. In their disappointment at the way in which the king was treating them, in 1469 they formed an alliance against Edward IV, fled to France in 1470 and became reconciled to Margaret of Anjou.

THE BATTLE OF LOSE-COATS FIELD (1470)

Edward defeated the Lancastrian rebels at the Battle of Lose-Coats Fields on 12 March 1470. But then he discovered that the rebellion had in fact been started up at the instigation of Warwick and Clarence, in order to show that Edward was not really in command of his kingdom. Warwick knew then that he would not be pardoned a second time. He would be condemned as a traitor, and in a struggle to survive he tried to raise an army. Instead he was forced to run for his life to France – naturally, with Clarence.

Once he was in France, Warwick came to the extraordinary decision that he would reinstate the feeble-minded Henry VI, simply because it gave him his best chance to become England's ruler. He gained the support of Queen Margaret and her French supporters, as well as the Lancastrian party in England; he could also depend on the support of his own extensive and influential family. Warwick had the advantage of surprise, by arranging to land in the West Country in September 1470 when Edward was not expecting it. Edward IV and his (totally loyal) youngest brother Richard, Duke of Gloucester, were very nearly captured, but they managed to escape to Ghent in the Low Countries.

Warwick marched into London, released a befuddled and elderly Henry VI from the confines of his prison, and placed him back on the throne, no wiser or more competent than before – but nevertheless being given his third turn at being king. It was of course not Warwick's intention that Henry VI should in any sense rule England: Warwick himself would do that. Henry VI was back on the throne, and Warwick was his chief minister.

Warwick managed to achieve this remarkable coup without any violence at all. He reversed the result of the previous Wars of the Roses. This was how Warwick achieved the nickname 'the Kingmaker'. Warwick called for a Parliament with a view to deposing Edward IV and replacing him with Clarence, or even himself. While Warwick waited for Parliament to assemble and respond, the Lancastrians took advantage of the unstable and uncertain situation to mount a rebellion on the Scottish border.

Edward IV was in exile and in effect deposed, but he had plenty of support. On the strength of a considerable loan from the Duke of Burgundy, he was able to assemble an army and he re-invaded his kingdom in the middle of March, 1471, landing in Yorkshire. Warwick was able to brings huge forces against Edward, but Edward was such an outstanding military leader that he was able to overcome them. By causing his small army to make sudden deceptive movements and feints on the battlefield, he was able to confuse his enemies, scatter them and open the road to London.

Once Edward was back in London, on 11 April he recaptured poor Henry VI, who was now deposed again and returned to the Tower. Once the Lancastrian king was safely locked up, Edward rushed to Westminster to see his wife and children, who had been living in sanctuary for their own safety for several months. Edward's disloyal and shallow brother Clarence saw that he had made a terrible mistake, and took his troops over to his brother and asked for his forgiveness. Now that his army was considerably enlarged, Edward was able to move back to deal with Warwick.

THE BATTLE OF BARNET (1471)

The two armies, Yorkist under Edward IV and Lancastrian under Warwick, collided near Barnet on Easter Day, 14 April 1471. There was a dense fog, and because of the poor visibility the divisions of each army fought entirely independently of each other, and virtually blind. At one stage in the battle, one Lancastrian division attacked another Lancastrian division by mistake. Edward IV was able to take advantage of the confusion and push the Lancastrian forces back. Edward was greatly helped at Barnet by the leadership qualities of his youngest brother, Richard, Duke of Gloucester, even though Richard was still only twenty-one years old. The battle became a rout. It was also decisive in that Warwick the Kingmaker was killed on the field of battle.

THE BATTLE OF TEWKESBURY (1471)

Ironically, it was at that moment that Queen Margaret and her son Edward arrived in England from France. It might have been better for them if they had not. She heard about the disastrous defeat of the Lancastrian army at Barnet and, instead of admitting defeat and returning to France at once, she set about raising another army. With this she confronted Edward IV's army at Tewkesbury on 4 May. The queen and her Lancastrian army were not equal to doing battle with Edward and his army. They were quickly defeated. The loss was doubled when, after the battle was over, the Lancastrian heir, Prince Edward, was stabbed to death in cold blood by Gloucester. Several other leading Lancastrian lords were similarly executed. Queen Margaret herself was captured.

Her misery and despair must have been acute. She had not only lost the battle and the war, she had lost her son and within days she would finally lose her husband, too. Edward IV was determined to bring the factional war to an end and destroying the opposing dynasty was the clearest, simplest, most expedient way of doing it. Henry VI must be killed, too. When Edward IV returned to London, and almost certainly on his direct orders, Henry VI was killed in the Tower. Richard Duke of Gloucester, was present and may even have carried out the execution himself. It was an act of cruelty, but also from the nation's point of view an act of mercy. The direct line of the House of Lancaster was now extinct; there was no obvious and conspicuous rival to Edward IV; the peace of the realm was ensured.

Queen Margaret was ransomed by the king of France and she died in obscurity a few years later. The collateral heirs of the House of Lancaster remained, living in poverty across the Channel, and seeming to be no further threat to the stability of England. It did look as though the Wars of the Roses were really over in 1471.

THE YEARS OF PEACE

After that, a decade of peace followed, during which there was a strengthening of the administration, a reorganization of finance and an end to the Hundred Years War with France. Edward IV looked like a king. He had the public persona of a king, and knew how to win over a crowd; he was extremely popular. He had two healthy sons – and heir and a spare – so his position looked secure.

There were only two rumbles of dissent. One was a general dissatisfaction at the way the king gave preferment to his wife's relatives, who were given lucrative government positions. The other, more personal, was the dissatisfaction of his shallow younger brother, George Duke of Clarence, at the way Edward was giving preferment to their youngest brother, Richard, Duke of Gloucester. Characteristically, Clarence had not noticed that while he himself had been treacherously conniving to overthrow Edward, Richard gave Edward continuous and unquestioning support. Edward was now, quite properly, rewarding Richard's loyalty; it was also safer to put power in the hands of someone of proven dependability.

In those years of peace, Richard, Duke of Gloucester, became the single most powerful lord in England. He had proved himself able, sensible, competent as a soldier and general, and completely loyal to his brother the king. Among other offices Richard was Chamberlain of England and Warden of the Western Marches, the Middle Marches and the Northern Marches (giving him control over the Welsh and Scottish borders). He also became very wealthy as he was given the estates of several dead Lancastrian lords.

Clarence felt aggrieved that he was not sharing equally in these honours. He complained ceaselessly and interfered in government. In 1477, he went a step too far when he interfered in the king's plan for a family marriage alliance in Europe. At the same moment he recklessly accused the king's wife, Elizabeth Woodville, of being a witch. Edward had pardoned his brother for treachery before, but he was now exasperated beyond toleration. He had Clarence tried before Parliament for treason. He was found guilty and executed privately in the Tower on 18 February 1478. Shakespeare has Clarence secretly murdered by Gloucester as part of Gloucester's plan to inherit the throne, but it is clear that Gloucester had nothing to do with it. The death of Clarence was a formal execution following his condemnation by Parliament. He was drowned in a barrel of Madeira, as in Shakespeare's *Richard III*, but that was Clarence's death of choice.

THE SUDDEN DEATH OF EDWARD IV

Then, on 9 April 1483, completely out of the blue, Edward IV suddenly died. He was only forty years old and appeared to be perfectly healthy, so there had been no reason to anticipate this turn of events. The elder of the two boys, who was twelve, was immediately proclaimed King Edward V, but the country would nevertheless be governed by his uncle Richard for some years to come.

Then Richard did something which looks on the face of it completely disloyal and out of character: he moved to claim the throne for himself. First he arranged for the young king to be escorted from Northampton to Stony Stratford, where he took personal charge of the two boys. He accompanied them to London and lodged them in the Tower, then still more a royal residence than a prison. He took the precaution of arresting Richard Neville, Earl of Warwick, the heir of the dead Kingmaker, who was the young king's guardian, and imprisoning him at Pontefract Castle for plotting to kill the young king.

Richard, Duke of Gloucester, declared himself Lord Protector and Chief Councillor. Something even more extraordinary followed. At a meeting of the Royal Council in the Tower on 13 June 1483, Lord Hastings was arrested for treason. He was a known anti-Ricardian, and Richard wanted him out of the way. A few minutes later, Hastings was executed by beheading outside. Three other alleged conspirators, Lord Rivers, Richard Grey and Sir Thomas Vaughan, were executed elsewhere.

After ruthlessly and systematically removing all possible opposition at court, Richard had a detailed statement read out, declaring that he was the rightful king, that his brother Edward IV had been illegitimate and that therefore the two princes were excluded from the line of succession. Edward IV's illegitimacy had almost certainly been common knowledge within the family. Clarence and Gloucester were small, slight men, just like their father the Duke of York, but Edward was an unusually big man; it was easy to believe that he had a different father. It was an open secret in court circles that he was the result of an affair between the Duchess of York and an English archer called Blayborne.

Obviously, while Edward IV was alive it would have been foolhardy to mention his illegitimacy, but once he was dead, Richard had nothing to lose by telling the truth. Richard's declaration was startling for many reasons – not least that Richard was not just denouncing the boy-king as illegitimate but his elder brother as well, the brother he had served with unswerving loyalty.

Some days later, evidence was produced, probably by the Bishop of Bath and Wells, to show that Edward IV's marriage to Elizabeth Woodville had been bigamous, and therefore all their children were bastards anyway. If Edward's two sons were illegitimate they could have no right to the throne. The children of George Duke of Clarence had lost their place in the line of succession on account of their father's treason. That left Richard. He was crowned King Richard III at Westminster Abbey on 6 July 1483. He had to explain publicly why the two princes had been disinherited; both he and Parliament wanted an uncontested, undisputed succession to the throne of England. With Lancastrian stirrings both in France and in the English West Country, there was a great fear of war breaking out again. The last thing Parliament wanted was a rift within the House of York.

Richard III then placed the two disinherited princes, his nephews, in the Tower. They were seen a few times during the summer, playing in the Tower garden, then no more. It is generally assumed that the boys were murdered that autumn, in secret in the Tower, but they may have been moved elsewhere, to a place of safety where they would be less visible, perhaps, like Richard himself as a boy, to the Low Countries. Richard's reign was very short, and when Henry Tudor usurped the throne in 1485 at Bosworth he had even less title to the throne than Richard III. He therefore had a very strong motive for removing the princes if they were still alive. When Henry Tudor's mother heard a report that the two princes were dead, she was pleased because she supposed 'that the deed would without doubt prove for the profit of the commonwealth.' The Crowland Chronicler noted that it suited the Tudors to spread the rumour that 'King Edward's sons, by some unknown manner of violent destruction, had met their fate.' Certainly the Tudor propagandists put great emphasis on Richard III as the murderer of the two princes; it made him seem a monster, unfit to be king, and by contrast Henry Tudor became the knight in shining armour who came to England's rescue.

THE DUKE OF BUCKINGHAM'S REBELLION

Regardless of the fate of the princes, Richard III was to find it very hard to hold onto his throne. By October 1483, he was putting down by force a rebellion from the Duke of Buckingham. It is not clear what Buckingham's motive was in opposing Richard. Up until the coronation, Buckingham had been a strong supporter of Richard. Perhaps he was expressing disgust at what may have been seen as Richard's usurpation of the throne, or at Richard's ruthless methods in acquiring the throne; perhaps he was dissatisfied with the rewards that came his way and felt that he had not been adequately paid for his services.

Whatever the reason or reasons for this rebellion, it did not last long. Richard was able to suppress it. Buckingham was executed. Richard's hold on the throne then appeared secure and he was able to resume the firm, strong and purposeful style of his half-brother.

THE SURPRISE LANCASTER CLAIMANT

But by the middle of 1485 a Lancastrian claimant was emerging on the European mainland. He was Henry Tudor, an obscure claimant to the earldom of Richmond and one of the few surviving collateral heirs of the House of Lancaster. His claim to the English throne was weak, but he was clever enough to enlist the support of Elizabeth Woodville, the Queen Mother, who had in effect been slandered and humiliated by Richard III's pronouncements on the succession. Queen Elizabeth supported Henry Tudor's claim that he was 'the very heir of Lancaster'. Perhaps, at the time, any claimant would do. Richard's harsh treatment of the Woodville lords had alienated them, and they made ready supporters for Henry's cause. Then he found he had the support of the French king.

With this level of support, Henry Tudor took a chance and on 7 August 1485 he landed at Milford Haven in south-west Wales with a small army. He chose Pembrokeshire as it was a county with strong anti-Ricardian feelings; he would be safe there. His small army quickly expanded as supporters joined him, and Henry advanced to do battle with Richard's army.

THE BATTLE OF BOSWORTH FIELD 1485

The two armies met at Bosworth Field in Leicestershire. Richard fought courageously and skilfully and would probably have won the battle if the Stanley family and their troops had not suddenly changed sides during the course of the battle. It was this defection, taking Richard completely by surprise, which lost him the battle. Richard refused to retreat, fighting on until he was killed.

Richard III was the last Yorkist king and, because Henry Tudor's pedigree was poor and he was not a well-connected Lancastrian, he was the last of the Plantagenets as well. Reflecting his status as a usurper, Henry Tudor was the first king of an entirely new dynasty, the House of Tudor. Henry moved at once to London, where he was accepted as King Henry VII and crowned. In the following January, Henry made a clever marriage, making Elizabeth Plantagenet his wife. She was the sister of the two Princes in the Tower; in this way, his marriage was supposed to represent the fusion of the two houses of Lancaster and York. The Tudor badge consisted of the two roses, the one superimposed on the other. These were symbolic statements that the Wars of the Roses were finally over.

TROUBLESOME CLAIMANTS

As far as major formal battles were concerned, the Wars of the Roses were over, but there were some troublesome claimants to the throne. Given Henry VII's weak pedigree, he was particularly sensitive to any suggestion that there might be a subject with a better claim than his.

In 1487, a young man by the name of Lambert Simnel appeared, claiming to be the son of the Duke of Clarence. He gathered supporters in Ireland, where there had been a lot of support for the Yorkist cause, and sailed with them to the English West Country. There was a final pitched battle against the Yorkists at the Battle of Stoke on 16 June 1487. Henry VII put down this last remaining resistance brutally, executing as many of these militants as he could. For some reason, possibly in a display of black humour, Henry allowed Simnel himself to live, keeping him as a servant in his household.

Potentially more dangerous, because of who he claimed to be, was Perkin Warbeck. This young man turned up claiming to be Richard, Duke of York. As the son of Edward IV, he had a strong claim to the throne, but only if he was who he said he was. He had supporters, but not enough. It was never established whether he was an impostor or genuinely Richard of York, but there were many things about him that convinced people that he was genuine. He too was kept for a time in the king's household, but he made the mistake of attempting to escape; then Henry had Warbeck executed.

From time to time during the reigns of Henry VII and his son Henry VIII surviving high profile members of the Yorkist clan were weeded out. Trumped-up charges of treason were brought and the unfortunates were judicially murdered. It was brutal, but it did ensure that the Wars of the Roses did not break out again.

Consequences

The ultimate result of the Wars of the Roses was the launching of the Tudor dynasty. The Tudor monarchs were extremely good at self-presentation, and because of this they convinced succeeding generations that they were the rightful heirs to the throne, though Henry VII's claim to the throne was in reality very weak. The Tudor propagandists were also skilled at blackening the name of the last Yorkist king, Richard III, who in fact had a superior claim to the throne, by making him out to be a usurper and the murderer of his nephews.

3
RENAISSANCE CONFLICTS

DISPUTING THE SUN
(1543–1992)

A very different kind of conflict is the conflict of belief, the conflict of ideas. The weapons are words, but the feelings of hostility run just as high. One of the fundamental principles of European Christianity in the Middle Ages was that the human race was the central organic creation of the universe and the Earth, its home, was the fixed the centre of the universe. Everything else revolved round it. It was Nicolaus Copernicus (1473–1543) who dared to propose that instead the *Sun* was the centre of the universe, and that the Earth revolved round it. Today, we would see cosmology, the study of the universe, as a purely scientific pursuit. In the sixteenth century, it was regarded as the preserve of theologians.

The Bible, on which Christianity was founded, includes a few references to the nature of the Earth. That automatically made cosmology the interest area of theologians. The Church's view of the universe was not really derived from the Bible at all but from Ptolemy. Ptolemy's book *Almagest* was compiled in about AD 150. The Ptolemaic system was really an amalgam of previous theories that put the Earth as a stationary object at the centre of a universe that revolved round it. Revolving close to the Earth were small concentric spheres, each with a planet or the Sun or Moon embedded in it. Outside was a larger sphere which had the stars embedded in it.

Because the medieval Church had decided on the Ptolemaic model, in other words that the Earth was at the centre of the universe, Copernicus's statement that it was not automatically counted as a heresy. Some centuries before, the scholars of other cultures had put the Sun at the centre, for example in India and ancient Greece, but Copernicus was the first to oppose the Church's view of the universe with such an idea.

COPERNICUS

Copernicus had a remarkably broad educational background. He studied law and medicine at the universities of Bologna and Padua. His uncle, who financed his education, hoped that he would go into the Church and become a bishop. But while he was studying law at Bologna, Copernicus met the famous astronomer Domenico Maria Novara da Ferrara. Copernicus was inspired by Novara's lectures and became his assistant; Copernicus helped Novara with astronomical observations, starting in 1497. In that year, the uncle was made Bishop of Warmia and Copernicus was named a canon at Frombork Cathedral. He lingered in Italy, even so, going to Rome to lecture on astronomy. Copernicus continued his programme of studies and in 1503 received his doctorate in canon law.

It is thought that while he was in Padua he read some pages in Cicero and Plato reporting the opinions of the ancient world on the movement of the Earth. In the third century BC, Aristarchus of Samos described some of the theories of Heraclides Ponticus (the daily rotation of the Earth on its axis, the revolution of Mercury and Venus round the Sun) to propose the very first scientific model of a Sun-centred solar system. The Earth and all the other planets revolved round the Sun, the Earth rotated on its axis once a day, the Moon revolved round the earth once a month. The detail had not survived, so it was and still is only possible to speculate about the evidence that led Aristarchus to his conclusion. Interestingly, even in antiquity, this idea was seen as heretical. Plutarch, who was a contemporary of Aristarchus, accused Aristarchus of impiety because he was 'putting the Earth in motion'. So the heliocentric (Sun-centred) idea created conflict even in antiquity.

In 1504, Copernicus started to gather observations and ideas that were relevant to the hypothesis of a Sun-centred universe. From that date he went on carrying out astronomical observations, making calculations and drawing inferences, but always as a sideline, a hobby; he never earned his living as a astronomer. Instead, he was employed for years as a civil servant by the Prussian government and was adviser to the Polish king on monetary reform. As governor of Warmia, he also administered taxation and justice.

In 1514, Copernicus wrote a *Little Commentary*, a handwritten summary of his developing ideas on a heliocentric universe, and circulated it among his friends. In 1533, Johann Widmannstetter delivered a series of lectures in Rome, outlining Copernicus's theory. Among those attending and listening with great interest, were Pope Clement VII and a number of cardinals. At this stage there seems to have been no overt criticism, only excitement at a wonderful new idea.

In 1536, the Archbishop of Capua wrote to Copernicus about the ideas he was circulating.

> *I began to have a very high regard for you... For I had learned that you had not merely mastered the discoveries of the ancient astronomers uncommonly well but had also formulated a new cosmology. In it you maintain that the Earth moves; that the Sun occupied the lowest, and thus the central, place in the universe... With the utmost earnestness I entreat you, most learned sir, unless I inconvenience you, to communicate this discovery of yours to scholars, and at the earliest possible moment to send me your writings on the sphere of the universe.*

Rumours were spreading all over Europe about Copernicus's new idea, which scholars were hearing about second-hand. He was urged to publish his theory in a book, but he was frightened – and justifiably so – of the consequences. He was probably worried about the possible denunciation of his work by scientists. On the other hand, other people had openly discussed the scientific evidence for the precise movements of the Earth, such as Nicole Oresme and Nicolaus Cusanus, and they had not fallen foul of the Church. He had no particular reason, at that stage, to fear the response of the Church.

The ramifications of his theory were enormous, and Copernicus was intelligent enough, and had a background that was broad enough, to realize that a great deal was at stake. It was a new idea, or a very old idea resuscitated, that had extraordinary importance. It has often been said that few other people have exerted such a far-reaching influence on human civilisation in general and on science in particular. Copernicus knew that many things were going to be changed by his idea. There is a conspicuous parallel here with Darwin and his big new idea, the evolution of species, in the nineteenth century. Both men were acutely aware of the importance of their ideas and of the upset they would cause; both shrank from the controversy and conflict that would follow; both delayed definitive publication for a long time, postponing it until late in life.

But in spite of the revolutionary nature of his idea, Copernicus was not looking for conflict. It was not in his nature. He was a modest and moderate man. This is very clear from his writings.

> *I am not so enamoured of my own opinions that I disregard what others may think of them. I am aware that a philosopher's ideas are not subject to the judgment of ordinary persons, because it is his endeavour to seek the truth in all things, to the extent permitted to human reason by God. Yet I hold that completely erroneous views should be shunned. Those who know that the consensus of many centuries has sanctioned the conception that the Earth remains at rest in the middle of the heaven as its centre would, I reflected, regard it as an insane pronouncement if I made the opposite assertion that the Earth moves.*
>
> *When a ship is floating calmly along, the sailors see its motion mirrored in everything outside, while on the other hand they suppose that they are stationary, together with everything on board. In the same way, the motion of the Earth can unquestionably produce the impression that the entire universe is rotating.*
>
> *So I feel no shame in asserting that this whole region engirdled by the moon, and the centre of the Earth, traverse this grand circle amid the rest of the planets in an annual revolution around the Sun. Near the Sun is the centre of the universe. Moreover, since the Sun remains stationary, whatever appears as a motion of the Sun is really due rather to the motion of the Earth.*
>
> *At rest, however, in the middle of everything is the Sun. For, in this most beautiful temple, who would place this lamp in another or better position than that from which it can light up the whole thing at the same time? For, the Sun is not inappropriately called by some people the lantern of the universe, its mind by others, and its ruler by still others.*

> *The Thrice Greatest labels it a visible god, and Sophocles' Electra, the all-seeing. Thus indeed, as though seated on a royal throne, the Sun governs the family of planets revolving around it.*

In 1539, the mathematician Georg Rheticus arrived in Frombork, where Copernicus was working on his definitive book. Rheticus became Copernicus's pupil and stayed with him for two years. During that time he wrote his own book, called *First Account*, which gave an outline of Copernicus's theory. Although Copernicus was writing a book himself, he was not at all sure he wanted to publish it. The favourable reception of *First Account*, together with Rheticus's enthusiasm, finally brought Copernicus round. He agreed to publish. He would give the book to his close friend the Bishop of Kulm, who would deliver it for printing in Nuremberg.

Copernicus died in May 1543, and it is said that the first printed copy of the book was put into his hands just before he died. In an early manuscript copy of the book, Copernicus specifically quoted Aristarchus and Philolaus as sources of his idea. He wrote, 'Philolaus believed in the mobility of the Earth, and some say that Aristarchus of Samos was of that opinion.' For reasons that Copernicus never explained, he cut that passage from the final version for publication. It is likely that he was unwilling to lean on pre-Christian scholarly sources for fear that opponents could quickly develop that into 'Copernicus subscribes to un-Christian or pagan ideas.'

GALILEO

The next phase in this strange but powerful conflict of ideas came with the arrival of Galileo Galilei, who was to become the great champion of the Copernican heliocentric theory. After being appointed to the chair of mathematics at the University of Pisa in 1589, Galileo moved to Padua where he taught geometry, astronomy and mechanics until 1610. It was at that time that Galileo made many of his discoveries. It was in 1610 that Galileo published his observations of the moons of Jupiter, made with the telescope, which had been invented only two years before and then refined and improved by Galileo himself. He saw that the moons were arranged in a line but one by one disappeared periodically, then reappeared. The only possible explanation was that they were disappearing behind Jupiter, that their movements corresponded to regular orbits and that the line of moons was in effect the common plane of their orbits. Galileo used these observations to argue in favour of Copernicus's heliocentric universe, and against the old Ptolemaic geocentric universe. The geocentric view of the universe had all celestial bodies revolving round the Earth, but Galileo's observations of the moons of Jupiter clearly demonstrated that they (the 'Galilean' moons) were revolving round Jupiter, not the Earth. Later, his observations of the phases of Venus similarly showed that Venus must be revolving round the Sun.

The telescope was giving the lie to the ancient Ptolemaic model which had its roots in Aristotle. Using his telescopes, Galileo became the first person to see mountains and craters on the Moon. He even tried to estimate the heights of the mountains from the length of their shadows. He described the surface of the Moon as 'rough and uneven, just like the surface of the Earth itself'. This was another departure from the teaching of Aristotle, who saw the Moon as a perfect sphere. But all these departures from the accepted view of the universe were leading Galileo towards conflict with the Church.

He went to Rome to demonstrate his new telescope to the distinguished philosophers and mathematicians there. Not long after, in 1612, the first opposition was voiced to the Sun-centred universe. Then, in 1614, came the critical moment when a priest formally and publicly denounced it as heresy. It was Father Tommaso Caccini who denounced Galileo's opinions from the pulpit of Santa Maria Novella, one of the great churches of Rome; he declared Galileo's theory dangerous and heretical. Galileo was ready to defend himself against this accusation, but in 1616 he was handed a formal reprimand by Cardinal Bellarmino, warning him not to advocate or teach the Copernican theory. The Church's position was made clear; the Pythagorean doctrine of the Earth's movement and the immobility of the Sun 'is false and altogether opposed to the Holy Scripture.'

Cardinal Bellarmino insisted that the Copernican system could only be vindicated if there was proof, 'a true physical demonstration that the Sun does not circle the Earth but the Earth circles the Sun.' Galileo thought the tides provided just this proof and circulated his account of the tides in 1616. But Galileo's arguments regarding tides fall over themselves in their determination to prove the 'Galilean' relationship between the Earth and the Sun, and dismiss the Moon as of no importance. Now, we know that both the Sun and the Moon exert their separate pulls on the oceans, which is why tides vary in height.

In 1630, Galileo was in Rome again, to apply for a licence to publish *Dialogue Concerning the Two Chief World Systems*, which appeared in Florence two years later with the full permission of the Inquisition and the Pope. But then he was ordered to present himself at the Holy Office in Rome. It was nothing less than an inquisition. Galileo led a rather irregular life, producing children out of wedlock, but he tried to be a good Catholic, to remain loyal to the teachings of the Church. This led him into an interior battle, because his observations and experiments were leading him to contradict Church teachings. Within Galileo, science and religion were separating, just as they were to separate in Christian Europe generally during the next four centuries. Both Albert Einstein and Stephen Hawking were later to describe Galileo as responsible for the birth of modern science.

Galileo entered into a dispute with a Jesuit called Grassi regarding the nature of comets. The debate became polemical. Grassi wrote *The Astronomical and Philosophical Balance*. Galileo wrote *The Assayer* as a riposte. Galileo's book is regarded as a masterpiece of polemical literature and it was widely acclaimed at the time. It even pleased the new pope, Urban VIII, who was the dedicatee. But this was a short-term victory. Because Grassi was a Jesuit and Galileo had in effect publicly humiliated him, Galileo alienated the Jesuits in general. How influential the Jesuits were in orchestrating the major trouble Galileo found himself in later is hard to tell, but Galileo and his friends became convinced that the Jesuits were responsible for bringing about his condemnation.

Galileo had to face the Roman Inquisition. The Church had decided that Aristotle and Ptolemy were right, that the Earth was fixed, stationery, and the rest of the universe turned round it. It leant on certain Biblical references in Psalms, Chronicles and Ecclesiastes, which said things such as 'the world is firmly established, it cannot be moved,' and 'the Lord set the Earth on its foundations; it can never be moved.' Galileo stood his ground, arguing that heliocentrism does not contradict those passages. He took the view that many modern people have taken subsequently, which is that the scriptural verses in question should not be taken as teaching but as poetry. The men who wrote those passages wrote from the vantage point of the terrestrial world, and about how things appeared from that vantage point.

Pope Urban VIII had asked Galileo to include arguments for and against a Sun-centred universe; he also asked for his own views to be incorporated. Galileo included a character called Simplicius to present the Earth-centred universe view in his *Dialogue Concerning the Two Chief World Systems.* Galileo could not resist outwitting Simplicius in order to make the case for a Sun-centred universe appear stronger. It was unfortunate that this made Simplicius, who was actually voicing the Pope's views, look a fool. Pope Urban was intelligent enough to realize that Galileo was making fun of him, and did not like it. Nor did he like the very obvious bias of the book, which was not what he had agreed to when he gave Galileo consent to publish.

This was how Galileo found himself standing trial for heresy in 1633. He was required to recant his Sun-centred universe ideas, which were formally denounced as 'absurd, philosophically false, and formally heretical'. He was found guilty of 'following the position of Copernicus, which is contrary to the true sense and authority of Holy Scripture.' His *Dialogue* was banned and he would not be allowed to publish any more works at all. He was also sentenced to imprisonment, though this was later commuted to house arrest. It seems an extraordinary event to have taken place in Renaissance Europe, though it is perhaps no more remarkable than the current refusal of the 'scientific community' (ironically not the Church any more) to countenance the possibility that global atmospheric temperature might be controlled by some factor other than carbon dioxide; the so-called contrarians who believe that the Earth's temperature has varied – certainly since Galileo's time – with solar variations are today's heretics. They may one day be seen as today's Galileos.

Stung by this incredibly reactionary experience, Galileo stayed for a while in the home of the Archbishop of Siena, who was a friend. Then he was allowed to return to his own home at Arcetri not far outside Florence. There he lived out the rest of his life under house arrest. He died in January 1642. There was conflict even after his death. The Grand Duke of Tuscany wanted to bury him in style in the nave of the basilica of Santa Croce, with a magnificent marble monument. Pope Urban VIII protested, so he was instead buried in a small chamber next to the novices' chapel at the end of a corridor leading out of the basilica's south transept – in other words, very pointedly outside the church.

But the Catholic Church could not turn its face from the reality of the universe for ever. Science moved on, increasingly independently of the Church, and of religious belief, finding out many new things about the cosmos that were not in the Bible. Eventually the Church had to come to an accommodation with the scientific perception of the universe, and with the memory of the deeply wronged Galileo. In 1718, the Inquisition's ban on printing Galileo's books was lifted; in 1741, Pope Benedict XIV gave permission for the publication of an edition of Galileo's complete works. In 1737, there was a gesture which look like a partial recantation on the part of the Church. Galileo's body was exhumed and reburied in the main body of the basilica and a monument to him raised there.

The final trace of official Church opposition to a Sun-centred universe vanished in 1835, when the uncensored original versions of Galileo's *Dialogue Concerning the Two Chief World Systems* and Copernicus's *On the Revolutions of the Celestial Spheres* were removed from the Catholic Church's Index of banned books. In October 1992, Pope John Paul II said that he regretted the way the Galileo controversy had been handled.

Aftermath

Copernicus's book, *On the Revolutions of the Celestial Spheres*, is often seen as the starting point of modern astronomy. Seeing the Sun as the centre of the solar system, and the Earth and the other planets as revolving at different distances round it, was not only a true observation – it made other deductions and the building of new knowledge possible.

The Copernican view of the universe opened a new view of man's relationship with it; religion was bound to enter the picture. With the Copernican universe came the idea of immanence. This is the idea that a divine force or being pervades everything that exists. It is an idea that has persisted through into modern philosophy. Belief in immanence led on to subjectivism, the principle that perception creates reality, that there is no objective underlying reality independent of perception. This was perhaps an inevitable outcome. The Earth, the Sun, the stars all looked exactly the same after Copernicus as they did before, but they meant something quite different. It was human perception that changed their meaning utterly, therefore it was perception that meant everything. That loss of absolutes meant that the foundations of medieval science and metaphysics had been removed. This was a key moment in human history, after which science would move on without religion.

The poet and polymath Goethe said:

> *Of all discoveries and opinions, none may have exerted a greater effect on the human spirit than the doctrine of Copernicus. The world had scarcely become known as round and complete in itself when it was asked to waive the tremendous privilege of being the centre of the universe. Never, perhaps, was a greater demand made on mankind – for by this admission so many things vanished in mist and smoke! What became of our Eden, our world of innocence, piety and poetry; the testimony of the senses; the conviction of a poetic – religious faith? No wonder his contemporaries did not wish to let all this go and offered every possible resistance to a doctrine which in its converts authorized and demanded a freedom of view and greatness of thought so far unknown, indeed not even dreamed of.*

THE SPANISH CONQUEST OF PERU (1532–72)

THE INCA CIVIL WAR

In the early sixteenth century, the Inca Empire had a strong leader in the person of Huayna Capac. But when he and his named heir, Ninan Coyuchui, died of smallpox a war of succession broke out between rival royal houses, or Panakas. This in-fighting seriously weakened the Inca leadership. At the centre of the power struggle were two claimants, Huascar and Atahualpa, both sons of Huayna Capac.

It is possible that Huascar was proclaimed emperor, though there is no document to prove that he was the rightful heir. He was known to be cruel, yet he was popular in the southern provinces of the empire. His brother Atahualpa was allocated the northern territory, the kingdom of Quito (now Ecuador and Colombia), to govern.

There were a few years of uneasy peace within the Inca Empire, but then civil war broke out, generated by the rivalry between the two brothers. An estimated 100,000 people were killed in this war. Eventually Atahualpa won, defeating his brother. Atahualpa rivalled his brother in cruelty and seems almost to have lost his reason. He treated the conquered people with appalling savagery. Some had boulders dropped on them to cripple them; bodies were stuck on poles for display; almost 1,500 members of the royal family were dismembered in front of Huascar – even his own children. Huascar himself was imprisoned.

Atahualpa paid a high price for his victory and his cruelty. He seriously weakened the Inca Empire just at the moment when the Spanish conquistadors arrived under the leadership of Francisco Pizarro.

THE ARRIVAL OF PIZARRO

Francisco Pizarro and his three brothers, Gonzalo, Hernando and Juan, were drawn to the Inca Empire by rumours of a fabulously rich kingdom. Motivated entirely by financial gain, they arrived in the Inca lands in 1531. They named the territory Peru, which is not an Inca name and appears to be a made-up part-Hispanic word.

It took Pizarro three protracted expeditions to establish the first Spanish settlement in the north of 'Peru'. He called it San Miguel de Piura. In July 1532, Pizarro sent another of the conquistadors, Hernando de Soto, to explore the territory. He returned with an envoy from Atahualpa, bearing gifts and an invitation to meet.

THE CAPTURE OF ATAHUALPA

After his victory over his brother, Atahualpa made his way gradually south to claim the Inca throne in Cuzco. On his way, he heard stories of 'white bearded men', and he was keen to meet them.

Atahualpa and his warriors met the Spaniards at Cajamarca on 15 November. Preferring not to meet Atahualpa himself, Pizarro instead sent Hernando de Soto, a friar called Vincente de Valverde and a native interpreter. De Soto explained to Atahualpa that they were envoys from Charles I, King of Spain, and he also said that they came in peace and were prepared to help him fight his enemies. Atahualpa was unimpressed by all of this, and thinly disguised his contempt for the Spanish. Their behaviour and demeanour were clearly not those of envoys. He knew in any case of some earlier atrocities committed against the female temple servants of the Inca god Inti in his temple. He insisted on having a full explanation of their behaviour in his territory – and an apology from Pizarro, their leader. He also agreed to meet them again the following day.

De Soto saw that his horses frightened some of the Incas. He was an able horseman and performed a number of tricks, including charging towards Atahualpa and stopping only inches away from him. Intriguingly, the Inca attendants were frightened, but Atahualpa did not even blink. It showed that Atahualpa was a man of enormous courage and nerve – unlike Montezuma in Mexico.

The next day, Pizarro stationed his men round the square where the meeting was due to take place. Then Atahualpa arrived with 4,000 unarmed soldiers and attendants. The friar tried to explain to Atahualpa the principles of the Catholic faith, which cannot have made much sense, especially when filtered through an unskilled translator. The friar offered Atahualpa a bible. The implication was that the emperor and his retinue must convert to Christianity or be considered enemies of Spain. This was one manifestation of the great conflict of faiths that has surfaced in one century after another.

Atahualpa remarked that he was nobody's vassal and asked the Spaniards where their authority came from. It is said that Friar Valverde pointed to the bible and said that it contained God's word. It is also said that Atahualpa held the book to his ear and shook it, complaining that he could hear no words. He had certainly never seen anything remotely like a book before. He threw the book aside with contempt. This may have been the trigger for the Spanish attack, though impatience and the desire for looting were probably to the fore.

THE BATTLE OF CAJAMARCA 1532

The attack, on 16 November 1532, was the Battle of Cajamarca. Enormous numbers of Incas were killed in this pitched battle. The Spanish victory is explained in a variety of ways. Although they were seriously outnumbered, the Spanish had the advantage of horses and superior weapons. A major factor seems to have been the mindset of the Incas. The empire functioned on a highly centralized chain of command that had the emperor as its focus. The emperor's well-being and success in battle reflected how the gods viewed the Inca people. When the Spaniards appeared holding the emperor hostage, many if not all of the Inca people must have thought that the gods had turned against them.

Pizarro then executed Atahualpa's twelve-strong bodyguard and took the emperor himself prisoner, confining him in a 'ransom room'. Then Pizarro's real motive for being in Peru emerged: he demanded an enormous sum in precious stones, silver and gold in exchange for Atahualpa's release. But then, in the most dishonourable episode of all, Pizarro had Atahualpa garrotted.

The Inca people were eventually defeated as a whole. This was in part because they had inferior weapons, lacked metal shields or armour, were unaccustomed to open battle tactics, and were still deeply unsettled by the recent civil war. The captivity and death of their emperor must also have been profoundly bewildering, a major blow to morale. These factors explain the similar success of other small bands of Europeans who attacked the Aztecs and other Andean cultures. But in later developments (the Mixton Rebellion, Chichimeca War and Arauco War) the conquistadors found it expedient to form alliances with friendly tribes.

Atahualpa offered as his ransom, the condition of his release, the filling of a large room with gold; in addition he would give the Spanish twice as much again in silver. Pizarro tacitly accepted his offer, but had no intention of giving Atahualpa his freedom in exchange for it. He needed Atahualpa in his possession, in his power, if he was going to have any control over the Inca generals. Atahualpa's incarceration dragged on for months, and he realised that Pizarro had no intention of releasing him, so he called on his generals to attack Pizarro. At that point, the Spanish began to see Atahualpa as a liability, not an asset. They charged him with a series of crimes, including revolting against the Spanish, practising the worship of idols and murdering his brother Huascar. He was found guilty and garrotted on 29 August 1533.

After that, pandemonium broke out. There were rebellions in many parts of the empire, some against the Spanish, some joining forces with the Spanish against their own local rulers. There were strategic alliances forged by some local groups with the Spanish, but these were misjudged, as the success of the Spanish conquest only meant – the Incas could not have known this – that more and more Spanish incomers would arrive. The conquest was not a finite visitation, but the beginning of a long-term political and cultural takeover. The conquest of the Inca Empire was the shape of things to come, not only in Latin America, but in North America and Africa, too.

THE SIEGE OF CUZCO 1536–7

Diego de Almagro, who was a member of Pizarro's party, explored Chile to the south, but returned to Peru to report that there was no wealth there comparable to that found in Peru. Charles I of Spain awarded the city of Cuzco to Pizarro, but Almagro decided to challenge his claim. Manco Inca thought he would be able to exploit the major rift between Pizarro and Almagro and recapture Cuzco for himself in the spring of 1537.

The siege of Cuzco went on for a year, but it was unsuccessful in ridding the city of Spaniards. The Inca leadership did not have the full support of the Inca people, and the disintegration of Inca morale following the execution of Atahualpa made Manco Inca realize that he would not succeed in recapturing Cuzco. Manco Inca eventually fell back to Vilcabamba after ten months of fighting. When the Spanish reinforcements arrived from the Caribbean under the command of Diego de Almagro, they were able to retake the city without any fighting.

After Almagro took Cuzco, Manco Inca and his army fell back to the fortress of Ollantaytambo. When he realized that they were critically outnumbered and would be defeated, he took his army further into retreat, into the mountain region of Vilcabamba. There, Manco Inca held onto some residual power for several decades. His son, Tupac Amaru, was the last Inca emperor. After a confrontation with the Spanish, he was murdered in 1572.

Aftermath

The aftermath of conquest was as horrific in its way as the process of defeating and annihilating the Incas; the conquest took about forty years to complete. From then on the Spanish colonised and exploited the former Inca Empire.

The Spanish displaced most of the Inca past, imposing Spanish culture on the native population. They destroyed virtually every Inca building in Cuzco. They built a replacement city in Spanish style on top of the old foundations. What the Spanish did to Cuzco was in a very real way a symbol of conquest and empire everywhere – a wanton display of cultural chauvinism and cultural destruction.

THE ANGLO-SPANISH WAR
(1585–1604)

The Anglo-Spanish War was an on-off, reluctant and undeclared conflict between England and Spain that dragged on through the last two decades of the reigns of Queen Elizabeth I of England and King Philip II of Spain.

BACKGROUND: THE CAUSES OF THE WAR

The conflict between England and Spain was partly religious, partly commercial. As early as the 1560s, King Philip II of Spain was trying to obstruct English policies. Philip of Spain was a staunch Catholic. Elizabeth of England was a Protestant. She angered English Catholics by making attendance at (Protestant) Church of England services compulsory and making attendance at Catholic mass illegal; Catholics faced imprisonment if they worshipped publicly. Just across the southern North Sea from England was the Netherlands, where a struggle between Protestantism and Catholicism broke out in 1560; England was seen to be supporting the Protestant cause there – against a Spanish Catholic government. At this point Philip II's uneasy misgivings about the Protestant regime in England turned into positive hostility. Philip's priority was to end the Protestant rebellion in the Netherlands, but some of his advisers alleged that that had been instigated in London; they wanted to invade England and overturn the Protestant regime there as a necessary step towards stamping out the rebellion in the Netherlands. But at the same time it would be much easier to invade England from the Netherlands than from Spain – an enormous logistical undertaking at that time.

The commercial conflict arose mainly from the activities of English privateers on the *Spanish Main*. These privateers were little more than the pirates the Spanish believed them to be – except that they were either approved or ignored by the English Crown. The privateers attacked and robbed Spanish ships and made a significant dent in the Spanish economy. In 1562, Sir John Hawkins began the English slave trade across the Atlantic, and this too was given Elizabeth's approval. The Spanish accused Hawkins of running a racket and represented his trading with Spanish colonies as smuggling. In 1568, Sir John Hawkins and Sir Francis Drake were running a slaving expedition when they were taken by surprise by the Spanish. The English slavers lost several ships near Veracruz in Mexico. The incident produced a serious worsening of Anglo-Spanish relations. The English were determined to get their own back on the Spanish and in 1569 they stopped several of the treasure ships sent by Spain to supply its army in the Netherlands. The English saw the Spanish as having an unfair monopoly on trade across the Atlantic, and responded to this by intensifying their privateering activity.

THE OUTBREAK OF WAR

Friction, small-scale raids, tit-for-tat acts of piracy – the conflict between England and Spain simmered on this level for a long time before open and large-scale conflict broke out. That happened in 1585, when Drake sailed to the West Indies and attacked a series of Spanish colonies in the Caribbean region. He sacked Santo Domingo, Cartagena de Indias and San Agustin. At the same time, England committed itself to a military expedition to the Netherlands, led by Elizabeth's favourite, the Earl of Leicester. The English intervention was in support of the Dutch Protestant United Provinces against Habsburg rule. This amounted to open support for the revolt led by William the Silent against Spanish rule in the Netherlands. So Spain was being struck twice by the English, once in the Caribbean and once in the Netherlands.

Philip of Spain planned to invade England and assembled the ships to do it. In April 1587, these preparations were seriously spoilt by a remarkable attack undertaken by Sir Francis Drake. He penetrated the harbour at Cadiz and succeeded in setting fire to thirty-seven Spanish ships. The attack incensed the Spanish.

Just two months earlier in the same year and an even greater offence, as far as Philip was concerned, was the execution of the Catholic Mary Queen of Scots. Mary Queen of Scots was Elizabeth I's cousin and, because Elizabeth was childless, also her heir; she would succeed to the English throne when Elizabeth died. Philip of Spain had looked forward to that day, as it would mean that England would once again become Catholic under a Catholic queen.

However, there were several plots by Catholics to hasten that day by assassinating Elizabeth and it was believed that Mary, who stood to gain her freedom as well as the throne of England with Elizabeth's death, was implicated. Elizabeth was persuaded by her advisers that she would never be safe while Mary lived and the evidence was found (or forged) which showed that Mary knew about and encouraged one of the plots to rescue her and assassinate Elizabeth in order to put her on the throne. So, in the end, and with great reluctance, Elizabeth signed her death warrant. Mary was beheaded at Fotheringhay Castle on 28 February 1587.

Philip wanted to invade England now to avenge the killing by the English establishment of the Catholic Queen of Scotland. But his case was stronger still. In her will, Mary passed her claim to the English throne to Philip. It is not clear whether she was within the law in doing this, as she had a living son, James VI of Scotland, who on Elizabeth's death was to become James I of England as well. But in 1587, Philip was nominated by the dead Mary as her champion, the official Catholic claimant to Elizabeth's throne. Mary presumably named Philip with the specific intention of throwing the cat among the pigeons. She wanted life for Elizabeth to be made as difficult as possible, and wanted to give Philip another reason to invade.

The execution of the Catholic Queen of Scots was not popular in the Vatican and, on 29 July, Philip was given the authority by the pope to overthrow Elizabeth, already excommunicated by Pope Pius V, and put the monarch of his choice on the English throne.

THE SPANISH ARMADA

The earliest scheme for an invasion of England dates from 1559. It was suggested to Philip while on a voyage down the English Channel towards Spain that he could make an armed landing on the south coast of England. He rejected the idea as too rash, and he went on being cautious about invading for two decades. One reason for his delay was that he had many other obligations and responsibilities, most of which were set above his obligation to protect English Catholics from what he saw as persecution by a Protestant queen. He was also well aware of the strength of England's navy. But the Enterprise of England, as it was known in Spain, was a continuing project. Spain would invade, and overthrow the new Protestant regime of Elizabeth.

Philip had already tried to organize the sending of an Armada up the English Channel in 1574, but this project failed before it started. Philip continued to plan and reconsider, never quite bringing his Armada to fruition. The plight of the imprisoned Mary Queen of Scots gave him a new reason to invade – the rescue of an imprisoned Catholic queen – and he prepared more plans. In 1583, the English government heard about some of them, and this nudged Elizabeth into ordering an open military intervention in the Netherlands in 1585 and a parallel expedition to the West Indies. Philip saw these actions as tantamount to a declaration of war on Spain. He decided that the time to invade and get a quick decisive victory over England had come.

The Armada preparations took two years, starting in 1586. Drake's Cadiz raid set the preparations back, delaying the Armada's sailing from 1587 to 1588. Philip's governor in the Netherlands, the Duke of Parma, was uneasy about mounting an invasion against England from the Dutch coast, because he did not yet have full control of it. Philip's solution was to sail the invasion fleet from Spain, land in Kent, then ferry Parma's army across to England from the Dutch coast. Another element in Philip's plan was to make no attempt to land on the English coast before reaching Kent, and he made no provision for a sea battle with the English or an English attack of any kind in the Channel before making landfall. It was a classic case of a war planned on a map as if it was a board game, a closed system with clear and simple rules. The reality was to be very different.

The 122 ships of the Armada eventually arrived off Land's End in July 1588. The Duke of Parma had by then given up expecting Philip's fleet, and had sent his own ships' crews off inland to work on canals. The English fleet had by then made a couple of attempts to intercept the Armada but failed because they were beaten back by storms. The English fleet fell back to Plymouth and was there, taking on new supplies in port, when the Armada unexpectedly appeared off the coast. The English were taken by surprise. Drake, like Parma, did not really believe that Philip's Armada would ever reach English waters.

The sixty-six ships of the English fleet were able to get out of Plymouth, but then had an unrewarding stern chase up the Channel as they followed the Spanish. A lot of ammunition was fired, but to little effect. The Spanish ships held to their formation and only two ships were lost, both by accident. The Spanish admiral, the Duke of Medina Sidonia, unexpectedly decided to drop anchor off Calais on 6 August. This gave the English an equally unexpected opportunity to send in fireships which dispersed the Spanish fleet; strong westerly winds blew it into the North Sea. Four Spanish ships were lost there, but most escaped by sailing north along the east coast of England.

The only way home for the Spanish fleet was the long detour round the north coasts of Scotland and Ireland, where another thirty-five ships were lost, either sinking or running aground. There was great relief in England that the invasion plan had failed, but also disappointment that so few Spanish ships had been sunk or captured. Elizabeth's appearance at Tilbury to speak to the troops was an enormously popular event. Above all, she had shown that she was Philip of Spain's most effective and dangerous enemy.

AFTER THE ARMADA

The defeat of the Spanish Armada was by no means decisive. In 1589, an English fleet commanded by Sir Francis Drake and Sir John Norreys succeeded in setting fire to the Spanish Atlantic navy, which had survived the Armada expedition unscathed. The Spanish navy was being repaired and refitted at Santander, Coruna and San Sebastian in northern Spain. The Drake-Norreys expedition was also intended to capture the Spanish treasure fleet when it arrived and eject the Spanish from Portugal. If these latter objectives had been achieved, Philip would almost certainly have had to concede defeat, and the war would have come to an end. But the English fleet was poorly organised and too cautious – a very different situation from the English response to the Spanish Armada. As a result the English fleet was repulsed by the Spanish, who inflicted heavy casualties. The treasure ships were not captured. Lisbon was not taken. The expedition was then hit by illness, and finally the squadron taken by Drake towards the Azores was dispersed by a storm. It was a major fiasco. English historians have always made much of the Spanish Armada (a Spanish failure) and glossed over, often not mentioned at all, the English Armada (an English failure). The result of the failure of the Drake-Norreys expedition was that Elizabeth's treasury made a serious loss; she had been pushed into being a major stockholder to fund the expedition, and so had to shoulder the loss.

The Spanish refitted their navy, to an extent incorporating modernizing features learnt from the disastrous Armada experience. The fleet had twelve brand-new galleons, which were enormous; they were called *The Twelve Apostles*. The Spanish navy was now far more effective than before the Armada year. A convoy system was adopted along with new intelligence networks. The result was a much greater resistance to English privateering in the 1590s. This in turn meant that the expeditions of Hawkins, Frobisher and the Earl of Cumberland to seize Spanish treasure failed. The English squadron that attempted to ambush the treasure fleet off the Azores in 1591 failed; it was in that sea battle that Sir Richard Grenville was killed and his flagship, the *Revenge*, was captured by the Spanish. The effect on the English treasury was significant, as less money was going into it.

The situation worsened in 1595 and 1596, when the English launched an expedition against Spanish possessions, Panama and Puerto Rico among them. This campaign, too, was a failure. The English lost many ships and men, including Drake and Hawkins. Not surprisingly, given the provocation and the recovery of the Spanish navy, the Spanish retaliated. A force led by Don Carlos de Amesquita patrolled the English Channel, looking for an opportunity, and landed troops in Cornwall. They seized supplies, sacked Penzance and the surrounding villages, then sailed away before any English force could be mustered to oppose it.

An Anglo-Dutch expedition succeeded in raiding the port of Cadiz again in a repeat performance of Drake's earlier exploit. This left Spanish ships destroyed and the city of Cadiz in ruins. The Spanish commander had nevertheless had the foresight and the vision to scuttle the treasure ships that were in port. This meant that the treasure, twelve million ducats' worth of it, went safely to the seabed, where the English could not get it. Spanish divers got most of it back later, after the raiders had sailed away virtually empty-handed.

Then a new front opened in this long war between Spain and England, the coast of northern France. A substantial Spanish force landed in Brittany, where they ejected the English who were there. The Anglo-French forces successfully held onto the port of Brest, but now there was a clear threat of a Spanish invasion of England launched from the coasts of Brittany and Normandy. Elizabeth sent another 2,000 troops across the Channel when the Spanish took the port of Calais, which was dangerously close to the coast of England. Over the next two years there were further battles.

In 1598, following the conversion of the French king to Catholicism, the French and the Spanish made peace. This left England in a worse state than ever. By then a nine-year-long war in Ireland had started: an attempt by the English to put down a rebellion by the Irish lords. This was not only a distraction for the English, but an opportunity for the Spanish to engage in subversion. The Spanish gave the Irish rebels a certain amount of support. While the English were occupied with containing the Irish problem, the Spanish launched two more Armadas against England.

The 1596 Armada was destroyed when it was hit by a storm off the coast of northern Spain. The 1597 Armada was more successful. It reached the English Channel and came very close to making landfall undetected. It was only adverse weather conditions that stopped this fleet from landing. The following year Philip II died, and then the Spanish determination to invade England petered out. The new king of Spain, Philip III, carried on with the war against England, but less wholeheartedly.

The last Armada was sent against the English towards the end of 1601. This was an expedition to deliver Spanish troops in the south of Ireland. They were to help the rebels in their struggle against the English. The 3,000 Spanish soldiers entered the town of Kinsale, where they were immediately surrounded by English troops. Before the English could annihilate them, Irish rebel forces arrived and surrounded the English. This should have put the English in an impossible position, but because the Irish and Spanish forces acted without co-ordination the English were able to win the Battle of Kinsale. The Spanish could then have opted to stay in Kinsale and hold onto it as a base from which to harass English ships in the area. But instead they surrendered and went home. The Irish rebels, now left unsupported by their fitful allies, were only able to continue for a year or so before they too surrendered, just after the death of Elizabeth in 1603.

When James VI of Scotland travelled south to take the throne of England as James I, the last thing he wanted was to have the Anglo-Spanish War draining his treasury. One of the first things he did was to negotiate a peace with Philip III, which was concluded in the Treaty of London in 1604.

Aftermath

The very real threat of a Spanish invasion of England hung over the greater part of the reign of Elizabeth I. It preoccupied her and her advisers. A successful invasion and occupation by a Catholic nation, and the most powerful one in Europe at that, would certainly have meant a conversion back to Catholicism.

England was run into serious debt by the war. It also had its colonial plans thwarted. The Spanish were able to stop English commercial shipping plying on the Atlantic, and that made colonisation extremely difficult. England wanted to develop colonies in North America, and the war with Spain delayed the establishment of those colonies until the Stuart period. This delay gave Spain the opportunity to consolidate and strengthen its Spanish Empire in the New World, which went on for another 200 years.

The English defeat of the Spanish Armada had a major effect on the future conduct of naval warfare. The high seas were also cleared by the 'English Armada' for further privateering, and the English were able to go on supporting the Protestant cause in the Netherlands and France. It is interesting to reflect that the conflict between England and Spain would have vanished overnight if Elizabeth I had converted to Catholicism. The enormous financial and commercial cost of the war with Spain was a direct result of Elizabeth's fierce loyalty to the Protestant cause.

The focal defeat of the Spanish Armada in 1588 was major blow to Philip of Spain's reputation. He was well known to be the architect of the project, both in general and in detail, and it was well known that he had disregarded the advice of experts. He was therefore rightly held to be personally responsible for the failure of the Enterprise. The English defeat of the Spanish Armada was not enough in itself to enable England to replace Spain as Europe's dominant power, nor to clear the Atlantic for an American colonisation programme. But it was an event of great symbolic value and it did an enormous amount to enhance the popularity of Elizabeth I in the closing years of her reign. It was an iconic event which became an important component in England's national myth. As such it remained an inspiration to succeeding generations of English people, in spite of the fact that in the historical Anglo-Spanish War the English victory of 1588 was followed by a series of miserable defeats and failures; they have been forgotten.

THE TYRONE REBELLION IN IRELAND

(1594–1603)

The Tyrone Rebellion is also known as the Nine Years War. This rebellion of Gaelic Irish chieftains was mounted against the advance of the English government of Ireland, and led by Hugh O'Neill, the Earl of Tyrone, whose political aspirations were being curtailed by English interference. The advance of the English state in Ireland under Elizabeth I inevitably meant the spread of Protestantism, so O'Neill was able to raise support among Catholic chieftains who wanted to stop the spread of Protestantism. Although fighting went on all over Ireland, the main focus was in the north, in the province of Ulster.

O'Neill himself had been sponsored by the English authorities as a reliable lord. In 1587 he persuaded Elizabeth I to make him Earl of Tyrone, although in Ireland his real power was to rest in his position as The O'Neill, the chief of the clan O'Neill, which enabled him to command the obedience and support of all the O'Neills in central Ulster. Hugh O'Neill managed to gain this position, by force, in 1595. O'Neill in effect turned his peasants into serfs, which enabled him to force them into military service. He also hired both Irish and Scottish mercenaries. From 1591, O'Donnell, acting on O'Neill's behalf, was able to enlist Spanish support for an Irish rising. In this way, O'Neill was able to feed and arm an army of 8,000 men, which was unheard of for an Irish lord and which made it possible for him to thwart any attempt by the English to govern Ulster.

The rebellion had its beginning in 1592, when Red Hugh O'Donnell drove one of the English sheriffs, Captain Willis, out. O'Donnell and his allies began attacking English outposts along the southern border of Ulster. At first, O'Neill stood apart from the rebellion in the hope that he would be seen as a compromise candidate for the position of Lord President of Ulster. Elizabeth I had no illusions about O'Neill's ambitions, though; she knew that he would not be content to act as a simple landlord but would seek to usurp her authority. When she appointed Henry Bagenal as president, O'Neill openly joined his Irish allies in an open rebellion, attacking the English fort on the Blackwater River.

The English authorities in Dublin did not appreciate at first how serious the rebellion was, and so acted slowly.

THE BATTLES OF CLONTIBRET (1596) AND THE YELLOW FORD (1598)

Negotiations failed in 1596. Then an English army tried to force its way into Ulster, but was pushed back by a trained army including musketeers in prepared positions. The English were not expecting this level of warfare at all, and at the Battle Clontibret they were roundly defeated by the Irish rebels.

In the years that followed, the English army mounted one offensive after another, each driven back. At the Battle of the Yellow Ford the English army was ambushed during the march on Armagh; as many as 2,000 English soldiers were killed. The rest were surrounded in Armagh, but were able to negotiate a safe passage out after agreeing to evacuate the town. Henry Bagenal, O'Neill's personal enemy, had been in command of the English army; he was killed in one of the earlier engagements of the rebellion.

The Battle of the Yellow Ford was the most serious setback so far for the English in Ireland. Victory gave hope to Irishmen everywhere and there were risings all over the country, which led to a major escalation in the rebellion. In Munster as many as 9,000 men came out in revolt. The so-called Munster Plantation, the English colony in Munster, was completely destroyed. Hugh O'Neill appointed his supporters as chiefs and earls. James Fitzgerald was made Earl of Desmond; Florence MacCarthy was made the MacCarthy Mor. Only a small number of

Irish lords remained loyal to Elizabeth I, although all the fortified cities and market towns were on the side of the English colonial government, in spite of O'Neill's attempts to win them over.

THE EARL OF ESSEX

In 1599, Robert Devereux, Earl of Essex, arrived in Ireland with an army of 17,000 troops. The Irish Privy Council advised him to settle the south before attempting the north. This had the disadvantage of dissipating his forces. Essex made slow progress through Munster and Leinster, losing many men along the way.

The military expeditions Essex organised were disastrous, notably the one directed across the Curlew Mountains into Sligo; at the Battle of Curlew Pass, Essex's troops were mauled by O'Donnell's men. Essex lost thousands of men shut up in garrisons, where they died of typhoid and dysentery. When Essex finally did go into Ulster, he negotiated with O'Neill and agreed a truce, a tactic that was severely criticised by Essex's enemies in London.

Essex expected to be recalled to London to give an account of the expedition as a whole, but he was not. Instead, Essex decided to return without the queen's permission, which was very rash. When he burst in upon the queen she was extremely angry with him. He found himself under house arrest. His response to this was to attempt to take over the English government, with the inevitable result that he was tried for treason and executed.

THE BATTLE OF KINSALE

The Earl of Essex was replaced in Ireland by Mountjoy, an abler military commander. The rebellion in Munster was under control by the middle of 1601, with most of the rebel forces scattered. Mountjoy penetrated the interior of Ulster by way of coastal landings at Derry and Carrickfergus. The English troops brought the local people into submission by devastating the countryside and killing civilians at random, with the idea of damaging both food supply and recruitment.

In 1601, the long-delayed relief expedition from Spain arrived. This consisted of 3,500 men landing at Kinsale. Mountjoy immediately went to Kinsale with 7,000 men and besieged the Spaniards. Then O'Neill and O'Donnell arrived, with their own armies in the hope of trapping Mountjoy's force between themselves and the Spanish force. On 5 January 1602, O'Neill and O'Donnell decided to attack the English. A series of pitched battles followed, known collectively as the Battle of Kinsale, in which the Irish forces were routed.

The Irish rebels retreated to Ulster, where they hoped to re-group, but they lost even more men there due to extreme environmental conditions – flooding and freezing weather. The last rebel stronghold in the south was taken at the Siege of Dunboy. Red Hugh O'Donnell fled to Spain, where he died in 1602; he was replaced as clan chief. O'Neill was reduced then to guerrilla warfare against Mountjoy and his troops.

Mountjoy smashed the O'Neill's inauguration stone kept at Tullaghogue, in a gesture that vividly symbolised the destruction of the O'Neill clan. Then, as a result of the scorched earth policy, famine struck Ulster and one by one O'Neill's sub-lords surrendered during 1602. O'Neill himself held out until March 1603, when he surrendered to Mountjoy.

Aftermath

By this point Elizabeth I was dead. The rebels must have been surprised when they received favourable terms from the new king of England, James I. O'Neill, O'Donnell and the other chieftains of Ulster who had survived the fighting were given full pardons; they were even given their estates back. The conditions were that they must give up their Irish titles, disband their private armies, release their people from serfdom and swear undivided loyalty to the English crown. The apparent leniency shown by the English is explained in purely practical terms; the English simply could not afford to carry on fighting the Irish any longer, particularly when it was engaged in another war in the Spanish Netherlands.

Fighting the Tyrone Rebellion cost the English exchequer an enormous amount of money and by the close of Elizabeth's reign the exchequer had come close to bankruptcy. The rebellion is believed to have cost as many as 60,000 Irish lives – in the Ulster famine of 1602–3 alone. The overall death toll on both sides is likely to have been 130,000.

O'Neill and his allies were treated leniently, but they were still not trusted by the English. O'Neill and the other Gaelic lords decided to leave Ireland for the European mainland in 1607. This so-called 'Flight of the Earls' was organised with the intention of setting up an expedition to restart the war, sponsored by a Catholic kingdom. In the event, they were unable to find any country prepared to sponsor them. Spain, for instance, might have invaded Ireland in the reign of Elizabeth, but Spain was easier with the idea of a Stuart dynasty in power. Inevitably, in their absence, the land that had belonged to the absentee earls was confiscated. It was settled in what became known as the Plantation of Ulster. The Tyrone Rebellion was therefore an important, though unintended, stepping stone on the way to the English and Scottish colonization of Ulster; that different status for Ulster was to prove a major problem in the twentieth century, when the rest of Ireland, including three counties of Ulster, was declared independent.

4
CONFLICTS OF THE ENLIGHTENMENT

THE THIRTY YEARS' WAR
(1618-48)

The Thirty Years' War, fought across Germany and neighbouring territories, was mainly a religious conflict between Catholics and Protestants but it also involved rivalry between the Habsburg dynasty and other European powers. Mainly Catholic France, ruled by Cardinal Richelieu, supported the Protestant side in this conflict with the aim of weakening the Habsburgs; this in turn had the effect of making France the dominant political power in Europe and aggravating French-Habsburg rivalry to the point of generating a later war between France and Spain.

Spain was involved because it held the Spanish Netherlands, a territory which bordered on the German states. France was menaced by two neighbouring Habsburg states, Spain to the south and the Holy Roman Empire to the east, and also wished to establish its supremacy over the weaker German states. Denmark and Sweden were involved because they wanted to gain control over the states of northern Germany that bordered the Baltic Sea. The Holy Roman Empire covered the area of present-day Germany and neighbouring regions, and consisted of a hotch-potch of independent states. The Holy Roman Emperor headed a confederation of princedoms, including Austria, Bohemia and Hungary and a huge number of small duchies and free cities. Of these principalities, probably only Austria was large enough and sophisticated enough to function politically as a nation in its own right.

In the early seventeenth century, southern Germany was mainly Catholic and northern Germany mainly Lutheran (Protestant), though there were minority creeds almost everywhere. In some lordships the numbers of Calvinists, Catholics and Lutherans were about the same.

The Habsburg emperors Ferdinand I, Maximilan II, Rudolf II and Matthias were ready to condone and support their subjects' choice of religion, in accordance with the spirit of the Peace of Augsburg of 1555, which had established that princes, at least, could choose the religion of their territories and that Lutheran subjects would be allowed to practice their religion.These emperors avoided wars of religion by simply allowing their subjects a free choice. This angered the Catholic rulers of Spain and others who wanted to impose religious uniformity. Denmark and Sweden were Lutheran kingdoms and wanted to support the cause of Protestantism in the empire to the south, while also hoping to gain political influence there.

OUTBREAK OF FIGHTING

Growing religious tension erupted in violence in Donauwörth in Swabia in 1606, when the Lutheran majority prevented the Catholic minority from mounting a religious procession. The riot prompted intervention from outside by Duke Maximilian of Bavaria, who wanted to help the Catholics. After that, German Calvinists expected a backlash; feeling threatened, they formed the League of Evangelical Union in 1608, under the Palatine elector Frederick IV. This in turn prompted Catholics to band together to form a Catholic League in 1609, led by Duke Maximilian. The battle lines were being drawn up.

THE BOHEMIAN REVOLT

It was apparent by 1617 that Holy Roman Emperor Matthias, King of Bohemia, would die without leaving an heir. His nearest male relative and therefore successor was Ferdinand of Styria, a staunch Catholic who wanted to impose uniformity. He was consequently a very unpopular candidate for the succession among the Bohemian Protestants.

The Protestant leaders of Bohemia preferred Frederick V, Elector of the Palatinate, as their candidate for Holy Roman Emperor: he was a Protestant. When he was elected crown prince of Bohemia in 1617, King-elect of Bohemia, Ferdinand sent his two representatives to

Hradcany Castle in Prague in order to govern in his absence. The Bohemian Protestants threw them from a window, 21 metres (71 ft) above the ground. They survived the fall by landing, the Protestants said, on a heap of manure. This Protestant insult to Catholic officials, the Second Defenestration of Prague, led directly to the outbreak of war.

The conflict between Protestant and Catholic quickly spread through Bohemia, Silesia, Lusatia and Moravia, and eventually across much of Europe. The Bohemian Revolt might have remained a local conflict if Ferdinand had only been king-elect of Bohemia, but he was also in effect Holy Roman Emperor in waiting. When Emperor Matthias died, Protestant leaders over a wide area were ready to join forces against him. Ferdinand was forced to call on his nephew, Philip IV of Spain, for help.

The Bohemians applied for admission to the Protestant Union, led by Frederick V, Elector of the Palatinate, and half-promised to make Frederick king of Bohemia. Unfortunately the Bohemians had made similar half promises to others. When the Austrians, who intercepted the mail coming out of Prague, made these deceitful manoeuvrings public, support for the Bohemian Protestants began to evaporate.

Initially the Bohemian Revolt went in the Bohemians' favour, with a siege of Vienna in 1619, but they suffered a major reverse at the Battle of Sablat (10 June 1619), in which Count Bucquoy commanding the Imperial army defeated the Protestant Union's army. This severed the Protestants' communications with Prague and the siege of Vienna by Count Thurn had to be called off. The capture of the Protestants' field chancery after the battle meant that Savoy's large-scale secret funding of the Protestant revolt was now no longer a secret. Once this Savoyard plot was uncovered, Savoy had to withdraw from the war.

On 17 August 1619, Ferdinand was formally deposed as King of Bohemia, and replaced by Palatine elector Frederick V. The Transylvanians succeeded in driving the Imperial armies out of Transylvania by 1620.

The Spanish sent an army under Ambrosio Spinola to support the emperor. Then the Saxons invaded, though the Spanish army in the west stopped the Protestant Union forces from intervening. The Catholic League army under General Tilly pacified Upper Austria; the emperor's army pacified Lower Austria. Then the two Catholic armies united and moved north into Bohemia. On 8 November 1620, in the Battle of White Mountain, not far from Prague, Ferdinand II's forces inflicted a decisive defeat on those of Frederick V. Bohemia was forced to become a Catholic state, and stayed in the hands of the Habsburgs for the next three centuries. The League of Evangelical Union was broken up, Frederick was outlawed from the Holy Roman Empire and his lands were given to Catholic aristocrats. His title Elector of the Palatinate was given to Duke Maximilian of Bavaria. The now-landless Frederick became a conspicuous exile, but he continued to try to raise support for the Protestant cause.

The collapse of the rebellion in Bohemia led to widespread confiscation of property, the suppression of the Bohemian nobility. The war continued in the Palatinate, mostly as a series of small battle and sieges carried out by the Spanish. Mannheim and Heidelberg fell to the Spanish in 1622, leaving the Palatinate in (Catholic) Spanish hands.

Remnants of the Protestant armies fled to Holland under the leadership of Mansfeld and Christian of Brunswick. Mansfeld was allowed to remain in Holland, but the Dutch would not give refuge to the soldiers, who had to move on to East Friesland. Christian tried to engage Catholic forces in Saxony and eventually Tilly's army pursued them back to the Dutch border. On 6 August 1623, in the Battle of Stadtlohn, Tilly's highly disciplined army annihilated Christian's 15,000-strong army, killing 80 per cent of the soldiers. This was a disaster for those directly involved, and also for Frederick V, who had to abandon any hope of mounting future campaigns. The Protestant revolt was over.

THE DANISH INTERVENTION

It was Christian IV of Denmark who restarted the war. Christian was a Lutheran. He wanted to help the Lutherans of Lower Saxony (the adjacent region of Germany) by leading an army against the Holy Roman Emperor. Denmark had a vested interest in opposing the empire; it was a Protestant nation and was threatened by an overstrong Catholic neighbour. Christian had also established an unparalleled stability and prosperity for Denmark by collaborating with his German neighbours.

The Danish enterprise was supported financially by France and England. Christian declared himself war leader and raised a mercenary army of 20,000. Against this new threat, the emperor appointed Wallenstein, a wealthy Bohemian aristocrat, as commander-in-chief. Wallenstein pledged his own army, which may have numbered as many as 100,000 soldiers, in return for the plunder from captured territories. Christian had no idea what he was up against, but as soon as he encountered the combined forces of Wallenstein and Tilly he retreated. Christian was let down by his allies, who turned out to be weak; France was divided by civil war, England was similarly internally divided, and Sweden was engaged in its own war with the Polish-Lithuanian Commonwealth.

Wallenstein defeated Mansfeld's army at the Battle of Dessau Bridge in 1626. Tilly defeated the Danish army at the Battle of Lutter in the same year. Mansfeld died shortly afterwards; he was ill, exhausted and humiliated that defeat in this one battle had cost him half his army. Wallenstein marched northwards, into Jutland, though he was unable to take the Danish capital, Copenhagen, on the island of Zealand. Wallenstein was invincibly strong on land, but had no fleet. Neither the Poles nor the Hanseatic League would allow the Holy Roman Empire to build a fleet in the Baltic ports. Wallenstein besieged Stralsund, the one Baltic port with the facilities to build a large fleet.

The cost of continuing was too great, though, and Wallenstein settled for a peace with Denmark, which was concluded in the Treaty of Lubeck in 1629. This stated that Christian IV could remain king of Denmark so long as he abandoned support for the Protestant states in Germany. The port of Stralsund continued to hold out against Wallenstein and the empire.

THE SWEDISH INTERVENTION

There was some distrust of Wallenstein within court circles in the empire. It was thought that he might defect and join forces with the German princes. Because of this fear, Emperor Ferdinand II dismissed Wallenstein in 1630, but he would later recall him when the Swedes invaded under Gustavus Adolphus, King Gustaf II.

Gustavus Adolphus invaded, just like Christian IV, to assist the German Lutherans and to gain economic influence in the German states bordering the Baltic Sea. Again like Christian IV, he was subsidized by Richelieu, the Chief Minister of Louis XIII. The Swedish armies were successful from 1630 to 1634 in pushing back the Catholic forces; the Protestant lands were regained. At the Battle of Breitenfeld in 1631 Gustavus Adolphus defeated Tilly's Catholic League army. In a sequel a year later, Gustavus Adolphus was victorious again, with Tilly himself being killed.

Now that Tilly was dead, Ferdinand II recalled Wallenstein and his large army. Wallenstein's tactic was to try to sever Gustavus Adolphus' supply chain. This resulted in a confrontation at the Battle of Lutzen in 1632, which the Swedes won, but Gustavus Adolphus himself was killed. In 1634, at the First Battle of Nördlingen, the Protestant forces were defeated; they lacked the firm leadership of Gustavus Adolphus.

In 1633, Ferdinand II again became suspicious of Wallenstein's loyalty when the latter was trying to arbitrate between Catholics and Protestants. Fearing that Wallenstein was about to change sides, Ferdinand had him arrested. Then one of Wallenstein's officers, Captain Devereuz, killed him when he tried to contact the Swedes in Eger Town Hall on 25 February 1634.

A negotiated Peace of Prague (1635) protected the interests of the Lutheran rulers in north-east Germany, but not the Lutheran rulers of the south and west. It also banned German rulers from setting up alliances among themselves or with foreign powers. The French were dissatisfied with this because it gave renewed strength and power to the Habsburgs. At this point France decided on military intervention.

THE FRENCH INTERVENTION

Although France was predominantly Catholic, politically it was a rival of the Holy Roman Empire and Spain, so it came into the war on the Protestant side. Richelieu was interested in reducing the power of the Habsburgs. France allied itself with Sweden and Holland. In retaliation, Spain invaded France, ravaging Champagne and Burgundy and even threatening to take Paris in 1636. The Spanish were repulsed by Bernhard of Saxe-Weimar at the Battle of Compiègne and pushed back.

Then there were major changes within the French power structure. Richelieu died in 1642 and Louis XIII in 1643, leaving an infant Louis XIV on the throne and a new chief minister, Cardinal Mazarin, ruling France. Mazarin worked towards peace. In 1645, the Swedish marshal Torstensson won a victory over the Imperial army at the Battle of Jankau, and the Prince of Conde defeated the Bavarian army in the Second Battle of Nördlingen. One of the major Catholic military commanders, Count Franz von Mercy, was killed in the battle.

On 14 March 1647, Cologne, Bavaria, France and Sweden signed the Truce of Ulm. In the following year, a combined French and Swedish army defeated the Imperial army at the Battle of Zusmarshausen. By this stage only the Imperial territories of Austria now remained securely in the Habsburgs' hands.

Aftermath

The mercenary armies used during the war paid no heed to the land or property they were fighting over, and they laid waste to huge tracts of Germany and the Low Countries. This in turn led to famine and disease, and much higher than normal death rates among the civilian populations. Germany's population was reduced by fifteen or twenty per cent. In Brandenburg, the population was halved. In the Czech lands population was reduced by one-third. The level of destruction was almost unimaginable; the Swedish armies destroyed 2,000 castles, 1,500 towns and 18,000 villages. The appalling destruction did much to bring to an end the age of mercenary armies and ushered in the age of well-disciplined and responsible national armies. The war bankrupted many of the powers involved and failed to resolve most of the issues that had brought about the conflict in the first place.

The war ended with the Treaty of Munster, which was part of the Peace of Westphalia (1648). The Peace of Westphalia laid the foundations for what are still regarded in the twenty-first century as the basic tenets of the sovereign nation-states. The Peace established fixed territorial boundaries for many of the countries involved, and changed the relationships between subjects and rulers. Up to that time, there were overlapping religious and political loyalties. From the Peace of Westphalia on, it was agreed that the citizens of a particular state are subject first and foremost to the laws of their own state government, not on those of neighbouring powers – whether religious or secular. An important principle was established, that a state has a right to govern its own affairs and may not be invaded by another power unless it has invaded or threatens to invade. This has been cited in recent years in relation to the Iraq War, in which foreign powers, notably Britain and America, blatantly invaded Iraq in spite of the fact that there was no threat of invasion whatever; according to the Peace of Westphalia, the Iraq War is an illegal and unwarranted war. At the time, this principle hampered and weakened the Holy Roman Empire, which depended on interference in the affairs of neighbouring states.

Huge numbers of people died, not just in the fighting but as a result of famine and disease – typhus, bubonic plague, scurvy and dysentery. Bloodbath though it was, the Thirty Years War was the last major religious war in Europe.

THE BRITISH CIVIL WAR
(1639–51)

The Civil War was a series of political quarrels and armed conflicts between supporters of Parliament and supporters of the monarchy, particularly in the person of King Charles I. One major feature of this internal conflict is that it was concerned with the way in which Britain was ruled; it was not so much a power struggle between individuals, like the civil war between Stephen and Matilda, or between dynasties, like the Wars of the Roses. But the most striking feature of all was the climactic rejection and execution of Charles I and the establishment of a brief republic.

The term 'English Civil War' has often been used, but the conflict spread to Scotland and Ireland, too, so some historians prefer to call it the 'War of the Three Kingdoms' instead. Other historians describe it as the 'English Revolution', which tells us a great deal about the character of the conflict, but the phrase 'Civil War' is now too deeply ingrained in the national culture to be cast aside lightly.

BACKGROUND

The rapid development of such a strong anti-monarchist movement in England seems surprising, in view of the enormous popularity of Elizabeth I. But after her death in 1603 an entire stratum of the English aristocracy was left stranded. Elizabeth's favourites found themselves marginalised when James VI of Scotland arrived in London with his own court. There were also many who saw the Stuart family as interlopers, parvenus who had no real right to rule in England. Sir Walter Raleigh was one of the Elizabethan courtiers stranded by the regime change. While imprisoned in the Tower by James I, Raleigh wrote his *History of the World*, in which he attempted to demonstrate that just kings have the right to rule. He sensibly and understandably did not write down what he thought about James I, who had put him in the Tower, but the implication was clear: James was a bad king who had no right to rule. Raleigh's unfinished book, with its powerful anti-Stuart subtext, became a foundation of the English Revolution and Raleigh himself, the peacock of the Elizabethan court, became an unlikely iconic hero of the rebellion against James I's son Charles I, who acceded to the throne in 1625.

One of Charles I's aspirations was to complete the welding together of the three kingdoms of England, Scotland and Ireland into a single homogeneous state. The union under one crown concealed many important differences; the Scottish legal system, for instance, remained different from the English. Many English Parliamentarians were suspicious of this drive to integration. Charles I was an absolutist, and they feared that in the process of creating a new kingdom the king would sweep away the limitations that the English constitution imposed on the monarch. They were right to be suspicious, as both Charles and his father thought of themselves as 'little Gods on Earth'.

Few Parliamentarians believed that kings had a divine right to rule. Charles's mildness of manner was deceptive – he regarded any questioning of his orders as offensive. Over a period of years, friction between Parliament and King gradually increased until open conflict broke out.

Further causes of concern were the king's Catholic sympathies, which emerged when he married Henrietta Maria, a French Catholic princess, and the king's eagerness to involve Britain in the Thirty Years War in Europe. Charles insisted on involving Britain in the religious war in France. He sent his favourite, the Duke of Buckingham, on an expedition that was a conspicuous failure. Parliament already hated Buckingham because of his excessive influence on the king, and tried to impeach Buckingham. The king retaliated by dissolving Parliament. This saved Buckingham, but frustrated and angered Parliament.

There was a stand-off. The king avoided calling a Parliament for a decade, a period referred to as Charles's 'Personal Rule' or 'the King's tyranny', according to people's view of the situation; but there was an intensifying polarization. Charles depended on Parliament for cash, so he was forced to resort to unusual methods. There was a war scare in 1635, and he demanded that inland counties in England paid Ship Money, a tax to support the British Navy. Charles was operating strictly within established English law, but it was one that had lain idle for hundreds of years and was therefore perceived as illegal by many of his contemporaries. Several prominent men refused to pay the tax and suffered reprisals.

Charles also antagonised Protestants by steering the Church of England towards Catholicism; he created what was called High Anglicanism. The system for fining people for non-attendance at church was reintroduced. People were severely punished for open criticism of the king's newly appointed Archbishop of Canterbury, William Laud. Two men had their ears cut off, which was a rare punishment for gentlemen; this too caused general anger against the king. Charles pressed on regardless of opposition. He tried to impose his new religious policies in Scotland, too, and met with violent opposition in Edinburgh in 1637. The following year a National Covenant was formulated in Scotland, outlining the Scots' 'loyal protest' against Charles's innovations. Charles appeared to back down, summoning a General Assembly of the Church of Scotland, but this rejected his new Prayer Book and declared the post of bishop to be unlawful. Then Charles demanded that the Assembly retract its proposals, the Scots refused and both sides began to arm. The first major step towards armed conflict had been taken.

Charles marched his army to the Scottish border in 1639 with the intention of suppressing the religious rebellion, which became known as the Bishops' War. But Charles's military campaign was inconclusive and he accepted the Scots' offer of a truce, the Pacification of Berwick; a second war followed in 1640. Then Charles was defeated by a Scots army which marched south and captured Newcastle. Charles was completely humiliated. He was obliged to agree not to interfere in religious matters in Scotland – and to pay war reparations, too.

The situation in England worsened when Charles had to go cap in hand to Parliament in 1640 to get the money to pay for the Scottish war.

John Pym, one of the new Members of Parliament, took the opportunity to air grievances against the king and declared his opposition to the king's invasion of Scotland. Charles was insulted by this and dissolved the 'Short Parliament'. It was after this that he resumed the attack on Scotland and provoked a Scottish invasion of northern England.

Thomas Wentworth had become Charles's Lord Deputy of Ireland in 1632. Wentworth successfully raised new taxes from Irish Catholic gentry in return for a promise of leniency relating to religious observance. In 1639, Charles recalled him, made him Earl of Strafford, and set him the task of achieving the same result in Scotland. But it did not work. The Scots invaded most of northern England and Charles was obliged to pay them £850 a day – a revival of the Danegeld - not to advance any further south. Charles was now in a desperate situation, both financially and politically. He had no choice but to recall Parliament in November 1640.

The new Long Parliament was hostile to Charles and took advantage of his weak position to force reforms on him. One major reform was a law stating that Parliament must meet at least once every three years, whether the king summoned it or not. Another was that the king was not to be allowed to raise taxes without Parliament's consent. Another was that the king was no longer to be allowed to dissolve Parliament without its consent. Feeling its own power quicken, in 1641 Parliament had the Earl of Strafford arrested subject to a Bill of Attainder and executed for treason. The Irish Catholics feared that this meant a crackdown from the Protestants, took up arms and Ireland sank into chaos. In England, Puritan Members of Parliament declared that they would shortly see the same thing happen in England.

In January 1642, Charles walked into the House of Commons with 400 soldiers, intent on arresting five of its members on a charge of treason. Charles asked Speaker William Lenthall, where the five members were. The speaker replied politely, 'May it please your majesty, I have neither eyes to see nor tongue to speak in this place but as the House is pleased to direct me, whose servant I am here.' He was telling the king that he was Parliament's servant, and not the king's. It was a turning point in the relationship between King and Parliament.

THE FIRST ENGLISH CIVIL WAR

Charles understood. Just a matter of days after failing to capture the five members of the Commons, he decided for safety's sake that he should leave London. As the spring of 1642 passed into summer, various towns and cities declared their support for the king or Parliament. Hull, for example, declared for Parliament and when Charles tried to acquire arms there he was turned away – twice, by force. The tension rose, though even as the open fighting broke out large areas were still neutral; by no means were all Members of Parliament were opposed to the king.

But Charles I fuelled the conflict. After being rebuffed at Hull, he travelled to Nottingham and raised his standard there. Initially he had only 2,000 cavalry and a small number of infantrymen, but built a larger army round this core. He moved on to Stafford and Shrewsbury, places where he knew royalist support was likely to be strong. The Parliamentarians who were against the king voted to raise an army of 10,000 on 9 June and appointed the Earl of Essex as its commander on 12 June. He was given orders 'to rescue His Majesty's person'; it was an interesting euphemism. Essex marched through the Midlands and by September he had 21,000 infantry and over 4,000 cavalry, including a Cambridgeshire detachment headed by Oliver Cromwell. On 14 September, Essex moved his army to Coventry and southwards, interposing it between the Royalist army and London. The first skirmish, between cavalry reconnaissance units, took place at a bridge over the River Teme near Worcester; it was the Battle of Powick Bridge. Prince Rupert's cavalry were involved in this skirmish, and after it he withdrew to Shrewsbury to discuss in a council of war whether the next action should be to march to confront Essex's army near Worcester or march on London. The decision was made to march on London, but to do battle if the opportunity arose; the Royalists took the view that it was better to attack and defeat Essex before his army grew too strong. The general temper of both sides meant that a large-scale battle could not be avoided for long.

The Royalist army left Shrewsbury for London on 12 October, which had the desired effect of provoking Essex to bring his army to intercept it. The first big battle of the Civil War, the Battle of Edgehill (23 October 1642), was inconclusive. A second action, at Turnham Green, forced Charles to withdraw to Oxford, which the king kept as his base for the rest of the war. The war went first one way, then the other. The Battle of Hopton Heath was inconclusive, though the Royalist commander Lord Northampton was killed; the Battles of Lansdowne and Roundway Down were Royalist victories. Then Oliver Cromwell formed his highly disciplined troop, the 'Ironsides', and used them to win the Battle of Gainsborough (July 1643). Then the Parliamentarian army gained the upper hand. The Royalist army was defeated at the First Battle of Newbury (20 September 1643). Charles negotiated a ceasefire in Ireland in order to release Royalist troops to use in England, while the Parliamentarians promised the Scots concessions in return for assistance. With that aid, the Parliamentary army won the Battle of Marston Moor (2 July 1644) and gained control of the north of England. It was above all Cromwell's skill as a military leader that made this a decisive battle.

In 1645, Parliament formally declared its determination to overwhelm the king. A Self-Denying Ordinance was passed, by which all the military commanders on the Parliamentary side surrendered their commands in the interest of a radical reorganization and the creation of a New Model Army. This was commanded by Sir Thomas Fairfax, with Cromwell second-in-command. The reorganization paid off at the Battle of Naseby (14 June 1645), in which Charles I's army was virtually destroyed.

The king then fell back on an attempt to consolidate a stable power base in the Midlands, based on the axis of the fortress towns of Oxford and Newark, both intensely loyal to him. In May 1646 Charles took shelter with a Scottish army at Southwell in Nottinghamshire. This brought the First Civil War to a close.

THE SECOND ENGLISH CIVIL WAR

During the lull that followed, on 28 December 1647 Charles – though now a prisoner – negotiated an agreement with the Scottish Church, offering promises of reform.

In the summer of 1648, there was a series of Royalist risings in England and also a Scottish invasion. These were relatively easily put down by the Parliamentarian forces, though there were exceptions. In Wales, Colonel Horton's Parliamentarian troops defeated Royalist rebels at the Battle of St Fagans (8 May 1648), and the rebel leaders surrendered to Cromwell in July only after a two-month long siege at Pembroke. Fairfax defeated a Royalist rebellion at the Battle of Maidstone in June, then turned to the county of Essex, where armed Royalists were gathering in considerable numbers under the charismatic leadership of Sir Charles Lucas. This led to a long siege at Colchester.

In the North of England there was a major Royalist rising under Sir Marmaduke Langdale in Cumberland. This was countered by a Parliamentarian force led by Major-General John Lambert. The most important action in the North was the Battle of Prestonpans near Preston in Lancashire (17-19 August) in which Cromwell defeated a combined Royalist-Scottish force and brought the Second English Civil War to an end. The Second War was very much a desperate rearguard action by a small number of Royalists who were in effect in breach of the parole granted at the close of the First War. As a result of their dishonourable behaviour, the Royalists who took up arms in the Second War were treated harshly. When the Royalists surrendered at Colchester, Sir Charles Lucas and Sir George Lisle were summarily executed. The leaders of the Welsh rebels, Laugharne, Poyer and Powel, were all sentenced to death. Three prominent peers who fell into the hands of the Parliamentarians were beheaded at Westminster: Lord Capel, the Earl of Holland and the Duke of Hamilton.

THE FATE OF THE KING

There remained Charles I himself, who had precipitated both the First and the Second Civil Wars. Even at this stage, there were still some Members of Parliament who wanted to see Charles I remain king and argued for negotiation. But the Parliamentarian army was determined that the king must be deposed. The army marched on London and on Parliament in particular. In 'Pride's Purge' (December 1648), troops arrested forty-five MPs and excluded 146. This allowed only seventy-five members in. The so-called Rump Parliament was given orders by the army to organise the trial of the king for treason, in the name of the people of England. The fifty-nine commissioners or judges at Charles I's trial found him guilty of high treason. He was declared a 'tyrant, traitor, murderer and public enemy' and was beheaded on a scaffold outside the Banqueting House at the Palace of Whitehall (30 January 1649).

THE SIEGE OF DROGHEDA

The rebellion in Ireland continued, with most of the island dominated by Irish Confederates. As the Royalist cause collapsed in England, the threat in Ireland from the English Parliamentary armies grew stronger. In 1648, the Irish Confederates formed an alliance with the Royalists in England. Their joint forces, led by the Duke of Ormonde, tried to overwhelm the Parliamentary army that controlled Dublin but they were defeated in August 1649. While Prince Rupert's Royalist fleet was blockaded in Kinsale, Cromwell was able to land an army at Dublin to destroy the Royalist alliance in Ireland.

Cromwell's siege of Drogheda, with his ensuing massacre of 3,500 people, is one of the most controversial episodes in his career. Cromwell justified his action by saying that the men in the town should not have been carrying arms after the town had surrendered. The English conquest of Ireland went on until 1653, when the last Royalist and Irish Confederate soldiers surrendered. By the close of this long war in Ireland, as many as one-third of the population of Ireland had gone; they had either died or emigrated. The Parliamentarians confiscated almost all the Catholic-owned estates, so the pattern of property-ownership in Ireland was completely transformed, too.

SCOTLAND

The death of Charles I changed the course of the civil war in Scotland, too. By 1649, the Royalists were in disarray and their leader, the Marquess of Montrose, had gone into exile. To begin with, Charles I's son, already regarded by some as Charles II, encouraged Montrose to raise an army in the Highlands to fight the Royalist cause, but when the Covenanters offered him the Scottish crown, Charles abandoned Montrose. By then, Montrose had landed with a force of mercenaries from Norway and was unable to turn back. After being defeated at the Battle of Carbisdale (25 April 1650), Montrose was captured and sentenced to death by the Scottish Parliament; he was hanged on 21 May 1650. He must have wondered whether Charles II's was a cause worth dying for.

With Charles I's son now formally recognised as Charles II in Scotland, Cromwell abandoned the suppression of the Irish Royalists to deal with this serious new threat. He arrived in Scotland on 22 July and besieged Edinburgh. He had to retreat because of disease and shortage of supplies. His Parliamentary army was pursued and brought to battle at Dunbar on 3 September. Cromwell won, and went back to take Edinburgh; by December he had taken most of southern Scotland.

By July 1651, Cromwell was pursuing Charles southwards into England, while General Monck finished off the Scottish campaign. In 1652, the Scots were given thirty seats in a unified Parliament in Westminster, and General Monck was Scotland's military governor. Cromwell, for all his ability as a military leader, was unable to stop Charles from penetrating further and further into England at the head of a Royalist army. Charles headed through the west of England, because he could rely on firmer support there. But eventually Cromwell brought Charles to battle at the crucial Battle of Worcester (3 September 1651), where the Royalists were finally defeated. Charles escaped from the field of battle, famously hiding in an oak tree and several safe houses before taking a ship across to France. The escape of the new king marks the end of the civil wars.

Aftermath and significance

Before the Civil War the English Parliament had no major, permanent role in government. It was summoned by the monarch as and when additional taxation was required, and it could be dissolved (dismissed) in the same summary way. After the Civil War, Parliament had far more power, and most significantly of all it was able to limit the power of the monarch. From that point on, Britain can be said to have had a constitutional monarchy. This development in effect meant that Britain would not join in the widespread republican movements that followed the French Revolution.

There was also a firming up of anti-Catholic feeling among Protestants in England, and in particular a feeling that the monarch could not be a Catholic. After the restoration of the monarchy in 1660, Charles II was apparently Protestant, but probably a secret Catholic. His brother and successor, James II, was openly Catholic and in a second revolution (the Glorious Revolution of 1688) Parliament ousted him.

The siege and massacre of Drogheda became an iconic bitter memory in Irish history, driving and intensifying the hatred between Catholic and Protestant, Irish and English.

Most conspicuously, the Civil War left England and Scotland not just without a monarch, but without a monarchy. For the first time in history, there were neither kings nor queens in these islands. The void was filled with various abortive attempts to set up a republic, none of them very successful. In the end, in a spirit of desperate frustration, Cromwell was approached with the idea that he should be king. It seems he seriously considered this possibility before rejecting it. Instead, he accepted the title Lord Protector and went through an inauguration ceremony that was similar to a coronation. Britain was not quite ready to become a republic. The experiment failed, and many who had been keen to be rid of Charles I were equally keen to see the monarchy restored and his son ascending the throne. When Cromwell died in 1658, there was a power vacuum. His son Richard briefly succeeded him, but he was not capable of filling his father's shoes and he was removed after seven months. Some twentieth-century historians have seen the Civil War as a class war, with the landed aristocrats and the churchmen on one side, the trading and industrial classes of town and country, yeomen and progressive gentry, and the relatively educated ordinary people on the other side. Some see it as a bourgeois revolution, a moment when a powerful and wealthy middle class annihilated a medieval absolutist system of government. Some see it as the result of a conspiracy by a cabal of aristocrats who were marginalised by Charles I's absolutism. Some see it in simple mechanistic terms as the result of an intolerant monarch trying to impose his will on several very different kingdoms.

THE JACOBITE RISINGS
(1690–1745)

The Jacobite Risings were a sequence of rebellions and wars that disrupted the peace in Britain and Ireland for more than half a century after 1688. That was the year in which James II of England, and James VII of Scotland, was deposed and exiled by Parliament in the Glorious Revolution. His supporters were called Jacobites - 'Jacobus' is the Latin form of 'James' – and they continually plotted and fought for the restoration of James II to the throne. After his death they went on fighting for the restoration of his descendants, the Stuart pretenders, or claimants to the English and Scottish throne. James II's son, also named James Stuart, became known as the Old Pretender and his son in turn, Charles Edward Stuart, became known as the Young Pretender.

There were two major risings, the First Jacobite Rebellion, which took place in 1715, and the Second Jacobite Rebellion, which happened in 1745. Though separated by thirty years, they were really part of a single long-term campaign to reinstate the Stuart dynasty and they were preceded by an earlier Jacobite rising in 1690.

In some ways, the Jacobite Risings were a continuation of the conflict that erupted in the Civil Wars of the mid-seventeenth century. When the Commonwealth collapsed and the monarchy was restored with the accession of Charles II in 1660, the Church of England was re-established. A closet-Catholic, Charles II managed to avoid stirring up major religious strife. When he died, he was succeeded by his brother who, as James II, was openly Catholic and attempted to impose the tolerance of Roman Catholics. This antagonised the Anglican establishment. When in 1688 the new king's wife gave birth to a boy the prospect of a Catholic dynasty loomed. At that point Parliament intervened, taking the drastic step of inviting James II's daughter Mary to rule in his place. She arrived with her husband William of Orange to rule England and Scotland as Mary II and William III. As William arrived at Torbay in November 1688, disembarking from a ship named *Brill*, James left hastily for exile in France. The so-called 'Glorious Revolution', the safe re-establishment of a Protestant monarchy, had been achieved.

But James still had many supporters. Naturally many Catholics supported him, but there were also many Tory royalists who supported him because they impartially regarded him as the legitimate monarch: they saw deposing James II as unconstitutional. The Stuart dynasty was descended from Mary Stuart, Mary Queen of Scots, and in Scotland there was a strong antipathy towards William and Mary, who were with some justification seen as interlopers and usurpers. The coronation of William and Mary nevertheless took place in May 1689.

In Edinburgh, a Convention of the Estates was summoned by William in March 1689, at which a conciliatory letter from William was discussed. James's supporters were represented by John Graham of Claverhouse, Viscount Dundee, who attended the start of the convention but withdrew once it became clear that there was general support for William. The convention expressed its formal approval and William and Mary were proclaimed king and queen in Edinburgh in April 1689. The Scots had, therefore, formally accepted the regime change.

THE JACOBITE WAR IN IRELAND

The opening conflict in James II's attempt to get his throne back took place in Ireland. On 1 July 1690, outside the town of Drogheda, the major and, as it turned out, decisive battle of the conflict took place. The Battle of the Boyne was in a very real and literal sense a shoot-out between the new king and the recently deposed king. The new King William III and the ex-King James II acted as commanders of their two armies as they faced each other across the River Boyne. In recent Irish history, the battle has been portrayed as a crucial moment in the struggle between Irish Protestant and Catholic interests; in fact the composition of the two armies was thoroughly mixed and there were both Catholics and Protestants in both armies. At the time there was no religious motive in the battle. It was very simply a power struggle between two kings over which of them should sit on the English throne, and therefore about power over the British Isles as a whole, Ireland included.

James was an experienced and able military commander, and had shown conspicuous bravery when fighting on behalf of his brother, Charles II, for instance at the Battle of the Dunes in 1658. On occasions, he could panic and make rash decisions. William was also a seasoned general, though his battles tended to degenerate into stalemates with a high death toll. The two commanders were well matched. Their armies were not. James led an army of 23,500, while William had an army of about 38,000. The difference in numbers was not decisive, but the difference in training would prove to be so. Many of James's soldiers were poorly trained Irish peasants who had been pressed into service; they were also poorly equipped.

William had landed at Carrickfergus in Ulster and marched south to capture Dublin. The Jacobites would have done well to block his advance in the rough country round Newry, on what is now the Irish border. Instead, James chose to put his line of defence on the River Boyne, about 50 km (30 miles) north of Dublin. The day before the battle, William was very nearly killed; he was wounded by James's artillery as he inspected the fords his troops would use to cross the river. It is an interesting example of the random element in warfare. How different would the course of British and Irish history have been if William III had been killed at the Battle of the Boyne? Might the Jacobites have been encouraged to fight harder? Might James II have won?

The battle itself was fought specifically for control of a ford. William's cavalry managed to cross the Boyne and engage the Jacobite cavalry, who fell back in an orderly way. William had an opportunity to trap them as they retreated across another river, the Nanny, at Duleek, but his forces were held off by a successful Jacobite rearguard action.

Considering the scale and importance of the battle, the casualty figures were surprisingly low. Of 50,000 soldiers, about 2,000 were killed. About three-quarters of the losses were Jacobites. The reason is that most losses are incurred in the pursuit and rout of an already beaten enemy. At the Battle of the Boyne this did not happen because the rearguard actions on the part of the Jacobite cavalry were very effective, screening the retreat of the rest of the Jacobite army. The Jacobites were demoralised in defeat, the Williamites triumphant in victory; two days later, William led his army into Dublin and the Jacobite army abandoned the city.

James did not linger in Ireland after that. He rode to Duncannon and returned to France, even though his army had left the battlefield more or less intact. He lost his nerve and his hasty exit from the battlefield earned him the contempt of his Irish supporters, who referred to him as 'James the Shit'. His son behaved in a similar way twenty-six years later, when he abandoned his supporters at Montrose, and fifty years on his grandson Bonnie Prince Charlie did the same at the Battle of Culloden. Bolting ran in the family.

At the time, the Battle of the Boyne was overshadowed as a news story by the Battle of Beachy Head, a sea battle just two days afterwards in which the French defeated an Anglo-Dutch fleet in the English Channel. On the European mainland the great significance of the Boyne was more fully appreciated. It was the first real victory for the League of Augsburg, the first alliance between Catholic and Protestant countries. By achieving a resounding victory, William III was seen as laying to rest the superstition that such an alliance was blasphemous. The victory encouraged more states to join the alliance and this ended the very real prospect that France would conquer Europe.

Within the British Isles the Battle of the Boyne had great significance because it ended any hope James had of getting his throne back by force of arms. The Jacobite defeat in Ireland was a factor in making the Scottish Highlanders give up their support for Dundee's rising. In Ireland, the British Protestant power in Ireland was established, and this is why today the Battle of the Boyne is still celebrated by the Protestant Orange Order. Irish Nationalists have tended to see the Boyne as a black day, a major step towards the total British colonisation of Ireland; this is why in 1929 the statue of William III standing outside Trinity College Dublin was destroyed by the IRA.

DUNDEE'S RISING

In Scotland, Claverhouse, Lord Dundee, had not accepted the new king. He raised ex-King James's standard on the summit of Dundee Law. It was a grand gesture, but he had under fifty supporters. He had become known as 'Bluidy Clavers' because of his role in dealing harshly with Covenanters, but now he would be transformed into 'Bonnie Dundee', at least after Sir Walter Scott wrote a sentimental ballad about him in 1830.

By this time, James II was in Ireland and he wrote a letter promising to send Irish troops to support the rising in Scotland. Dundee was having trouble in raising military support for this cause and the 200 promised Irish troops made a difference. He got some support from Catholic clans in the Western Highlands. By July 1689, Dundee had mustered eight battalions and two companies, mostly from the Highlands. Dundee had considerable diplomatic skills, understanding the need to treat the clan chiefs with circumspection; their feelings about clan loyalty, precedence and etiquette were more important to them than the Jacobite cause and Dundee won them round by showing their concerns due respect.

The Highlanders' battle technique consisted of precipitate charges on foot armed with broadswords, shields, pitchforks and axes. This simple and ancient technique proved devastatingly effective against troops with modern weaponry; musketeers could easily be overcome while they were struggling to fix their bayonets or reload their muskets. It was this kind of primitive charge that enabled a small Highland Jacobite force to overwhelm and defeat a larger Lowland force at the Battle of Killiecrankie in July 1689, though a third of the Highlanders died in the action, as did Dundee himself. The Battle of Dunkeld in August 1689 was a street fight in which the Jacobite Highlanders were defeated.

The Jacobites were heavily defeated again at the Haughs of Cromdale in May 1690. Then in July the news came from Ireland that King William had defeated James II at the Battle of the Boyne. It was clear that the Jacobite cause was lost.

On 17 August 1691, William offered the Highland clans a pardon for their action in the rebellion, on condition that they took an oath of allegiance to him before 1 January 1692. The oath had to be sworn in front of a magistrate. The Highland chiefs were honourable men and they needed to be formally released from their loyalty to James before they could take such an oath. James, who was then in France, was unable to decide how to respond to their request. Eventually he agreed that his clan chiefs could take the oath, but his message only reached them in the middle of December. In spite of the severe winter weather, some chiefs succeeded in taking the oath before William's deadline. The Massacre of Glencoe was an example to those who were hesitating and by the spring of 1692 all the previously Jacobite clan chiefs had sworn allegiance to King William.

THE 'FIRST' JACOBITE RISING (1715)

With French support, the ex-King's son, James Stuart, sailed from Dunkirk in 1708 with 6,000 French troops and ships of the French navy. Rather than risk landing in England, they headed for Scotland. But the intended landing in the Firth of Forth, near Edinburgh, was prevented by the British navy under Admiral Byng. James's fleet was chased northwards round the north of Scotland. Many French troops and French ships were lost on the long way back to Dunkirk.

The objections to the installation of William and Mary as British monarchs were raised all over again when the first of the Hanoverian monarchs was imported from Germany. George I arrived from Hanover in 1714, and this prompted the Jacobites to organise an armed rebellion against the new regime. Initially there was an conspiracy among English Tories to overturn the new regime, but they were neither decisive enough nor courageous enough to carry it through. In Scotland it was a different matter.

James Stuart, the Old Pretender, had continued to plot for a Stuart restoration. He corresponded with the Earl of Mar and in the summer of 1715 he instructed Mar to raise the clans. Mar travelled from London to Braemar to summon the clan chiefs to 'a grand hunting match' in August 1715. Encouraged by this gathering, Mar proclaimed James Stuart as their 'lawful sovereign' on 6 September and symbolically raised the old Scottish standard. Equally symbolically, the gold finial immediately fell from the top of the flagpole. Mar's call to arms brought together an alliance of clans from all over Scotland.

The Jacobites took Perth on 14 September and the army grew to 8,000. Even so, a much smaller force under the Duke of Argyll, about a quarter the size of the Jacobite army, held the Stirling area for the Hanoverian government. Mar hesitated and stayed in Perth, waiting for the Earl of Seaforth to come with reinforcements from the northern clans. But Seaforth was held up by attacks from clans loyal to the Hanoverian government.

Separate local risings planned in Devon, Cornwall and Wales were pre-empted by the arrest of the local Jacobites. A rising in northern England got under way, led by Thomas Foster, a Northumberland landowner, and this joined forces with a rising in southern Scotland led by Lord Kenmure. Mar sent troops under Brigadier Mackintosh to aid them. Mackintosh's troops left Perth on 10 October and were ferried across the Firth of Forth. They were tempted into attacking Edinburgh, which was on their route, but they were chased off by Argyll's forces. Mackintosh's 2,000 strong force met their allies at Kelso on the Scottish Borders on 22 October, where several days were spent arguing over possible future actions. The Scots wanted to direct an attack on Dumfries or Glasgow, while the English wanted to march on Liverpool, arguing that as many as 20,000 men might be recruited in Lancashire. The Highlanders were unhappy about marching into England and some defected, though the march south was begun. The English Jacobites had seriously overestimated the level of support they would get. By the time they reached Preston in early November, they had gathered only 1,500 new recruits. Then government forces closed in on them, defeating them at the Battle of Preston. The Jacobites who survived this defeat surrendered on 14 November. The Highlanders had been right.

Meanwhile, at the Battle of Sheriffmuir in Scotland on 13 November, Mar had been unable to defeat the Duke of Argyll's smaller army. Mar went back to Perth. Too late, the Old Pretender arrived by sea at Peterhead on 22 December. He was not only too late, he was in too depressed and sickly a state to inspire his supporters. He set up court at

Scone in Perthshire for a time, visited his troops in Perth and demanded the burning of villages to obstruct the advance of Argyll's troops. The Highlanders were ready to do battle for him but James and his advisers decided to desert. They gave as a pretext that they were falling back to a stronger position, but in fact James was abandoning his followers, falling back to the coast in order to board a ship and escape. He boarded a ship at Montrose and sailed for France on 4 February 1716.

THE SPANISH-SPONSORED JACOBITE INVASION (1719)

While Britain and France were formally at peace, the Jacobites could not depend on France for help. The Jacobites found a new ally in Cardinal Alberoni, the Spanish king's minister, who sponsored an invasion force. A fleet of twenty-nine ships set sail in 1719, two sailing for Scotland where the clans were to be raised and twenty-seven carrying 5,000 troops to raise rebellion in England. However, the larger fleet was dispersed by storms and never reached Britain. The two frigates bound for Scotland landed with 300 Spanish soldiers and they held Eilean Donan Castle, but there was little support this time from the Highland clans. There was a battle at Glen Shiel, and the Spanish soldiers were obliged to surrender.

After the collapse of the First Jacobite rising, the Hanoverian government attempted to make future rebellion impossible. A Disarming Act and a Clan Act were passed, but these parliamentary measures were ineffectual. Government garrisons in the Highlands were built or reinforced and they were joined more effectively to the south by new military roads (Wade roads) built under the direction of Major-General Wade.

THE SECOND JACOBITE RISING (1745)

The War of the Austrian Succession brought Britain and France into open warfare with each other once more in 1743. English Jacobites saw their opportunity to enlist the aid of France against the Hanoverian government of England. The French king's Master of Horse came to England and visited Tories in southern England to discuss their proposals for a coup facilitated by a French invasion. Following that impudent reconnaissance, in November 1743 Louis XV gave his consent for a large-scale invasion of England in February 1744. It was to be a surprise attack. Charles Edward Stuart, known as the Young Pretender, was to be ferried to Maldon in Essex, where he and the invasion force would be met by local supporters for a march on London. As late as 13 February the British government was unaware of this invasion plan.

Once the plan was known, many English Jacobite suspects were arrested. Then the French invasion fleet was scattered by one of the worst storms of the eighteenth century. The barges carrying the troops were extremely vulnerable under these weather conditions, and some sank with the loss of all hands. Charles was informed by the French at the end of February that the invasion was cancelled. The British made a formal protest regarding the French support of Charles Edward Stuart, and the French gave him no further aid.

In spite of this debacle, Charles went on thinking that he could reclaim the British Crown for himself and his dynasty. Early in 1744, he had a message from a small number of Highland clan chiefs to say that they would rise in his support if he came with as few as 3,000 French troops. Charles had a problem now in enlisting French support. The earlier invasion had been a fiasco, and the French government was unlikely to sponsor another. He went on pestering government ministers to help him mount an invasion, and they became increasingly irritated; they were after all giving him substantial personal support already.

Charles negotiated not just privately but secretly with a group of privateers based at the port of Nantes, to fit out two ships to enable him to sail to Scotland to lead a rising. The ship of the line *Elisabeth* and the frigate *Du Teillay* with Charles on board sailed from Nantes in July 1745. Charles left behind a letter to Louis XV telling him he was sailing to Scotland to begin a rebellion and (again) asking for help. The *Elisabeth* encountered HMS *Lion*. After an exchange of fire, the badly damaged *Elisabeth* turned back. The frigate went on and successfully landed Charles on the Hebridean island of Eriskay on 2 August 1745.

The Scottish clan chiefs were unenthusiastic about this appearance of the Young Pretender in their midst: no troops, no weapons, no munitions, just Charles Edward Stuart. Two clan chiefs, Alexander MacDonald of Sleat and Norman MacLeod of MacLeod were so disgusted that they refused to meet the prince. Ever-optimistic, Charles raised the standard at Glenfinnan, announcing the second rising in his father's name. This drew about 1,200 men from four clans. As this small force marched south it soon doubled in size. By chance, most of the British army was abroad, leaving only an inexperienced force of 4,000 under Sir John Cope in Scotland. This government force marched into the Highlands, but then, because of general hostility towards it and George II, and because the Jacobite army was believed to be much larger than it actually was, it avoided doing battle and withdrew northwards to Inverness.

The Jacobites were left free to capture Perth and march on towards Edinburgh, where there was panic and the City Guard melted away. When the city gate was rashly opened at night to let a coach pass through, a band of Camerons rushed the sentries and seized the city. The following day King James VIII was proclaimed and Charles (his son) triumphantly entered the palace of Holyrood.

Cope's government army sailed from Aberdeen south to Dunbar with a view to engaging the Jacobite army. They finally closed with the Jacobites to the east of Edinburgh in the Battle of Prestonpans on 21 September 1745. This resulted in a surprising rout of government forces. Charles wrote off to France, begging for a speedy invasion of England where, understandably, there was by now considerable alarm. Charles held court at Holyrood palace for five weeks, basking in his success but failing to maintain a significant local military power base. He was still not in possession of Edinburgh Castle and he had not raised a local regiment.

The French sent some money and weapons, and promised to invade England by the end of the year. Lord George Murray, Charles's principal military adviser, warned against marching south, but Charles was able to sway the Council of War by telling it that he had been assured by English Tories that he would gain support in England if he marched south. As a result, the Council agreed to the march south by a margin of one vote. As events turned out, that was two votes too many – and Charles would live to regret the strategic lie.

The Jacobite army, numbering over 5,000 men, set off on the march into England on 3 November. During Charles's lengthy stay at Holyrood, the government had ordered experienced soldiers back from the European mainland to deal with Charles Edward Stuart. A government army led by General Wade gathered at Newcastle in north-east England. Charles was all for confronting them in battle, but Murray and the rest of his Council advised against this. Instead, they advanced through north-west England, heading for Carlisle. Very few Englishmen joined the Jacobite army along the way, perhaps 250 in all. Then as November came to an end, French ships landed 800 men in Scotland: not enough to make any difference.

The Jacobite army had now shrunk to less than 5,000 as men deserted. Murray wheeled it round to the east of another government army led by the Duke of Cumberland and headed for Derby. The Jacobites reached Derby on 4 December. They were now only 200 km (125 miles) from London, where panic was mounting. What Charles needed now above all else was the French invasion. He was told that the French invasion fleet was being assembled at Dunkirk, but he lost considerable ground at his Council of War when he had to admit that he had previously lied about assurances that had been given about support in England. It then began to look as if the entire march south had been a fool's errand, and Prince Charles Edward, Bonnie Prince Charlie, was the fool. The members of Charles's Council of War were disillusioned.

Murray led the Council in making the case against going any further. The promised support from the English had not materialised; the armies of both Wade and the Duke of Cumberland were closing in on them; a third government army was also approaching. The third army turned out to be fictitious. It was an effective piece of disinformation supplied by a government double agent. But the evidence available to Charles's Council pointed towards a strategic withdrawal. The Jacobite army must go back to join the growing Jacobite numbers in Scotland. The matter was put to the vote. This time only Charles voted to continue. He threw a tantrum when he was overruled and told his Council members he would never consult them again.

On 6 December, the dejected retreat began. Charles sulked and refused to play any part in the withdrawal. This had the benefit of leaving Murray in complete control, and Murray had the leadership skills needed to retreat effectively. He planned the perilous journey back through England with care and dash, and managed to get the army back into Scotland virtually intact, which was a major achievement. The English Tories now, just too late, sent a message pledging their support if Charles reached London. The French invasion was now, again just too late, ready to sail. If Charles had gone on from Derby, it looks as if he just might have succeeded. Certainly many officials in London thought so. There was no defensive force responsible for protecting London, the Jacobite army was only two or three days' march away, and many of the rich and powerful in London had made plans for their escape. But now that Charles was in full retreat, only disaster lay ahead.

By Christmas, the Jacobite army reached Glasgow and re-provisioned. On 3 January it left to seize Stirling. Reinforcements from the north swelled the army and at the Battle of Falkirk the Jacobite army was able to rout General Hawley's government army. Charles resumed control of the army after this and his unimaginative defensive style proved fatal to his cause.

On 16 April 1746, the Jacobite army was finally defeated at the Battle of Culloden near Inverness. The victorious army was composed of English and Scottish troops commanded by the Duke of Cumberland. The Highland sword charges that had worked in earlier battles could not work on the boggy, tussocky moor perversely chosen as a battlefield by Charles. His tactics were indecisive. His men were relatively untrained compared with those of Cumberland's regulars. The battle was going badly for the Jacobites, when Charles abruptly left the battlefield and blamed the failure on the treachery of his officers.

In the aftermath of the Battle of Culloden, the Duke of Cumberland's men ruthlessly massacred as many survivors as they could find, combing the battlefield for survivors and finishing them off, searching the streets of Inverness for rebels who were hiding there and butchering them on the spot. The crazed soldiers butchered onlookers, too, innocent by-standers, even children. It was a terrible ending to a battle, even by the customs of the time. And by the customs of the time, Charles Edward Stuart should have been brought to trial for treason, as the Duke of Monmouth had before him, and ended his life on the scaffold. As it was, with the help of Flora MacDonald, he escaped through the Hebrides disguised as a woman and made it back to France alive.

The implementation of the Duke of Cumberland's orders shocked many people at the time. The Duke, whose forename was William, was reviled by many under the nickname Stinking Billy, though flattered by his supporters as Sweet William. The brutality of Cumberland's suppression of the Jacobites after Culloden effectively brought Jacobitism to an end as a political and military cause. Charles himself did not accept this. He went on, even after Culloden, trying to enlist support.

Prince Charles Edward Stuart may have lived out the remainder of his life in frustration, but the consequences of his Jacobite Rebellion, the '45, for Scotland were truly devastating. The Hanoverian government was now determined, after two major Jacobite rebellions, that there should never be another. Clans that had supported Prince Charles suffered severely for it. Their lands were confiscated, clansmen were evicted and their homes burnt down. The Scottish Highlands were seen as a hotbed of sedition and a systematic clearance of the Highlands got under way. Huge areas were emptied of people. The evicted people were in some cases to drift to the towns in the Central Lowlands, accelerating the process of urbanisation and industrialisation there. In others they were to emigrate, many to Canada and America. Over the next 200 years the process continued as Highland areas became so depopulated that the surviving communities were no longer viable; the emptying continued long after the original motive disappeared. The emptiness of the Scottish Highlands today is not, as some people assume, due to the rigour of the physical environment. It is man-made.

There was a concerted attempt to destroy clan culture. Clansmen were forbidden to carry weapons and to wear Highland dress, which was perceived as a kind of military uniform. The bagpipes were outlawed, because they were used, like bugles in England, to give military signals; the pipes were not a musical instrument, but an accoutrement of war. The onslaught on Highland people and their culture was quite unlike anything that has happened anywhere else in north-west Europe in modern times. We have to look to central Europe and the Jewish Holocaust to find an analogue.

The Jacobite cause removed itself from the political scene by the oldest form of natural wastage: the family simply petered out. Prince Charles Edward Stuart married in 1772 with a view to providing a dynastic heir, but it was said that he was by then impotent, and he died in 1788 without issue. He did have a daughter, Caroline, by his mistress Clementina in 1760, but Caroline was illegitimate and in any case died without issue herself. Charles's brother Henry became a cardinal and he too died without issue in 1807. Later claimants to be Stuart descendants depend on unverified stories of secret births and smuggled babies; the House of Windsor is probably safe enough.

THE AMERICAN WAR OF INDEPENDENCE
(1775–1783)

The American War of Independence, or American Revolutionary War as it is also known, was fought between Great Britain and thirteen British colonies on the north-eastern seaboard of North America. This war occupies an important, almost mythic, role in the popular ideology of America and as such it has often been simplified (when it was in fact extremely complex). It has also been exaggerated: some of the 'battles' were little more than brawls. One feature of the war that later generations of Americans forget is that it was as much a civil war as a war between the colonies and Britain. During the war, many of the colonists remained loyal to the British Crown, and at the war's close as many as 100,000 of these loyalists fled abroad, not wanting to have any part of the mutiny. Another aspect of the war that is often glossed over is that it was a world war: Canada, France, Spain and the Netherlands were all involved in the fighting, as well as the thirteen American colonies and Britain.

ORIGINS – THE DEVELOPING POLITICAL CONFLICT

The Revolutionary War, like so many others before and since, had its origins in an earlier war, the Seven Years War. In North America this was known as the French and Indian War. Several countries were involved, with France and Britain being on opposite sides. At its end, the 1763 Treaty of Paris ceded French territory in North America to Britain; General Wolfe's victory at Quebec had helped to secure Canada for the British Crown. As a result of this British show of military strength in Canada, the colonists of the thirteen American colonies further south could feel much safer than before from any territorial threat that came from the French.

The French and Indian War that made the colonists safe had cost the British a great deal of money, yet the American colonists took for granted this British foreign policy which provided them with defence. They had no army or navy of their own and relied entirely on the British army and navy to defend them. In the wake of the war, the British government decided, logically, to press the colonists to pay more towards the high cost of defending them. Britain had run up a war debt. This additional taxation was deeply resented by the colonists, who portrayed it as an unwarranted imposition. The fanning of this resentment to the point of revolution was engineered by American propagandists. But their task was made easier by the inept and insensitive way in which the British government introduced one tax after another.

In 1764, the Sugar Act was passed by the English Parliament, putting additional duties on imported sugar, textiles, coffee and wine. The duties on foreign goods reshipped out from England were doubled. At a town meeting in Boston in May 1764, James Otis raised an objection to 'taxation without representation' and urged a united resistance to the imposition of taxes from England. Shortly afterwards, Boston merchants started to boycott British luxury goods.

In March 1765, the English Parliament passed the Stamp Act, the first direct tax on the American colonists. Under this measure, all printed matter was taxed, including newspapers, pamphlets, legal documents and licences. The colonists objected very strongly to this. In the same month, an equally objectionable but very different requirement was made in the form of the Quartering Act. This required colonists to house and feed British troops. That same year an underground organisation opposed to the Stamp Act was founded, called the Sons of Liberty; violent intimidation was used to compel the British stamp agents to resign. Then a formal Stamp Act Congress was convened in New York. This sent a resolution to George III petitioning the repeal of the Stamp Act and stating that taxation without representation was a violation of the colonists' civil rights. In 1766, the New York assembly

Queen Boudicca was the warrior queen of the Iceni, a British tribe which rose in revolt against the Romans in 61 AD*. He she can be seen attempting to rouse her countrymen.*

The Templar knights, in their distinctive white mantles each with a red cross, were among the best fighting units of the Crusades.

King Charles I (centre) kneeling on scaffold at his execution during the English Civil War (1639–1651).

Members of the British 13th Light Dragoon surround Colonel Doherty (centre, with beard) as he gives a speech during the Crimean War.

British troops, using horse-drawn transport, move up the line during the Second Battle of Ypres during World War I.

Pearl Harbor battleship row in 1941 during World War II.

Moslems waiting to leave for Pakistan in September 1947, as they seek protected transport to Dot Purana Qila, an ancient fort in Pakistan, where many refugees had gathered during the period of partition in India.

During the Gulf war (1990–91), retreating Iraqi forces set fire to more than 600 Kuwaiti oil wells, which continued to burn for up to nine months.

refused to comply with General Gage's request to enforce the Quartering Act to house his troops. Then the British backed down a little. The Stamp Act was repealed. In America there were celebrations when the news arrived, but also riots as the New York colonists refused to quarter British troops.

The so-called Boston Massacre in 1770 was a step along the way to the demand for independence. This was an incident in which British troops fired on a mob that had attacked a British sentry outside the State House in Boston. Another, and far more famous, step along the way was the Boston Tea Party of 1773, when British-taxed tea was emptied into the harbour. Less obtrusively, but probably more decisively, was the gradual takeover of the colonial militias by officers who were sympathetic towards the American revolutionary cause, replacing those who were sympathetic to the pro-British loyalists. The militias were, in other words, being politicised in the run-up to a revolutionary war. But while all of this was going on, huge numbers of ordinary American colonists remained loyal to the British Crown and had no interest in rebellion.

In 1775, revolutionaries took control of the governments of each of the thirteen colonies, set up the Second Continental Congress and formed a Continental Army. When the war started, there was no American army or navy. Each colony had its own local militia, not very well trained, not very well equipped and usually without uniforms. The militias served for only short periods and were reluctant to travel very far. They were therefore in every way unsuited for the task of concerted action against a professional 'enemy' army and navy. The Continental Congress founded a regular army in June 1775, but only on paper. Throughout the war the regular army was being developed by George Washington, its newly appointed commander-in-chief.

At the end of the war, both the Continental Army and the Continental Marines were disbanded. Altogether, during the course of the war, 250,000 colonists served as fighters of one sort or another in the revolutionary cause, though there were no more than 90,000 serving at once and the largest number of men that Washington commanded in the field was under 17,000. By comparison, in 1775, the British army was also relatively small, only 36,000 regulars in all, and more had to be recruited during the war. These were supplemented by the hiring of 30,000 German mercenaries. The British (and German) troops stationed in North America amounted to over 60,000 men, though they were spread over a huge distance from Florida to Canada. In terms of general numbers, the two sides were fairly evenly matched.

THE MILITARY PHASE

In the run-up to the war, Boston was the scene of a good deal of revolutionary activity. Lieutenant-General Thomas Gage, the British commander-in-chief for North America, had his headquarters there; he commanded four regiments, consisting of approximately 4,000 men in all, from Boston.

On the night of 18 April 1775, General Gage sent 700 men to seize munitions that were being stored by the colonial militia at Concord in Massachusetts. When the colonists realised what was about to happen, riders including Paul Revere alerted people out in the countryside. When British troops entered Lexington the next morning they were met by seventy-seven minutemen formed up on the village green. (A minuteman was a soldier because he was ready to march at a minute's notice.) Shots were exchanged and several of the minutemen were killed. The British troops moved on to Concord, where they were routed by a force of 500 minutemen. The British were obliged to retreat all the way back to Boston, and they were attacked by thousands of colonial militiamen as they went.

These skirmishes, which are rather grandly referred to as the Battles of Lexington and Concord, were the opening actions of the war. With the British already in rapid retreat, the militia surrounded Boston to bottle them up. British reinforcements arrived by sea and on 17 June 1775 the British under General Howe took the Charlestown peninsula at the Battle of Bunker Hill. The outcome was unclear, as the Americans fell back but the British suffered so many casualties that they could not follow the action through. The Boston siege was left unbroken and Howe replaced Gage as commander-in-chief.

In July, the new American commander, Washington, arrived on the outskirts of Boston to take command of his colonial forces. He realised at once that supplies of gunpowder were inadequate; by the end of the following year nearly all of the gunpowder was imported from France. Meanwhile there was a military stand-off that lasted several months. In the spring, cannon captured at Fort Ticonderoga were positioned on hills overlooking the British positions. Howe's situation then become untenable, and he and his troops withdrew in March, sailing to the naval base at Halifax, Nova Scotia.

During the military stand-off, the Continental Congress tried another initiative. Congress had already tried and failed to get the French Canadians to join as a fourteenth colony. When that was turned down, Congress instigated an invasion of Canada, with the idea of getting the British out of Quebec. The expedition that followed was a disastrous failure in military terms, and also in political terms. Invading Canada changed the views of many people in Britain who had been sympathetic to the American colonists' cause. Now that the Americans showed that they were aggressors, they lost such support as they had in Britain and the majority in Britain were ready to see violent measures freely used against them.

Howe had withdrawn from Boston and tried to capture New York. Washington's defence of the city consisted of 20,000 troops divided between Manhattan and Long Island. Meanwhile, British troops assembled on Staten Island. Washington had the newly written *Declaration of American Independence* read to his troops, to inspire them and show that there was no going back. The British landed 22,000 troops on Long Island on 27 August 1776, pushing the much smaller American force back to Brooklyn Heights. This was the biggest battle in the entire war. Though retreating, Washington successfully transferred his army to Manhattan. On 15 September, Howe landed 12,000 men on Manhattan, quickly taking control of the city. Washington fell back to Harlem Heights and then back again as Howe advanced. Then, instead of pursuing and destroying the American army, as he could have done, Howe returned to Manhattan. In fact Howe missed several opportunities to crush the dwindling American army.

General Cornwallis did give chase through New Jersey until, in early December, Washington and his army withdrew across the Delaware into Pennsylvania. That seemed to bring the campaign to a close for the year, and the British army settled into its winter quarters. There was every prospect that the British would finish off the American army in the spring. The outlook for the Continental Army was poor. The army was down to only 5,000 men fit for duty. When enlistments ran out at the year end, that number would drop to 1,400.

But Washington was a genius. He decided to do the unexpected. On Christmas night he crossed the Delaware by stealth and made a surprise attack. At the Battle of Trenton (26 December 1776) he captured both Trenton and 1,000 German mercenaries. Cornwallis set off to retake Trenton, but Washington surprised him again by attacking the British rearguard at Princeton (3 January 1777). After giving the Americans a major boost to morale, Washington entered his winter quarters.

The American cause was greatly advanced by the incompetence of the British military commanders and their political masters. The plan for military operations for 1777 should have involved a co-ordinated strategy for the two British armies in North America, Carleton's in Canada and Howe's in New York. Instead of a single unified, integrated campaign, two campaigns were approved in London by Lord George Germain; because of poor planning, poor communication and personal rivalry, these campaigns did not work in conjunction. Howe captured Philadelphia, but the northern army was forced to surrender at Saratoga. After this disastrous 1777 campaign, both Howe and Carleton were to resign.

The first of the 1777 campaigns by the British was General Burgoyne's expedition from Canada to seize the Lake Champlain and Hudson River corridor. With that corridor in British hands, New England would be isolated from the rest of the colonies. Burgoyne led the main force of 10,000 men along Lake Champlain towards Albany in New York State, while a smaller second force moved along the Mohawk Valley to meet Burgoyne at Albany. Burgoyne started out in June, and recaptured Fort Ticonderoga. After that his progress was slowed down by Americans who felled trees in his path. Meanwhile the smaller force laid siege to Fort Stanwix. Half of this force consisted of Native Americans led by

Joseph Brant, the Mohawk leader. After interventions by American militiamen, the British broke off the siege and retreated to Canada.

Burgoyne's army was now down to 6,000 men, but he was determined to press forward to Albany, a controversial and perhaps reckless decision. General Gates with an American army of 8,000 were entrenched 16 km (10 miles) south of Saratoga in New York State. Burgoyne tried to move round the Americans, but was drawn into battle at the First Battle of Saratoga. Burgoyne's situation was now very serious indeed. He hoped that Howe's army from New York City was on the way, but it was not. In a catastrophically unco-ordinated action, Howe had sailed away to capture Philadelphia. American militiamen arrived to reinforce Gates's army. By early October he had 11,000 men. At a Second Battle of Saratoga, Burgoyne surrendered on 17 October.

It was the fulcrum, the turning point of the war. The confidence of the Americans was boosted. More important still, the Saratoga victory encouraged the French to join the war on the American side. It more than compensated for the loss of Philadelphia, where Howe for once outmanoeuvred Washington, who had to retreat and let Howe enter Philadelphia unopposed.

Washington wintered at Valley Forge, 32 km (20 miles) from Philadelphia. During that 1777–78 winter, 2,500 men, a quarter of Washington's army, were lost through disease and exposure. Yet the following spring the surviving soldiers emerged in good fighting shape, thanks to a modern Prussian training programme introduced by Baron von Steuben. Howe was replaced by General Clinton as British commander-in-chief, and Clinton had different ideas. He abandoned Philadelphia so that he could reinforce British control over New York City, which, now that the French were in the war, was suddenly vulnerable to French naval power.

Washington shadowed Clinton as Clinton withdrew from Philadelphia and forced him into battle at Monmouth (28 June 1778). The battle was indecisive, but significant in being the last major battle in the north. Clinton arrived in New York in July. He was right about the French threat; he arrived just before a French fleet arrived under Admiral d'Estaing. Washington, still shadowing, returned to White Plains to the north of New York City. The two armies were where they had been two years earlier, except that now the war was international.

France signed the Treaty of Alliance with the United States on 6 February 1778. Spain entered the war as a French ally in June 1779, though Spain had initially not been keen to recognise the independence of a colony; Spain was a state with colonial possessions of its own. The Netherlands became involved in the war in 1780. All three countries had been giving the Americans financial support since the start of the war, all three with a view to weakening the power of Britain. It was a clear case of 'my enemy's enemy is my friend.'

In England, King George III realised that there was no hope of defeating the American colonists while Britain was engaged in a war in Europe. But he was determined to punish the rebel colonies by keeping 30,000 British troops garrisoned at various points in North America indefinitely, and having them blockade and attack the colonists' ports. He wanted to encourage the Native Americans to attack civilians in frontier settlements. He wanted 'to punish [the colonists'] contumacy by the indefinite prolongation of a war which promises to be eternal.' He 'would keep the rebels harassed, anxious and poor, until the day when, by a natural and inevitable process, discontent and disappointment are converted into penitence and remorse.' In the end, the king of England thought, the Americans would plead to return to his authority, like a justly punished child. How wrong he was!

At the outbreak of the American War of Independence, Britain ruled the waves. The Royal Navy had more than 100 ships of the line in service as well as many smaller vessels, though the ships were ageing and in poor condition. In the early stages of the war, Britain used these ships mainly to ferry land troops to North America and move them along the American coastline. The Americans by contrast possessed no ships of the line at all, and depended on privateers to molest and worry the British ships, a tactic that proved very effective. In October 1775, the Continental Congress authorized the building a small Continental Navy, to be used mainly for raiding. The first conspicuous action by this new navy was the capture of HMS *Drake* in April 1778.

Once the French came into the war the supremacy of the British fleet was contested. Initially the Franco-American alliance did not work very well, partly because the French had a much wider perspective; they hoped to capture British colonies in the West Indies before assisting the Americans in their struggle for independence. In fact French military aid did not yield any results at all until the arrival in July 1780 of an army led by the Comte de Rochambeau. The Spanish too had an agenda of their own in joining the war. They wanted an opportunity to capture Minorca and Gibraltar from the British. In February 1782, a joint French and Spanish attack successfully took Minorca, which Spain then kept; they never did get Gibraltar.

This widening of the Revolutionary War saw a great deal of action taking place in the West Indies. Several islands changed hands. In April 1782, at the Battle of the Saintes a British fleet under Admiral Rodney defeated a French fleet under Admiral de Grasse. This battle brought to an end any possibility that France and Spain were going to take Jamaica and other Caribbean colonies away from the British.

The open conflict between France and Britain in North America and the Caribbean increased the tension between the two countries, sparking a conflict over India. This started a Second Anglo-Mysore War in 1780. This war was fought between the British government of Madras and Tipu Sultan, who was the native ruler of the kingdom of Mysore and a major ally of France. This war closed with the Treaty of Mangalore; it was the last occasion when a native Indian prince or king was able to dictate terms to the British.

The Revolutionary War also led directly to conflict between Britain and the Netherlands. In 1780, the British made a pre-emptive strike against the Dutch in order to stop them from taking part in the League of Armed Neutrality. This was a declaration by several European states that they would continue neutral trade during the American War of Independence. The British saw this as giving aid to the American rebels. The fact that the Dutch government was openly displaying a friendly attitude towards the American colonists also inflamed the British. The Anglo-Dutch War that resulted went on until 1784, and proved to be disastrous to the Dutch economy.

Meanwhile, in the southern part of North America, Clinton and the British army had some successes. In December 1778, a British expedition from New York succeeded in capturing Savannah in Georgia. In October the following year, a combined French and American attempt to retake Savannah failed. Clinton then laid siege to Charleston and captured it in May 1780. It then looked certain that Clinton would completely conquer the South. Organised military action by the American colonists was collapsing. By August, General Cornwallis was set to invade North Carolina.

Then one wing of Cornwallis's army was completely defeated at the Battle of Kings Mountain in October 1780. There was another decisive defeat of a British army at the Battle of Cowpens in January 1781. Gradually, in a series of battles, the British were worn down. The American colonists were led by General Nathanael Greene, who memorably said, 'We fight, get beat, rise and fight again.'

Cornwallis moved north into Virginia. In March 1781, Washington sent General Lafayette to organise the defence of Virginia against Cornwallis. Lafayette skirmished with the British, not wanting to risk a major confrontation in a set-piece battle until he had reinforcements. Frustrated that he could not bring Lafayette to battle, Cornwallis moved his forces to Yorktown in July, so that he could, as he thought, transport them by sea on British naval vessels back to New York.

THE END OF THE WAR

A critical moment in the ending of the war came at Yorktown in October 1781. The previous month a French naval force defeated a British fleet at the Battle of the Chesapeake. This cut off Cornwallis's planned escape route by sea. Sensing that he had Cornwallis trapped, Washington rushed to get American and French soldiers from New York to lay siege to Cornwallis at Yorktown. A combined French and American force numbering 17,000 began the siege of Yorktown in early October. Cornwallis saw immediately that his position was hopeless and surrendered on 19 October 1781.

News of the Yorktown surrender came as a political thunderbolt in England. The peace party gained the ascendancy at Westminster and there were no further military campaigns on North American soil. The war continued at sea in the West Indies between the French and British fleets. In the commercial shipping lanes around the world, American ships repeatedly attacked British merchantmen, and this had a noticeable effect on British trading; merchants applied increasing pressure on politicians to get the war stopped.

Lord North, the British prime minister who had presided over the war, resigned in March 1782. Within weeks, there was a Commons vote to end the war. The formal end did not come until the signing of the Treaty of Paris in September 1783; this was ratified by the US Congress in January 1784.

Aftermath

The death toll in the American War of Independence is not known for certain, but relatively few men died in battle. Of an estimated 25,000 American colonists who died in active military service, 17,000 died of disease (or of neglect while British prisoners of war). Of 19,740 British servicemen who died, 18,500 died from disease, mainly of scurvy. About 42,000 British sailors deserted during the war. The cost to the British in money was also considerable: £80 million.

The War of Independence was a war that the British might have won, but there were several reasons why they did not. One was the logistical problem created by the army's distance from home, not only in transporting supplies but in communicating reports and orders; instructions from London were often two months out of date by the time they arrived in America. Another was the low quality of the political and military leadership. Another was the fact that the colonies had not been centrally organised before the war, so there was no clear power centre, the capture of which would have meant victory and the decisive end of the war. Another was the involvement of France as an American ally. It is certain that the colonists would have lost but for the financial and military support given by France.

The war played a significant role in the development of race relations in America. Washington lifted the existing ban on black enlistment in his Continental Army in 1776, leading to the recruitment of 5,000 black soldiers; over 20,000 black soldiers served on the British side. Most

Native Americans were opposed to the colonists as their activities encroached on native land. An estimated 13,000 Native American warriors fought on the British side, with the Iroquois contributing the largest contingent.

The greatest significance of the war lay in its outcome. The thirteen colonies were colonies no longer but an autonomous state, the United States of America. In a very real sense, the war marked the beginning of the history of the United States.

The new nation was created with unusual suddenness, and it was necessary to explain to the colonists who were going into battle, perhaps to die in battle, what it was they were fighting for. In 1776, Thomas Jefferson wrote it down for them. His *Declaration of Independence* became the foundation stone of the new state. It is full of the powerful new ideas and ideals of the Enlightenment, fresh from Revolutionary Europe. Some sections of the Declaration are a specific attack on George III and his government, and these are very time- and situation-specific, but the more general statements still have a powerful resonance today.

> *We hold these truths to be self-evident, that all men are created equal, that they are endowed by their Creator with certain unalienable Rights, that among these are Life, Liberty and the pursuit of Happiness . . . That to secure these rights, Governments are instituted among Men, deriving their just powers from the consent of the governed . . . That whenever any Form of Government becomes destructive of these ends, it is the Right of the People to alter or to abolish it, and to institute new Government, laying its foundation on such principles and organising its powers in such form, as to them shall seem most likely to effect their Safety and Happiness.*

THE FRENCH REVOLUTION

(1789–95)

One of the commonest types of conflict in history is the revolt, the attempt by a group of people or sometimes an entire population to resist or overturn a government decision – or indeed to overturn the government itself. A revolution is a much larger-scale conflict, one that usually involves a large proportion of a country's population, and is aimed at overturning and replacing the government. It is usually highly organized rather than spontaneous. One momentous afternoon, on 14 July 1789 in the palace of Versailles, the Duc de La Rochefoucauld-Liancourt went to the French king, Louis XVI, to tell him that the people of Paris had stormed the Bastille, the stronghold of Paris. Louis XVI exclaimed, 'Why, this is a revolt!' The duke replied, 'No, sire. It is a revolution.' The duke was right. It was the French Revolution.

The French Revolution, which was in its special way one of the greatest conflicts in history, was different from any other previous revolution. It contained within itself several revolutions. The background to it was, as in other revolutions, a desire to put right perceived evils in the system of government. But the successive waves of revolution that followed represented successive efforts by different people and different factions to replace an unsatisfactory system of government with an ideal government. It was idealism more than anything else that marked this revolution out as different. Robespierre was one of the great ideologues of the French Revolution, and he asked himself the question, 'What does this mysterious science of government and legislation amount to? To putting into the laws the moral truths culled from the works of the philosophers.' That view was widespread among the revolutionaries, but Robespierre was the most rigid, extreme and fanatical in pursuing it.

The French Revolution was prompted by the survival into the late eighteenth century of a virtually unaltered and unevolved medieval system of government. It was an extraordinary anachronism, an absolute monarchy, with a monarch dispensing feudal privileges. The beneficiaries of these privileges were the aristocracy and the Catholic clergy, and the privileges were enjoyed on a grand scale and flaunted before an impoverished lower class and an increasingly resentful and restless middle class. Whereas in England the absolutism of monarchy had been eroded away over several centuries, with power increasingly diverted to Parliament, in France it had somehow survived unmodified. What happened during the complexity, chaos and carnage of the Revolution was that the old system of governing France, the *ancien régime*, was completely swept away. Instead a new system was put in place based on the principles of the Age of Enlightenment, principles that included republicanism, citizenship and inalienable human rights. It was a great irony of the Revolution that, in the pursuit of these high ideals, people stooped to committing acts of barbarity, terrible atrocities that even now, after the horrors of the Third Reich, are still hard to believe.

CAUSES

There is endless disagreement among historians about the precise way in which the French Revolution came about. One widely held view is that the unacceptable levels of privilege and luxury enjoyed by the upper class (the aristocracy and the clergy) provoked an alliance of revolt formed by the rising middle class (the bourgeoisie), the under-privileged rural peasants and the wage earners in the towns and cities. That comes close to the idea of a Marxist class struggle. Another view is that the revolution began in a different way entirely, with various movements for social and political reform, some activated by the middle classes, others activated by enlightened and well-meaning aristocrats. These movements for reform then spiralled out of control.

Either way, the provocation came from various unsatisfactory features of the *ancien régime*. One was the burden of successive wars that France had been involved in during the eighteenth century. That burden was felt in the absence of any social services or pensions for war veterans, and it was also felt in an unmanageable national debt. The debt exaggerated the effects of what was already a grossly unfair system of taxation. The Catholic Church levied its own tax on agricultural production, the *dîme*, which struck hardest at the poorest peasants, many of whom were malnourished as a result.

The upper class noblemen and noblewomen flaunted their wealth and privilege. The lavishness of court life at Versailles was in itself a great provocation to revolt, given the plight of the poor and the weak state of the French economy. There were high levels of unemployment and high prices for bread, resulting in high levels of malnutrition, famine and starvation; this situation worsened in the months leading up to the Revolution.

There were political factors, too. In the Age of Enlightenment, there was increasing resentment of absolute monarchy among educated middle class people such as merchants and doctors, who were well aware of the very different status of their peers in countries like the Netherlands and Britain. The peasants resented their lords; both peasants and bourgeois resented the privileges of the clergy. There was general dissatisfaction with Catholic control over institutions, especially by the large numbers of Protestants. There was a general aspiration for liberty, by which was meant things like rights of citizenship, justice and freedom of thought and belief. This in turn led increasingly to the desire for a republic.

The focus for these many dissatisfactions became the king himself, when he dismissed two financial advisors, Jacques Necker and the Baron de Laune, who had represented the interests of the people. These dismissals pointed up the miserable failure of Louis XVI and the people around him to address any of France's problems. A background problem was the character of Louis XVI, who was a well-meaning though not very intelligent and rather unworldly man.

THE ESTATES-GENERAL OF 1789

The serious worsening of France's financial predicament led to the calling of an Assembly of Notables in February 1787 by Loménie de Brienne, Louis XVI's finance minister. This was a meeting of government officials, bourgeois, clergy and nobles who had been selected to make a think tank. The group was asked to approve a new land tax which, for the very first time, would apply to the property of nobles and clergy. The assembly rejected the new tax, instead calling for the king to call the Estates-General. In August 1788 the king agreed; the Estates-General was to be convened in May 1789. By then, Jacques Necker was Louis' finance minister.

In the run-up to the 1789 Estates-General, books of grievances were prepared across France. These were lists of complaints from the different orders of society; anyone could write about their problem in the local book of grievance. The process, which lasted for some months, created an atmosphere of expectation that improvements and reforms were on the way at last. At the same time, there was concern that the government would constitute the assembly in such a way as to produce a result that it liked. To forestall this, the *Parlement* of Paris insisted that the Estates-General must meet according to the forms of the previous meeting, which had been way back in 1614. The people who made this demand were probably unaware what the forms of 1614 had been, but the demand created a great stir. In fact there had, in 1614, been equal numbers of deputies representing the three estates, with each estate being given a single vote. The First Estate was the clergy; the Second Estate was the nobility; the Third Estate was the middle and lower classes. The estates voted by order, the First Estate first, and so on. A group of Parisian liberals agitated against voting by order. Instead they wanted the Third Estate doubled and they wanted the voting to be by headcount. Necker agreed that the Third Estate should be doubled, but wanted to leave the matter of voting by headcount until the meeting of the Estates.

Disputes and debates like these raised the temperature, and fuelled the general resentment. Pamphlets were produced by liberal members of the First and Second Estates arguing the importance of the Third Estate, among them the Abbé Sieyès and the Comte d'Antraigues. The count wrote, 'the People is the foundation of the State; it is in fact the State itself.' The Abbé Sieyès wrote, 'What is the Third Estate? Everything.'

There was a great sense of anticipation and excitement when the Estates-General finally met in May 1789, but the gathering was a great disappointment. There were speeches by Necker and Lamoignon, who was the keeper of the seals, though these gave little guidance to the deputies. The matter of voting by headcount was put aside for the moment, and the meeting ground to a halt on a technical procedural issue – how the Third Estate would provide its credentials.

THE NATIONAL ASSEMBLY (1789)

On 10 June, the Abbé Sieyès proposed that the Third Estate should verify its own powers and invite the other two estates to attend, though not wait for them. Two days later, they did so. Then, as if feeling their new-found power, the Third Estate went on to vote a much more radical issue. They declared themselves the National Assembly. They invited the other estates to join in, but made it clear that they would debate and govern the nation's affairs whether the others attended or not.

The king tried to keep control of what was happening. In particular he wanted to stop the Assembly from meeting, so he provocatively ordered the Salle des Etats to be cleared on the feeble pretext that it needed to be got ready for a royal speech in two days' time. The weather was poor, so an outdoor meeting was impossible. Instead the Assembly met in an indoor tennis court nearby. There on 20 June 1789 they swore the Tennis Court Oath, an oath not to disband until they had delivered France a constitution. Most of the representatives of the clergy joined them, and nearly fifty members of the nobility.

The king did not intervene directly, but troops began to gather in large numbers round Versailles and Paris. Indications of support arrived at the Assembly from Paris and other cities round France.

THE NATIONAL CONSTITUENT ASSEMBLY (1789–91)

On 9 July 1789, the National Assembly reconstituted itself as the National Constituent Assembly. Necker had by this time come to be regarded as a class traitor at the French court. Marie Antoinette and the king's younger brother, the Comte d'Artois, along with other members of the Privy Council, pressed the king to dismiss Necker. The climax came on 11 July, when Necker asked the king to ensure that the royal family lived within a budget in order to save money – and the king sacked him.

News of this was heard in Paris the next day and it was interpreted as a Versailles coup, with some sort of reactionary clampdown shortly to follow. There was also a fear that the arrival of the king's troops meant that the National Constituent Assembly was about to be dispersed. The Assembly went into continuous session in order to prevent any possibility of eviction (as before). Open rebellion erupted in Paris, with rioting and looting. The Paris mob soon had the French Guard on their side, because the militia along with the city had in effect been abandoned by the king.

The rioters in Paris realised that they needed more weapons and ammunition to keep the revolution going, and set their sights on the substantial stores in the Bastille, the fortress of Paris. As it happened, the Bastille was also a powerful symbol of monarchical tyranny. The huge, massive stone castle looked like a symbol of oppression, and it had also been used for at least 100 years for the incarceration of political opponents of the *ancien régime*. Storming the Bastille on 14 July was the iconic moment of the French Revolution, the single action that summed up the whole complicated process.

The struggle to take the stronghold went on all day. A ceasefire was ordered by the prison governor, the Marquis de Launay, to prevent a mutual massacre. But his humanity did not save him from the anger of the mob. He was beaten, stabbed and beheaded. This was an omen of what the Revolution was to bring to Paris, and the rest of France; more, much more, of this was to follow. The mob went back to the Hotel de Ville, where it accused the mayor, Jacques de Flesselles, of treachery. He was to be taken to the Palais Royal for a show trial, but the mob killed him on the way there. Alarming atrocities of this kind were to mark every phase of the Revolution from now on.

In the face of this, the king backed down. Lafayette took control of the National Guard in Paris. The president of the Assembly, Jean-Sylvain Bailly, became the new mayor of Paris. The king travelled to Paris on 27 July. When he accepted the red, white and blue tricolor cockade symbolising the Revolution, he was greeted with shouts of 'Vive le Roi!' Louis handled the situation well, and even backed down to the extent of recalling Necker to office. Necker then went too far in demanding, and getting, a general amnesty. This lost him a good deal of popular support. The nobles were unimpressed with the way things were going and began to leave the country to become *émigrés.* Some of them plotted against the Revolution from abroad, trying to organise a European coalition against Revolutionary France. This did the image of the nobility no good, and it was a line of activity that in the end would lose the king his life.

As the month of July wore on the idea of the Third Estate ruling France took hold. In the countryside, a general revolt called the Great Fear (Grand Peur) got under way. People got hold of the title-deeds of properties belonging to the privileged and wealthy, and burnt them. In some places, they set fire to the chateaux themselves.

On 4 August 1789, the National Constituent Assembly put an end to feudalism. These so-called August Decrees abolished the special privileges of the nobility and the tithes collected by the Church. Using the *American Declaration of Independence* as a model, the Assembly issued a *Declaration of the Rights of Man and of the Citizen.* This was a statement of principles on which a constitution could be built. A Senate was proposed, but there was disagreement as to its composition. Some wanted members to be appointed by the king after being nominated by the people. The nobles naturally wanted an aristocratic upper house, like the English House of Lords, but elected by the nobles. In the end, the idea of an upper house was abandoned and France was to have a single assembly. The king was to have a suspensive veto; in other words he could put a temporary stop to a measure's progress, delay legislation but not prevent it.

On 5 October 1789, working women from Paris marched to Versailles to protest at the difficulty of their economic circumstances. They suffered from bread shortages while the king and his court enjoyed rich banquets. One of their demands was that the king and his court should move to Paris; there they would be closer to the problem, see it for themselves and be more likely to address it. The very next day the king took his family from Versailles to Paris, accompanied by 20,000 soldiers of the National Guard.

The National Constituent Assembly abolished the historic provinces of France, replacing them with eighty-three *départements*, which were to be roughly similar in their populations and identical in administration. But the financial crisis was still there, unaddressed. It was Honoré Mirabeau who initiated the move, and Necker was given wide powers to resolve the problem.

THE CHURCH

Given its previous large-scale privileges, the Church was bound to be affected powerfully by the Revolution. Under the old regime, the Church was the biggest landowner in France. The *dîme* was abolished. Declaring Church property to be henceforth the property of the state went some way towards solving the acute financial crisis. To turn the vast estates into money, the government introduced paper currency, called *assignats*, the equivalent of British banknotes, which were backed by confiscated land. Monastic vows were abolished and the Church became a limb of the state. This made the clergy employees of the state; as such they would be required to take an oath of loyalty to the new constitution. As with many other aspects of the French Revolution, this was going much too far much too fast. Two leading clerics, the Archbishop of Aix and the Bishop of Clermont, walked out of the Assembly in disgust. The Pope did not accept the new arrangement and a rift developed between those clergy who swore the oath of loyalty and those who refused.

In the wake of these stern and draconian measures, there was violent action against the clergy during the next few years. Resentment that had been accumulating for decades against the privileges of the clergy boiled over. Throughout France, priests were thrown in prison, murdered or massacred. The Revolutionary de-Christianisation of France formally ended in 1801, when Napoleon established new guidelines for the Church-State relationship that lasted through the nineteenth century.

FACTIONS AND CLUBS

At the onset of the Revolution there was a convergence of views, an agreement that the old regime was unsatisfactory. Inevitably, as the new state was built virtually from scratch, differences of view emerged more and more strongly. These were expressed in the formation of factions. A right wing emerged under the leadership of Jacques de Cazalès and the Abbé Maury, and this was opposed to revolutionary change. Then there were the Royalist democrats, such as Necker, who wanted to see France re-organised along the British model as a constitutional monarchy. The so-called National Party was at the centre, and this included men like Mirabeau and Lafayette. Then there was the left, and at this stage there were very few revolutionaries who were as radical as this; Maximilien Robespierre, the little lawyer from Arras, was more or less on his own.

As the Assembly worked on to scrap more and more of the past, the conservative nobles were increasingly alienated. Armorial bearings and livery were abolished. More and more nobles emigrated. On 14 July 1790, crowds gathered in the Champ de Mars in Paris to celebrate the fall of the Bastille. A mass was celebrated, in which participants swore an oath of 'fidelity to the nation, the law and the king.' The king was trying his hardest to be seen to go along with the Revolution, however unpalatable he might have found it. He was there, in the Champ de Mars, with his family, celebrating the fall of the Bastille with the rest of Paris. But behind the scenes, with or without his knowledge, his court was encouraging every anti-revolutionary enterprise. In late 1790, there were several small-scale counter-revolutionary risings. They all failed.

This was the time when political clubs appeared. The best-known, and by far the most notorious, was the Jacobin Club. By August 1790,

152 clubs were affiliated with the Jacobin Club. There were also a Club of '89, a Club of the Impartials and a Monarchic Club. Members of the Monarchic Club tried to curry favour with the masses by handing out bread. It did not work. In fact there were so many protests about the club and so many riots directed against it that in January 1791 the Paris authorities closed it down.

In the winter of 1791, the Assembly considered legislating against the *émigrés.* In the debate on the subject, the argument in favour of legislation hinged on the safety of the state, and the argument against on the freedom of individuals. Mirabeau argued that the proposed legislation was too draconian, and the legislation was dropped. But then, in April 1791, Mirabeau died and his voice of reason and moderation had no successor; now the legislation went through.

THE KING'S FLIGHT AND THE CONSTITUTION

The most famous would-be *émigré* was Louis XVI himself. But the new legislation meant that he was stopped (near the border) and taken back to Paris. At night on 20 June 1791, the king and his family secretly left the Tuileries Palace dressed in servants' clothes. The king was recognised at Varennes. That he was recognised at all was remarkable. In the days before television, before photography, before mass travel, very few people would have had a chance to see the king at close quarters. Yet he was recognised. The king and his family were taken back to Paris under guard, still in their disguises. Representatives of the Assembly (Pétion, Latour-Maubourg and Barnave) met them at Epernay and accompanied them. From this moment, Antoine Barnave became a supporter of the royal family, and a valued advisor. When they reached Paris, the royal family was met by a silent crowd. The Assembly suspended the king and both he and the queen were held under guard.

Most of the Assembly was still in favour of a constitutional monarchy, not a republic, and the compromise was a constitutional monarchy that left Louis XVI as little more than a figurehead. Jacques Brissot drew up a petition which made the point that in trying to leave the country, and nearly succeeding, the king had in effect abdicated already; in the eyes of the French people he was already deposed. A huge crowd gathered to sign Brissot's petition. There were big public demonstrations, fuelled by rabble-rousing speeches from Georges Danton and Camille Desmoulins. The Assembly summoned the National Guard under Lafayette to keep order. Lafayette was reduced to firing into the crowd and as many as fifty people were killed. The authorities shut down many of the political clubs, as well as newspapers like *l'Ami de Peuple*, published by Jean Paul Marat. Marat went into hiding in the Paris sewers; Danton fled to England.

There was an invasion threat. Holy Roman Emperor Leopold II together with the king's brother the Comte d'Artois and Frederick II of Prussia, issued a declaration that they considered the cause of Louis XVI to be their own and they demanded his liberation. They also demanded the dissolution of the Assembly. If their demands were refused, they said, they would invade. But this threat was extremely ill-judged. The French people had no respect for foreign kings and their wishes. The threat meant militarising the frontiers of France – and a new reason for hating Louis. The threat put him in more serious danger than ever. If he was seen as promoting the invasion of France by the kings of other countries, he could be portrayed as a traitor.

But still there was restraint on the part of the Assembly, not only in overlooking the king's flight to Varennes but in debarring themselves from service in the Legislative Assembly they were setting up. The new constitution was now ready, and it was submitted to the restored Louis XVI. He accepted it and wrote, 'I engage to maintain it at home, to defend it from all attacks from abroad, and to cause its execution by all the means it places at my disposal.' Louis addressed the Assembly, where he was enthusiastically applauded. Had the Assembly survived, so perhaps might Louis have survived. As it was, the Assembly voted itself out of existence on 29 September 1791.

THE LEGISLATIVE ASSEMBLY (1791–92)

Louis now had to share power with the an elected Legislative Assembly, but he still retained the right to choose his ministers. The new Assembly was a shambles. It proved unable to govern; it emptied the treasury and left the navy, army and general populace in an undisciplined state. It consisted of Feuillants (supporters of a constitutional monarchy), Girondists (liberal republicans), Jacobins (radical revolutionaries) and unaffiliated independents. In numbers, the Assembly was dominated by the Girondists and Jacobins.

One measure the new assembly attempted threatened *émigrés* with death. As a would-be *émigré* himself, the king vetoed that. Over the next few months, disagreements like this escalated into a constitutional crisis. The Revolution was ratcheted up to a more extreme level.

The events within France inevitably led to conflict with other countries, such as Austria. The king was keen on war, as he anticipated it would increase his personal popularity if there was a French victory; he could also see that his position might be strengthened if the Revolutionary government was defeated. He had nothing to lose by war and much to gain, whether France won or lost. France declared war on Austria in April 1792. Prussia joined in as Austria's ally. The Prussian army advanced until it was stopped at the Battle of Valmy in September 1792; then it retreated. But by then, Louis was in no position to gain anything from the outcome of the fighting.

CONSTITUTIONAL CRISIS

At night on 10 August 1792, a revolutionary mob attacked the Tuileries Palace in Paris, supported by the new and anarchic Paris Commune. The king and queen were taken prisoner and a session of the Legislative Assembly suspended the monarchy; only a third of the deputies were in attendance and most of them were Jacobins.

The national government by the Legislative Assembly was by now in obvious disarray, and it only functioned with the support of the Commune, which was in favour of insurgency. The Commune sent gangs of thugs into the prisons to murder prisoners, and sent a circular letter round to other French cities encouraging them to do the same. This outrageous and totally lawless behaviour brought virtually no response from the Assembly.

THE NATIONAL CONVENTION (1792–95)

A National Convention met in the autumn of 1792 with the brief to create a new constitution and, because of the power vacuum, the Convention became France's government by default. Nor did it hang back from tackling major issues. On its second day in session (20 September 1792) it abolished the monarchy and declared a republic. Now even the calendar had to be revolutionised; this was the start of Year One of the French Revolutionary Calendar.

The Austrian and Prussian armies threatened France again. The Brunswick Manifesto promised armed attack unless the monarchy was reinstated. Louis was now seen in France as a traitor, conspiring with France's enemies. On 17 January 1793, Louis XVI was condemned to death for 'conspiracy against the public liberty and the general safety' in the Convention, but by a small majority. He was nevertheless executed in the public square outside the Tuileries Palace four days later. The queen, Marie Antoinette, shared his fate on 16 October.

These executions inflamed France's enemies. The foreign wars multiplied, prices rose in France because of the disruption to production and trade, rioting flared up and counter-revolutionary activity started in some areas. The Jacobins took this as their opportunity to seize power, helping things along by whipping up popular antipathy to the Girondists among the Paris mob. It was a parliamentary coup – and also a revolution in itself.

THE TERROR (1793–94)

In June, Jacques Roux and Jacques Hébert took over the leadership of the National Convention. They demanded purges in the administration and a fixed low price for bread. They got the backing of the National Guard to arrest the leaders of the Girondists, including Jacques Brissot. Within a week, on 10 June 1793, the Jacobins had succeeded in winning control of the Committee of Public Safety. On 13 July, one of the Jacobin leaders, Jean Paul Marat, was assassinated in his bath by Charlotte Corday, a Girondist. This was a gift to the Jacobins, who were able to exploit the murder to increase their hold on power even further. The Revolutionary government became even more radical. Georges Danton was seen by Robespierre as a man who enjoyed luxury too much. He was removed from the Committee. On 27 July, Robespierre appeared, and soon became the more powerful member of the Committee as it became ever-more radical. Robespierre had the gift of eloquence. He could make almost any decision, however nasty or illogical, sound like the most natural and ethically sound outcome. He talked in poetic and flowery generalisations, which made everything he said sound highly idealistic.

The Convention adopted another new constitution, the first republican constitution of France. This was the Constitution of Year One. It was approved by a public referendum, but it was never actually applied. By that stage, normal legal processes had been suspended. The foreign wars demanded urgent responses and in August the Convention voted for general conscription. All citizens of France could be ordered to serve as soldiers or ancillary workers in the war effort.

On 5 September, bowing to pressure from the Paris mob, formally inaugurated the Reign of Terror. This was the systematic and brutal extermination of all enemies of the Revolution and marked the most radical phase of the Revolution. In less than two years over 18,000 people and perhaps as many as 40,000 were put to death in Paris and other cities. The guillotine had been devised just before the Revolution as a humane instrument of execution. It was now to become a killing machine that would facilitate execution on an industrial scale. It was easy to kill scores of people each day. The only problem was the way people living in the streets nearby complained about the stench of blood. The people who were sent to the guillotine were those accused of counter-revolutionary activity. This included voicing any thoughts that might hint at counter-revolution. It even included, in the case of Hébert, radical revolutionary zeal which exceeded that of Robespierre. Many were sentenced to death just because someone else had something to gain by their removal. The removal of Danton can only really be explained as a convenience for Robespierre. The conduct of the trials was irregular and often highly emotive in tone; they were little more than show trials, with the verdict and sentence a foregone conclusion.

Most of the victims were taken on open carts (tumbrils) through the Paris streets, where they were subjected to taunts and jeers from the crowd. Their journey ended in the middle of what is now the Place de la Concorde, where the guillotine had been erected on a scaffold. By this stage in the Revolution any dissent with the approved Jacobin line was described as counter-revolutionary. Now extremists like Hébert, the so-called *enragé*, and moderates like Danton were sent to the guillotine in the early months of 1794.

Chaotic and terrible though this purging episode was, the new government seems to have known how to organise warfare. The new Republican army was able to withstand and push back the armies of the Austrians, Prussians, Spanish and British. By the end of 1793, the Republican army was in the ascendancy. The problems of the poor were eased by the Ventôse Decrees (of February and March 1794), which arranged the confiscation of goods belonging to *émigrés* and other enemies of the Revolution; they were to be given to the needy.

On 7 June 1794, Robespierre introduced a new and completely artificial state religion. He asked the Convention to ratify the existence of God. The next day, he inaugurated the worship of the Supreme Being in a major public ceremony. It was an austere and threadbare affair, and it did not suit the red-blooded people of Paris, who watched this nonsense in hostile amazement. Robespierre's new religion and his executions of both moderate and ultra-radical Jacobins left him suddenly with very little support. He had, as they say, no constituency any more.

There was a reaction, a revolt, and it came on 27 July 1794. Robespierre and his associate Saint-Just were arrested and executed. The new government – in effect another revolution – was constituted mainly of Girondists, or at least those who had managed to survive the Reign of Terror. After taking power, they started to exact their revenge for the way they and their murdered associates had been treated. They even persecuted the Jacobins who had helped to topple Robespierre! They banned the hated and feared Jacobin Club and executed many of its members. This Girondist purge was known at the time as the White Terror.

The Convention gave its approval for another new constitution, the Constitution of the Year III. It was ratified by a plebiscite in September 1795. This final Revolutionary act created the Directory. It also set up the first two-chamber legislature in the history of France. The administrative structure consisted of a Council of the Five Hundred (with 500 representatives), a Council of Elders (with 250 senators) and five executive directors. These directors were to be named each year by the Elders from a list offered by the Five Hundred. And with this sober outcome, the French Revolution might have come to a peaceful close. The problem was that there had been too much blood-letting, too much change, too much instability. France was not ready to settle down just yet. It was in this uneasy and unstable aftermath of the French Revolution that Napoleon Bonaparte was able to seize his opportunity. Dictators often exploit conflict for their own ends.

Aftermath

By 1799, when the Directory was seen to have failed, the French Revolution itself seemed to be a failure. It led on to the career of Napoleon, which was a future none of the revolutionaries can have envisaged in their wildest dreams or nightmares. When Napoleon himself had gone in 1815, and bringing with his fall the ignominious defeat of France, the Revolution must have appeared to have been completely in vain. Tens of thousands of men, women and children had been cruelly killed – for nothing.

But there were far-reaching results that flowed from the radical sweeping away of the old regime. The tyranny of king, nobility and Church had gone. Instead the middle classes emerged as the dominant power, the merchants, the landowners, the professionals. Feudalism had gone, never to return. Social order was certainly not achieved by the French Revolution; that was only achieved by Napoleon's reaction to it in the Napoleonic Code.

The Revolution has been said to have unified France, but it must be obvious from what has been written here that it simply replaced one set of conflicts with another. It was an experiment in extreme political radicalism, and that experiment would be taken on a step further, on paper at least, by Karl Marx. It was an experiment in ultra-nationalist ideology, and that, too, would be taken a step or two further, by Adolf Hitler. The French Revolution had an extraordinary and profound influence on the way the modern world developed.

5

NINETEENTH-CENTURY CONFLICTS

THE NAPOLEONIC WARS

(1799–1815)

The Napoleonic Wars were to an extent a continuation and expansion of the European wars triggered by the French Revolution of 1789. One outstanding characteristic of these wars was their huge scale, which depended on a modern concept – mass conscription. The power of France rose rapidly as Napoleon Bonaparte's armies overran and conquered most of Europe. The Napoleonic Wars foreshadowed the rather similar wars precipitated by the dictator-led Axis powers. Like Hitler, Napoleon overreached himself by invading Russia; the collapse of Napoleon's military adventure had its beginning in his catastrophic invasion of Russia in 1812.

The second attempt to crush the French Republic came with the formation of the Second Coalition in 1798. This consisted of the Ottoman Empire, the Papal States, the Kingdom of Naples, Russia, Portugal and Britain. The French government, the Directory, was divided and corrupt, and there were inadequate funds to fight a war. Napoleon, who had already emerged as France's greatest military commander, was away campaigning in Egypt. As a result, France was repeatedly defeated by a coalition energised by British funding. Napoleon came back from Egypt in August 1799 and simply took over the reins of government in a coup on 9 November. He reorganised the French army and was able to catch the Austrians unprepared at the Battle of Marengo (1800), a conspicuous French victory. The decisive battle was the Battle of Hohenlinden (1800) on the Rhine, which led to a treaty under which Austria withdrew from the conflict, bringing the Second Coalition to an end.

Britain remained a strong political force in rallying resistance to France, and Napoleon understood that until Britain signed a treaty or was defeated France would not be left alone. For this reason he made Britain his next focus.

WAR BETWEEN FRANCE AND BRITAIN (1803–14)

The British felt safe from the French threat because of their supremacy at sea. Admiral Jervis declared to the House of Lords, 'I do not say that the French will not come. I say only that they will not come by sea.' The British were so strong at this time that they could hold off the French and simultaneously give long-term support to the Spanish in the Peninsular War (1808–14). Even so, the British signed the Treaty of Amiens in March 1802, though neither side appeared to have any intention of honouring it. The French went ahead and occupied towns along the Italian coast, while the British occupied Malta. Open hostilities between Britain and France broke out again in May 1803. By this stage the aim of the war had shifted. To begin with the British had sought to replace the succession of revolutionary governments in France, restoring the monarchy; now they only sought to oust Napoleon.

As if acknowledging that he had become the most feared man in Europe, Napoleon declared France an empire in May 1804 and on 2 December that year he crowned himself emperor in Notre Dame Cathedral in Paris.

In 1806, Napoleon set up what was called the Continental System. This was in effect a blockade directed against Britain; all French-controlled territories were closed to trade with Britain and the intention was to separate Britain from the European economy. The French army now looked infinitely stronger than Britain's. Britain had a standing army of at most 220,000 men, while the French army reached over 1.5 million. French agricultural production was far greater than Britain's. Where Britain was strong was in its navy (and therefore international commerce) and its industry. The Continental System never succeeded in isolating Britain.

THE THIRD COALITION

Napoleon was intent on invading Britain, mustering nearly 200,000 troops at Boulogne ready to cross the Channel. The only way he could get them across was by getting the British fleet out of the Channel. He devised a complicated decoy manoeuvre, which involved threatening British possessions in the West Indies. This failed when a British fleet under Collingwood managed to bottle the French fleet under the command of Admiral Villeneuve at Cadiz.

Nelson had earlier in the year been trying to keep Villeneuve bottled up in the Mediterranean, but he lost Villeneuve in March 1805 when he broke out into the Atlantic. Nelson had a hunch that Villeneuve had taken his fleet to the West Indies for safety and sailed there in pursuit. When Villeneuve heard that Nelson had arrived, he ran away again, taking his fleet hastily back across the Atlantic towards Europe, once more hotly pursued by Nelson. The French fleet was kept bottled up at Cadiz by Collingwood, while Nelson returned to England for a break. Then Nelson offered 'to give Monsieur Villeneuve a drubbing', an offer which the Admiralty accepted with alacrity, and Nelson left England for the last time.

He caught up with the French fleet off Cape Trafalgar, on the coast of Portugal, in late September 1805. The battle was one of those moments in history that becomes, in retrospect, a kind of pageant, because it is too colourful and melodramatic to be true. But it happened.

Villeneuve had orders from Napoleon to leave Cadiz in late September, but he judged that Nelson had thirty-one sail about 50 km (30 miles) west of Cadiz, more than a match for his fleet of thirty-three damaged ships. The main fleet was connected to the coast by a line of frigates; signals could pass from ship to ship so that Nelson knew when there was a change at Cadiz. Admiral Federico Gravina and his Spanish officers agreed on 7 October that the British fleet was a superior force, and that it was far too risky to engage it in battle. Nelson stayed far enough away to entice the Combined Fleet out. On 9 October, Nelson issued his famous Tactical Memorandum. He outlined a battle plan to break the enemy line in two places and destroy two-thirds of the

Combined Fleet, but left captains free to follow opportunities when they arose; 'no Captain can do very wrong if he places his ship alongside that of an enemy.' On 19 October, Villeneuve decided to go to sea. Nelson, now 70 km (45 miles) to the west, heard about it within three hours. On 20 October, the British had located the Combined Fleet, a regular line of twenty ships apparently making for Brest. Collingwood was summoned on board Nelson's flagship, the *Victory*, where he urged immediate attack. Nelson wanted to delay, partly because he was hoping for reinforcements, partly because the enemy was still too close to Cadiz, where another thirteen ships of the Combined Fleet lay in reserve. Nelson also thought that mid-afternoon was too late in the day for a decisive battle.

At daybreak on 21 October, Nelson was ready and he closed in. Villeneuve was horrified to see that Nelson had five more ships than he had thought. He formed his line of battle. During the next two hours, the British ships divided into two groups gradually forming into two parallel lines, one headed by Nelson in the *Victory*, the other by Collingwood in his recently re-coppered, and therefore fast, *Royal Sovereign*. Nelson led his line of ships straight at the centre of Villeneuve's line. Collingwood broke the line of the Combined Fleet about one-third from the back, and together they fulfilled Nelson's scheme to destroy the centre and rear of the enemy fleet.

Nelson was delighted. 'See how that noble fellow Collingwood carries his ship into action!' In the light wind, the British fleet closed on the Combined Fleet at a sedate walking speed while musicians played *Hearts of Oak, The Downfall of Paris* and *Rule Britannia* to stir the men. It was a festival day for Nelson, the day of the autumn fair at his home village of Burnham Thorpe. Oddly, he forgot to wear the sword given to him by his uncle, Maurice Suckling, that day; he had superstitiously worn it in every other action. Instead, as the British ships drew nearer and near the enemy, he sat in his cabin making adjustments to his will, leaving his mistress as a legacy for England to look after.

Just before the battle started, Nelson ordered the famous signal to be run up: 'England confides that every man this day will do his duty.' 'Confides' was meant in the sense 'is confident'. Then at the last moment, with his left hand he scribbled a change. It became 'England expects', which is how we remember it today. Collingwood was rather irritated by the nannying command, as it implied that there had been the possibility that they might not do their duty. He felt patronised by it, but was then struck by its personal warmth.

Nelson aimed for the fourteenth ship in the line, unsure where Villeneuve himself was because he had not shown his flag. As the enemy opened fire on Collingwood, Villeneuve and his admirals at last unfurled their flags. It was time for Captain Henry Blackwood, commander of the inshore watch and in effect Nelson's liaison officer, to leave and he was shaken when Nelson said, 'God bless you, Blackwood: I shall never speak to you again.' Then Nelson turned to attack Villeneuve, who was unexpectedly hiding in a frigate, and brushed past his stern. Suddenly the *Victory* was under heavy fire from all sides. Within moments fifty men were dead or wounded while the *Victory* had yet to open fire. Then she was able to fire a double broadside, damaging ships on both sides. The *Bucentaure* shook under the impact; Villeneuve was the only man left standing on her quarter-deck and a quarter of her guns had been wrecked.

Another enemy ship, the *Redoutable*, was blocking the *Victory*'s path, and Nelson's simple plan had misfired; he was suddenly trapped in the middle of the Combined Fleet and taking fire from all sides. Nelson asked Hardy, his captain, to choose a ship to ram, and Hardy chose the *Redoutable*.

Collingwood meanwhile had chosen one of the Spanish flagships, the *Santa Anna*, ran alongside her and fought a furious battle with her that went on for two hours. Twelve British ships were involved in this decisive phase of the battle, and the losses on them were very high. The highest losses were sustained by the *Victory* (132 dead), *Royal Sovereign* (141 dead) and *Bellerophon* (150 dead). But it was the death of Nelson himself that altered the character of the battle. While the *Victory* and *Redoutable* were locked together, Nelson continued to walk with Hardy on the quarter deck, dressed as always in full uniform, flamboyantly decorated with all his honours like a bird of paradise, while the French crew strafed the *Victory*'s decks with muskets and grenades, preparing to board. At 1.15 p.m. a shot fired from a French sharpshooter on the mizzen top of the *Redoutable* hit Nelson. Nelson was shot through the shoulder and mortally wounded. He languished in great pain for several hours in the cockpit, among the many other wounded and dying, receiving reports of the progress of the battle. He repeatedly muttered, 'Thank God I have done my duty', and died knowing that the battle was won. At the end he asked Hardy to kiss him.

The French meanwhile repeatedly tried to board and take the *Victory*, until they were beaten off by fire from the (British) *Temeraire*. Midshipmen on the *Victory* shot down Nelson's assassin. At 2.15 p.m., Villeneuve, his ship destroyed, surrendered to the captain of the *Conqueror*. He may have wished to die rather than surrender; in fact two of his rear admirals died in the action, and Gravina died of his wounds, months later. Nelson lived long enough to hear, at 3.50 p.m., that victory had been won and, after checking with Beatty the ship's surgeon that he really was dying, he composed his last remarks as he lay deep inside his ship. Finally, at 4.30 p.m., he died. There were 1,700 British dead and wounded, and 6,000 casualties in the Combined Fleet.

Among the 7,000 VIPs allowed into St Paul's Cathedral for Nelson's funeral in December was his opponent Villeneuve, now a British prisoner. Nelson was buried under a great sarcophagus made for, but not in the end used by, Cardinal Wolsey. The damage done to the French fleet by Nelson's ultimate victory ensured that the French could never contemplate an invasion of Britain. Although the Napoleonic Wars dragged on for another ten years after the Battle of Trafalgar, Britain was safe from any threat of a French invasion. Trafalgar also became a potent myth for Britain, raising national spirits for 150 years. Nelson himself, the sacrificial offering that made victory possible, became a great national hero. The painter Benjamin West even painted an allegorical picture, *The Apotheosis of Nelson*, in which Neptune supports the cloud on which Victory carries the dead Nelson up to the helmeted goddess Minerva; cherubs wait in the heavens with a laurel wreath. It sums up the unimaginable national hysteria that surrounded Nelson's death. But West was right; in winning Trafalgar and throwing his life away in the process, Nelson had become a national god. He had also, unwittingly, become a real-life Byronic hero.

Napoleon never again dared to challenge the supremacy of the British at sea, and knew that he could not ferry his invasion army across the Channel unmolested. He gave up the idea of invading Britain. He turned his attention back to his enemies on the mainland of Europe, and even before the *coup de grace* of Trafalgar he had ordered the invasion army at Boulogne to march off in the direction of Austria.

An Austrian army under Mack von Leiberich had invaded Bavaria, and the French army confronted them in the Battle of Ulm (September-October 1805). Napoleon surrounded the Austrian army and forced its surrender. Then Napoleon was able to occupy Vienna. There he faced a big Austrian-Russian army under the command of Kutuzov; the Russian tsar was also present. On 2 December, Napoleon won a great victory against the Austrian-Russian army in the Battle of Austerlitz in Moravia. After this, Austria once again signed a treaty, the Treaty of Pressburg, in December 1805 and retired from the Coalition.

Now Napoleon had an unbroken record of victories in land battles, but he had yet to experience the full weight of the Russian army.

THE FOURTH COALITION (1806–7)

As soon as the Third Coalition collapsed, a Fourth was formed, consisting of Saxony, Prussia, Russia, Sweden and Britain. At the same time, Napoleon created a Confederation of the Rhine out of many small German principalities in the Rhineland; his aim in joining these small states into a large unit was to make the control and administration of non-Prussian Germany easier. The process of course foreshadowed and prepared the way for the unification of Germany. Along the way, Napoleon raised the status of the rulers of the largest non-Prussian states, Bavaria and Saxony, to kings.

In August 1806, King Friedrich Wilhelm II of Prussia made the odd decision to go to war against France. It would have made more sense if he had done this the previous year, joining forces with Russia and Austria. The enlarged army just might have contained Napoleon, perhaps even reversed the outcome of Austerlitz. Napoleon personally led his army against a Prussian army at the Battle of Jena (14 October

1806), and defeated it. Another French army under Davout defeated a second and much bigger Prussian army at the Battle of Auerstadt on the same day. Napoleon advanced with speed, quickly annihilating the huge Prussian army, estimated to be 250,000 strong. It took only nineteen days in all. Napoleon entered Berlin on 27 October. He respectfully visited the tomb of Frederick the Great, saying to his own marshals, 'If he were alive, we wouldn't be here today.'

Napoleon's next step was to drive Russian troops out of Poland and create another new state, the Duchy of Warsaw. Then he turned north to engage the rest of the Russian army, which he routed at the Battle of Friedland on 14 June 1807. After that, Tsar Alexander was obliged to make peace with Napoleon at Tilsit.

In 1807, the British attacked Denmark, intent on capturing the Danish fleet. Given Napoleon's progress in the region, he could relatively easily have acquired the large Danish fleet, which would have changed the balance of sea power in France's favour. The French might have made good their losses at Trafalgar. The British successfully attacked Copenhagen and captured the Danish fleet, an action which angered the Danes and brought them into the war on the side of the French.

At the Congress of Erfurt (October 1808) Napoleon and Tsar Alexander agreed that Sweden should be compelled to join the Continental System. This led to the Finnish War, and this in turn to the splitting of Sweden into two countries, separated by the Gulf of Bothnia; the new country to the east of the Baltic became Finland.

THE FIFTH COALITION (1809)

The Fifth Coalition, an alliance of Britain and Austria against France, was set up as Britain fought against France in the Peninsular War. As before, Britain took the initiative and bore the brunt of the cost. As before, the sea was the main theatre of war between Britain and France, and the British navy won a series of victories around France's colonies as well as an important victory against 'neutral' Denmark in the Battle of Copenhagen (2 September 1807). There were also some land-based military campaigns. The Walcheren Expedition in 1809 was an attempt by the British army and navy to relieve an Austrian army beleaguered by the French. This was a British failure. The commander of the British army, John Pitt, the 2nd Earl of Chatham, failed to capture the French-controlled naval base at Antwerp. Most of the operations were guerrilla-style hit-and-run strikes by the British navy, delivering land troops where needed. The main problem throughout this phase was that Britain's allies continually failed to supply the troops they promised.

The conflict in Iberia (the Peninsular War of 1808-14) started when Portugal broke Napoleon's Continental System by continuing to trade with Britain. Spain too failed to support the system, so the Spanish alliance with France disintegrated and French troops invaded Spain. Eventually French troops occupied Madrid. It was this invasion of Spain that prompted British intervention. The French had little difficulty in defeating the Spanish, and forcing a British withdrawal from the peninsula at the Battle of Corunna (16 January 1809); the British were heavily outnumbered.

Meanwhile, renewed action by the Austrians forced Napoleon to withdraw many of his own troops, and his most talented generals, from the Iberian Peninsula, and they never returned. This weakened the French position in Spain to the point where the enormously talented British commander, Sir Arthur Wellesley (later Duke of Wellington), was able to regain ground when he arrived to take command; his predecessor had been killed at Corunna.

In the east, Napoleon assumed personal command for the counter-attack against Austria. He forced the Austrian army to withdraw from Bavaria and then advanced into Austria. The success of this well-organised campaign led Napoleon to move on too quickly. His hasty attempt at crossing the River Danube led to a major defeat at the Battle of Aspern-Essling (22 May 1809) – Napoleon's first significant defeat. But then his adversary, the Austrian commander Archduke Karl, did not follow up on his victory, leaving Napoleon to prepare for a new attempt to take Vienna.

Napoleon defeated the Austrian army at the Battle of Wagram (5-6 July 1809). It was during this battle that Napoleon demoted Marshal Bernadotte and ridiculed him in front of other officers. In doing so,

Napoleon made an enemy of Bernadotte, who accepted Sweden's offer to take the vacant position of Crown Prince, and then went on to take part in the war against Napoleon.

The Fifth Coalition came to an end with the Treaty of Schönbrunn (October 1809), with Austria once more withdrawing from the conflict. By 1810, Napoleon's Empire had reached its maximum extent. In the Iberian Peninsula, the war continued, but with the Portuguese and British forces driven back to the Lisbon area. Napoleon married an Austrian archduchess, Marie-Louise, with the idea of stabilising the alliance with Austria – and producing an heir, which his first wife Josephine had failed to do. Napoleon now controlled the Swiss Confederation, the Confederation of the Rhine, the Duchy of Warsaw, the Kingdom of Italy, Spain (ruled by Napoleon's older brother Joseph), Westphalia (ruled by his younger brother Jerome), Naples (ruled by his brother-in-law Murat), Prussia and Austria.

THE INVASION OF RUSSIA (1812)

Britain's attack on Denmark in 1807 led Russia to declare war on Britain. This war within a war, the Anglo-Russian War, ended with a strategic victory for Russia. The Russian army's successes on land meant that Russia was able to force Sweden to sign treaties with Russia in 1809 and France in 1810; Sweden then joined the Continental System, which strengthened the blockade against Britain. But then, in 1812, Britain, Sweden and Russia signed secret agreements that in effect were a coalition against France.

In 1812, Napoleon made his biggest mistake. He invaded Russia, with the intention of forcing the tsar to stay in the Continental System and to forestall the Russian invasion of Poland. Napoleon's army was huge, consisting of 650,000 men. When this Grande Armée crossed the River Niemen (23 June 1812), Russia proclaimed a Patriotic War. Napoleon proclaimed a Second Polish War, but disappointed the Poles by promising no concessions to them, even though they had provided 100,000 troops for the invasion.

The Russians pursued a scorched-earth retreat policy, determined to leave Napoleon without any supplies. There was one major confrontation, the Battle of Borodino (7 September 1812), which was fierce and bloody. It ended in a tactical draw, but the Russians were afterwards forced to withdraw. This left Napoleon with an open road to Moscow. On 14 September the great army had captured Moscow, which the Russians had abandoned, to the extent of releasing the inmates of the Moscow prisons to cause the French inconvenience. Napoleon had captured an almost empty city. Tsar Alexander refused to admit defeat, and Napoleon settled in, waiting for him to change his mind. Then the city's governor, Rostopchin, ordered the city burnt to the ground. An empty city was one thing, a city going up in flames was another. Napoleon withdrew from Moscow in bewilderment, without securing a surrender from the absent tsar and therefore without a conquest.

Then the long disastrous retreat from Moscow started. The Russian scorched-earth policy meant that there was no local food supply available for the retreating troops – and the Russian winter had set in. As a result of hunger and freezing weather, more than half of Napoleon's Grande Armée died before they could get back home. Another 200,000 soldiers were captured. After crossing the River Berezina, Napoleon abandoned his army to return to Paris to prepare plans to defend Poland against the Russian army. Napoleon's situation was by this stage serious but not desperate. The Russian army was also depleted, though they had the advantage of shorter supply lines.

THE SIXTH COALITION (1812–14)

Heartened by Napoleon's disastrous Russian campaign, several European states decided to rejoin the war against him. It looked now as if there was a good chance of defeating him. The Sixth Coalition saw Austria, Sweden, Prussia and several of the German states re-entering the war against Napoleon.

With astonishing resilience, Napoleon responded by rapidly rebuilding his armies in the east from 30,000 to 130,000, and then up to 400,000. The sheer waste of manpower in these Napoleonic campaigns is still breathtaking. Diversions to warfare (ie economic losses) on this scale would be seen as crippling today, but the situation was far worse in the more sparsely populated Europe of 200 years ago. At the Battles of Lutzen (2 May 1813) and Bautzen (20–21 May 1813), the total forces involved amounted to more than 250,000 men. These were two of the biggest battles of the wars so far, and in the course of those three days Napoleon inflicted 40,000 casualties on the Allied armies.

In the Peninsular War, Wellesley (Wellington) inflicted a decisive defeat on Joseph Bonaparte's army at the Battle of Vitoria (21 June 1813). This really terminated French power in Spain and the French troops had to withdraw across the Pyrenees.

The losses in battle suffered by both sides were so great that an armistice had to be declared (June-August 1813) to provide a period of recovery. During the armistice, Austria came out in open opposition to France, which added 300,000 soldiers to the Coalition armies in Germany. The Coalition forces now significantly outnumbered Napoleon's. The Coalition had 800,000 front-line troops and a strategic reserve of 350,000, while Napoleon had 250,000 front-line troops under his direct command and another 650,000 from Naples, Italy and the Confederation of the Rhine. So Napoleon was outnumbered by about 100,000 troops; but some of his contingents could not be relied on to remain loyal, such as those from Germany, and he was effectively outnumbered two to one.

In spite of this, Napoleon regained the initiative at the Battle of Dresden (August 1813), where his smaller army was able to inflict enormous casualties on the Coalition armies. Then came one of the greatest battles, the Battle of Leipzig (16–19 October 1813), which was called the Battle of the Nations. In this major confrontation, 191,000 French troops fought against 300,000 Coalition troops. Napoleon was defeated and he had to retreat into France. He fought battle after battle, but he was pushed relentlessly back by the sheer force of Coalition numbers. The success of the Coalition gave its members confidence; they agreed to persist now until Napoleon was totally defeated. Napoleon fought on, apparently unaware that he was doomed. He continued to order up now-non-existent troops, in much the same way that Hitler did in the closing stages of World War II, completely out of touch with reality.

The Coalition Allies entered Paris on 30 March 1814. Napoleon was forced to abdicate on 6 April 1814 and exiled to the island of Elba. The monarchy was restored in France (Louis XVIII), the Treaty of Fontainebleau was drawn up (11 April 1814) and the Congress of Vienna was set up to redesign the map of Europe.

NAPOLEON'S ESCAPE – TO WATERLOO (1815)

The Allies must have regretted allowing Napoleon to live, when not long afterwards he escaped from Elba; he landed at Cannes on 1 March 1815 and reopened the war all over again. In this final phase, often called the Hundred Days, a large number of European states joined forces to create a Seventh Coalition that was determined to defeat Napoleon. In view of the disastrous consequences of the later phases of his reign it was surprising that Napoleon was able to pick up any support at all in France, but there was a powerful bond between Napoleon and the French, and he was possessed of an extraordinary charisma. Using the same incredible daring with which he seized power in the first place, Napoleon marched to Paris, picking up supporters as he went, and overthrew Louis XVIII.

The Coalition Allies quickly gathered their armies to confront him in battle. As before, they raised colossal numbers of troops, something approaching one million, in order to overwhelm him. Napoleon miscalculated badly when he aspired to raise double that figure.

Napoleon took an army to make a pre-emptive strike against the Coalition in Belgium. His idea was to deal with their armies separately, before they could combine, and he certainly had the advantage of surprise. At the Battle of Ligny (16 June 1815), he defeated the Prussian army and forced them to retreat. At the same time, Marshal Ney fought a successful blocking action at Quatre Bras to stop the British army under Wellington from reaching and helping the Prussians. As the Prussians retreated, Wellington also retreated, to a carefully chosen low escarpment straddling the Brussels road where it emerged from woods just south of the village of Waterloo. He had been promised by Blücher that the Prussians would join him there for what promised to be the decisive battle. The road crossed the low ridge occupied by Wellington and descended into a broad shallow valley before rising on the south to a second ridge. In the valley below the first crest was La Haye Sante Farm, which became the focus for the Prussian troops. On the road below the crest of the second ridge stood La Belle Alliance Farm, which the French used as their headquarters. The Namur road crossed the Brussels road to the north of the first ridge, and the main British, Dutch, Belgian and German (Hanover and Brunswick) positions lay along that, just behind and therefore protected by the first ridge. In the valley, in front of Wellington's right wing, was Hougoumont Farm. Fighting continued there all day: it was the key to Wellington's right flank.

Napoleon took his army north to join Ney in pursuing Wellington, approaching from the south of La Belle Alliance. He sent Marshal Grouchy with troops to prevent the Prussian army from regrouping and returning, but Grouchy failed and the Prussian army was able to 'march towards the sound of the guns' at Waterloo. The battlefield at Waterloo was wet after a night's rain, and for several hours on the morning of 18 June Napoleon delayed the start of the battle; he was waiting for the ground to dry out so that he could move his artillery. But for the rain, Napoleon might perhaps have defeated Wellington before Blücher and the Prussians arrived. As it was, the two Coalition armies joined – and defeated him decisively. By the afternoon, Napoleon had still not succeeded in dislodging Wellington's army from the high ground Wellington had chosen for them. Then the Prussians arrived and attacked the French army's right flank. The French were driven into retreat.

The battle started at 11 a.m. with the French bombarding Hougoumont Farm and the British on the ridge behind it giving answering fire against the French infantry massing for attack on the far side of the valley. The French infantry assault on Hougoumont started. Then, at 1.30 p.m., Marshal Ney brought artillery over the ridge opposite La Haye Sante, along with 17,000 infantry, to launch an attack on Wellington's centre and left flank. The French cannonade began and the veterans on the British side said it was the heaviest they had ever known. Wellington ordered his infantry battalions to get back behind the ridge and lie down, to save them from the worst of the cannonade.

A Belgian Dutch brigade remained out on the exposed slope and it suffered terrible losses. The appalling barrage went on for half an hour.

Then there was a roar of drums as Ney ordered the French infantry columns to attack. They passed La Haye Sante, which was held by German troops until they were overwhelmed later in the day, and went on to the hedge at the top of the ridge. Then the line of British infantrymen stood up, fired and charged, driving back the French infantry.

A problem was that once an order to charge was given, especially to cavalry, it was difficult in the noise of battle to countermand it. The Union Brigade, commanded by General Ponsonby, continued to charge right across the valley and into the French lines where it was overpowered; Ponsonby himself died in the charge.

Around 3 p.m. there was a lull in the battle, when Blücher's Prussian army arrived on the battlefield from the south-east. From this moment the battle began to swing in the Allies' favour. Napoleon instructed Ney to attack La Haye Sante, which was a key British position. As he did so, Ney formed the impression that the British and their allies were retreating; it seems that what he actually saw were casualties being moved back. On this flimsy evidence, Ney unwisely launched a huge cavalry attack on the Allies, but the French Corps of Cuirassiers was unable to make any impression on the squares of British infantry. During the three hours that followed, Ney launched twelve cavalry attacks up the ridge at the non-retreating British. The last cavalry charge was sent at around 5.30 p.m. This, too, was a failure.

By this time the Prussian attack on the French right flank was a serious threat and Napoleon was deploying troops to drive the Prussians back from Plancenoit. After that, he intended to send them to relieve Ney, but by then it was too late: Wellington had further consolidated his position. Napoleon's troops, the Guard, marched to La Haye Sante ready to attack. Once there, Napoleon stood aside and let Ney take command – even though Napoleon thought Ney's initial cavalry attacks had been misjudged. As the five battalions of French infantry climbed the ridge they came under fire from British guns that were waiting for them, thanks to information from a French deserter.

By now it was 8 p.m. The French infantry were locked into a futile frontal attack on the British, while Blucher's Prussians were pressing in strongly from the east. The battle now looked like an inevitable defeat for the French. The French Guard regiments were repulsed one by one and after a shout of 'La Garde recule!' there was a general retreat. A few minutes later, Wellington appeared on the skyline and waved his famous hat, giving the signal for a general pursuit of the retreating French. British, Belgian, German and Dutch soldiers poured down the hill slope.

The French were routed. Three battalions of the Old Guard made a last stand, fighting to the death in order to give the emperor time to escape. They were invited to surrender, but they refused and were all killed. There were some rearguard actions around the battlefield, but once the emperor had fled the battle was clearly over. The Allied forces sustained 22,000 casualties, the French 25,000.

The battle was, as so often, 'a damned close run thing', and Napoleon might have defeated the British and Prussian armies at Waterloo. But there were 400,000 Austrian and Russian troops marching across from the east, and it is unlikely that Napoleon could have defeated them, too. Napoleon escaped from the battlefield in his carriage and arrived in Paris three days later. He still hoped to rally France, but the political mood had changed. On 22 June, the politicians forced him to abdicate a second time. Some fighting continued until a formal ceasefire was agreed on 4 July. On 15 July, Napoleon surrendered to a British squadron at Rochefort, and he was taken into exile on the South Atlantic island of St Helena, where he died, possibly of natural causes but more likely assassinated with poison, on 5 May 1821.

Significance and aftermath

The wars transformed Europe. Charlemagne had created a single empire in central Europe; now many centuries later Napoleon had for a short time achieved the same thing. But the cost in human lives, in human suffering, in damage to property, in economic damage, was very high. Napoleon had for a short time made France a superpower, but France had been the dominant power in Europe since the time of Louis XIV anyway. By the time of Napoleon's fall from power France was no longer the dominant power. Britain was instead, both politically and economically, and remained so for the next 100 years.

One positive legacy from the Napoleonic Wars was the spread of some of the ideals of the French Revolution, such as the abolition of privileges, democracy, a regular system of justice. After 1815 it was difficult for monarchs anywhere in Europe to go back to the old absolutist principles, and some of the reforms introduced under Napoleon were kept. Many countries in mainland Europe still operate systems of civil law based on clear codes that are based on the Napoleonic Code.

The conquests created a sharper sense of national self-awareness all over Europe and the ensuing spirit of nationalism would be a major factor in European history over the course of the next century. Napoleon himself began the aggregation of German states; this process of German unification became a major concern for the Germans themselves, ultimately leading to the creation of a Prussia-dominated German state. In Italy, too, unification became a major cause. The idea of an integrated, centrally controlled Europe also had its origins in Napoleon's empire, which was the precursor of the European Union. Napoleon mentioned more than once that he intended to create a single European state, though it may be that the aggressive way in which he tried to achieve it set back the cause rather than advancing it.

The Napoleonic Wars had a major effect on the way war itself was conducted from that time on. European states had customarily maintained small national armies and hired mercenaries to supplement them. During the eighteenth century there was a growing awareness that an alternative to this might be 'a nation in arms', a system in which conscription supplemented the national army. In the eighteenth century, armies were rarely larger than 200,000 men, yet at the peak of the Napoleonic Wars France had nearly three million combatants on land and sea. This was a major shift in the scale of warfare, and it was made possible by the Industrial Revolution; armaments factories were now capable of making mass-produced weapons to equip these huge military forces. Britain led the way with industrialisation and was the principal manufacturer of weapons for all the Coalition forces.

The French army also introduced new tactics, which often involved increased mobility to make up for low numbers. It used highly mobile artillery units which could be moved around independently of other units. It used standardised cannonball sizes to ensure compatibility between the supplies of ammunition and the artillery pieces; this idea of standardisation of equipment looks forward to the EU with, for instance, its standard container sizes. Many of these new military ideas came from innovators other than Napoleon; Carnot, who reorganised the French army at the time of the Revolution, must be given the credit for some of them.

BOLÍVAR'S WAR
(1811-25)

Bolívar's War was a series of independence wars fought in South America between 1811 and 1825 and led by Simón Bolívar, who was a member of an old aristocratic family in Caracas, the capital of Venezuela. The purpose of each of these wars was the same – emancipation. Each was a struggle for freedom from colonial rule by Spain. The situation was complicated by the fact that separate and independent freedom struggles were going on. They only fall under the heading 'Bolívar's War' for the period when Simón Bolívar (1783–1830) was commanding the revolutionary forces. It is nevertheless clear that Bolívar was the most powerful driving force behind and within – and very often at the forefront of – the liberation movements. The liberation movement in Venezuela began just a few months after Bolívar's return to Venezuela from Europe. In 1805, Bolívar had been to visit his old friend and tutor, Simón Rodríguez, in Rome; he gave a pledge to Rodríguez that he would devote his life to the freeing of Venezuela from Spanish rule.

The movement towards emancipation was a by-product of the Napoleonic Wars. After Napoleon invaded Spain, the Spanish were fully occupied with the business of ejecting him. There was little interest, for the moment, in what might be happening in the colonies. That led to a temporary power vacuum in the colonies in America. Consequently the Creoles held a congress, which was strongly influenced by the ideas of the European Age of Enlightenment, in the wake of the French Revolution.

The fight to win freedom from Spanish rule began unpromisingly in 1806. The Venezuelan revolutionary Francisco de Miranda gathered together a small band of foreign volunteer fighters, in the hope of inciting the people of Venezuela to rise up against Spanish rule. But he did not gain sufficient support. The Creole (mixed blood) population of the area wanted to expand the free trade environment, which was helping the plantation economy to flourish. But there was a fear that removing the Spanish and their colonial administration might bring on a revolution within Venezuela that would undermine their power.

This fear was well founded. There had been a large-scale slave revolt in the French colony of Saint-Domingue in the Caribbean. It had begun in 1791 and led to a general rebellion against the plantation economy as well as the French. The Saint-Domingue rebellion had degenerated into a civil war, with large-scale racial conflict and interventions by the English (who supported the white plantation owners) and Spanish (who supported the rebels). By 1805, the rebels had dismantled and transformed what had been a smoothly operating colony into the independent but poor state of Haiti.

Venezuelan slaves were encouraged by the success of the Saint-Domingue slave rebellion, and launched their own rising in the 1790s. Saint-Domingue was understandably a beacon of hope for slaves throughout the region, as well as a terrible warning to plantation owners. The owners of the cacao plantations in Venezuela were very nervous about any change that might take their country in the same direction as Haiti.

There was the same uneasiness among Creole plantation owners in the colony of New Granada. There, a strong faction loyal to Spain persisted, though not to the point of preventing a movement towards emancipation. In 1810, revolutionary governments were set up, proclaiming economic and social reforms. In 1811, the rebels declared a formal break with Spain. There were loyalist forces dominating large areas of the countryside opposing and fighting the patriots who held the capital. By 1812, the patriot armies in New Granada were in difficulties. The loyalist forces defeated the patriot armies and Bolívar was driven out.

Bolívar took part in many conspiratorial meetings, trying to organise a revolution in Venezuela. Finally in April 1810 the Spanish governor, Vicente Emparán, was deprived of his powers and expelled from Venezuela; a military junta was set up. Bolívar realised that he needed help if he and his revolutionary government were to withstand the might of Spain. Britain would help, he thought. He travelled to London where he explained the predicament of the newly independent colony and tried to get recognition, arms and financial support. It is not clear why he expected to get a sympathetic hearing – from a committed colonial power – and he did not get one. He returned empty-handed, though he did succeed in persuading Francisco de Miranda, who had tried single-handedly to liberate Venezuela in 1806 and was now living in exile, to return to Caracas and take command of the movement towards independence.

Venezuela was seething with excitement and anticipation as, in March 1811, a congress met in Caracas to draft a constitution. The congress unilaterally declared Venezuela's independence from Spain in July 1811. This declaration led immediately to a civil war which went on until 1823.

Bolívar then joined the army of the new republic and was given command of Puerto Cabello, one of the country's key ports. One of Bolívar's officers betrayed him, opening the fort to Spanish troops. Francisco de Miranda, who had assumed the dictatorship of Venezuela, was obliged to open negotiations with the Spanish commander. Three provinces rebelled against the revolutionaries and the new republic was seriously threatened. There was a Spanish blockade, funds were short, and there was an earthquake which was taken by many as a bad omen for the future of the republic. In July 1812, an armistice was signed which left Venezuela at the mercy of Spain and brought to an end the opening phase of the revolutionary war. Miranda was then handed over to the Spanish, it is said by Bolívar, and spent the remainder of his life in a Spanish prison.

Simón Bolívar and other leaders of the Venezuelan revolutionary army left the country for New Granada, intending to return later with more troops. Bolívar did not give up. He acquired a passport to leave Venezuela and travelled to Cartagena in New Granada (now Colombia). While he was there he wrote a defining political statement, the *Cartagena Manifesto.* In this, he urged the revolutionary armies to destroy the power of Spain in Venezuela. He emerged as the charismatic leader of the revolutionary movements of all the emerging ex-Spanish colonies in Latin America. He was named the leader of an expeditionary force to free Venezuela a second time from Spanish control.

With the approval of the Granadian congress, Bolívar returned to Venezuela in 1813, where he found the continuing struggle was mainly between blacks and mulattos (half-black, half-Caucasian). Bolívar's army fought fiercely, defeating Monteverde's loyalist army in a series of six major battles. Bolívar managed to gain control of Caracas. On 6 August 1813, Bolívar entered the capital, was given the title Libertador, the Liberator. This marked the formation of the Second Republic. He assumed political dictatorship and besieged Monteverde at Puerto Cabello in September.

But the war of independence was not yet won. The loyalists saw to it that Bolívar's victories were short-lived. In 1814, Spanish troops (now with reinforcements) inflicted a decisive defeat on Bolívar at La Puerta in June 1814, and defeated him again at Aragua in August. These were large-scale and violent engagements involving 10,000 men and causing 5,000 casualties.

The loyalist army commanded by José Boves included *llaneros*, cowboys, who made an important contribution to the army's mobility and effectiveness, harassing the patriots in the centre of the country. The cowboys were extremely mobile and aggressive fighters, and they played a major role in pushing Bolívar out of the country. Boves marched on Caracas, capturing the city and subjecting it to terrible atrocities. He forced the republicans to seek refuge in the east of Venezuela. Yet again, the republic had been stamped out. Bolívar and the other revolutionary leaders once more retreated to New Granada. Bolívar in this way narrowly escaped joining Miranda in a Spanish dungeon. He fled to Jamaica.

While he was in exile in Jamaica, Bolívar wrote a powerful document called the *Letter from Jamaica*. In this new manifesto he outlined a grand panoramic scheme for a new political geography of Latin America. He wrote, 'The bonds that united us to Spain have been severed.' In their place he proposed a suite of constitutional republics with governments that would be modelled on the British parliamentary system, with hereditary upper houses and elected lower houses. Unlike Britain, the head of state would not be a king but a president but, unlike other elected presidents, chosen for life. This last feature, to which Bolívar clung throughout his life, was the most questionable. It was uncomfortably close to the past dictatorships of ancient Rome; to us, today, it looks uncomfortably close to the tyrannical dictatorships of the twentieth century.

By 1815, the patriotic revolutionary movement throughout Spanish South America seems to have fizzled out. The Spanish sent in a large military expedition, which reclaimed Venezuela and much of New Granada for Spain. An attempt by Bolívar in 1816–18 to re-invade was a failure.

The Spanish had, by 1815, sent across the Atlantic to its troubled colonies the biggest army that had ever crossed the ocean. Its commander was Pablo Morillo. For three years the fighting went backwards and forwards, with indecisive victories and defeats on both sides. In 1817, Bolívar made the decision to set up his headquarters in the Orinoco region. This was an area that had not been spoilt by warfare, and an area that was not easily accessible to the Spanish; he was relatively safe there. He recruited several thousand foreign soldiers and established his capital at Angostura (which today is called Ciudad Bolívar).

He inaugurated a newspaper and set up liaison links with other revolutionary forces, including those led by José Antonio Paez and Francisco de Paula Santander. By early 1819, he had put together a master plan for attacking and conquering the colony of New Granada. It was among the most daring military campaigns in history. The plan entailed marching a fairly small army, of around 2,500 men, through the most inhospitable terrains imaginable – across swampy floodplains and over the high mountains of the Andes – along routes the Spanish would see as impassable and impossible. In that way, the Spanish forces were taken totally by surprise. At the epoch-making Battle of Poyaca (August 1819) the greater part of the Spanish and loyalist army surrendered to Bolívar. At the beginning of the following year, Bolívar and his army of 2,500 entered Bogota after capturing an entire country.

This was Bolívar's first resounding success in what had been a long and not always encouraging campaign. The Liberator, as he was justly known, then convened a conference at Angostura, which named him the first president of the new republic of Gran Colombia. This was a union of Venezuela, Colombia, Ecuador and Panama. But the reality was not to be quite so easy as the proclamation. The reality was that Bolívar had control of Colombia, but not Venezuela or Ecuador. The region was split by sharp divisions and Bolívar's hopes of creating a single nation out of the several former Spanish colonies were dashed. The area round Bogota refused to join the rest of New Granada; loyalist supporters were in control of large areas of Venezuela, the whole of Ecuador and parts of the Colombian Andes. But there was cause for optimism, as there was now a groundswell in favour of independence.

Bolívar knew now that a complete victory was within his grasp. The Spanish forces in South America had lost heart over events in Spain. There had been a revolution in Spain and this had obliged the king of Spain to acknowledge liberal ideals at home; it was now much harder for the army to have any faith in stamping out those liberal ideals abroad. Bolívar persuaded the Spanish commander in chief, Morillo, to begin negotiating an armistice. The two men met at Santa Ana in November 1820 and signed a treaty that provided for a six-month cessation of hostilities. When the fighting started again, Bolívar was easily able to defeat the Spanish force in Venezuela; he had superior numbers. With the Battle of Carabobo (June 1821), Bolívar was able to open the gates of Caracas and enter as his country's conqueror. At last Venezuela was freed from Spanish rule.

In the autumn of 1821, there was a congress at Cucuta to devise a constitution for Colombia. But the constitution was a disappointment to Bolívar. He thought it was too liberal, that it would not ensure the survival of the newly created state. For the moment, he was too preoccupied with more urgent military matters, so he accepted the weak constitution.

Bolívar put his trusted lieutenant, Francisco de Paula Santander, in charge of the newly constituted government in Bogota. Then he took the fighting up into the mountains, towards Ecuador and the central Andes. Once there, southern and northern armies converged, squeezing out the remaining loyalist resistance. In 1822, Bolívar and that other great resistance fighter, the Argentinian revolutionary José de San Martin, finally met one another in Ecuador. San Martin had been doing in the southern regions of South America what Bolívar had been doing in the northern regions. They had never met before. There are varied accounts of this meeting, but it appears that San Martin made the (honest and realistic) observation that only Bolívar could complete the liberation of the Andes. San Martin had entered the city of Lima and declared Peru independent, but the Spanish army had withdrawn into the Andes. San Martin had been unable to follow them into the mountains and decided he needed to consult Bolívar.

So, on 26 July 1822, the two revolutionary warriors met at the port of Guayaquil in Ecuador. Although it is not known what they discussed, it is likely that San Martin wanted Bolívar's advice and military aid. San Martin probably understood that only Bolívar had the military, political and psychological mastery to deal with the situation. If Bolívar was going to do that, he probably did not want San Martin in the area, complicating the situation. Whatever was said, San Martin left Guayaquil, resigned his office in Lima and went into self-imposed exile. He left Bolívar in sole charge of the war.

Spanish forces threatened to recapture all the territories that San Martin and his army had liberated. Now Bolívar moved to help the Peruvian Creoles in the city of Lima. Once he had helped to take Lima and organise the government there, he sent his army out to conquer the Peruvian Highlands. One of his lieutenants was Antonio José de Sucre, a Venezuelan like Bolívar. It was he who commanded the patriot army at Ayacucho in 1824; this turned out to be the final battle in the war, when the entire Spanish army surrendered. Although there was still some fighting after this, as pockets of loyalist resistance were tackled, but it was small-scale and sporadic. Then South America was free of Spain.

The following year, a bigger and more determined independence movement emerged. In May Venezuelan revolutionary forces under General de Sucre succeeded in defeating Spanish and colonial forces at Pinchincha in Ecuador. They had been defending Quito, which de Sucre was then able to take.

Simon Bolívar was now president of both Gran Colombia and Peru. A small area of Peru was still putting up rearguard resistance, but by 1825 that, too, had been 'liberated' by de Sucre. He reported that the task had been accomplished. The newly created independent nation was to be called, as it still is, Bolivia (after Simón Bolívar, the great Liberator).

Aftermath

Simón Bolívar had a remarkable ambition, which was not only to liberate all of the Spanish colonies in Latin America but to unify them into a single large independent sovereign state. He would call it Gran Colombia. It would be the South American equivalent of the United States. It was a bold and imaginative vision, but there were many obstacles in the way. One was the huge internal divisions within the colonies, divisions that were social, political, economic and ethnic. Even during the struggle for liberation from Spain there were internal rifts that jeopardised the fight for freedom. The coalition, once created, was extremely fragile and it soon collapsed. Gran Colombia was quickly to disintegrate into fragments and the small states that resulted were very vulnerable to interference and exploitation by outside interests. The failure of Bolívar's great enterprise was a great loss to Latin America, as it was doomed then to at least a century of political and economic instability. While the United States became richer and more powerful by the year, disunited Latin America became poorer and weaker.

THE ZULU WARS
1817–28

The Zulu in the 1820s were a people with an expansionist war-like culture. The wars of conquest were preceded by a civil war which is sometimes called the Ndwandwe-Zulu War. It broke out in 1817 in South Africa and was fought between the Zulu and the Ndwandwe peoples.

At the turn of the nineteenth century, the Zulu were a small tribe that had migrated onto the high eastern plateau country of South Africa. They were transformed into a strong and assertive tribal nation mainly through the personality and vision of their great chief, Shaka, who ruled from about 1787 until 1828. As a young man he was a rebel, estranged from his father, a Zulu chief called Senzangakona, and he became a warrior in the Mthethwa tribe. The paramount chief of the Mthethwa, Dingiswayo, supported and sponsored the young Shaka. He released him from service as a Mthethwa warrior and in 1816 helped him to become recognised as chief of the Zulu people when Shaka's father Senzangakona died.

The two chiefs, Shaka and Dingiswayo, remained friends and became allies. Their bands of warriors fought together side by side against common enemies. One of these enemies was the Ndwandwe tribe, which was ruled by King Zwide.

When Zwide murdered Dingiswayo, the Mthethwa were without a chief. In view of the relationship between Dingiswayo and Shaka and in view of Shaka's time with them as a Mthethwa warrior, they asked Shaka to be their chief. The Mthethwa took the Zulu name, so they were in effect absorbed into the Zulu nation.

Shaka had enormous powers of leadership, but he also had ideas on reorganising and modernising warfare. He modified the traditional Zulu way of fighting in a number of ways. He introduced a new weapon, a lightweight javelin with a short haft and a long blade: it was called an *assegai*. He also made change to the way the warriors were organised. When Shaka became the Zulu chief, the Zulu probably numbered only 1,500. They were one of the smallest of over 800 Eastern Nguni-Bantu clans. Shaka was a ruthless and dictatorial ruler who punished the slightest opposition to his rule with death. It was Shaka's single-minded ambition and determination that took this small and obscure tribe and made it the most powerful nation in southern Africa.

Shaka had new ideas about tactics, weapons and military discipline. He transformed his fighting force in a variety of ways. One was to organise the warriors into disciplined units that fought in close formation behind walls of cowhide shields. The effect was not unlike the tortoise or turtle formation that had been used by Roman infantry units 2,000 years before. The traditional method of tribal fighting had been a disorganised fray which involved a lot of spear-waving and gesticulating, and which was relatively brief and bloodless. Usually the outcome was decided by the side with smaller numbers of warriors submitting to the side with the larger numbers before too many casualties were inflicted. Shaka changed all that. Under Shaka, there was efficient killing and on a much larger scale than before. Shaka fought to extermination. He fought until the enemy did not exist any more, and this was probably a symptom of his insanity. He did not invent genocide, but he certainly used it to increase his power. Enemy tribes were reduced in battle, and then the remnants were absorbed into the Zulu nation.

Shaka instituted the regimental system. The regiments were organised according to age groups and they lived apart from one another, in separate *kraals* (fenced village enclosures). The regiments were distinguished from each other by uniform markings on their cowhide shields; they also wore different combinations of ornaments and headdresses. The principle was very similar to that of the distinctive multi-coloured uniforms used in European armies of his time.

Shaka also developed some original battle tactics, which were repeated in battle after battle, which was not unlike the rather rigid and formal approach adopted by the ancient Romans. Preparing to do battle, the regiments that were available, which were known collectively as the *impi*, were grouped into four units. The strongest unit was known as the 'chest'. This was placed at the centre and it was the unit that squarely confronted the enemy. On each side were the flanking 'horns'. These moved forwards rapidly to outflank the enemy and close in behind. The aim was encirclement. There was also a fourth unit, a reserve unit known as the 'loins'. This, rather oddly, was required to sit down nearby, facing away from the battle so that it did not become unduly excited. The loins could be sent for to act as reinforcements for any part of the ring of warriors that needed strengthening once the encirclement was accomplished.

The conduct of the battle was overseen by officers, *indunas*. They used hand signals, a kind of semaphore, to direct the warriors and this could be read above the noise of battle. A Zulu army or *impi* as organised by Shaka was extremely mobile. It could travel 80 km (50 miles) in a day and was empowered to take food requisitioned from kraals as it passed them. The impi on the march was accompanied by troops of boys, whose job it was to carry the sleeping mats and cooking pots for the warriors.

Shaka set about increasing his power and the power of the Zulu by first attacking and reducing the clans in his immediate neighbourhood. The first clan to suffer was the Langeni. He singled out the men from that tribe who had made his childhood a misery and impaled them on the sharpened fence-posts of their own kraals. By attacking and absorbing the neighbouring clans, Shaka quadrupled the size of the Zulu tribe and its army. In the Battle of Gqokli Hill in 1819, Shaka and his modernised Zulu army met the warriors of the Ndwandwe tribe. The Ndwandwe had far more warriors, but Shaka's tactics and the greater discipline of his warriors won the day.

The Zulu and Ndwandwe warriors met again at the Battle of Mhlatuze River in the following year. Once again the revolutionary tactics gave Shaka the victory. This time, Shaka attacked vigorously at a moment when the enemy army was divided while crossing the Mhlatuze River. After the defeat of the Ndwandwe army, Zulu warriors went to Nongoma, where King Zwide had his headquarters. He had not yet heard news of his army's defeat and the Zulu warriors approached the kraal singing Ndwandwe victory songs. Those in the kraal assumed the approaching warriors were their own and welcomed them into the camp. Once inside the kraal, the Zulu killed King Zwide.

After this disaster, most of the Ndwandwe tribe left their homeland and moved off to the north and east. This shift of population was the beginning of what became known as the *Mfecane*. It was a series of migrations, each leading to another in a kind of chain reaction, and involving enormous bloodshed. The *Mfecane* was very much the responsibility of the Zulu.

The Ndwandwe and the Qwabe were the only tribes in the area that were big enough to pose any serious threat to Shaka's expansionist plan. Once those two tribes had been defeated and their remnants either driven out or absorbed, Shaka had no local opposition to fear. After that, from 1820 onwards, he organised a series of annual campaigns to strike out at the complex networks of clans to the south of the Zulu territories.

By the year 1823, the Zulu had reduced a huge area, corresponding to modern Natal, to scorched earth. There was nothing left there but the smoking ruins of scores of kraals. The only people left there were a few terrified survivors of battles that were little short of massacres. Many survivors migrated out of the area, to break up the traditional tribal patterns as far away as Cape Colony. Although Shaka and the Zulu directly attacked a relatively small area, the knock-on effect was felt across huge distances. The Mfecane (literally, the Crushing) has been described as a deadly game of musical chairs. The displaced tribespeople had to find themselves new land, and they had to fight hard to get it; more people were deprived and displaced, and so on across the map of southern Africa. Two million Africans died in the process.

In 1827, Shaka's mother died. This event was so traumatic for him that he became deranged. He had a personality that was perhaps always psychotic. Now grief made him overtly and obviously insane. In his grief, he ordered the killing of 7,000 Zulu people. For a year no crops were planted, nor was milk to be used. Women found to be pregnant were killed along with their husbands. Thousands of cows were slaughtered so that their calves would know what it was like for Shaka to lose his mother. This was madness on the grandest scale.

At the beginning of 1828, Shaka sent his army south on a raid. The expedition took them all the way to the border of Cape Colony. The army returned exhausted after its expedition, anticipating the season-long rest they were normally allowed, but their insane king sent them off at once on another raid in the opposite direction, to the far north. This was going too far. Shaka had to go. In September 1828, two of his half-brothers, Dingane and Mhlangana, murdered Shaka with the help of one of the officers, an induna called Mbopa. That brought the Zulu Wars to an end.

Aftermath

The Zulu Wars broke up the traditional clan structure in the interior of South Africa. The tribal societies and economies of the region were left in tatters. The whole area was left depopulated and wrecked. When the Boers passed through the area on their Great Trek just a few years afterwards, in the 1830s, they were able to do so easily because it was empty and there was no tribal polity to organise any opposition.

It was often argued in the mid-twentieth century that African culture was disrupted to the point of no recovery by European colonisation. Certainly the interference in southern Africa by Europeans was very disruptive, but the Zulu Wars are a reminder that the native African history of the region also had its destructive side. South Africa was no Garden of Eden when the European settlers arrived there.

A handful of European settlers set up a trading post at Port Natal in 1824. They soon made contact with Shaka, even though his kraal lay 160 km (100 miles) away to the north at Bulawayo. Shaka was intrigued by them. He was certain that his Zulu civilisation was in every way superior to theirs, but he was interested in their artefacts and their customs. He let them stay. Two of them became fluent speakers of the Zulu language and it is through them that so much is known about the earlier history of the area.

THE DRESDEN REVOLUTION (1848–49)

REVOLUTION IN THE GERMAN STATES

The year of revolutions in Europe was 1848. Germany as such did not exist at that time, except as a collection of thirty-eight independent states loosely connected in a German Confederation. Nationalism had become a global idea. Partly as a result of the French Revolution and the American War of Independence, communities throughout the Western world were coming to think of themselves in nationalist terms. It was not a coincidence that ideas of a 'Celtic' heritage in Ireland, Wales and Scotland had their origins in the late eighteenth century. That awareness or perception was to lead eventually to demands for political separation. On the European mainland, on the other hand, rising nationalist sentiment was leading towards demands for national *unity*, for the little kingdoms and principalities of the German Confederation to be swept away altogether and replaced by a German nation. Side by side with this went the demand for democracy and freedom, and the abolition of the privileges of monarchy.

One step in this direction was the Hambach Festival in 1832. Inspired by the 1830 revolution in France, this was the culmination of a series of demonstrations organised by radicals and democrats who were growing restive about heavy taxation and political censorship. The Festival involved a student march to the Hambach Castle at Neustadt, where 30,000 people gathered to demand justice, freedom of expression and a republican government. The response from the reactionary German monarchs was predictably repressive – they tightened up security and clamped down on any further political demonstrations. One thing achieved by the Hambach Festival was the creation and adoption of the black-red-gold banner as a symbol of the republican movement and of the unity of the German people.

The rise of nationalism in Germany was intensified in 1840 by the fear that the French were about to invade the Rhineland. This generated a wave of anti-French feeling and there is nothing like a threat from outside to generate a feeling of national identity. It was a similar process to the forging of an English identity in the face of an external threat from the Vikings, 1,000 years before.

The very next year, 1841, the *Deutschlandlied* was written. This powerfully nationalistic song (*Deutschland über alles*) was eventually to become the German national anthem.

The liberal republican movement spread throughout the states that would later become Germany. Each one had its own revolution. Some monarchs cunningly accepted some of the revolutionaries' demands, at least until the revolutionary fervour had died down, and then renegued on their promises. The immediate triggers for the revolutions in Germany were harvest failures in 1846 and 1847, leading to widespread famine in Germany, and the 1848 revolution in France. A few weeks after the February revolution in France the March Revolution was under way in Germany. There were popular meetings and demonstrations. Generally the demands were the same: removal of press censorship, freedom of assembly and a national parliament for Germany. It was important that this parliament should be democratic; a federal council already existed, but that only represented the monarchs of the various states, not the people.

The German revolutions began on 27 February, when an assembly at Mannheim passed a resolution demanding a bill of rights. Similar resolutions were passed in other German states. The strength and uniformity of these demands seemed to take the German rulers by surprise and, in their surprise, they yielded to them with virtually no resistance. Republican agitators continued to encourage public disorder. The efforts of the Baden government to suppress these disorders with troops led to armed insurrection. But the insurrection was not well organised or well equipped and it was easy for the troops to quell it. The

Baden revolutionaries, led by Friedrich Hecker, were defeated on 20 April 1848. Disillusioned and unable to admit errors in leadership, Hecker emigrated to America in September 1848. He returned when the German revolutions boiled up again in the spring of 1849, but by the time he reached Strasbourg the revolution was already over, so he went back to America for good.

In Berlin, the Prussian people submitted their own list of demands, directed to the king of Prussia, Frederick William IV. The king gave in, agreeing to the demonstrators' demands, which included parliamentary elections, a constitution and freedom of the press. He went so far as to promise them that Prussia would be merged into Germany. As at Mannheim, this was followed by continuing public disorder, met by the intervention of troops. The crowds were fired on, leaving hundreds of people dead in the streets. The king tried to reassure the revolutionaries that government reorganisation would proceed. On 21 March he visited the cemetery where the victims of the demonstration were buried. He was attended by his ministers and generals – all wearing the revolutionary German tricolor, which has subsequently become the German flag.

REVOLUTION IN DRESDEN

In Dresden, the pattern of the revolution was similar. Dresden was a small city of 70,000, but a major cultural centre. It had a musical life second only to Vienna and was well-known as a lively centre of political debate, especially among liberals, democrats and anarchists. There was a radical newspaper called the *Dresdner Zeitung*, edited by the violinist and music director August Röckel, who also published a popular democratic newspaper called *Die Volksblätter*. Dresden also had left-wing political societies. The Dresden revolution began in the last days of February 1848 with demands for liberal reforms being made of the king of Saxony, Friedrich August II. The king responded positively and immediately. He dismissed his cabinet, promised to relax censorship, introduce trial by jury, guarantee electoral reforms and abolish feudal rights and tithes. The revolutionaries were not going to get their republic, but they were granted nearly everything else they asked for. The king was cheered on the streets. By the middle of March 1848 it looked as if the revolution had been accomplished; certainly everything, or nearly everything, had been promised.

Then, as the months passed, it became clear that the reforms were not to take place after all. Mikhail Bakunin, a high-profile anarchist and a great advocate of Karl Marx's new socio-political ideas, just published in *The Communist Manifesto*, arrived to drive the revolution forward in March 1849. He may have visited Dresden the previous summer, but the authorities were probably wrong (afterwards) to accuse him at his trial of being the ringleader of the revolution.

The composer Richard Wagner, who was the Royal Saxon Court Conductor, put music to one side for a while in order to be actively involved in leading the Dresden rising. He wrote articles, printed posters, gave speeches, made hand grenades. In October he wrote a newspaper article entitled *Germany and its Princes*, which included some fine rhetoric addressed to the German kings: 'Awake! Abandon your impotent and futile resistance. It can only visit suffering and ruin upon you!' It could almost be an excerpt from *The Ring*, which he was planning even then.

The central pivot of the revolutions in the German states was Frankfurt, where the newly created National Assembly met for the first time in May 1848. Its call was for a system of constitutional monarchy – for the whole of Germany. To set up the Assembly, elections were held across the German states; most of the members were in fact Saxon democrats. At the end of March 1849, the Assembly approved the first constitution for Germany and the next month the king of Prussia was offered the crown of a unified Germany.

Wagner was not a delegate at the National Assembly, but wrote to one of the delegates from Saxony, Dr Franz Wigard, threatening that there would be trouble if the Assembly failed to assert its supremacy over the governments of the separate states. It had to establish a citizens' army and form an alliance with France. Shortly after that, Wagner made a speech on *Republican Tendencies and the Monarchy* to a left-wing political society. He advocated a one-man-one-vote democracy and demanded the abolition of inherited wealth and power. He called on the aristocracy to abandon its privileged life style and share the life of the common people. Behind all this was the idea that money was the root of all the evils of society; society should rest on people, not on money. What he had to say was inspiring but without adding up to a political system. He had not yet read *The Communist Manifesto*, but some of the ideas in his speeches and articles are Marxist. Bakunin was certainly familiar with Marx's writings, so Wagner probably got the ideas by listening to Bakunin.

The National Assembly had seemed, until March 1849, to be making good progress. But it was an illusion. The Assembly had no power. It depended entirely on the co-operation and goodwill of the existing rulers, who were unlikely to hand over their authority to it. The king of Prussia contemptuously rejected the crown of Germany offered to him by the National Assembly. Then a new and violent phase of the German revolutions opened, as various movements sprang up to try to force the new constitution on the state governments. The National Assembly fell apart. In Saxony, King Friedrich August took heart from the Prussian king's stand; he had never recognised the new constitution, and now he disbanded the Saxon parliament. The Saxon town councillors tried to persuade the king to accept the constitution by making public speeches, but the king would not change his mind and called for order. This led to further unrest, and then the king called for Prussian troops to quell the revolt. There was an explosion of violence.

Wagner was one of the revolution's leaders, along with the anarchist Bakunin and the violinist August Röckel. The Dresden revolution was approaching its climax in the spring of 1849, when Wagner made his final mark on Dresden's musical life. He conducted a performance of Beethoven's Ninth Symphony on Palm Sunday. By then, there were only weeks to go before the fighting started. Wagner contributed several anonymous articles to Röckel's political newspaper *Die Volksblätter* urging the overthrow of capitalism and its replacement by a new world order. While Röckel went off to Prague in April 1849 to co-ordinate a revolution there, Wagner took responsibility for the publication of the paper in his absence.

Röckel returned to Dresden as the fighting broke out there on 3 May. The municipal guards were told to go home, but they were sympathetic to the revolution and the town councillors were able to organise them into units to defend Dresden against the anticipated arrival of Prussian troops. As people poured onto the streets, angry at the king's non-cooperation, the government retreated into the castle and armoury, protected by Saxon state troops. The municipal guard were now undecided whether to support the government or the people, who were threatening to use explosives to get the government out. The Saxon troops took the initiative by firing at the crowd. There were chaotic scenes in the streets as over 100 barricades were raised.

In the middle of the night, the king of Saxony and his ministers managed to escape, leaving the city for the stronghold of Königstein. The following morning, to the sounds of church bells and cheers from the crowds, the rebels appeared on the town hall balcony to proclaim a provisional government, led by three members of the now-dissolved democratic parliament: Samuel Tzschirner, who was a lawyer, Karl Todt, the Mayor of Dresden, and Otto Heubner, a state official who was also a member of the Frankfurt National Assembly. The next day, 5 May, there were skirmishes between the crowd and the police and disorder broke out afresh. The following night, Wagner was on duty as a lookout from a church tower, watching for troop movements.

On 6 May, Prussian troops arrived to reinforce the Saxon army in suppressing the revolt. The state troops planned to surround the armed revolutionaries and trap them in the Altmarkt (Old Market). Their task was made very difficult by the many barricades. They had to fight for each and every street; the fighting even continued inside the houses and became very violent.

Clara Schumann, the pianist and wife of the composer Robert Schumann, was in Dresden at the time. She noted in her diary:

We heard of the terrible atrocities committed by the troops. They shot every insurgent they could find. Our landlady told us later that her brother, who owned the Goldner Hirsch Inn on the Scheffelgasse, watched helplessly while the soldiers shot twenty-six students, one after the other, that they found in a room there. Then we heard that they thrown dozens of men out of third and fourth floor windows onto the street below. It is horrible to have to live through such things. This is the way men have to fight for their little patch of freedom. When will the time come when all men have the same rights?

On 7 May, the opera house was set on fire. More insurgents came in from the rural areas to man the barricades. Now Dresden had become a very dangerous place to be. That day, Wagner took his wife Minna, and their pet dog and parrot, to the safety of her sister's house at Chemnitz, 80 km (50 miles) away. When he got back to Dresden on 8 May he heard that Röckel had been arrested. Todt and Tzschirner had fled as troops began to gain the upper hand, and the rebels gave in that evening; the fighting suddenly stopped and the revolution was over. The revolutionaries numbered 3,000, compared with 5,000 government troops from Saxony and Prussia. The revolutionaries were outnumbered, but also untrained, militarily inexperienced, poorly equipped; they had really stood no chance of winning.

The Dresden revolution ended just like all the others, with its ineffectual liberal leaders unable to direct or control events and the state militia restoring order. Wagner was now a marked man and although he called Todt and Tzschirner cowards for running away he had little choice but to try to run away himself in order to avoid arrest. He left Dresden the next morning, 9 May, and made his way to Minna's sister's house. His brother-in-law ordered a carriage to take him to Weimar, where he knew the composer Franz Liszt would give him shelter and help. Meanwhile the police had searched for him in Dresden and issued a warrant for his arrest. It is surprising that he was not caught in Chemnitz, where both Bakunin and Heubner, two other revolutionary leaders, were identified by locals who reported them to the police. They were caught and arrested; Wagner was not.

Wagner was lucky. He spent many years in self-imposed exile in Switzerland. August Röckel was not so lucky. Along with Bakunin, Röckel was tried for treason and sentenced to death. The sentence was later commuted to life imprisonment and Röckel was released in 1862.

In his own account of what happened in Dresden, Wagner was careful to minimise his role in the unfolding of events. This was not due to modesty – Wagner had none! – but due to the fact that his memoir, *Mein Leben,* was being prepared for his new patron, the young King Ludwig of Bavaria, to read. By that stage, it suited Wagner to have a royal patron who was prepared to fund productions of his operas, and he was keen to play down his role as a revolutionary leader. He tried to play it down as youthful exuberance, an adventure, a *folie de jeunesse.* In the same way, Wagner had to gloss over his many sexual liaisons, simply because he was dictating *Mein Leben* to his newly acquired second wife, Cosima. His autobiography, like so many other historical accounts, has to be interpreted with the author's undisclosed personal interests in mind. The historical reality is that he seems to have been a member of the Dresden revolutionary leadership. Wagner mentions that he attended meetings of the left-wing political society; what he does not mention is that he *hosted* them! He was also centrally involved in the attempt to set up a republican government at Chemnitz, and if it had come to fruition there is no doubt that Wagner would have been near the top in the new power structure.

The leaders who were caught spent long periods in prison. If Wagner had been caught, he, too, would have been imprisoned, and that would have seriously curtailed his development as a composer. He was in fact very lucky indeed to have escaped from Saxony without being identified. If he had been identified, there is no doubt that he would have suffered the same fate as Röckel. Then there would probably have been no *Ring,* no *Tristan und Isolde,* no *Siegfried Idyll,* no *Mastersingers.*

Other Dresden revolutionaries left Europe altogether, along with revolutionaries from the other German states, many of them finishing up in Texas. There they became known as 'Latin farmers', because of their redundant classical education.

Significance and aftermath

Ultimately the Dresden revolution and the other German revolutions failed because they had no military backing and were poorly led. Many of the leaders were fundamentally peace-loving liberals who were simply not tough enough for the violent action required. But the aims of the revolution were very clear and well defined. The leaders of the German states were also expecting revolt and, at some level, they were prepared to acquiesce. They all gave in to the demands astonishingly quickly. It looks as if with stronger and more co-ordinated cross-state leadership the revolutions might have succeeded in forcing through some major reforms. The Dresden revolution, led by a group of ill-assorted high-minded liberals like Röckel and Wagner, allying themselves to the anarchist-extremist outsider Bakunin, was unlikely to be anything other than a fiasco.

Conflicts have always had a profound influence on art and culture. His involvement as a leader of the Dresden rising had a major and lasting effect on Wagner. In October 1848, in exile, he wrote the first prose sketch for the text of *The Ring*, which was to have an anti-capitalist message. He had to put writing the music for it to one side until several years later, by which time his views had changed, but the finished four-part cycle still has a powerful flavour of social revolution. Bernard Shaw described it as a clear allegory of Marxist ideas. The gods break their contract with lower orders of beings, and in doing so forfeit their right to rule. The Dresden experience affected Wagner more profoundly than he ever admitted. He wrote letters to his friend Röckel, as Röckel languished in prison, but he did not write a note of music for five years; there is no parallel silence in the career of any other great composer.

THE CRIMEAN WAR
(1854–56)

In the 1850s, Britain and France, allies for the first time in 200 years, drifted into a war against Russia. The reasons are obscure, but rooted in a completely false view in the West that Russia was an extremely powerful and aggressive expansionist power that had to be contained at any cost. It was an illusion that may have developed as a result of politicians and civil servants looking for too long at Mercator-projection maps of the world drawn with north at the top; these made Russia look colossal and overbearing. And Russia did have modest aspirations to expand in the direction of the Black Sea, to occupy Constantinople, with a view to gaining access to the Mediterranean. The British government saw this as a threat to the overland route from Britain to India. Constantinople belonged to the Turks, who were therefore supported by the British. A congress was held, arriving at a solution no-one understood and only the tsar accepted, and in July 1853 a Russian army occupied the Turkish territory north of the Danube.

The Russian fleet attacked and destroyed a squadron of Turkish ships in the Black Sea, and after this a war was inevitable. In March 1854, France and Britain formed an unlikely alliance against Russia. French and British troops assembled on the west coast of the Black Sea, the Russian troops withdrew, and suddenly there seemed to be no excuse for war. But now that Britain and France had mobilised their armies, they wanted to achieve something with them. They decided to invade the Crimean peninsula, which had Sevastopol, Russia's only naval base in the Black Sea, at its southern tip.

The Crimean War was badly planned from the outset, and based on very poor geographical knowledge. The French commanders were working from sketches rather than proper maps; the terrain was largely unknown. The British cabinet looked at a map and saw that Crimea was very nearly an island. It looked as if it could be very easily taken by commanding the isthmus, and as if this could be achieved by sending in ships and covering it with their guns. Unfortunately the extreme shallowness of the water was not taken into account. The sea was only 60–90 cm (2–3 ft) deep on each side of the isthmus, so ships could not get anywhere near it.

The problems multiplied when undertrained troops commanded by very elderly generals (actually described at the time as 'duffers') were landed and sent into action. The Russian army was also disadvantaged by being equipped with obsolete weapons, such as smooth-bored rifles, by contrast to the Allies' Minié rifles.

THE BATTLE OF THE ALMA

The Allied advance on Sebastopol began on 19 September, with the French moving along the coast and the British approaching by an inland route. There was no co-operation or co-ordination between the two armies, so in effect on 20 September two separate actions were fought. The French General Canrobert was profoundly impressed by the nonchalant way in which the British troops advanced, 'as though they were in Hyde Park!' Years later, he watched Queen Victoria carefully dancing a quadrille at a ball in Paris. It reminded him of the British advance at the Alma and he observed, 'The British fight as Victoria dances.' Yet, in spite of their inefficiency, the Allied troops succeeded in taking the Russian position defending Sebastopol.

THE BATTLE OF BALACLAVA 1854

The Allied armies could easily have gone straight on to occupy Sebastopol, but their imperfect knowledge of the area – lack of detailed maps again – led them to surround the base and lay siege to it. The British had occupied the harbour at Balaclava in the south and took the eastern flank, while the French set up their position at Kamiesch and took the western flank.

The fortifications at Sebastopol, designed by Todleben, its chief engineer, were formidable. The base was difficult to attack from the landward side. The Russians had also scuttled ships in the harbour mouth, making it hard for the naval vessels to participate in the attack.

On 17 October, Allied bombardment started, but it was not followed up by assault. In the lull that followed, the Russian army suddenly attacked the British from behind, with the aim of retaking Balaclava. The surprise attack by the Russians was held in check by a brilliant charge of the Heavy Cavalry Brigade. Unfortunately in the first stage of the action some Turkish batteries were overrun and captured and Lord Raglan, strongly influenced by Wellington's boast that he 'never lost a British gun', sent an aide-de-camp, Nolan, with orders that the Light Cavalry Brigade must retrieve the captured guns. There was a misunderstanding over the orders, and the Light Brigade charged in the wrong direction, along the wrong valley, and directly into the Russian artillery position. The Charge of the Light Brigade was one of the most heroic and futile actions in the history of British warfare.

The Battle of Balaclava ended with the advantage to the Russians, who had succeeded in cutting the one good road between the British army and its base at Balaclava.

The 1854–55 winter that followed caused immense suffering and misery to all the troops, with many British and French soldiers dying of cold and disease. The Russian troops garrisoned at Sebastopol suffered similarly. The Russian recruits who were sent from the interior to relieve Sebastopol suffered worst of all; two-thirds of them died on the road of sickness or starvation. The plight of the British was worsened when a great storm on 14 November sank their supply ships.

THE BATTLE OF SEBASTOPOL 1855

In the spring, the siege of Sebastopol was resumed. The Allied leaders could not agree on a new campaign to attack Kertch, the Russian base in east Crimea. General Canrobert agreed to it, was contradicted by Paris and so had to recall his troops; in exasperation, Canrobert resigned as French commander-in-chief, to be replaced by Pelissier. A new expedition to Kertch was mounted by the Allies, with complete success. An attempt to take Sebastopol on the anniversary of Waterloo was a complete failure. Todleben, the main Russian defender, was badly wounded; Lord Raglan, the British general, fell ill and died, to be succeeded by Simpson, his chief of staff. With this change of leadership on all sides, a new attack on Sebastopol was mounted on 8 September. This was successful, and the Russians withdrew to the north side of the harbour. Unaccountably, the Allies did not follow them. When Simpson was required to explain his inaction, he could give no reason. Queen Victoria was furious.

The Crimean War gradually petered out, until a formal peace treaty, the Treaty of Paris, was signed in February 1856. The war is remembered as perhaps the worst-managed war in British history, and an outstanding example of the difficulties and dangers of fighting a coalition war. The so-called Allies were at no point really working together; one British general repeatedly referred to the Russians as 'the French', which to him was synonymous with 'the enemy'.

THE AMERICAN CIVIL WAR
(1861–65)

The four-year American Civil War was the struggle by eleven states in the South to leave the Union; the states of the North were determined to prevent this secession, which would have meant the loss of slightly more than half the population of the United States.

Slavery was one of the root causes of the war. Black slave labour was an integral part of the economy of the cotton-growing South, and there was growing disquiet in the South about the drive (from the North) to abolish slavery. This led to a desire to secede from the Union. Another contributor to the Civil War was the so-called Second Great Awakening, a religious revival in the 1820s and 1830s that led to attempts at various kinds of social reform. The most notable of these reforms was the abolition of slavery. Several different groups of abolitionists emerged, the most extreme of which demanded the immediate abolition of slavery. There were also 'anti-slavery men', such as John Quincy Adams, who wanted to see an end to slavery yet did not belong to any abolitionist group. By the 1850s, America was polarising into those who condoned and favoured slavery and those who hated it and wanted to see it abolished; this was the fundamental cause of the Civil War.

HARPER'S FERRY (1859)

John Brown was an abolitionist. His legendary raid in October 1859 involved a group of twenty-two men who belonged to the anti-slavery group called the Secret Six. They seized the Federal Harpers Ferry Armoury in Virginia. John Brown thought the slaves in the South were on the point of an armed rebellion against their masters and that one spark would ignite the rebellion. The raid on Harper's Ferry was intended to set off a major revolutionary slave rising. In fact, nothing happened, at least as far as the slaves were concerned; not a single slave made an attempt to revolt.

Lieutenant-Colonel Robert E. Lee of the US Army went to suppress the raid. Brown was captured immediately, tried for treason and hanged. At his trial, Brown impressed everyone with his commitment and single-mindedness, fuelling the Southerners' belief that a slave revolt really was imminent. The Harper's Ferry episode did more than anything else to encourage belief in the South that secession from the Union was the right course of action.

THE SECESSION OF SOUTH CAROLINA (1860)

In December 1860, South Carolina seceded and by the following February six more states had followed its example. Their delegates met at Montgomery to set up the Confederate States of America with Jefferson Davis as president. At that time Buchanan was US president, and he operated a 'no coercion' policy, but things changed on 4 March 1862, when Lincoln was inaugurated as president in his place. He did not want to try coercion either, as he knew this would throw the eight remaining 'slave' states into the Confederacy. In the North, generally there was feeling that the states that had already seceded should be allowed to go their own way. The break-away states felt that Lincoln was threatening them with war, but they were unwilling to strike the first blow.

THE FALL OF FORT SUMTER (1861)

Fort Sumter at the mouth of Charleston Harbour was claimed by the Confederates and besieged. Like Buchanan, Lincoln was reluctant to send in troops to relieve the Union garrison stationed there under Anderson, but on 5 March Lincoln heard that Anderson might be starved into surrender. Lincoln's chief military adviser, General Scott, urged evacuation, but Lincoln had just pledged himself to 'hold, occupy and posses the property and places belonging to the government' and he felt bound to honour that pledge. He decided not to evacuate Sumter but send in food; if the Confederates intercepted the food, that would be tantamount to a declaration of war. Lincoln informed the Confederate governor, Pickens, of his intentions, and Pickens passed the ultimatum on to Davis. Davis issued orders that Confederate forces under Beauregard were to take Sumter, which they did; the Southern leaders wanted a military showdown with the North in order to rally flagging popular support for the secession in the South.

If Lincoln had ordered the (temporary) evacuation of Sumter, Southern interest in secession might have dwindled away. As it was, the fall of Sumter, seen as an insult to the national flag, roused the fury of the North, uniting Democrats and Republicans in condemning the secession and regarding it as insurrection. Suppressing insurrection was a constitutional function of the US Army. The free (non-slave) states freely responded to the call-up, but the governors of the seven slave states in the Union refused to raise contingent forces. The call to arms divided loyalties, and some of the slave states threw in their lot with the Confederacy. Lincoln proclaimed a blockade of the Confederate ports on 19 April, though controlling the highly indented and very long coastline – 4,800 km (3,000 miles) long – was going to be almost impossible to achieve.

THE BATTLE OF BULL RUN 1862

The two armies met at Bull Run on 21 July. After several hours of fighting the Federals (Northern) left the field in a panic-stricken flight back to the Potomac River. The Confederates were too disorganised to pursue them. Instead they advanced to Centreville, where they established a base and waited for the Federal army to make the next move. Bull Run was the first pitched battle of the Civil War, a spectacular defeat for the Federals, but it had no decisive strategic results. The Battle of Wilson's Creek on 10 August was similarly indecisive.

THE BATTLE OF SHILOH (1862)

Johnstons and Beauregard called up Bragg from Pensacola with 10,000 men, they concentrated an army of almost 40,000 at Corinth by the end of March 1862. Van Dorn was supposed to be bringing another 15,000 men from Arkansas, but they could not wait for him to arrive. The Battle of Shiloh on 6–7 April was one of the biggest, most fiercely fought and bloodiest battles of the entire war. Johnston was killed on the first day and Beauregard retreated to Corinth, which he was able to hold on to until 30 May, when he retreated again, to Tupelo. The Federal squadron attacked and destroyed a Confederate flotilla at Memphis on 6 June.

With the capture of Corinth and Memphis, the Federal offensive virtually came to an end. The Federals had cleared Kentucky and West Tennessee of the enemy, established control of the railway, and opened the Mississippi as far as Vicksburg. But the Confederate army of the west had got away, and was free to take the offensive.

THE FALL OF NEW ORLEANS (1862)

A small Confederate expeditionary force was sent up the Rio Grande to secure Arizona and New Mexico, with the long-term aim of bringing California into the Confederacy. It occupied Santa Fe but was forced to make a disastrous retreat to Texas in April 1862. The attempt to take in the south-west had failed.

But the biggest loss to the Confederates in the spring of 1862 was undoubtedly the loss of New Orleans, the great river port at the mouth of the Mississippi. The Gulf squadron under Farragut ran past the forts guarding the lower Mississippi and on 24 April it appeared in front of New Orleans. The city had been abandoned by its garrison and immediately surrendered to the Federal fleet. It was formally occupied by General Butler's troops on 1 May.

THE BATTLE OF HAMPTON ROADS (1862)

The Confederate ship CSS *Virginia*, an unwieldy ironclad commanded by Captain Buchanan, steamed into Hampton Roads on 8 March 1862, to break the Union blockade. She was accompanied by three other vessels and succeeded in sinking the USS *Cumberland* by ramming her below the water line. Then Buchanan turned his ship on USS *Congress.* After witnessing the fate of the *Cumberland,* the captain of the *Congress* grounded his ship in shallow water. The James River Squadron arrived and supported the *Virginia's* attack on the *Congress.* This battering lasted an hour, after which the *Congress* surrendered. While the surviving crew of the *Congress* were being transferred from her, a Union battery on the shore opened fire on the *Virginia.* In retaliation, the *Virginia* fired incendiary shells into the *Congress,* which later exploded in a fireball.

The *Virginia* had a very successful day, but ended up severely damaged. Part of her ram was embedded in the *Cumberland,* and Captain Buchanan lost a leg. She steamed off into safe, Confederate-controlled waters for the night, but she returned the next day with the intention of finishing off the remaining blockade ships. For the Union Navy, it had been a terrifying and demoralising day. But late that night the unique Union ship, USS *Monitor,* commanded by Lieutenant Worden, arrived in Hampton Roads. It was sent in a desperate attempt to protect the Union fleet and stop the *Virginia* from going on to attack Northern cities.

The next morning, 9 March, the *Virginia* returned to finish off the *Minnesota,* which had gone aground. Its way was blocked by the strange and sinister-looking *Monitor,* which was like a raft with a huge gun turret mounted on it. The two metal-clad ships fought each other for hours at close range without either being able to overcome the other. If anything the *Monitor* had the advantage, being smaller, more manoeuvrable and with a revolving gun turret. In the end the *Virginia* retreated. Victory was claimed by both sides; the battle was inconclusive, but if anything the strategic balance remained in the Union's favour.

The *Monitor's* guns were more powerful than the *Virginia's,* and succeeded in cracking the ironclad's plating in several places, while the *Virginia* only managed to make a few dents in the *Monitor's* armour, as photographs taken at the time show. The *Monitor's* designer, Ericsson, was furious that the *Monitor's* crew had used solid shot and aimed at the *Virginia's* upper works. He cried that they should have used explosive shells and aimed them at the water line; then the *Virginia* could have been sunk very easily.

Over the next two months, the *Virginia* returned to Hampton Roads several times in the hope of drawing the *Monitor* into battle. The ship steamed up and down, while a huge number of Union vessels waited for the *Virginia* to steam towards Fort Munroe – into Union-controlled waters. The *Monitor* was held back. The president had given express instructions that the *Monitor* was not to engage in battle unless it was unavoidable. Twice the *Virginia* ventured into Hampton Roads, trying to entice the *Monitor* out to fight, but the two ships never fought each other again. It was the most anticipated naval battle of its time, and it never happened. Neither the *Virginia* nor the *Monitor* was to play any further role in history. To save the *Virginia* from being captured, Captain Tattnall deliberately ran her aground and set her on fire; after an hour of burning fiercely, she was engulfed in an enormous explosion. Later the same year, 1862, the *Monitor* encountered a gale while under tow by the USS *Rhode Island*; she sank on the last day of 1862 off Cape Hatteras in North Carolina. Her wreck was discovered, in surprisingly good condition, in 1973. One outcome of the remarkable encounters in the Hampton Roads was that the age of wooden fighting ships was clearly over; from that point on, iron would rule.

THE BATTLE OF FREDERICKSBURG (1862)

McClellan was seen to be too cautious when he failed to follow up his advantage after the Battle of Antietam, so he was replaced by Major-General Ambrose Burnside. But Burnside's Union army was soon defeated, at the Battle of Fredericksburg on 13 December 1862. Over 12,000 Union soldiers were killed or wounded when they futilely and repeatedly tried a frontal assault on Marye's Heights. After this spectacular Union defeat, Burnside was replaced by Major-General Joseph Hooker, but Hooker, too, was unable to defeat Lee's Southern army. Even though his army was more than double the size of the Confederate army, Hooker was subjected to a humiliating defeat at the Battle of Chancellorsville in May 1863. Hooker was replaced by Major-General George Meade when Lee and his army invaded the North for the second time, in June.

LINCOLN'S EMANCIPATION PROCLAMATION (1862)

In September, Lincoln made the freeing of slaves in the South a formal goal of the war. This was not universally popular in the North, but it reduced the likelihood of intervention from France or Britain on the side of the Confederates. It also allowed the Union to recruit Afro-Americans as fighters.

THREE BATTLES IN 1863

In the East, General Robert E. Lee took command of the Confederate Army of North Virginia and gained a sequence of victories over the Union Army of the Potomac. He suffered a major loss, though, at the Battle of Chancellorsville in May 1863, when his ablest general, 'Stonewall' Jackson, was killed. Meade did finally succeed in gaining a major victory over Lee at the landmark Battle of Gettysburg in Pennsylvania on 1–3 July 1863. This marked the end of Lee's invasion of the North, and he was lucky to escape from the battle alive. This was the bloodiest battle of the Civil War, and it was also its turning point; from then on, there was a development towards an overall Northern (Union) victory.

The Confederate stronghold of Vicksburg fell to Union forces under General Ulysses S. Grant the day after the Battle of Gettysburg. Vicksburg's location on a commanding bluff above the Mississippi made it an important point from which the Mississippi river traffic could be controlled, so the Confederates' loss of Vicksburg was highly significant, especially after the Union's earlier capture of New Orleans. In the Battle of Vicksburg, Lee's army suffered 28,000 casualties; Meade's suffered 23,000. This was very much a war of attrition, with crippling losses on both sides. One reason for the heavy losses was the dangerous mixture of modern weaponry including guns with rifled barrels, with old-style strategies that included charges.

In spite of Meade's victory, Lincoln was angry with him for failing to block Lee's retreat. When Meade consolidated that failure by running an inconclusive campaign that autumn, Lincoln looked towards the Western Theatre for new leadership.

CONFEDERATE RETREAT AND DEFEAT

Grant fought several fierce battles against Lee in Virginia in the middle of 1864. Lee's strategy was effective in inflicting high rates of casualties on Grant's army, but he lost in the end because he could not replace his own casualties and was forced to fall back into trenches round his capital at Richmond, Virginia.

General William Sherman, who led the Union's Military Division of the Mississippi, captured Atlanta in Georgia. The fall of Atlanta on 2 September 1864 was a major factor in seeing the re-election of Lincoln as president. After that Sherman began his 'March to the Sea', in which he destroyed a swathe 160 km (100 miles) wide across the state of Georgia. He did this in imitation of a similarly ruthless but effective action carried out by General Philip Sheridan in the Shenandoah Valley, where there was a systematic destruction of the Confederate agricultural base. The Civil War thus came very close to what we think of as total war. The armies and their generals did not set out to kill the civilian population directly – they stopped short of that – but they systematically set about destroying the non-military infrastructure: houses, farms, railway tracks.

THE BATTLE OF FIVE FORKS (1865)

By the spring of 1865, Lee's army had thinned dangerously as a result of casualties and desertion; it was now much smaller than Grant's and it was only a matter of time before defeat had to be formally admitted. There was a decisive victory by the Union forces at the Battle of Five Forks on 1 April 1865. This obliged Lee to abandon Petersburg and Richmond. Richmond, the Confederate capital, fell to the Union XXV Corps, which was appropriately made up of black soldiers. Those Confederate units that were left fled to the west. The Confederate leaders were forced to admit that it was all over; on 9 April General Lee formally surrendered to General Grant at the Court House in Appomattox. In a gesture of respect and reconciliation, Grant allowed Lee to keep his officer's sword and his horse; Grant wisely had one eye on the difficult task ahead of rebuilding the Union. Johnston surrendered to General Sherman on 26 April at Durham, North Carolina.

The first and last President of the Confederacy, Jefferson Davis, was captured, charged with treason and was disgraced by having his US citizenship taken away. Davis's intransigence prolonged the war, and after it was over, he was displaced in the affections of the South by the war hero, General Robert E. Lee. Davis was clapped in irons for three days, and then spent two years in prison, from where he managed to sell his estate – to one of his former slaves, Ben Montgomery. Davis lived on until 1889, when the South gave him the biggest funeral ever seen there.

CONSEQUENCES OF THE CIVIL WAR

All slaves in the Confederate states were freed in the spring of 1865, as a result of Lincoln's (partly tactical) Emancipation Proclamation. Four million black slaves were freed that year. There was also a noticeable strengthening of the Union, with a permanent ending of the question of secession.

The most obvious feature of the American Civil War was the very high death rate. It is estimated that there were altogether 970,000 casualties, in other words three per cent of the population of the United States. The census figures reveal that 18 per cent of white Southern males aged 13-43 died in the Civil War – a very high death rate indeed, compared with 6 per cent for the equivalent age and race group in the North. About 620,000 soldiers died, one-third in battle, two-thirds as a result of disease.

Disease was rife during the war; many of the fatalities were the result of diseases like dysentery. The experience led to the publication of a six-volume review of medical procedures and a change in the design of military and civilian hospitals. So, in spite of, or perhaps because of, the carnage of the Civil War, medical care improved radically afterwards.

There were also major economic repercussions. The northern blockade naturally decreased the markets for Southern cotton. Many Southern farmers switched from cotton, diversifying into food crops. The mobilisation of troops in the Union led to the abandonment of many farms for the duration of the war; afterwards the farms were mechanised. There was also a marked slump in industrial development during the war. There was a recovery afterwards, but even by 1910 economic development was not where it would have been if the Civil War had never happened; the war did America lasting damage.

THE FRANCO-PRUSSIAN WAR

(1870–71)

After the victory of Prussia in the Austro-Prussian War of 1866, Napoleon III of France became increasingly apprehensive: Prussia had established itself as the leading power in Germany and the thrust towards German unification was well under way. In Germany, Bismarck encouraged the developing rift between France and Germany; with a perception of France as the enemy at the gates, the southern states of Germany would be more readily drawn into a national union. Bismarck made sure that Italy and Russia remained neutral; he also shrewdly (and accurately) calculated that Britain would remain neutral, too. Preparations for war went forward in both France and Prussia; very thoroughly in Prussia, and very inefficiently in France.

The unlikely pretext for the war was the candidate for the Spanish throne. The throne was offered to a prince of the Prussian ruling family. This was accepted on Bismarck's advice, then rejected after the French made a strong protest. The French foreign minister, Duc de Gramont, then foolishly insisted on further assurances from Prussia, which the Prussian king, Wilhelm I, declined to give. Bismarck then fanned French hostility by publishing the famous Ems telegram. This was a report by Heinrich Abeken (Prussian Foreign Office) of the altercation between the Prussian king and French diplomats. The telegram made clear that the king was irritated by the importunate demands of the French: 'I rejected this demand somewhat sternly as it is neither right nor possible to undertake engagements of this kind for ever and ever.' Abeken went on to say that the king proposed that both the demand and its rejection 'might well be communicated to both our ambassadors and the Press.' Bismarck did indeed release an edited version of the telegram to the

Press, and without warning the French. On 19 July 1870, France ill advisedly declared war.

As Bismarck intended, the southern states of Germany saw France as the aggressor and joined the North German Confederation. The military conduct of the war was masterminded by the gifted Helmuth von Moltke. In France, Napoleon III took command, but this quickly devolved on to Marshal Bazaine. On 4 August, the Germans crossed the French border into Alsace, defeating the French army under Marshal MacMahon at Wissembourg and then pushing it to Chalons-en-Champagne. The Germans then forced a wedge between the forces of MacMahon and those of Bazaine, which were centred on the town of Metz.

THE BATTLES OF VIONVILLE, GRAVELOTTE AND SEDAN (1870)

Marshal Bazaine tried to rejoin his forces with those of MacMahon, but was defeated in two battles, one at Vionville on 16 August and the other at Gravelotte on 18 August. After these two defeats, Bazaine returned to Metz.

The German army began its march on Paris. The Battle of Sedan on 1 September represented an attempt by Napoleon III and MacMahon to rescue Bazaine. The battle was a complete disaster for the French. The French were not merely defeated, they were humiliated - 100,000 French soldiers and the emperor himself were captured. When news of the great military disaster reached Paris, there was a very quiet coup d'état. Napoleon III was deposed and a provisional government was set up under the leadership of Jules Favre, Leon Gambetta and General Trochu. But the abandonment of the emperor did not in any way resolve the situation in Paris. The city was surrounded by German troops on 19 September, which marked the start of a long siege.

THE SIEGE OF PARIS

There were some determined attempts to throw off the Prussian yoke in the provinces, notably by Faidherbe on the River Loire. But Marshal

Bazaine and his garrison of 180,000 were still surrounded, and when on 27 October 1870 they surrendered, any further resistance elsewhere was pointless. The Prussian invasion had succeeded and France was a defeated, occupied, conquered country.

Showing a certain amount of spirit, Gambetta escaped from the siege of Paris in a balloon, with a view to organising resistance to the German occupation from the provinces. The people of Paris suffered several months of severe hardship and famine. The city held out until 28 January 1871 before surrendering. Bismarck and Adolphe Thiers signed an armistice on that day, though the fortress of Belfort held out against the Prussians until 16 February.

Aftermath

The Prussians held a short victory parade in Paris. To sweeten the bitter pill of defeat for the French, Bismarck organised the transport of trainloads of food to the starving Parisians and the withdrawal of Prussian troops to the east of Paris. The troops would be withdrawn altogether, he said, one France agreed to pay Prussia five billion francs as a war indemnity. Having declared war and lost, France was now expected to pay for it.

Prussian troops were withdrawn from the Paris region and posted in the border provinces of Alsace and Lorraine. Parisians no longer felt confident or safe in their city, did not know what to expect next, and many left. Around 200,000 people left Paris for the rural areas. The remaining Parisians were greatly helped by the British, who supplied them with free food and fuel. Gradually, normal life resumed in the French capital.

There was a national election which returned a conservative and rather reactionary government. Under President Thiers, this was set up at Versailles, because the political climate in Paris was too volatile. This new government passed several laws which angered the Parisians. One was the Law of Maturities, which decreed that all rents in Paris, which had been postponed since September 1870, and all public debts everywhere in France, which had been suspended in November 1870, now had to be paid in full, at once and with interest. Parisians were in addition shouldering a disproportionately high proportion of the indemnity payments to Prussia. The people of Paris were furious with Thiers and his government.

Paris had been left under the protection of the revolutionary National Guard, so it was possible for left-wing political leaders to set themselves up in the Hotel de Ville and establish the Paris Commune. In Versailles, the decision was made to suppress this revolution with brute force. The Commune was annihilated with astonishing violence and 20,000 people were killed.

The Treaty of Frankfurt formally stated that Alsace and the northern part of Lorraine were to become German territory. The loss of this mineral-rich territory as spoils of war was a major source of resentment in France. It contributed enormously to anti-German feeling in the twentieth century, and meant that there was widespread public support in France for World War I. France's main aim in involving itself in that conflict was to regain its lost territories. As so often in history, one conflict fuels another.

The Franco-Prussian War had the primary result that Bismarck had intended – the unification of German states into one nation. The creation of the united German Empire changed the power structure of Europe; it disrupted the balance of power that had been devised with the Congress of Vienna after the removal of Napoleon I. Germany very quickly established itself as the main political and military power in Europe, with one of the most powerful armies, though Britain remained the main political and military in the world as a whole. This shift in the power balance made a military confrontation between Germany and Britain almost inevitable.

In the Franco-Prussian War, the seeds of World War I can be seen germinating.

THE ANGLO-ZULU WAR (1879)

BACKGROUND

The Zulu king Mpande had two sons, Cetshwayo and Umtonga. When Umtonga fled to the Utrecht district, which was occupied by Boers (white farmers), Cetshwayo assembled an army along its border. Cetshwayo offered the farmers a strip of land along the border in exchange for his brother. The farmers agreed, but on condition that Umtonga would not be killed. In the same year, 1861, king Mpande duly signed a deed of transfer for the land Cetshwayo had promised. The southern boundary of this new Boer territory ran from Rorke's Drift to the Pongola River.

The new boundary position was marked with a beacon in 1864. The next year Umtonga fled from Zululand to Natal. Then Cetshwayo felt that he had given away the land for nothing. He also felt insecure, as it was possible that he might be supplanted by Umtonga, just as Dingane had been murdered and supplanted by Cetshwayo's father Mpande in 1840, and the great Shaka had been assassinated by Dingane in 1828. To be safe, he needed to assert his authority. Cetshwayo ordered the beacon to be moved. Not long afterwards some Boer troops under Paul Kruger were posted to defend the newly acquired border country; an army under Cetshwayo moved to defend it from the Zulu side. The Zulus took back some more land and questions were raised about the validity of the documents signed by the Zulus relating to the Utrecht strip. In 1869, both sides in the land dispute agreed to accept the lieutenant-governor of Natal as an arbiter, but they still could not agree on a settlement.

That was the situation as it stood when Mpande died and Cetshwayo succeeded him in 1873. Cetshwayo revived the military culture of his uncle, the great warrior king Shaka. He stirred up a revolt in the Transkei and ruled his own people with ruthless tyranny. He was a cold, proud, cruel and untruthful man, according to one white missionary, though that was obviously a powerfully biased view. On the other hand there are well-provenanced accounts of specific atrocities that were carried out at his orders. In 1876, he either ordered or acquiesced in the massacre of a large number of girls. He had ordered them to marry men from an older regiment; they had disobeyed in order to marry youths of their own age. This atrocity brought a strong protest from the Natal government, which was unusual at a time when colonial governments tended to leave subject nations to do things in their own way.

The tension between Cetshwayo and the Transvaal went on. Sir Theophilus Shepstone had supported Cetshwayo over the border dispute, but in 1877 Shepstone visited the area of the Transvaal that was under dispute and began to see the situation from the Boer side. The lieutenant-governor of Natal ordered a commission to report on the border question in 1878, and its report found in favour of the Zulus. The High Commissioner for South Africa, Sir Henry Bartle Frere, disagreed with the report's findings and insisted that if the Boers were forced out they should be compensated by the Zulus.

Cetshwayo was by now in a defiant mood and spoiling for a fight. There were some incidents along the border that may have been intended as deliberate provocation to the white settlers. In two separate incidents two wives of chief Sihayo tried to run away into Natal, where they were caught by the chief's brother and sons; the unfortunate women were later executed according to Zulu law. In another incident, two white men surveying a road went down to a ford and, without crossing the stream, found themselves surrounded by up to twenty armed Zulus. They were taken away, roughly treated and threatened for some time before being let go.

These were minor incidents, scarcely sufficient to warrant an invasion of Zululand. As far as the women were concerned, there was nothing for Cetshwayo to answer for. The executions were barbaric by European standards, but all had been done according to Zulu law and custom, so Cetshwayo was above reproach, though Mehlokazulu and

Bekuzulu, who were the ones who had led the party to seize the women in Natal territory had certainly committed an offence. A message was sent to Cetshwayo to that effect. Cetshwayo treated the matter lightly in his letter of reply, referring to 'a rash act of boys who in their zeal for their father's house did not think of what they were doing.' He agreed that they needed punishing. It was Sir Henry Bartle Frere who raised the temperature by using blustering language like, 'an insult and a violation of British territory which cannot be passed over'. He demanded that 'the leaders of the murderous gangs shall be given up to justice.' He also introduced a reference to an ultimatum.

By the time of the meeting to discuss the findings of the Boundary Commission, more issues had arisen. One was an apparently broken promise given to Shepstone in 1872. Another was a demand for the surrender of Mbelini, the son of a Swazi chief who had unsuccessfully disputed his brother's succession and had been exiled. Cetshwayo had given him refuge and granted him land in what he may have regarded as a useful buffer zone between himself and the Boers. Mbelini took up the life of a brigand, descending from his lair on the Tafelberg to raid Boers and Zulus in his area.

Frere was convinced that Mbelini was being sponsored by Cetshwayo to make trouble, and that was why the demand for his surrender was included in the ultimatum, which now contained a list of no less than *thirteen* demands. Frere seems to have been determined to pick a fight with the Zulus, and he seems to have exploited the long return time for information and instructions to pass to and from London, which gave him considerable freedom of action. London was disposed not to show aggression towards Cetshwayo, but Frere was pursuing a one-man foreign policy of his own. Hicks Beach, in a memorandum to Disraeli in November 1878, wrote, 'I cannot really control him without a telegraph (I don't know that I could with one). I feel it is as likely as not that he is at war with the Zulus at the present moment.'

Cetshwayo rejected Frere's demands, as Frere intended that he should, by simply not responding by the end of December 1878. After 11 January 1879 the British declared that a state of war existed.

THE BATTLE OF ISANDLWANA

General Lord Chelmsford led a British force of over 13,000 soldiers in an invasion of Zululand. The conflict was significantly one-sided, with Cetshwayo commanding a force of 40,000 men. Three British columns went in, from the Lower Tugela River, Rorke's Drift and Utrecht. They were to converge on the royal kraal at Ulundi and at first they marched unopposed. The centre column, advancing from Rorke's Drift, made camp near Isandlwana on 22 January. Lord Chelmsford divided his troops and went off with a scouting party, leaving the camp in the hands of the 1st Battalion of the 24th Foot under the command of Lieutenant Colonel Pulleine. Orders were sent to Colonel Durnford to bring his column up to reinforce the camp. Early in the morning on 22 January, Chelmsford joined Dartnell. The Zulus had vanished. Chelmsford started searching the hills for them, but they had already bypassed him and were bearing down on Isandlwana.

It seems the Zulu attack was in part provoked by Durnford's activities in the hills. Durnford's mounted troops had combed the hills, looking for Zulus. They followed a party of Zulus as they retreated, and suddenly saw an entire Zulu army in a fold of the ground. The Zulus were startled into action when the British troops appeared, forming up into an attack formation. Durnford sent a man back to the camp to warn of the imminent attack. The British troops in the camp were unprepared when Zulus appeared first on the hills to the north, and then to the east. Pulleine had been given no indication by Durnford of the likely scale of the attack. Pulleine was caught completely unawares by the appearance of a Zulu army 20,000 strong. Pulleine ordered his troops to form up facing the Zulus, thinking he was simply supporting Durnford, and sent a message to Chelmsford that he was threatened with imminent attack.

As the main front of the Zulu assault appeared over the ridge, outlying units of British soldiers fell back towards the camp, firing as they went. The main front was slowed down by the terrain, a hill side broken up by many gullies. The main danger to the British in the camp was now from the flanks, the 'horns' which raced down unstoppably to encircle the British flanks. Then the warriors of the 'chest', in the centre, recovered and pushed the advancing British line back into the camp. A Zulu regiment surged in between the retreating British centre and the camp, the horns closed in and the British line disintegrated.

At the height of the battle, at about 2.30 p.m., there was a solar eclipse, which plunged the carnage into an eerie twilight. The breaking line collapsed into informal groups, each making a stand while their ammunition lasted. A group of Natal Carbineers commanded by Durnford gave the Zulus heavy fire until they ran out of ammunition; even then they fought on with their pistols and knives until they were all killed. A few soldiers managed to escape the Zulu encirclement and make their way back towards Rorke's Drift. The Zulus saw what they were doing, blocked the road and forced the escaping soldiers to make a detour up into the hills, where they were hunted down and killed like animals. It was only men on horseback who were able to escape; they reached the River Tugela and crossed it to safety.

The last man to survive the main battle, which was a massacre, escaped up to a cave in the hillside. He carried on fighting single-handed until he ran out of ammunition, then he too was shot down. At the end of the battle, escaping British soldiers were trapped and killed by the Zulus along the banks of the Tugela.

At about 3.30 p.m., Lieutenant Melville of the 1st Battalion, the 24th Foot, collected the regimental flag, the Queen's Colour, from a tent near the end of the battle and rode off towards the Tugela River, which was in flood after rain. Melville plunged in. Halfway across the swirling river he came off his horse, but still clung on to the colour. Lieutenant Coghill went into the river straight afterwards and tried to help Melville. Zulus lining the river bank fired at them and Coghill's horse was killed and the precious colour was swept away. Melville and Coghill reached the Natal bank of the Tugela, where they were killed out of hand by Natal natives, incited by the Zulus. Later, the Queen's Colour was retrieved from the river and survivors from the battle presented it to Queen Victoria.

One thousand three hundred and twenty-nine soldiers were killed on the British side, and about 2,000 Zulus, but it was a total defeat for the British. Chelmsford had made some serious mistakes. He had refused to set up a defensive camp, and ignored intelligence that the Zulus were not far away. The outcome of the Battle of Isandlwana was a foregone conclusion. The British were undefended, outnumbered and unprepared. It was the greatest victory the Zulus were to achieve.

When Chelmsford was told of the disaster he was staggered. All he could manage to say was, 'But I left 1,000 men to guard the camp.' He took his troops to the battlefield to save what could be saved: the Zulus had taken 1,000 rifles and a great deal of ammunition. In the distance he could see smoke rising. It was the supply station – Rorke's Drift.

RORKE'S DRIFT

In the aftermath of the Battle of Isandlwana, a party of 4,000 Zulu warriors raided the British border post of Rorke's Drift. After ten hours of fierce fighting, the Zulus this time were not victorious, but withdrew. The British defence of Rorke's Drift became one of the legends of British military history.

Three men came tumbling down from the Oscarberg, a hill that overlooked the supply station, with the news that a Zulu army was fording the river 'no more than five minutes away.' Then a native scout reported that the Zulus were a minute away. At that moment the natives at the station made a run for it; they had already seen the slaughter at Isandlwana and they wanted no more of it. They deserted, a few British soldiers firing after them. In that instant the force defending Rorke's Drift halved and 140 men had gone.

Chard saw at once that the perimeter of the camp had to be shortened and gave orders for the post to be bisected. Private Hitch, on the storehouse roof, reported a column of 4,000–6,000 Zulu approaching. The south wall, joining the hospital to the storehouse was attacked first. Sergeant Gallagher shouted, 'Here they come, thick as grass and as black as thunder!' The firing started and a pile of Zulu dead started building up. A large force attacked the hospital and the north-west wall and those defending the barricades were engaged in hand to hand fighting.

The Zulus were unable to get over the wall, so they tried crouching beneath it and snatching up at the rifles, or slashing at the British with their spears. Some climbed over the bodies of dead Zulus to drive the

British off the walls, but were pushed back with bayonets. Inevitably, some of the Zulu firing found its mark and several men were shot or wounded. Corporal Scammel was shot in the back and Private Byrne was shot in the head while trying to help him.

It eventually became clear to the British that the front wall could not be held, so the defenders were pulled back into the yard. The front two rooms of the hospital were abandoned as well. The hospital was becoming very dangerous. It was possible for Zulu warriors to poke their rifles through the loopholes and fire into the rooms; British rifles poked out could be grabbed by Zulus outside. The abandonment of the hospital was messy. During the retreat, some of the wounded men were pulled out in time, but not all. Four of them were left behind to be stabbed to death by the Zulus.

The Zulus carried on attacking into the night, only stopping at 2 a.m. After that there was only harassing fire from a distance, and that ended at 4 a.m. Inside the compound virtually every surviving soldier had some kind of wound, and they were all totally exhausted after fighting non-stop for ten hours.

At dawn, the British expected a final attack to finish them off, but the Zulus had gone. All that remained was the piles of bodies. At about 7 a.m. a contingent of Zulus appeared. The exhausted redcoats raised their rifles ready to fight again, but no attack came. Instead they withdrew. Various explanations have been given for this, but the likeliest is that the Zulus were exhausted. They had been on the march for six days before the battle and had not eaten for two; they were several days away from supplies. At 8 a.m. another army appeared. It was Lord Chelmsford. Of the 139 defenders of Rorke's Drift, eleven were awarded the Victoria Cross.

THE SIEGE OF ESHOWE

The right flank column, which was on the coast under Colonel Pearson, crossed the Tugela River and fought a Zulu group at the Inyezane River. Then he advanced to the deserted missionary post of Eshowe, which he fortified. Once Pearson heard the news about the disaster at Isandlwana, he decided to drop back across the Tugela River. Before he could act, the Zulus had surrounded him and the Siege of Eshowe began.

The left flank column at Utrecht was commanded by Colonel Wood. His original orders had been to occupy the tribes of north-west Zululand, to stop them from interfering with the progress of the central column towards Ulundi. Wood set up camp at Tinta's Kraal, close to a force of 4,000 Zulus, which he planned to attack on 24 January. Like Pearson, when he heard about the disaster at Isandlwana, his instinct was to fall back. He withdrew to Tinta's Kraal. So, within a few weeks of the invasion, only one of the three invasion columns remained effective in military terms, and that was not enough to achieve anything on its own.

If Cetshwayo had wanted to invade and conquer Natal, he could have done so at this moment, but that was never his intention. However black he has been painted, Cetshwayo wanted only to defend his own kingdom. As a result, it was possible for Chelmsford to bring in a fresh invasion force. The first priority was to relieve Pearson. The British government sent reinforcements in the shape of seven regiments to Natal. The first new troops disembarked at Durban on 7 March. Three weeks later Lord Chelmsford led a new column of 5,700 soldiers to relieve the siege of Eshowe. Each night when he stopped to set up camp, he ordered defensive entrenchments to be dug. He had learned something from Isandlwana.

Chelmsford ordered Wood to attack the Zulu stronghold from which he had been holding back. It was Lieutenant Colonel Redvers Buller (later to be British commander in the Boer War) who led the attack on 28 March. This initiative, too, was doomed, as a force of 26,000 Zulus arrived, the main Zulu army, to relieve the besieged Zulus. The British troops were scattered. The next day the huge Zulu army descended on Wood's camp at Kambula, without Cetshwayo's consent. In the Battle of Kambula, in which the British were outnumbered by a ratio of ten to one, the Zulus backed off after five hours of heavy fighting. About 2,000 Zulus were killed, but only 29 British soldiers. The unexpected outcome of this battle turned out to be decisive.

Meanwhile, Lord Chelmsford was marching towards Eshowe when he was intercepted at Gingingdlovu on 2 April by a Zulu force. The

Zulus again suffered heavy losses while only two British soldiers died. Chelmsford arrived at Eshowe the next day and relieved Pearson.

THE BATTLE OF ULUNDI

Lord Chelmsford was conscious that in spite of recent successes, he was really only back where he started. He wanted to press on and redeem himself before he was replaced. He knew Sir Garnet Wolseley was being sent to replace him, and he was determined to defeat Cetshwayo before he was relieved of his command. More reinforcements arrived and Chelmsford relaunched his invasion in June.

Another disaster for Chelmsford was the death of the exiled heir to the French throne, Prince Imperial Napoleon Eugène. As he embarked from Southampton, the press commented, '[His mother's] fears for his safety in Zululand may not be totally unfounded. After months of intensive training, it appears that he has yet to master even a simple salute. We hope that no harm will befall him there.' The prince had volunteered for British army service and was killed on 1 June while on a scouting expedition.

Cetshwayo anticipated that the reinforced British army would be very powerful, so he tried to negotiate a peace treaty. But Chelmsford was in no mood to talk now. He marched his men as fast as he could to the royal kraal at Ulundi with every intention of destroying Cetshwayo and his army. On 4 July the two armies met at the Battle of Ulundi. Cetshwayo was decisively defeated.

Aftermath

Most of the Zulu chiefs surrendered and the army dispersed. Cetshwayo himself fled. He was captured on 28 August and sent to Cape Town. The British reported to the Zulus that he had been deposed and Sir Garnet Wolseley drew up plans for a replacement government of Zululand. The royal dynasty was deposed in its entirety, and the country divided under eleven Zulu chiefs, one of whom would be Cetshwayo. Sir Henry Bartle Frere's role in the war had not gone unnoticed by the British authorities, nor forgotten, and he was relegated to a minor post in Cape Town. A cloud hung over him. A bronze statue of him was nevertheless raised on the Thames Embankment; he had become part of the myth of empire.

The new arrangements in Zululand were unsatisfactory, and internal conflicts quickly developed. In 1882, the British decided to reinstate Cetshwayo. The country between the Tugela River and Natal was set aside as a reserve for those Zulus who could not accept the rule of Cetshwayo. This arrangement did not work very well either. The civil war culminated in a raid on 22 July 1883, in which disaffected Zulus led by mounted Boer mercenaries descended on Cetshwayo's kraal, massacring everyone incapable of running away. Though wounded, Cetshwayo himself managed to escape. He moved to Eshowe, where he died not long afterwards.

The breaking up of the traditional polity of the Zulu nation was a major blow to its survival; once the polity was disrupted, the society and the culture disintegrated, too. The war and its aftermath are in a sense emblematic of what happened in Africa as a result of European intervention.

It is clear, in the cold light of day, that the Anglo-Zulu War was a completely unnecessary war. It has nevertheless acquired a cultural importance all its own. This is partly due to the visual contrast between the British soldiers in their Western uniforms, equipped with modern Western weaponry, and the Zulus in traditional African costume and wielding assegais. It is also partly due to the asymmetry of the battles. In several of the major battles the British were seriously outnumbered. 'Impossible odds' were the stock in trade of boys' adventure stories 100 years ago. It is also to do with the astonishing bravery shown by men on both sides. The appeal continues, as is shown by popular films like *Zulu* (1964) about Rorke's Drift and *Zulu Dawn* (1979) about the Battle of Isandlwana.

6

WORLD WAR I:

'The war to end wars'

WORLD WAR I
(1914–18)

TENSIONS

After the final defeat of Napoleon at Waterloo in 1815 there was a long period of peace in Europe which lasted until 1914, but it was a fragile peace disturbed by several ominous small-scale armed conflicts, which hinted that large-scale, continent-wide war could easily break out again. There were the Crimean War, the Italian War of 1859, the Seven Weeks War of 1866, the Franco-Prussian War of 1870–71 and the Russo-Turkish War of 1877–78. These were significant conflicts in themselves, but they were also sinister symptoms of a deep and widespread political instability.

The run-up to World War I was a long period of developing globalisation. The railway age, the age of the steamship and the era of the telegraph were elements in a great Victorian revolution in communications, which was centred on Britain. Springing from this there was also increasing interdependence among countries. By 1914, exports accounted for up to 25 per cent of the economic output of Germany, France and Britain. At the same time, this was an age of empire. Empire-building involved large-scale movements of people, with people emigrating to colonise Australia and North and South America. By 1914, an astonishing 84 per cent of the Earth's surface was inhabited by people of European origin. Europe was at the hub of a demographic, cultural, political and economic dynamo that had run away with itself. The links of interdependency among European states ensured that local wars were likely to generate European wars; the outreach of Europe to the world as a whole ensured that a European war would become a world war.

Within Europe the rulers of the Austro-Hungarian Empire became nervous, feeling critically encircled and jeopardised by the development of neighbouring states, and the rulers of Germany were similarly fretful and edgy about shifts in the European balance of power generally, and this state of mind expressed itself in a frantic arms race against Britain. So there were major regional tensions developing within the continent-wide tensions.

THE TRIGGER

The trigger to the open conflict came from what now looks like a very local act of terrorism, committed in Sarajevo, the capital of Bosnia, a province of the Austro-Hungarian Empire. On 28 June 1914, a group of young conspirators planned the assassination of the Archduke Ferdinand, who was the heir to the throne. It was Gavrilo Princip, a nineteen-year-old Bosnian Serb, who shot the Archduke and his wife. It was a symbolic act. Even the date chosen was symbolic; it was the anniversary of the Battle of Kosovo in 1389, a disaster for the kingdom of Serbia, and in the turbulence following the battle a Serb had assassinated the Turkish sultan.

The assassination was a personal tragedy for the Archduke and his family, but it was an internal matter, something happening between rulers and subjects within the state, and should not have led to war. What made that happen was the response of the Imperial family. A promise was secretly obtained from Germany to support drastic retaliation. Then on 23 July the Austrians gave neighbouring Serbia an ultimatum alleging that the assassination had been planned in Belgrade and demanding a crackdown on subversives in Serbia. Under the circumstances, the Belgrade government responded well. Just within the forty-eight-hour deadline given, they accepted nearly all the demands made so far, even consenting to an Austrian-led inquiry into the assassination conspiracy – as it was consistent with Serbia's constitution and international law. Because of the conditions Belgrade made, Vienna broke off relations with Belgrade at once and three days later declared war on Serbia.

Because the whole of Europe was entangled in defensive alliances, with this country agreeing to go the aid of that in the event of war, it took only a matter of weeks for all the major powers to find themselves at war – over Sarajevo. When Austria-Hungary declared war on Serbia, France and Russia began mobilising their armies. This led to Germany declaring war on Russia on 1 August and France two days later. When the German army marched into Belgium on 4 August, Britain declared war on Germany. Turkey had just signed a defensive alliance with Germany, so in September it, too, joined the war, siding with Germany against Britain, France and Russia.

THE WAR ON LAND

There were several theatres of war, including the Atlantic, the North Sea, the Middle East and Northern Italy, but the fiercest fighting was on Germany's Eastern and Western Fronts. Fighting on the Western Front went on along a system of opposing trenches, breastworks, gun emplacements and fortifications that stretched for a distance of 600 km (370 miles), and separated from each other by a dangerous no man's land. For many soldiers and onlookers the Western Front defined World War I. The Eastern Front was huge and, partly because of limited rail access, less well defined, but the conflict there was just as violent. The Italian and Middle Eastern Fronts were also the scenes of heavy fighting.

THE FIRST BATTLE OF THE MARNE (1914)

The advance of German troops through Belgium and into northern France immediately made that region one of the main theatres of war. It became known as the Western Front.

The British Expeditionary Force, 70,000 strong, under General Horace Smith-Dorrien, arrived in France on 14 August 1914. It was on its way to join the French Army at Charleroi when it met the advancing German force at Mons, along a front 40 km (25 miles) long. Sir John French was in command of the British infantry, while the cavalry division under

General Edmund Allenby was kept in reserve. With the idea of stopping the German advance into France, the Royal Fusiliers were ordered to destroy the bridges over the Mons-Conde Canal. These men came under heavy German fire. Five of them received the Victoria Cross.

On 23 August, the 150,000 soldiers of the German army under General Alexander von Kluck attacked the British positions. The Germans suffered heavy losses, but Sir John French was obliged to order his men to retreat. French wanted to retreat to the Channel coast, but the British war minister, Lord Kitchener, ordered him to retreat to the River Marne, south-east of Paris instead. The French Fifth and Sixth Armies were in retreat, too.

The German invasion force was divided into three armies, all sweeping south to reach Paris. Von Kluck, commanding the German First Army, had orders to surround Paris from the east. The French government expected the Germans to capture Paris imminently and fled to Bordeaux; about half a million civilians had also left Paris by 3 September. Joseph Joffre, the French commander-in-chief, ordered the French troops to fall back to a line roughly following the River Seine and River Marne valleys. Joffre intended to attack the advancing German army on 6 September and, with that in view, replaced General Lanrezac with the more aggressive General Franchet d'Esperey. Sir John French agreed to join in the French attack on the German army.

As planned, the attack on the German First Army was launched on 6 September. In response, von Kluck wheeled his whole army round to face this attack, which opened a gap 50 km (30 miles) wide between his own army and the German Second Army commanded by General Karl von Bulow. Seeing this an opportunity to weaken the German advance, the British army and the French Fifth Army moved into the gap. For three days the Germans were unable to break through the Allied lines. At one point the French Sixth Army came close to folding and it was only saved by rushing 6,000 reservists to the battle using a fleet of Paris taxis.

On 9 September, the German commander-in-chief, General Helmuth von Moltke, ordered Generals von Bulow and von Kluck to retreat. This allowed the British and French armies to cross the Marne. Even though the Germans were retreating, the Allied advance was slow, covering only 20 km (12 miles) on the first day. Because of this slowness, von Kluck's army was able to reunite with von Bulow's in the valley of the River Aisne.

By sundown on 10 September, the Battle of the Marne was over. The French has suffered 250,000 casualties, and it is believed German casualties were on a similar scale, though the German authorities never revealed how many men they had lost on the Marne. British losses amounted to 12,733.

The most significant consequence of the Battle of the Marne was that the French and British armies had made it clear that Germany was not going to win a quick, decisive victory. The German army had nevertheless not been decisively defeated either, and the war was evidently going to be protracted. It was going to be a long war. The British soldiers' slogan 'Home by Christmas' quickly turned into black humour.

The most important consequence of the Battle of the Marne was that the French and British forces were able to prevent the German plan for a swift and decisive victory. However, the German army was not beaten and its successful retreat ended all hope of a short war.

THE BATTLE OF TANNENBERG (1914)

At the start of the war, General Alexander Samsonov was given command of the Russian Second Army with the order to invade East Prussia. This opened another theatre of war, the Eastern Front. Samsonov advanced slowly into the south-west corner of the province, with the intention of linking up with General Paul von Rennenkampf who was advancing from the north-east. Faced with this Russian advance, General Maximilian Prittwitz, commanding the German army, ordered his men to retreat. He was immediately dismissed. Instead, Generals Paul von Hindenburg and Erich Ludendorff went out to meet Samsonov.

The two armies met on 22 August 1914. For almost a week the Russians were making progress – they had superior numbers – but by 29 August Samsonov was surrounded. Samsonov tried to retreat, but he was now in a noose and most of his troops were killed or captured. Of the 150,000 troops he started out with, only 10,000 escaped. Samsonov was so shaken and humiliated by the disaster that he killed himself. The Germans lost 20,000 men in the Battle of Tannenberg, but took more than 92,000 Russian prisoners.

The Battle of Tannenberg was such a disaster for the Allies that all news of it was suppressed as far as the British press was concerned. Censorship was a major feature of the war, right from the beginning.

THE BATTLE OF YPRES (1914)

Ypres, a Belgian town, was captured by the German army early on, but by the beginning of October 1914 the British Expeditionary Force was able to retake it. The first serious attempt by the Germans to get the town back again came on 15 October. Experience British riflemen managed to hold their positions, but sustained heavy losses.

The Germans attacked repeatedly during the following four weeks, but thanks to the arrival of French troops the British were able to hold out. The weather worsened and on 22 November the Germans decided to abandon their attack on Ypres. The Germans suffered 135,000 casualties. The British lost fewer – 75,000 men – but the British Expeditionary Force was in effect destroyed as a professional army. Ypres went on being a bone of contention during the war; there were to be two more major battles there, the Second Battle of Ypres (April-May 1915) and Passchendaele (July-October 1917).

GALLIPOLI (1915)

The British attacked Turkish forts in the Dardanelles, the entrance to the Black Sea, on 19 February 1915. The attack opened with a long range bombardment, then continued with heavy fire at close range. The immediate effect was that the outer forts were abandoned by the Turks. Then British minesweeper went in, penetrating 10 km (6 miles) inside the Dardanelles straits, to clear the channel of mines. But further advance into the straits was impossible as the inner Turkish forts were too far away to be knocked out by the Allied warships. The minesweepers were sent on to clear the next reach of the straits but were forced back when they came under fire from the Turkish batteries.

The First Lord of the Admiralty, Winston Churchill, was impatient at the slow progress Admiral Carden was making in the Dardanelles. He demanded to know when Carden was going on to the next stage in the campaign. Carden was extremely stressed by the situation; now that he was under pressure from Churchill he headed towards nervous breakdown. In mid-March 1915, he was sent home and replaced by Vice-Admiral Sir John de Robeck, who did not hesitate to order the Allied fleet to advance through the still-mined Dardanelles.

On 18 March, eighteen British and French battleships entered the enemy waters. Initially they made good progress. Then the French battleship *Bouvet* hit a mine, capsized and sank; shortly afterwards the British warships *Irresistible* and *Ocean* hit mines too. The Allied fleet had to retreat, with three major warships and 700 men lost, and three more warships seriously damaged. Churchill had made an expensive mistake. De Robeck advised Churchill that he could not take the Gallipoli peninsula, on the European side of the Dardanelles, without the aid of the army. General Hamilton, commanding the troops on the nearby island of Lemnos, had watched the naval fiasco and agreed. Plans were then made for landing troops at Gallipoli.

Greek army officers, who knew the terrain and knew the Turks, told Kitchener it would need 150,000 troops to take Gallipoli. Kitchener decided that half that number would suffice and they were duly sent to Lemnos. It was another terrible mistake. The Turkish commander, Liman von Sanders, heard that 70,000 troops were about to arrive on Lemnos and positioned his 84,000 men along the Gallipoli coast where he anticipated they would attempt to land.

The Gallipoli landings began on 25 April 1915, establishing two beachheads at Helles and Gaba Tepe. On 6 August, another beachhead was established at Sulva Bay. But attempts to send these troops in sweeps across the peninsula were a failure. General Hamilton asked for another 95,000 men. Churchill agreed with this tactic, but Kitchener was unwilling to send any more troops into the area. In October, Hamilton was replaced by General Munro. After looking at the situation on the ground, Munro advised that withdrawal was the best strategy. Kitchener himself arrived two weeks later, and he agreed, recommending the withdrawal of all 105,000 men. The evacuation started at Sulva Bay on 7 December. The last of the Allied troops left a month later, on 9 January 1916. About 480,00 Allied troops took part in the Gallipoli campaign, of which 43,000 of the British contingent were killed, 11,000 of the Australian and New Zealand contingents were killed and 5,000 of the French contingent were killed. Some 65,000 Turks were killed, but all to no avail. Gallipoli was an unmitigated disaster, largely due to major errors of judgement by Churchill and Kitchener.

THE ARTOIS OFFENSIVE (1915)

During the Second Battle of Ypres, Joffre decided he would attempt to break through the German lines on the Western Front at Artois. There was a preliminary bombardment of German positions that lasted for five days. Then, on 9 May 1915, Pétain led the French Ninth Army into the attack. The main objective was Vimy Ridge, but Pétain was unable to hold it. Gneeral Sir Douglas Haig led a simultaneous British attack at Neuve Chapelle, and he too failed to make a breakthrough.

On 25 September, the British and French launched another attack on the German line at Artois. General Dubail managed to reach the crest of Vimy Ridge, but the German Sixth Army pushed him back again. Haig attacked at Loos and made some progress, but was similarly forced back. After a second British attack on 13 October resulted in heavy losses, Sir John French decided to end the Artois offensive. It had been an expensive failure, with 50,000 British and 48,000 French casualties.

THE BATTLE OF VERDUN (1916)

Verdun was a fortified French garrison town on the River Meuse. In December 1915, the German Chief of Staff, General Erich von Falkenhayn, decided that the German army would attack Verdun. He believed that it was impossible for the German troops to take Verdun, but that the offensive would be worthwhile, because defending the town would 'bleed the French army white'. The German assault began on 21 February 1916, with a spectacular assemblage of one million German soldiers attacking a town defended by 200,000 French troops. By the second day, the French had fallen back from their first line of trenches to the second. By 24 February, they had fallen back to the third line of trenches, just 8 km (5 miles) outside Verdun itself.

On that day, General Petain was given command of the Verdun sector. He arranged that every spare French soldier was diverted to this section of the Western Front; 259 out of the 330 infantry regiments in the French Army fought at Verdun. Halted at the end of February, the German army made a new onslaught on 6 March. Major French strategic points fell at the end of May and the first week in June, after a long siege.

The German made repeated attacks on Verdun during the summer and autumn of 1916, but they had to scale down their attacks as they needed to transfer troops to defend the German front line on the Somme. The French now made a courageous counter-attack under General Charles Mangin, in which they managed to recapture the lost forts in November.

Verdun was the longest battle in World War I and one of the largest in scale. It ended on 18 December 1916. The French army lost about 550,000 men there, but the Germans also suffered heavy losses – 434,000 casualties. Nothing was achieved in this battle other than the gradual wearing-down of both sides. It did indeed bleed the French army white – but it did not prevent them from winning both the battle and the war.

THE BATTLE OF THE SOMME (1916)

The idea for the Battle of the Somme came from Joffre and was accepted by Haig, even though Haig would have preferred to mount a large-scale attack in Flanders. Joffre was motivated by the idea of territorial gain in the Paris Basin, but he also intended the battle to destroy German manpower. Initially, Joffre proposed to use French troops, but the huge German attack on Verdun, which came in February

1916, prompted an escalation of the Somme; it was to be turned into a major diversionary attack by the British Expeditionary Force. As such, overall responsibility for the battle passed over to General Haig; Haig and General Sir Henry Rawlinson devised a plan of attack.

Haig's strategy was to begin with an eight-day bombardment that would, he believed, completely destroy all the forward German gun emplacements. After that, Rawlinson and the Fourth Army were to advance towards Bapaume. North of Rawlinson, General Allenby and the Third Army were to break through the German line. Cavalry standing by would pass through the gap Allenby created. To the south, General Fayolle was to advance towards Combles with the French Sixth Army. On paper it looked foolproof, especially with the large forces Haig had in view; he was going to use 750,000 men.

The Battle of the Somme went wrong for the Allied forces right from the start. The preliminary bombardment was a failure. It did not knock out the German defences at all. It was useless against the barbed wire; it was ineffectual against the concrete bunkers protecting the German troops. This meant that when the British and French troops marched forward at 7.30 a.m. on 1 July, the Germans were still ensconced in good defensive positions, and the barbed wire was still there to impede the Allied infantry. The losses on the Allied side were horrific. The British Expeditionary Force suffered 58,000 casualties, about a third of which were fatalities. It was the single worst day in history for the British army. And it was only the first day of the Battle of the Somme.

Strangely, Haig was not disheartened or dismayed by this huge loss of human life on the first day of the battle. He ordered Rawlinson to go on attacking the German front line. There was a temporary breakthrough during a night attack on 13 July, but German reinforcements quickly sealed the gap in their front line. There was another, minor, victory on 23 July, when the Allies captured Pozières, but this was not sustained. Haig persuaded himself that the Germans were close to exhaustion and ordered more attacks, all of them very costly in lives.

On 15 September, General Micheler joined the battle in the south. With his twelve divisions, and using tanks for the first time, Micheler succeeded in gaining a few kilometres.

Haig went on and on ordering attacks until deteriorating winter weather put an end to one of the most ill-conceived battles of modern times. In all, the British army suffered 420,000 casualties and the French something approaching 200,000. German casualties are estimated at 500,000. At some points the front was pushed back, but only by a maximum of 12 km (7½ miles).

THE NIVELLE OFFENSIVE (1916)

Joffre was replaced by Robert Nivelle in December 1916 as Commander-in-Chief of Allied forces on the Western Front. Nivelle straight away devised a plan for a major offensive on the German front line. One important element of the plan was to capture Vimy Ridge. Nivelle argued that because the ridge was 60 metres (200 ft) high, Allied control of it would guarantee a panoramic view of German activity behind the front line.

On the evening of 8 April 1917, 30,000 troops belonging to the Canadian Corps were moved up to the front line. Early the next morning, Allied guns opened heavy fire on the German trenches as a preliminary. Then the Canadian infantry went over the top and out across No-Man's-Land. The advance was supported by a carefully planned creeping barrage; the gunfire was aimed just ahead of the steadily advancing infantry, to destroy enemy positions just before they reached them. Within thirty minutes, the Canadian Corps had captured an important German trench system, and after another hour another trench system was under Canadian control.

The operation was not without mishap, though. Several German German machine-gun posts survived the barrage because they were built of concrete, and these inflicted heavy casualties on the Allies. More than half of the men in the 87th Battalion of the Canadian 4th Division were lost in just a few minutes of German machine-gun fire.

Allenby led the British Third Army in an attack on each side of Arras, and made good progress on the first day. But after that the Germans resisted strongly. General Gough tried to overstretch the German defences by taking the British Fifth Army into the offensive further south. Gough used tanks, but was still stopped as Bullecourt. Australian troops who assisted in this attack suffered very heavy losses.

By 12 April, the Canadians were in firm control of Vimy Ridge. Now disadvantaged down on low ground, the Germans retreated under cover of night. By the time the offensive was halted in May, the British had suffered heavy losses – around 160,000 casualties in all. The Canadian Corps lost 11,300 men, killed, wounded or missing.

THE BATTLE OF PASSCHENDAELE (1917)

The Battle of Passchendaele was the third major battle fought at Ypres during World War I. It was another long battle; it went on from July until November 1917. As at the Somme, Haig was convinced that the German army was close to collapse, and equally convinced that all that was needed was a major offensive to make the breakthrough.

It was General Gough who led the opening attack with the British Fifth Army. To his right he had General Plumer leading the Second Army; to his left he had General Anthoine and the French First Army. There was a preliminary bombardment lasting ten days, a barrage of over four million shells. Then the British infantry went in at 3.50 a.m. on 31 July 1917. The German Fourth Army held the British advance back. The Allied attacks continued regardless of heavy rain, which turned the low-lying land into a muddy swamp. The heavy bombardment by the British destroyed both the natural and the artificial drainage of the landscape. The bombardment also helped to liquefy the surface layer of the land, making progress by infantry and tanks almost impossible. Many wounded men drowned in the mud. Eventually Haig called off the attacks, resuming in late September.

The attacks of 26 September and 4 October were successful as far as the Allies were concerned; British troops occupied the ridge east of Ypres. Heavy rain resumed, but Haig wanted to continue, ordering attacks towards the Passchendaele Ridge. The new attacks failed. Now the British soldiers had to contend with mustard gas as well as mud and bullets. On 6 November the village of Passchendaele was finally taken by British and Canadian troops, but at a cost of 310,000 casualties.

It was a small victory at a very high cost. General Haig was severely criticised for continuing attacks that had no real strategic value.

THE CAMBRAI OFFENSIVE (1917)

After the bad experience at Passchendaele, in which tanks had become inoperable in thick mud, Colonel Fuller, chief of staff to the Tank Corps, proposed a large-scale raid on dry ground, between the Canal du Nord and the St Quentin Canal. The commander of the Third Army, General Byng, accepted Fuller's plan, though it had originally been vetoed by Haig.

His failure to break through at Ypres led Haig to change his mind. He ordered a mass tank attack at Artois. This time there was no preliminary bombardment, and therefore no prior warning to the Germans. The attack, at dawn on 20 November, took the Germans completely by surprise. Using nearly 500 tanks and six infantry divisions, the assault gained more than 6 km (3¾ miles) on the first day. This was added to on subsequent days, until there was a German counter-offensive.

By the time the Battle of Artois came to an end on 7 December 1917, the German troops had won back all the ground they had lost. There had been 45,000 British and 50,000 German casualties. Haig saw the Cambrai Offensive as a failure. He was unconvinced about the new-fangled tanks; they were bizarre; the infantrymen thought they looked like giant toads. The failure at Cambrai made him sure that tanks could never win the war. This was an odd conclusion, in that if he had viewed the Battle of the Somme objectively he must have deduced that a combination of artillery and infantry could not win the war either. And no less a person than the German general, Paul von Hindenburg, was deeply impressed by the performance of the British tanks at Cambrai, as he wrote in his autobiography:

The English attack at Cambrai for the first time revealed the possibilities of a great surprise attack with tanks. We had had previous experience of this weapon in the spring offensive, when it had not made any particular impression. However, the fact that the tanks had now been raised to such a pitch of technical perfection that they could cross our undamaged trenches and obstacles did not fail to have a marked effect on our troops. The physical effects of fire from machine guns and light ordnance with which the steel Colossus was provided were far less destructive than the moral effect of its comparative invulnerability. The infantryman felt that he could do practically nothing against its armoured sides. As soon as the machine broke through our trench lines, the defender felt himself threatened in the rear and left his post.

THE SECOND BATTLE OF THE MARNE (1918)

The Second Battle of the Marne took place close to the end of the war, in the summer of 1918. In its Spring Offensive, the German army advanced across the River Aisne (late May), reaching the River Marne on 5 June. By this stage in the war, the French army was in a poor state. Its commander, Pétain, knew that the British were resisting a German offensive at Lys, but nevertheless needed British aid. Haig eventually agreed to let Pétain have four divisions of British troops and two recently arrived American divisions. In this way, more than 85,000 US soldiers took part in the Second Battle of the Marne.

The German attack was launched by General Erich von Ludendorff on 15 July. He hurled a huge force at the Allies: 23 divisions attacked the French Fourth Army to the east of the city of Rheims, 17 divisions attacked the French Fifth Army to the west of the city. In spite of these huge forces, the Germans were unable to break through. General Foch counter-attacked with 24 divisions of the French army together with troops from Italy, America and Britain. On 20 July, the German retreat began and by the first week in August the Germans were back where they were before they launched their Spring Offensive.

The tide had turned in favour of the Allies, though the cost was huge. American casualties numbered 12,000, British 13,000 and French 95,000. But the German army is believed to have suffered 168,000 casualties in the battle. The Germans had fought the Second Battle of the Marne to win the war; their defeat proved that they could not do it. Although the fighting would go on for a while longer, it was from that point on a rearguard action.

THE MEUSE-ARGONNE OFFENSIVE (1918)

This Allied offensive opened on 26 September with an attack on the German front line at the Canal du Nord. This was perhaps the most difficult section of the Hindenburg Line that the Allies had to attack; there were marshes on each side of the road between Arras and Cambrai, and the Germans were occupying a high position, giving them a major advantage.

Canadian soldiers led the attack on the canal, supported by covering fire from heavy artillery. British troops led by General Byng moved forward along a front 20 km (12½ miles long to the north. The Allies made good progress with their offensive when, on 1 October, it was called off.

THE WAR AT SEA

The sea war was given its distinctive character by the new developments in battleship technology. It was the British Admiral John Fisher who was the main driving force behind the development of HMS *Dreadnought*, launched in 1906. This ship was the most heavily armed ship in history, with ten 12-inch guns; they were mounted higher than usual, in order to increase their range and improve their accuracy. The *Dreadnought* had many smaller-calibre guns and also five torpedo tubes. She was also very heavily armoured; along the waterline she was protected by armour plates 28 cm (11 in) thick. Powered by four sets of Parsons turbines, the *Dreadnought* was faster than any other warship of its day, with a maximum speed of twenty-one knots. This was a brand-new fighting machine, very much a product of the arms race between Britain and Germany.

The revolutionary design was quickly copied to produce a whole class of great battleships called dreadnoughts. By 1914, the British shipyards had completed nineteen of them, with another thirteen under construction. Germany copied the design and by 1914 had thirteen dreadnoughts, with another seven under construction. America and France had eight dreadnoughts each. The design was still developing during the war. In 1915, Britain built the *Queen Elizabeth*, a super-dreadnought with eight 38-cm (15-in) guns; four more were built to this design: *Warspite, Barham, Malaya* and *Valiant*. All five of these ships survived World War I to serve in World War II, one of the many ways in which World War II was a continuation of the First.

Another major new piece of marine technology was the military submarine. The first submarine used by the British navy was designed by John P. Holland and launched in 1902. From 1905, it was Germany that took the lead in designing submarines with real fighting ability. By 1913, the German designers had produced the first diesel-powered Unterseeboot (U-boat). By 1914, Germany had ten U-boats, with seventeen more under construction. Britain had fifty-five submarines and the French seventy-seven.

These early submarines were slow (eighteen knots on the surface, eight underwater), fragile and could only stay under water for a couple of hours. They were nevertheless a very serious threat to conventional shipping because they were fitted with torpedoes – and could move about unseen.

The German U-boats, with their orders to sink Allied shipping at will, were a major danger during the war. They succeeded in sinking 192 ships, killing over 5,400 people. The scale of the killing was very small by comparison with that of the great land battles, but it had a profound psychological effect in Britain; suddenly being on an island surrounded by U-boat-infested waters seemed perilous. In the first six months of 1915, German U-boats were responsible for destroying 750,000 tons of British shipping. In 1916, the convoy system was devised to reduce the danger, and the scale of the losses.

THE BATTLE OF HELIGOLAND BIGHT (1914)

In August 1914, the British Admiral Sir David Beatty conceived a plan to draw the German navy into a major battle in the North Sea. Beatty provoked the Germans by sending two light cruisers, the *Fearless* and the *Arethusa*, with twenty-five destroyers to raid German ships near the German naval base at Heligoland. Once the German navy responding to this provocation, Beatty sent in two battleships, the *New Zealand* and the *Invincible*, along with three battlecruisers. The idea was to bring on a major sea battle that would decisively trounce the Germans. The British fleet was designed for major set-piece confrontations of this kind.

In the Battle of Heligoland Bight which followed, the Germans lost three cruisers and a destroyer. Of the British fleet, no ships were lost; the *Arethusa* was badly damaged but was towed safely home for repair.

The success of the battle and Beatty's aggressive strategy played a large part in his appointment as Jellicoe's successor as Commander of the British Grand Fleet in December 1916.

THE BATTLE OF THE FALKLAND ISLANDS (1914)

The British navy sent two battlecruisers, the *Inflexible* and the *Invincible*, to protect the Falkland Islands in the South Atlantic. A fortnight later they were followed by five cruisers, which headed for the Port Stanley naval base. The Germans seem to have been unprepared for a major British military presence in the Falklands, when five German cruisers arrived there on 7 December with the intention of taking Port Stanley. Presumably seizing this remote British possession was planned as a major, but easy, propaganda victory.

The German commander, Admiral von Spee, saw at once that he was outnumbered and outgunned – and fled. The British ships steamed after him and eventually caught up. The British ships gave the German cruisers a heavy pounding and the cruisers *Scharnhorst* and *Gneisenau* were sunk quickly. The *Nurnberg* and the *Leipzig* tried to make a run for it, but they were chased and destroyed. Only the *Dresden* managed to get away.

Admiral von Spee and his two sons were among the 2,200 German sailors who died in this violent but one-sided battle. The Falkland

Islands remained under British control – for the rest of the twentieth century – and the Battle of the Falkland Islands turned into a British rather than a German propaganda victory.

THE BATTLE OF THE DOGGER BANK (1915)

In December 1914, Admiral Franz von Hipper made an ill-judged decision. He took his German High Seas Fleet to the North Sea coast of England and bombarded defenceless civilian populations in the towns of Scarborough, Hartlepool and Whitby. The attacks killed only eighteen people, but generated enormous anger and contempt in Britain for Germany. Hipper planned to make further raids of the same kind in January 1915, but British outrage prompted Admiral Beatty to take some pre-emptive action.

Beatty took six battlecruisers and a flotilla of destroyers to intercept Hipper's fleet. In an exchange of fire in the middle of the North Sea, the German ships *Sydlitz* and *Blucher* were damaged and in retaliation the Germans damaged Beatty's ship, the *Lion.* Both sides claimed the Battle of the Dogger Bank as a victory.

THE BATTLE OF JUTLAND (1916)

In May 1916, the commander of the German fleet, von Scheer, decided he would take on the British navy in a pitched sea battle. He offered as calculated bait a fleet of German ships steaming along the coast of Denmark. When Admiral Jellicoe heard about it at Rosyth, he gave orders for the Grand Fleet to put to sea.

Neither Jellicoe nor von Scheer had the advantage of reconnaissance aircraft to locate their enemy's position, so they both sent out scouting cruisers. As it happened, it was the scouting cruisers that made contact, and there was a brief exchange of gunfire before they returned to their respective fleets. Meanwhile, Beatty had sailed from Scapa Flow in the Orkneys with fifty-two ships. He was on his way to join Jellicoe and the Grand Fleet. It was Beatty who first came in contact with the forty-strong German fleet commanded by Admiral Franz von Hipper, west of

Jutland and south of Norway. The two fleets opened fire at each other at a range of 15 km (9 miles).

Visibility was poor, owing to haze, and the position of the sun gave the Germans an advantage. The British battlecruiser *Indefatigable* took five shells fired by the German battlecruiser *Von der Tann*; there was a magazine explosion on the *Indefatigable* and she sank with the loss of over 1,000 lives. That happened at 4.03 p.m. and only twenty minutes later the *Queen Mary* also blew up after being hit, and sank in just ninety seconds. Two destroyers from each fleet were also sunk.

Beatty's situation became more serious still when Admiral von Scheer arrived at the scene with the German High Seas Fleet. Jellicoe and the British Grand Fleet were 20 km (12½ miles) away from Beatty when the battle started and, before Jellicoe could reach Beatty, at 6.33 p.m. the *Invincible* became the third of Beatty's battleships to blow up after being hit by a German shell. Jellicoe ordered his ships to fire the moment the Grand Fleet arrived. Now it was von Scheer who was in serious danger. He ordered his fleet to turn north and steam away from the battle. Jellicoe feared that von Scheer was leading him towards a submarine trap or a minefield, and did not follow. Instead he ordered his ships to head south-east with the idea of intercepting von Scheer as he took his ships home.

At 7.10 p.m., the two fleets met once more. Von Scheer gave the order for the admiral to charge the Grand Fleet with his battleships, while ordering his own ships to turn away from the fighting. But after twenty minutes of firing, Hipper too headed for home. Once again, Jellicoe was unwilling to follow directly. This time he headed south-west, and successfully intercepted Hipper's ships at 8.15 p.m. In this encounter, Jellicoe succeeded in sinking the *Lutzow* and severely damaging the *Sydlitz* and *Derfflinger* before the German fleet withdrew; once again, Jellicoe did not follow.

The result of the Battle of Jutland was ambiguous. Victory was claimed by both sides. Admiral von Scheer and the German Navy claimed they had won on the basis of the number of ships destroyed. The British had lost three battlecruisers, three cruisers and eight destroyers, and suffered 6,100 casualties; the Germans had lost one battleship, one battlecruiser, four light cruisers and three destroyers, and suffered only 2,550 casualties. On the other hand, strategically the Battle of Jutland was a British victory in that the German fleet hardly ventured out of port for the rest of the war.

Jellicoe was naturally criticised in Britain for being over-cautious in not pursuing the enemy each time it retreated, but he saw it as his primary duty to protect and maintain the size of the Grand Fleet. He was able to report to the British government on 2 June that the Grand Fleet was ready for action again. On the other hand, the German High Seas Fleet had to be rebuilt and was never in a position to risk another naval engagement. Jellicoe rightly claimed that his tactics were right and that Jutland was a tactical victory for the British.

THE WAR IN THE AIR

Flight was still in its infancy when World War I broke out, and the use of aircraft was naturally tentative and experimental. There were, in total, fewer than a thousand aircraft involved in World War I.

As well as aircraft there were airships, though fewer than fifty of these. In January 1915, two (German) Zeppelin airships flew across the East Anglian coast and dropped bombs on King's Lynn and Great Yarmouth, killing twenty-eight civilians. Following this trial raid, the Germans launched bombing raids on London and the Midlands. In all only 600 people were killed in these raids, but they had a profound psychological effect on Britain. In 1917, the Germans stopped using Zeppelins for bombing raids, because they were very vulnerable to adverse weather conditions and were relatively easy to attack. Technical advances in planes had by that stage made them infinitely preferable.

The style of fighting in the air was at first usually a duel between two planes, known as a 'dogfight'. The first fighter planes did not have inbuilt guns, only machine guns that were bolted on top of the wings. The planes were fitted with two seats, one behind the other. The front seat was for the pilot, the rear seat for the gunner. The first dogfight, the first battle in the air of any kind, took place on 28 August 1914; Lieutenant Norman Spratt used his (unarmed) Sopwith Tabloid to force down a German plane.

The dogfights generated a special breed of war heroes, men with film star status. Louis Strange was one of the first British star pilots. He invented a system of safety straps which enabled his gunner to 'stand up and fire all round over the top of the plane and behind'. Strange's gunner was a man named Rabagliati. By 1915, fighter planes were in regular use in the skies over the Western Front. A major technical advance was made by Anton Fokker, a Dutch designer who devised a machine gun that had a blocking device to stop the gun from firing whenever it was in line with the propeller blades. Until then it was possible for the gunner to shoot down his own plane.

Pilots who were able to claim eight kills or more were known as flying aces. German flying aces included men like Max Immelmann and Oswald Boelcke. Boelcke brought down forty Allied planes before he too was killed in October 1916. Mick Mannock, the leading British ace, scored seventy-three kills before he was killed in July 1918. The death rate was very high, and by the end of the war nearly all the pilots were under the age of twenty-one. By 1917, tactics were changing, and it became commoner for British planes to hunt in packs of six, often in V formation; German pilots preferred larger formations which were known as circuses.

The contribution made by the war in the air was inevitably slight. But it was a highly significant episode because of the impetus the war gave to technical innovation. The technology of flying advanced enormously during those four years.

Consequences and aftermath

The Allied or Entente Powers (France, Russia, Britain and its colonies) finally defeated the Central Powers (the Austro-Hungarian, German and Ottoman Empires) in 1918. The Allied Powers were joined by Italy in 1915 and the United States in 1917; they were abandoned by Russia after the Russian Revolution in 1917.

It was a great shock to Europeans generally when Germany decided to march two million men out across its frontiers and into the agricultural and industrial landscapes of neighbouring states. It was a shock that Germany was to repeat in 1939. The German people have, in a sense, had to live down their reputation after 1945. That enactment of war was an enormous folly in itself – a mistake. The second major mistake that Germany made was in declaring unrestricted submarine warfare. Without that, better terms for surrender might have been procured as the war closed. Embittering her enemies, Germany ensured that the peace terms would be crippling and humiliating for her – and those terms led on to a sense of frustration and grievance that contained the seeds of World War II. If the Treaty of Versailles had been more lenient, there would have been less resentment for Hitler to tap.

Of all the countries in Europe, Russia was in the most troubled and unstable state. Fighting a major foreign war was the catalyst that made the Russian Revolution possible. This was foreseen by some Russians even before the war began. In 1914, Peter Durnovo, a former interior minister, wrote to Tsar Nicholas II to say that the war would end in defeat for Russia and a cataclysmic social upheaval. He was right. The tsar himself accelerated the process by quixotically making himself personally responsible for his army's defeat; this led inevitably to calls for his abdication. He was duly deposed and executed, along with his family. World War I therefore had as two of its consequences the inauguration of a socialist state in Russia and the rise of Stalin.

There was a parallel shift in Germany. The kaiser was deposed and exiled, and his autocratic regime was replaced by a more democratic one. Four dynasties with their four ancillary aristocratic elites were all swept away at the end of the war: the Hohenzollerns, the Habsburgs, the Ottomans and the Romanovs.

The Treaty of Versailles in 1919 made a formal end to the war. Germany was held under blockade until its leaders had signed the treaty. Under duress, Germany was obliged to admit moral responsibility for the war and agree to pay huge war reparations. The only way these could be paid was by borrowing from the United States, which went on until the payments stopped in 1931. The terms of the treaty seriously damaged the German economy, contributed to runaway inflation and economic collapse. There was no question among the Allies that Germany had to shoulder the consequences of its guilt, but one of the consequences was enormous bitterness. It was easy for extreme nationalist groups like the Nazis to exploit this bitterness for their own ends.

The Treaty of Sèvres in 1920 arranged for the punishment of Turkey by the partitioning of the Ottoman Empire. This treaty was never agreed to by the sultan, and the republican movement in Turkey rejected it, too. There was a Turkish War of Independence, which led to a 1923 Treaty of Lausanne. The Austro-Hungarian Empire was similarly dismembered, mainly along ethnic lines, in the terms of the Treaties of Saint-Germain and Trianon. It was no exaggeration to say that the map of Europe had been redrawn. The continental order that had been established at the end of the Napoleonic Wars was over and a new order set up. No other war has had such a major political impact.

To an extent the map of the world was redrawn, too. A popular view in Britain was that World War I, at the time called the Great War, had been a struggle between two empires, German and British, and the British Empire had won. A major atlas was published in Britain in 1920, which included a special sequence of historical maps showing the extent of the British Empire (in red) and the German Empire (in green), at different dates during the preceding two centuries. The propagandist maps needed scarcely any captions; they showed that the British Empire was slow-growing and enduring, while the German Empire was a flash in the pan, a parvenu, a Johnny-come-lately. The message was clear: the upstart German had been given his comeuppance – and seen off the world map.

New national identities were established. Russia was replaced by the Soviet Union. The war also stimulated a wave of nationalism in the colonies of the British Empire. In Australia and New Zealand, Gallipoli was known as a 'baptism of fire', a major rite of passage on the way to nationhood. This effect was even more strongly felt in Canada. For Canadian soldiers it was fighting for Vimy Ridge that made them feel that Canada was a nation 'forged from fire'. The heroic conduct of the Canadian soldiers, fighting on where British and French soldiers were failing, gave a spur to independence. Canada entered the war a dominion, and emerged with full independence.

World War I had a powerful mythic effect on the world as whole, certainly for the next two decades, though this was to a great extent overwhelmed by the experience of World War II. One major difference between the two wars was the lower death tolls in the military operations, with fewer killed in each World War II engagement; though even in this respect there were exceptions. The 1944 Battle of Normandy resulted in more casualties than the Third Battle of Ypres.

There were profound social and cultural effects, though some of these have been oversimplified and exaggerated. It has been said that 'modern art' movements were stimulated by the shock effect of the war. Yet movements in painting such as Cubism, Futurism and Expressionism had their origins back in 1908, well before the outbreak of war. The same is true of music. Perhaps the most 'modernist' piece of the period was Stravinsky's *Rite of Spring*, and that was written in 1913. The same is true of architecture. Adolph Loos's *House Without Eyebrows* in Vienna was built in 1910. The anarchic Dadaist movement in Germany and Switzerland nevertheless did have its origins during the war.

An argument can be made in the opposite direction. War has a tendency to make people more conservative and culturally defensive. In wartime, German music was conspicuously less popular in Britain, a development in taste akin to the stories of people kicking dachshunds (German dogs) in the street and withdrawing custom from shopkeepers with German-sounding names. In the end the British royal family decided to change its name from Saxe-Coburg-Gotha to something more English-sounding – Windsor. Picasso, the great modernist and innovator, reverted to a more traditional style during the war. Even so, the vigorous development of new art during the 1920s may have been helped by the massive social and psychological shake-up of the war.

Another cultural effect was the euphemising of the war that went on especially in France and Britain. The war was referred to in general, archaic, sentimental and patriotic terms, such as Laurence Binyon's famously moving line, 'They shall grow not old, as we that are left grow old.' The reversal of the normal word order (which often passes unnoticed) was a way of putting the whole dreadful experience back into a stirring mythic past. Men were said to have 'given their lives.' It was 'the war to end wars' and the emphasis was on king and country. As little as possible was said. Alan Bennett has commented that there is an irony in the tight-lipped phrase on many municipal war memorials, 'Lest we forget'; the memorials were erected so that honour was satisfied and people did not need to remember: the monuments did that for them. The war memorials were bland, monolithic, understated, often deploying the visual pun of a sword superimposed on a cross. Just occasionally a war memorial came closer to reality; there is one, unusually realistic, that shows a British soldier flinging up his arms in a wild gesture of triumph – or could it be the moment when he was shot? That is real. That is war.

The sheer loss of people was a major impact. France had to cope with the loss of 1,400,000 soldiers, killed, not counting other casualties. Russia and Germany were similarly affected. Taking all the countries involved and all the theatres of war, there were 37.5 million casualties in all, and of those more than 8.5 million died. More than two-thirds of those mobilised became casualties. There were huge demographic, economic, social and psychological consequences of these losses. Many wives lost their husbands. Many young women lost their boyfriends. And after the war there was a great shortage of men, which meant that a great many women remained single. It was a lost generation. Win Ellis, who lived at the village of Sevenoaks Weald all her life, had a boyfriend, Curly Long, who was killed in World War I; she died, single, as recently as 2003 at the age of 104. Characteristically, she said very little about her loss, but a long quiet shadow of bereavement had stretched right across the twentieth century and beyond.

7
WORLD WAR II

WORLD WAR II
(1939–45)

This global military conflict involved the merging of two initially separate conflicts, one that started in the East in 1937 as the Second Sino-Japanese War, the other in the West in 1939, when Germany invaded Poland. The European war was to an extent a continuation of World War I. World War II polarized the world, with most countries joining one of the two opposed alliances, the Axis and the Allies. The conflict was large in scale, resulting in the deaths of more than 70 million people and must, from that statistic alone, be regarded as both the worst and the most important conflict of all time.

THE BEGINNINGS OF THE WAR IN EUROPE

The march towards war began in Europe in 1933, when Adolf Hitler became the leader of Germany. The way had been to an extent prepared by developments in Italy, where as early as 1922 Benito Mussolini had taken control of Italy. Mussolini invaded Abyssinia in Africa in a gesture of conquest; he was evidently looking for a weak victim. Mussolini and his Fascist Party supplied Hitler with role models for his own dictatorship and the Nazi Party, though Hitler was to prove far more daring in terms of the countries he picked to invade.

Both Hitler and Mussolini gave active military support to their opposite number in Spain, where Francisco Franco led his fascist Falange Party against the Second Spanish Republic, which in turn was supported by the Soviet Union. The Spanish Civil War was in some ways a kind of rehearsal for the much larger and bloodier European war that was to follow, with both fascist and communist sympathisers from various countries going to Spain to fight as volunteers.

The civil unrest caused by severe economic depression in Germany made it easier for a figure like Hitler, proposing radical solutions, to rise to power. Under Hitler's leadership, Germany broke the terms of the Treaty of Versailles by beginning a major rearmament programme. Hitler pursued an aggressive nationalist foreign policy. In this nationalist spirit he annexed German-speaking Austria. By 1937, Hitler was demanding the annexation of territories that had formally been German territory, such as the Sudetenland (the German-speaking part of Czechoslovakia), Gdansk and the Rhineland. Britain and France tried initially to defuse Germany's increasingly aggressive demands through policies of appeasement. Both countries were acutely aware of the enormous costs they had carried in World War I and were anxious to avoid an expensive military confrontation. This appeasement policy culminated in the 1938 Munich Agreement. This allowed Germany to keep the Sudetenland on condition that it would make no further territorial claims – at least within Europe.

In March 1939, Hitler annexed the rest of Czechoslovakia, sensing that the British and French would not intervene. Not to be outdone, in April 1939 Mussolini invaded and annexed Albania. It became obvious to Britain and France now that appeasement was not going to work and the two countries began to prepare for the military conflict they had both hoped to avoid. Hitler evidently had his sights on Poland. On 19 May 1939, France and Poland formed a mutual defensive alliance; if either was attacked, the other would give military assistance. Three months later, in August, the British made Poland the same guarantee. Britain and France were in effect now committed to war. At the same time, Germany and the Soviet Union agreed the Molotov-Ribbentrop Pact. This anticipated a British blockade like the one that had starved Germany into surrendering at the end of World War I, by providing for the sale of Soviet food and oil to Germany. There was also a secret section of the pact, an agreement that provided for the division of Central Europe between Hitler and Stalin, including the partition of Poland. Each of the two powers, Germany and the Soviet Union, would have complete freedom of action within its own sphere of influence.

One week after the signing of the Molotov-Ribbentrop Pact, on 1

September 1939, German troops invaded Poland. They used as a pretext a fake Polish attack on a German border post. France and Britain still held back for a moment in the hope that Hitler could be persuaded by a diplomatic initiative into more moderate behaviour. On 3 September Britain sent Germany an ultimatum, but Hitler did not respond and Britain had no alternative but to declare war; Australia and New Zealand declared war at the same time, France declared war later the same day. In spite of the formal promises they had made to Poland, neither France nor Britain had the stomach for a full-scale invasion of Germany, which we can now see is probably what the moment required. The French mobilised as if in a trance, mounting a slow and negligible offensive in the Saar. The British failed to send land forces in time to save the Poles. It was an episode that did no credit to either Britain or France, but the German blitzkrieg offensive was startlingly swift, determined and efficient. Within one week, on 8 September, the German troops were in Warsaw. Nine days after that, as agreed, the Soviet army invaded Poland from the east and by 6 October the entire Polish army had surrendered. It was all over, and Britain and France had done nothing about it, apart from the British navy's imposition of a blockade; it started intercepting German ships.

There was little in the way of overt military action in the winter of 1939–40, a phase described in Britain as the Phoney War. The Soviets started to occupy states with Baltic coastlines, which led to a confrontation with Finland. This was resolved by Finland conceding some land to the Soviets. In April 1940, both Allied and German forces launched operations along the north coast of Norway over access to Swedish iron ore. The richest iron ore field in Europe lies round the town of Kiruna in northern Sweden. Kiruna is just inside the Arctic Circle and the only all-year access is by rail, west to the warm-water Norwegian port of Narvik. The struggle for control went on for two months, and the result was German control of both Norway and Denmark, though the Germans suffered considerable losses to their navy. The fall of Norway was profoundly depressing for the British. It led to a 'Norway Debate' in the House of Commons, and resulted in the resignation of Neville Chamberlain as prime minister and his replacement by Winston Churchill.

On 10 May 1940, German troops invaded Belgium and France. A British Expeditionary Force and the French army advanced into Flanders in what looked as if it might become a re-run of the Western Front of World War I. The Allied strategy was to fight a mobile war in the northern section of the front, but hold a static front along the Maginot Line in the southern section. This was foiled by a surprise German offensive through the hill country of the Ardennes, which divided the Allied forces in two. The British and French forces in the north were surrounded and had to be evacuated from the beach at Dunkirk. The Allied defence of France was a disaster. The German blitzkrieg invasion resulted in the surrender of France on 22 June 1940; this in turn led to the German occupation of Paris and the setting up of a German puppet regime known as Vichy France, as its headquarters in south-eastern France. The Vichy government was headed by Marshal Pétain and it was sustained only by obedient collaboration with the Germans, up to and including the deportation of Jewish children to concentration camps.

Italy joined the war, on Germany's side, attacking France just before the French surrendered. Hitler had thus far been amazingly successful, and he turned his attention at once to Britain, the only remaining opponent in Europe. The timing appeared favourable for such an operation, in that the British army had lost most of its heavy weaponry and supplies in the retreat from Dunkirk. The plan to invade Britain was code-named Operation Sealion. Hitler tried to blockade Britain, to cut off vital supplies from outside, but the British navy was still more powerful than the German navy. He tried instead to gain superiority in the air as a preliminary to a seaborne invasion – to destroy the Royal Air Force by deploying the Luftwaffe – but was unable to achieve this. The Battle of Britain, fought mainly in the skies over Kent and Sussex during the summer of 1940, was a critical defeat for the German Luftwaffe.

Hitler and his Luftwaffe commander, Goering, were angered by the RAF bomber raids on German cities and decided to give the British the same treatment. In particular, the German bombing raids were to be directed at London in a major offensive, the Blitz. Although this was a major challenge to British morale, and a great deal of property was destroyed especially in East London, the diversion of attention enabled the RAF to rebuild their damaged airfields. Restored, these enabled the RAF to function normally again. Hitler gave up, deciding to postpone indefinitely the planned invasion of Britain by sea.

Because France was now German-occupied, the British forces were unable to engage the German forces on the European mainland, so instead they concentrated on fighting Italian and German forces in the Mediterranean theatre of war. They fought to a stalemate in the Sahara, but had more success in the Mediterranean, where they did a lot of damage to the Italian navy.

The Italian war effort in the Mediterranean was foundering. Hitler was sufficiently alarmed by this failure to send a substantial German force to North Africa. The British meanwhile started redeploying their troops, sending soldiers from North Africa to Greece. To secure transport lines, the Allied navy managed to engage the Italian navy in a pitched sea battle, the Battle of Cape Matapan, in which significant damage was done to the Italian fleet. In North Africa, by April 1941 General Rommel's forces successfully pushed British Commonwealth forces eastwards into Egypt, except for the port of Tobruk, which he surrounded. British oil supplies were at the same time endangered by a coup d'état in Iraq. The British responded to this by invading and occupying Iraq in order to secure their future oil supplies. German forces were at the same time moving southwards through the Balkans, capturing first Yugoslavia, then mainland Greece, then the island of Crete. This impressive and continuous sweeping conquest pushed all British and Commonwealth forces out of the area.

In June, a combined force of British Commonwealth and Free French troops invaded Syria and Lebanon, at that time controlled by the Vichy regime. This invasion was prompted by the fact that the Vichy regime was allowing Axis forces through the Levant and the Allies sought to control the Middle East oilfields. At the end of August, following the surprise German invasion of the Soviet Union, the British and the Soviets jointly invaded Iran in order to secure the Iranian oilfields, at least in the short-term for Soviet use.

The impact of the new German-Soviet war on Europe was so powerful that it caused a lull in the fighting in the Mediterranean theatre, which seemed less important. During this lull both British Commonwealth and German troops regrouped. On 18 November, Allied forces launched Operation Crusader, a major offensive in the Western Desert. This succeeded in pushing Rommel right back to his starting point in Libya. The entry of Japan into the global conflict in December 1941 led to another regrouping, as many Commonwealth troops were withdrawn from units in North Africa to be taken to Burma. Rommel was able to turn this weakening of the Allied force to his advantage. On 21 January 1942, he launched an offensive which pushed the British Commonwealth forces back towards Tobruk. Another diversion was created by a Japanese raid in the Indian Ocean. More British Commonwealth forces were diverted to Madagascar (controlled by the Vichy regime) and stationed there to stop the Japanese navy from using the island as a base for further attacks. Rommel was again able to exploit the situation, launching his own attack in May 1942 and pushing the British right back into Egypt, where they only stopped at El Alamein. In London, a change of command was seen as necessary in North Africa; Montgomery was to take over Montgomery built up his forces and then in October launched a major offensive, pushing the German forces back across the desert. Gradually Rommel's troops were cornered in Tunisia and in May 1943 they were forced to leave Africa for good.

THE BATTLE OF THE ATLANTIC

Out in the Atlantic Ocean, a parallel war was fought that started just after the Soviet-German invasion of Poland and lasted until 1945. The first event in this long campaign was the sinking of the British liner, the *Athenia*, which was torpedoed by a German U-boat. U-boat raids were familiar to the British from World War I, when they learnt that escorted convoys were the best way of protecting ships. Convoys were organised but some had to sail without any other protection as there was a shortage of naval vessels to act as escort ships. Initially, the U-boat campaign was restricted to the shallow waters close to Britain, while German surface vessels patrolled the open Atlantic. German sea power was greatly enhanced by the conquest of Norway and France. The French navy was out of the way and the French seaports were of particular value to the German warships and submarines, effectively increasing their range.

The British navy became overstretched, needing to reserve a significant force to defend the English Channel against a German invasion of Britain. The situation improved slightly in late 1940, when it was agreed with the United States that Britain would offer several overseas bases in exchange for fifty destroyers, for convoy escort duties.

The German surface ships had some successes, but some spectacular losses, too. The early loss of the *Admiral Graf Spee* was one of these. The Battle of the River Plate (1939) was the first British victory in World War II. The British commander in the action, Harwood, was made a knight and rear-admiral even before the situation was resolved: the *Graf Spee* was still afloat in Montevideo Harbour. The *Graf Spee* was a heavy cruiser fitted with 28-cm (11-in) guns. The Germans described her as a Panzerschiff, while the British described her as a pocket battleship. Weight was saved by using arc welding instead of rivets, and she was unusually fast for her time. She sailed from Wilhelmshaven on 21 August with orders to carry out raids on British merchant shipping in the South Atlantic, but to avoid combat with superior forces. She was provided with fuel by a supply ship, the *Altmark*. She was a major danger to the British war effort, destroying valuable British supplies and shipping, and diverting British naval units to deal with her.

In the period September-December 1939, the *Graf Spee* sank nine merchant ships in the South Atlantic and adjacent Indian Ocean. Her Captain, Hans Langsdorf, was a scrupulous and humane figure, a good man; he saved every single crew member from each of the ships he sank. Captured crews were transferred to the *Altmark*, and they were later freed in Norwegian territorial waters in a raid by the destroyer HMS *Cossack*.

The British navy assigned a hunting group to track the *Graf Spee* down. Hunting Group G consisted of the cruiser *Exeter* and the light cruisers *Ajax* and *Achilles*, which found the *Graf Spee* on 13 December. The Battle of the River Plate followed. The *Exeter* was very badly damaged and had to break away. The *Graf Spee* was hit repeatedly by 15-cm (6-in) shells from the *Ajax* and *Achilles*, which did a lot of superficial damage. The *Exeter*'s 20-cm (8-in) shells penetrated the *Graf Spee*'s armour and exploded inside the vessel amidships, causing crippling damage. The *Graf Spee* made for the neutral port of Montevideo for repairs. In fact, Langsdorf knew that the serious fuel leak could not be repaired, that he and his ship were not going any great distance. The British were keen not to allow the *Graf Spee* to escape. According to the Hague Convention of 1907, Langsdorf's ship could stay for only twenty-four hours. After that it risked internment. But the same convention stipulated that as a warship the *Graf Spee* had to give any enemy merchant ship leaving port twenty-four hours' start. The British consul in Montevideo organised it so that merchant ships would sail every twenty-four hours, locking the *Graf Spee* in port. The Uruguayan government gave Langsdorf an ultimatum: he must sail within seventy-two hours of arriving or lose his ship.

At the same time Harwood faked plans to send in five cruisers to assist the two British ships guarding the *Graf Spee*. The *Graf Spee*'s Captain Langsdorf was convinced by Harwood's ploy, and expected an annihilating confrontation with an overwhelming British squadron in a day or so. He made his decision. He wrote a last letter home to his family. He decided he could not send his men to their death unnecessarily, and he wanted to retain the honour of his ship. He had had no clear orders from Berlin, so he went ahead with his own extraordinary plan. He sailed the *Graf Spee* out of the harbour into open water, took his crew off and scuttled the ship. He said goodbye to his son, then crossed the harbour to Buenos Aires with his crew. There, in the night, he shot himself. He was buried with full military honours.

The Battle of the River Plate was the first great media event of the war. It was full of poignancy, heroism on both sides, moral dilemmas, destruction, deception, wasted lives. Only 108 men altogether died in the Battle of the River Plate. It was a small action, but it was somehow the epitome of World War II as a whole.

The German battleship *Bismarck* was destroyed in the North Atlantic as a sequel to the Battle of Denmark Strait, which was fought on 24 May

1941. During the battle, the *Bismarck* and her escort the *Prinz Eugen* had sunk the British battlecruiser *Hood* and forced the battleship *Prince of Wales* to retreat. The *Hood* was seen as the pride of the Royal Navy, so her loss was deeply felt by the British. In the battle the *Bismarck*'s fuel tanks had been damaged and her captain intended returning to Brest for repairs; the *Prinz Eugen* left to steam out into the Atlantic. The British were determined to destroy the *Bismarck.* They pursued her with ships and planes for two days. For a while the *Bismarck* steamed ahead undetected. Then inexplicably Admiral Lutjens transmitted a half-hour radio message, which allowed the British to work out his approximate position and heading. Thanks to incompetence on board the *King George V*, the *Bismarck*'s position was incorrectly calculated, which gave her time to head closer to France – and safety.

Finally, in the evening of 26 May 1941 she was sighted by an RAF plane that happened to be passing; the position was reported to the Admiralty. She was then crippled by a torpedo bomber attack launched from the aircraft carrier *Ark Royal.* This jammed her rudder, which made her a sitting target. She was shadowed and harassed through the night by British destroyers, the constant firing exhausting and demoralising the *Bismarck*'s crew. The next day, starting at 9 a.m., she was pounded by British fire from the battleships *Rodney* and *King George V* and supporting cruisers until after about ninety minutes she sank. It seems that in spite of all the shells and torpedoes, the *Bismarck*'s hull was still intact. She only sank, in the end, because Captain Lindemann decided to scuttle her, with many men still below decks. No British vessel was lost during this action. British ships picked up 110 survivors, leaving as many as 2,000 men to die when they withdrew after a U-boat sighting was reported. The British ships withdrew under attack from the Luftwaffe, which resulted in the loss of the destroyer *Mashona.* A German weather ship arrived at the scene and picked up just five more survivors from the *Bismarck.*

The loss of the *Bismarck* had deep implications. Hitler ordered all the big surface ships back to Norwegian waters, where they were assembled to protect Scandinavia from an anticipated Allied invasion.

The British had a lucky break in May 1941 when they captured an

Enigma machine. This code-maker made it possible to break German codes and find out in advance where the U-boats would be stationed; then avoiding action could be taken. Shortly after that the Soviet Union came into the war on the side of the Allies, but the German invasion meant that they lost a great deal of their military equipment. The Allies tried to help Russia by sending Arctic convoys round the North Cape to Archangel. Inevitably these convoys ran the gauntlet of German attacks. In December 1942, a substantial surface force of the German navy attacked an Allied Arctic convoy but failed to destroy a single vessel. As a result of this failure, Grand Admiral Raeder, the supreme commander of the German Navy, was required to resign. He was replaced by Commander of Submarines Karl Doenitz, who naturally diverted resources to building new U-boats.

By the spring of 1943, the Battle of the Atlantic had swung in the Allies' favour. In May, because of improved Allied anti-submarine tactics, the Germans lost a quarter of their active U-boats. With fewer U-boats patrolling, more supplies were getting through to Britain, which was vital for the supply build-up needed to source the invasion of Western Europe in the middle of 1944. In December 1943, the Germans lost their last battlecruiser in the Battle of North Cape.

THE GERMAN INVASION OF THE SOVIET UNION

The scale of the European war increased enormously when, in June 1941, the Germans invaded the Soviet Union. The Soviets immediately went into an alliance with Britain. To begin with, the Germans had great success. Stalin was completely unprepared for the invasion psychologically; he had made a pact with Hitler and was stupefied when he realised that Hitler had betrayed him on this scale. Hitler had the huge advantage of total surprise.

The Eastern Front was the biggest theatre of war in history, measured in the numbers of soldiers involved, war gear, levels of destruction, casualties, loss of life. Five million Axis soldiers were killed; over ten million Soviet soldiers died, three million of those in German captivity; around seventeen or eighteen million civilians died. More people fought, and more people died, on the Eastern Front than in all the other theatres of war added together. It was at the Eastern Front that the outcome of World War II was determined, because it was there that the German army was crippled.

Of Stalin's Russia, Hitler declared that Germany had only to 'kick the door in and the whole rotten structure will come down.' He nevertheless assembled a huge invasion army, including 3,000 tanks and 2,500 aircraft. The Red Army was poorly maintained, poorly trained and weakened by a 1937 purge of its experienced senior officers. Hitler was justified in expecting his invasion to succeed. Germany's army was divided into three groups, functioning independently of one another. Army Group North went through East Prussia to secure the Baltic states and Leningrad. After encountering Soviet tanks and two major river crossings, it approached Leningrad. Army Group Centre's target was Moscow, and it found itself opposed by four Soviet armies. In a complex manoeuvre, the Germans encircled and destroyed the Soviet armies; 135,000 Soviet soldiers were killed or wounded, 290,000 were captured, 250,000 fled. Army Group South went through southern Poland and Romania towards the Caucasus oilfields. The Battle of Brody, a fierce four-day affair, was a German victory but at heavy cost.

Smolensk was attacked next, but the progress of the invasion made Hitler lose faith in battles of encirclement. He then decided to cripple the Soviet war effort by inflicting serious economic damage. This meant diverting troops to the Baku oilfields (the Caspian Sea) and Leningrad. Hitler's generals tried to dissuade him from this deviation from plan, not least because Army Group Centre was very close to Moscow and an attack there could end the war quickly. Hitler could not be persuaded.

By 8 September German troops had encircled Leningrad, which was put under a 900-day siege (ending on 27 January 1944) that would result in one million civilians dying of cold and starvation. Conditions in Leningrad were primitive; there was no heating, no water supply, and almost no food. In spite of the poor conditions, the war industries of the city kept functioning. By 16 September, German troops had encircled Soviet forces in the city of Kiev. The trapped Soviets fought hard for ten days, at the end of which Hitler captured half a million Soviet soldiers.

Now the German army outnumbered the Red Army. Stalin had only 800,000 men left to defend Moscow and on 2 October the Germans resumed their drive towards Moscow. The Germans captured huge numbers of Soviet soldiers, leaving only 90,000 defending the Russian capital.

But the Russian winter was getting steadily more severe, slowing German progress to 3 km (2 miles) per day. The Germans decided on a reorganisation, which gave Stalin time to muster new armies by transferring troops across from the East. When the Germans resumed their attack, they found Moscow defended by six Soviet armies – over 500,000 men. The Germans prepared to encircle Moscow, but the intense cold brought the operation to a standstill. The Germans were suffering more casualties from disease and frostbite than from combat; the Luftwaffe was grounded. Hitler had not equipped his armies for the intensity of a Russian winter. On 5 December, the Soviets launched a powerful attack which pushed the Germans back 320 km (200 miles).

In January 1942, Stalin ordered a counter-offensive. In May, the Soviet troops tried to retake the city of Kharkov in the Ukraine. The German response was launch its own offensive, encircling the whole Soviet army as it attacked Kharkov. The Soviet troops were trapped; 70,000 of them were killed, 200,000 were captured and only 22,000 escaped.

Stalin did not know where the main German offensive of 1942 would be directed, though he was convinced it would be towards Moscow. As a result, he moved more than half of the troops in the Soviet Union to the Moscow region; only a small number remained in the south. The German offensive began on 28 June 1942, and it was directed towards Stalingrad and the Caucasus oilfields. The Germans attempted to capture Stalingrad in order to protect their troops in the Caucasus.

German bombers killed more than 40,000 people and demolished large areas of the city. By this stage, Stalin realised that Hitler was aiming to secure the Baku oilfields and started sending troops south to reinforce those at Stalingrad. General Zhukov was put in command at Stalingrad in September, and he launched a series of attacks which delayed the Germans. On 13 September, German troops advanced into the city's southern suburbs. Then days later the industrial zone was surrounded. There was fierce and barbaric hand-to-hand street fighting among the ruins of Stalingrad. The ferocity of the German onslaught was such that a newly arrived Soviet soldier had a life expectancy of less than a day, but still the Soviet's fought with determination.

Hitler became obsessed with Stalingrad. Withdrawal would have been the most sensible strategy, but he refused to allow it. On his behalf, General Paulus launched a November attack, and by then the Germans were in control of nine-tenths of the city. But this had been achieved at a terrible cost; the German troops were now mostly inside the city and Axis satellite troops were left outside, guarding the city's flanks. The Soviets launched their attack on 19 November, which culminated in the encirclement of the German troops in Stalingrad. The Germans asked Hitler for permission to break out. He refused, saying they would be supplied by air until rescued.

Meanwhile, in the Caucasus the German invasion stalled. Soviet troops had destroyed the oil production plant and it would take a year to repair it. Just before he surrendered to the Red Army on 2 February 1943, General Paulus was promoted to the rank of field marshal. This was a sinister coded signal from Hitler, because it was well known that no German field marshal had ever surrendered his troops or been taken alive. Of Paulus's Sixth Army, once 300,000 strong, only 91,000 survived to be taken prisoner – and only 5,000 of them returned to Germany after the war was over. Although Paulus did not dare to defy Hitler by breaking out of Stalingrad, he did defy him over the tacit demand to commit suicide. He surrendered, became a Soviet prisoner-of-war, and while he was in captivity he freely voiced his criticisms of the Nazi regime and joined the Soviet-sponsored National Committee for a Free Germany; he was released in 1953.

The Battle of Stalingrad was the greatest battle in human history in terms of the number of lives lost. About two million people, soldiers and civilians, were killed altogether. Stalin commented grimly, 'They want a war of annihilation. We will give them a war of annihilation.' After Stalingrad, the Soviet army launched several offensives along the River Don. These made some gains until the Germans counter-attacked and recaptured the city of Kharkov. This was the last big strategic victory for Germany in World War II.

By 4 July the biggest concentration of German fire power in all of World War II had been assembled for the attack on the Soviets at the Kursk salient. The Soviets knew in advance that this attack was coming, and prepared with a huge system of defensive earthworks. The Germans attacked from each side of the tongue of land occupied by the Soviet army, north and south, cutting it off and encircling the sixty Soviet divisions. The Battle of Kursk that followed was the biggest tank battle of the war. The Germans had used up their armoured forces and were unable to halt the Soviet counter-offensive; they were forced back.

After their victory at Kursk, the Soviet troops captured Kharkov. Hitler agreed to withdraw his troops to the Dnieper line in August, but during the next two months, they found they were unable to hold the line as the Soviet bridgeheads strengthened. In November, the Soviet troops broke through and recaptured Kiev, the Ukrainian capital. By the end of 1943, the Soviets had advanced as far as the original 1939 border between the Soviet Union and Poland.

Then, in January 1944, the Soviets launched an offensive in the north to relieve the appalling siege of Leningrad. The Germans retreated in stages, with the Soviet army following them across Eastern Europe. In March 1944, as the Soviets approached, German troops occupied Hungary. The Soviets decided to clear the Crimean peninsula of Axis troops; some had been cut off and stranded there during the German retreat from the Ukraine. In May, the Red Army attacked the German force in the Crimea – a battle easily won by the Soviets.

After clearing the Crimea, the Soviets launched their summer offensive (June 1944). This huge operation, involving 2.5 million soldiers and 6,000 tanks, had as its objective the removal of German troops from Belarus and crushing German Army Group Centre. This offensive was designed to coincide with the Normandy landings in Western Europe, but unintended delays caused its postponement for some weeks. In the battle that followed, the German division was annihilated, suffering more than 800,000 casualties; it was the biggest single defeat for the German army in the entire war. The Soviet army swept on to reach the outskirts of Warsaw at the end of July.

The Poles in Warsaw thought they were about to be liberated by the

Soviet army and launched a revolt on 1 August. Forty thousand Polish resistance fighters attempted to take over Warsaw. But the Russians stayed where they were, outside the city, and German troops put down the revolt and destroyed most of what was left of the city.

Once the Soviets had driven the Germans out of Ukraine they advanced on German-occupied Romania. The Battle of Romania was an overwhelming victory for the Soviet army, and Romania moved from the Axis to the Allies. In September 1944, Bulgaria surrendered to the Soviets, after which they went into Hungary, where the German Sixth Army stopped them; they failed to capture Budapest. But it was Germany's last victory on the Eastern Front. The Red Army marched inexorably westwards, an Bulgaria fell in September; German troops fled from Greece in October. Then in December the Red Army liberated Belgrade and went on to encircle Budapest in the last days of 1944, bottling up 188,000 German troops. The siege of Budapest became one of the bloodiest of the war, with the Germans holding out until 13 February 1945. One by one the cities and countries conquered by Germany were being 'liberated' by the Russians.

On 17 January, Marshal Zhukov took Warsaw from the Germans. Two days later another Soviet force reached Germany's prewar eastern border; now the invasion of Germany, the Soviet counter-invasion, could begin. The Soviet army was unstoppable now. By the end of January, it was only 65 km (40 miles) outside Berlin. Then there was a slowing down, partly because Soviet supply lines had been over-extended, partly because there was a last-ditch German resistance to total defeat. Himmler, in command of a new Army Group Vistula, tried a counter-attack against the Red Army's flank but failed. Hitler made ever more unrealistic demands of his army; now he insisted that his troops regain the Danube.

On 30 March the Red Army entered Austria, where it captured Vienna on 13 April.

THE WAR IN THE EAST

When World War I ended, the Allied victors in Europe adopted policies that tacitly recognised Japan as a colonial power. From that point on, both politicians and military leaders in Japan developed expansionist policies, and in particular the idea that their country had a right to conquer Eastern Asia and unify it under Japanese control.

The war in the Far East began in September 1931, when the Japanese invaded Manchuria on a pretext, taking it from the Chinese. The principal reason for doing this was economic; Japanese was not rich in resources and suffered from a high density of population. This opening step was followed up nearly six years later by a large-scale Japanese invasion of China. The invasion began with the bombing of Shanghai and Guangzhou and continued with a massacre at Nanking. Shanghai fell to the Japanese in December 1937. The Japanese occupation of China was particularly harsh and inhumane, with many atrocities committed against the civilian population.

The Japanese invasion of China interrupted a major civil war in China, one that had been going on since 1927. The internal war was fought between the Chinese Nationalist Army, led by Chiang Kai-shek, and the Communist Chinese Army, led by Mao Zedong. The Japanese invasion made them collaborate, to an extent, to deal with the invaders. They called a truce. Mao's soldiers became the New Fourth Army and the Eighth Route Army within the Nationalist Army.

By the spring of 1939, the Japanese army and Soviet forces met and fought in Mongolia. The Soviet Union saw Japanese expansion in the East as a major threat to its security, and there was a danger of having to fight a war on two fronts. Fear of a two-front war was one of the motives for signing the Molotov-Ribbentrop Pact with Germany. The Japanese invasion of Mongolia was halted and reversed by Soviet troops under the command of General Zhukov. Following this, the Soviet Union and Japan maintained an uneasy peace until World War II ended. In 1941, Japan and the Soviet Union signed a non-aggression pact. The Soviet Union was then able to focus on its European front, made necessary by Hitler's treachery, while Japan looked elsewhere to create its empire – the islands of the Pacific. This in turn led to conflict with the United States over the Philippines and the control over shipping lanes, and with Britain and America over colonies in the South Pacific.

Several countries in the West tried to coerce Japan into ending this undeclared war and withdrawing from the mainland of Asia by applying economic sanctions. Britain, the Netherlands and the United States introduced economic sanctions against Japan. This had no effect, though, and in December 1941 the war escalated further. In spite of being in the fifth year of its war with China, Japan launched unprovoked and unannounced attacks against the United States (at Pearl Harbour) and British assets in South-East Asia. The surprise air attack, launched from a Japanese carrier fleet, came on 7 December. It succeeded in destroying most of the American aircraft on the island and disabled the main American battle fleet. Three battleships were sunk, five were heavily damaged. Of these capital ships, only the *Arizona* and *Oklahoma* were completely wrecked, though: the other six were repaired and went back into service. The four American aircraft carriers were at sea and therefore escaped damage. Although the damage might have appeared spectacular, it was not crippling; the fuel storage facilities, for instance, remained untouched.

The next day, 8 December 1941, the United States and Britain declared war on Japan. On the same day, the Japanese invaded the Philippines. Filipino and American forces, under the command of General MacArthur, were caught unawares, and had to retreat to the Bataan Peninsula. They fought on, stubbornly resisting the Japanese until April, when they were forced to surrender. The survivors were taken on what became known as the Bataan Death March. MacArthur was ordered to retreat to Australia but vowed to return. On the same day as the Philippines invasion, the Japanese invaded Hong Kong. Not long afterwards came Japanese invasions of Malaya, Borneo and Burma, all of them successful.

On 10 December 1941, the British suffered a spectacular loss at sea. Two huge warships, the *Prince of Wales* and the *Repulse* were both sunk after being attacked by Japanese bombers and torpedo planes flying out of Saigon – 840 sailors were lost. Churchill was stunned. The loss was incomprehensible. It now seems that although the ships were fitted with torpedo bulges – double skins along their waterlines – they may have exposed their single skins to torpedoes while turning, which entailed heeling over slightly. It was a great loss shortly to be followed by another even more devastating for British morale. But before that came, the Allies came into official being, in a Declaration by the United Nations on 1 January 1942. Shortly after that, the American-British-Dutch-Australian Command (or ABDACOM) was created to create a co-ordinated Allied force in South-East Asia and a co-ordinated response to the Japanese offensive.

Then, on 15 February 1942, Singapore fell to the Japanese. Around 80,000 British and Commonwealth troops were rounded up and sent to Japanese prisoner-of-war camps. It was a devastating and humiliating defeat for the British, the biggest ever surrender of British personnel.

Political and military leaders in Japan thought that the Allies were fully occupied with the war against Hitler and that America was several years away from being ready to fight a war; they therefore launched an ambitious Pacific war which involved simultaneous invasions of Malaya, Thailand, Hawaii, Hong Kong and the Philippines. The Japanese assumed the Americans would be ready to negotiate and compromise sooner than go to war. The invasions were also (thinly) disguised as an economic crusade. The aim, so the Japanese claimed, was to create a Greater East Asia Co-Prosperity Sphere that would be free of European or American domination and create self-determination. The reality was that the invasions were straightforward military invasions and the occupied territories were entirely subordinated to Japanese control.

Four days after the Japanese attack on Pearl Harbour, Germany declared war on the United States. This in effect closed the circle, bringing both Japan and the United States into the larger conflict. After Pearl Harbour, what had been two relatively separate wars, one in the West, one in the East, became a single world conflict. The huge co-ordinated attack following Pearl Harbour was a spectacular success for the Japanese. Within six months the Japanese had achieved most of their naval objectives. While keeping their fleet of eleven battleships, ten aircraft carriers and thirty-eight cruisers intact, they had either sunk or damaged all the American battleships in the Pacific, they had destroyed the British Far Eastern fleet, and made the Australian Navy run back to port. With a daring and far-sighted strategy, the Japanese had established an arc of conquered territories that extended from Burma through New Guinea to the Central Pacific.

In May 1942, the Japanese launched Operation Mo. Its aim was to capture Port Moresby in New Guinea. In the Battle of the Coral Sea the combined navies of Australia and the United States blocked the Japanese. This was the first battle fought between aircraft carriers, and the first to be fought between fleets that never made visual contact with each other. The Americans suffered serious losses – the aircraft carrier *Lexington* was sunk and the *Yorktown* was badly damaged. The Japanese lost the carrier *Shoho* and another carrier, the *Shokaku*, was seriously damaged. The *Shokaku* and the *Zuikaku* were unable to take part in the major battle that followed a few weeks later, the Battle of Midway. It can be argued that the Japanese won the Battle of the Coral Sea, in that they inflicted heavier losses than they suffered, but the Allied fleets won a strategic victory in that the Japanese were stopped from taking Port Moresby.

The military leaders in both the United States and Japan regarded it as inevitable that there would at some point be a decisive battle between aircraft carriers. This came on 5 June 1942, at the Battle of Midway. Midway Island was one of the outermost islands of the Hawaiian group. The Japanese sent a task force towards Midway with the intention of drawing what was left of the American Pacific fleet out to do battle. The Battle of Midway was a major victory for the Americans, who lost the aircraft carrier *Yorktown* in the action but succeeded in sinking four of the finest carriers in the Japanese fleet. This battle was the turning point in the war in the Pacific, and was predicted with startling accuracy by the Japanese Isoruku Yamamoto at the time of Pearl Harbour. With Midway, the United States gained the initiative. After being surprised by Pearl Harbour, American production of planes and ships now outran that of the Japanese.

Next the Japanese tried to take Port Moresby by land, along the Kokoda Track, which was literally a path through the forest and mountains. A small Australian force found itself fighting a losing battle as it retreated in the face of a larger Japanese force. Meanwhile, the Americans and the Japanese fought a six-month battle starting in August 1942 for control of Guadalcanal, an island in the Solomon Islands group.

In late August, Japanese marines were landed at the eastern tip of New Guinea, and they were defeated by Australian troops at the Battle of Milne Bay, the first land defeat the Japanese had experienced in the Pacific War. In late January 1943, Australian and American troops regained control of the Japanese beachheads in eastern New Guinea, and in early February the Americans were in control of Guadalcanal. It then became clear that, if they were going to win the war in the Pacific, the Allies were going to have to chase the Japanese out of each island between New Guinea and Japan. In June 1943, the Allies launched Operation Cartwheel, which was a comprehensive strategy for the Western Pacific, involving isolating and neutralising the big Japanese base at Rabaul before the island-hopping expedition to Japan.

By October and November 1943, American casualties were mounting so high that there were protests in the United States. The Battle of Tarawa in particular was seen as futile – how could such huge losses be justified in gaining such a small island? From then on the Allied military leaders decided to bypass some Japanese-held islands, leaving them to wither away through isolation as their supply routes were intercepted.

The new American strategy worked. Gradually, during the early months of 1944, they captured one island after another from the Japanese, knocking out one air base after another. The Japanese invested their remaining naval strength in the Battle of the Philippine Sea, but lost many ships and aircraft. After this battle the Japanese carrier fleet was no longer a fighting force. Once the Americans had captured Saipan, the Americans had Tokyo within the range of their B-29 bombers. The war, as far as Japan was concerned, was as good as lost. Yet still the Japanese fought with undiminished energy and determination. The Americans won the Battle of Guam (21 July-10 August 1944), but it was fiercely fought, and Japanese stragglers went on fighting long after the real battle was over.

After the Pearl Harbour offensive, the Japanese launched a major offensive in China with the aim of taking the important city of Changsa. The Japanese had tried twice before and failed to take it. For this determined attack, the Japanese military command mustered 120,000 troops, but the Chinese responded with 300,000; the Japanese were surrounded and had to retreat. From the Changsa offensive on, there was a stalemate. The Japanese army had been reduced by heavy casualties and were fully occupied controlling the territory already conquered; they could not carry through the conquest of China. The Chinese on the other hand did not have the strength to drive them out.

The stalemate continued until 1944. Then the Japanese launched Operation Ichigo. The aim was to seize the railway from Peking to Nanking and clear the American airfields in the south of China. This was a successful operation, but did not destroy Chiang Kai-shek's army. Then the Japanese were distracted by the American acquisition of the Marianas; from bases in those islands, the Americans could bomb the Japanese mainland.

On 20 October 1944, General MacArthur returned to the Philippines, landing on the island of Leyte. The Japanese again fought with incredible determination, using up the last of their naval forces in the Battle of Leyte (23–26 October 1944). This has been described as the biggest naval battle in history. It was also the first battle in which suicide bombers were used, with their notorious Japanese kamikaze pilots; HMAS *Australia* was the first Allied ship to be attacked in this way. During the battle, the Japanese *Musashi*, one of the largest battleships ever to have been built, was sunk – by seventeen bombs and nineteen torpedoes. In January 1945 American troops landed on the main island of the Philippines, Luzon, and the capital, Manila, was retaken in March.

The island of Iwo Jima was captured by the Americans in February 1945. This was a major psychological step in the war, as it was long-established Japanese territory, not newly conquered; it was administered from Tokyo. In spite of its heavy defences, it was captured after US Marines took Mount Suribachi. Iwo Jima had airfields that could be used to launch American fighters towards the Japanese 'home islands'. Tokyo and other cities were firebombed; around 90,000 civilians died in the initial firebombing attacks on Tokyo alone. Still the Japanese did not surrender.

A major part was played in the Pacific War by Allied submarines. After Pearl Harbour, the Americans had no compunction about waging unrestricted submarine warfare on Japanese shipping. One motive was to deprive Japan of the raw materials it had gone to war specifically to obtain. The principal targets were oil tankers, and by the end of 1944 Japan had been virtually starved of oil. American submarines destroyed more than half of the Japanese merchant ships that were sunk. The rest were sunk by mines or destroyed, at the end of the war, by planes. US submarines were responsible for sinking nearly thirty per cent of the Japanese warships that were destroyed. The submarines were also very useful in gathering reconnaissance information.

DEFEAT FOR THE AXIS

In 1943, Germany experienced two major disasters on its Eastern Front. The Battle of Stalingrad was a siege the Germans expected to win, and they were unprepared for the ferocious, self-sacrificing defence the Soviets offered. The result was that the Germans had to withdraw after suffering devastating losses. This defeat was followed by another at the Battle of Kursk, the greatest tank battle in history.

German forces were pushed out of Africa, and then had to retreat through Italy, steadily pursued by British and American troops from Sicily northwards. The Allied Italian Campaign began in July 1943 with the invasion of Sicily. The ongoing series of defeats under Mussolini's leadership led to his dismissal by Victor Emmanuel III, the King of Italy. Mussolini was arrested and replaced by Pietro Badoglio, who started peace negotiations with the advancing Allies. On 3 September, the Allied troops invaded Italy, but the Germans had anticipated such a move and seized northern and central Italy. Shortly after that, Mussolini was rescued by the Germans. The Italian government was obliged to sign an armistice in September 1943.

In the Far East, the Japanese fought a fierce rearguard action as American troops captured island after island in the Western Pacific Ocean, in effect chasing the Japanese back to Japan.

By the spring of 1944, the situation favoured the Allies. Germany was looking increasingly surrounded and besieged. The victorious Soviets on the Eastern Front were now pressing westwards, out of Russia and into Poland and Romania. On the Western Front, Allied preparations for the liberation of Western Europe (code-named Operation Overlord) were complete. About two million soldiers had been assembled, of which about half were American, the rest British, Free French, Polish and Canadian. The invasion itself is usually called D-Day, though it was code-named Operation Neptune at the time, and it came on 6 June 1944, at a moment when nearly ninety per cent of Germany's troops were on the Eastern Front.

The Allied D-Day forces were under the overall command of General Eisenhower, who had launched an elaborate and successful deception, to make the Germans believe that the landings would be in the Calais area. As a result, many German troops were diverted away from the actual landing places, along the Normandy coast, where only 50,000 German troops remained. In spite of these advantages, Allied losses were heavy. The Americans lost many lives on Omaha Beach, as the Germans had fortified that stretch of coast. Even so, the Allied objectives were achieved and the Germans did not counter-attack because Hitler believed the landings were a decoy. It was three days before Hitler and his generals realised that the Normandy landings were the real thing, and by then the Allies were well established. The deep-water port of Cherbourg was captured by the Americans on 26 June, but the Germans had sabotaged many of the installations and it would be a month before the port was usable again. The Allies made several attempts to take the city of Caen, and they did not succeed until 9 July. As the Allies moved inland, the Germans were forced out of their camouflaged defensive positions, and this rendered them vulnerable to attack by the RAF. The Americans slowly encircled the Germans in the Falaise area; 50,000 of them were captured, but twice as many managed to escape.

From then on the Allied forces sped eastwards across France, chasing the retreating Germans into Belgium and Holland. The Free French received the surrender of the German forces from General von Choltiz and liberated Paris on 25 August.

At about this time, apparently in desperation, the Germans started launching V-1s, the flying bombs nicknamed 'doodlebugs' by the British. These very inaccurate missiles could only target large areas such as

London and some of them fell well short, in open country. They had no real military effect; their main purpose was to menace and intimidate the civilian population.

As the Allied troops approached the German border, their supply lines became overstretched. Activity was diverted to capturing ports on the Rhine Delta in order to bring in supplies from the north. Progress was also slowed by the River Rhine itself, a wide and deep river with relatively few bridges; it made a natural defensive line for the Germans. The Allies had nursed hopes of ending the war by Christmas 1944, but the Rhine stopped them and the war dragged on through the winter.

Hitler planned a counter-offensive on the Western Front; it was really a last-gasp attempt at victory as defeat loomed ever-larger. The aim of it was to capture Antwerp, and so prevent supplies from reaching the Allies. It would also divided the Allies into two, which would seriously weaken them and, Hitler hoped, force the leaders to negotiate. Hitler directed his forces to attack through the Ardennes, the heavily wooded hill country in Belgium where he had had a major victory in 1940. Hitler was helped in this operation by dense cloud cover, which restricted the Americans' use of aircraft for reconnaissance and attack.

In the Battle of the Bulge which followed, the Germans were able to break through some stretches of the American line. But they were delayed at St Vith and Bastogne, which the Americans stoutly defended. Then the sky cleared and Allied aircraft were able to attack as the German initiative came to a full stop at Dinant. In a kind of destructive diversion, the Germans launched an air raid on Allied airfields in the Low Countries on 1 January 1945. In this attack, the Germans succeeded in destroying 465 Allied planes, but in doing so lost 277 of their own. The Allies were sufficiently resilient to repair these losses in a matter of days, but the Luftwaffe was now disabled for the rest of the war.

The Rhine was finally crossed by ground troops in late March 1945, thanks to the capture of the Ludendorff Bridge at Remagen. At the same time there was a major parachute drop of airborne troops on the east bank of the Rhine. Once the Rhine had been crossed, the Allied troops fanned out across Germany, moving on towards Hamburg and Denmark. In the middle of April, the American First and Ninth Armies reached the River Elbe; this was the historic moment when the American troops met Soviet troops.

Hitler thought the Soviets would strike towards Prague, not Berlin, and in this mistaken belief sent the last German reserve troops to defend Prague. But it was Berlin the Soviets wanted and by 16 April the Red Army was preparing to make its final attack on the German capital. In the Battle of Berlin, Marshal Zhukov sent his forces across the River Oder from the east, but came under heavy fire from German troops. There were three days of heavy and desperate fighting, which left 33,000 Soviet soldiers dead, but after that the German defences of Berlin were broken. Soviet troops under Konev's command had crossed the Oder and were within striking distance of Berlin from the south, but Stalin sent orders that Konev was to protect the flank of Zhukov's army instead of attacking Berlin. Stalin had in fact promised Zhukov the treat of taking Berlin.

It was only a matter of time before the Soviet flag would be flying on the roof of the Reichstag in Berlin. The city was encircled. Still Hitler did not surrender. He called on civilians, even boys and old men, to fight in the Volkssturm militia to defend the city. Some tattered remnants of the German army outside Berlin linked up and went to relieve Berlin, but it was impossible. There was fierce street fighting in Berlin as the Red Army entered, and the Germans were able to take a heavy toll on the Soviet tanks as they picked their way along the rubble-filled streets. The population of Berlin fought for their survival, and some of the fighting was hand-to-hand. In the capture of Berlin, the Soviets sustained 350,000 casualties, the Germans 450,000. In the midst of this carnage, Hitler and his associates moved for safety into a concrete bunker under the Chancellery.

On 30 April 1945, as the Russians inexorably closed in, Hitler shot himself. Grand Admiral Doenitz became Hitler's successor as Führer, but not for very long: the German war effort had already crumbled away. The Germans surrendered Berlin to the Red Army on 2 May 1945. On the same day, the German forces in Italy also surrendered. Two days later, German forces in northern Germany, Netherlands and Denmark surrendered. The war in Europe was over.

The Japanese had a successful offensive in China, but in the Pacific their navy suffered heavy losses and the Americans captured airfields that put them in bombing range of Tokyo.

The final Allied conference of World War II was held at Potsdam, outside Berlin (July-August 1945). During the Potsdam Conference, the Allies agreed on policies for occupying Germany after the war. An ultimatum was also issued to Japan to surrender unconditionally. In the Far East, the Japanese refused to surrender. But then, after US President Truman ordered the dropping of atom bombs on two Japanese cities, Japan finally surrendered. On 6 August 1945, an American B-29 bomber called Enola Gay dropped a bomb called Little Boy on Hiroshima. It destroyed the city. There was no surrender from the Japanese government. On 9 August, a second bomb was dropped on the port of Nagasaki. On 8 August, the Soviets invaded Manchuria, in fulfilment of their Yalta pledge to attack the Japanese within three months of the war ending in Europe. Within a fortnight the one million strong Japanese army in Manchuria was annihilated by Soviet soldiers toughened by fighting the Germans. Japan surrendered on 15 August 1945 ('V-J Day') and the formal Instrument of Surrender was signed on 2 September. The Japanese troops in China surrendered to the Chinese a week later. This Japanese admission of defeat marks the end of World War II.

Significance and aftermath

Because of the geographical spread of the war and the huge number of soldiers involved – over 100 million – World War II was one of the most important conflicts of all time, with many ramifications, many consequences. The number of people who died in the war is roughly equivalent to the current total population of the UK, Ireland and the Netherlands. Curiously, in view of the fact that the Allies won, there were far more deaths on the Allied side than on the Axis side: 85 per cent of the deaths in the war were on the Allied side (mainly Soviet and Chinese), only 15 per cent on the Axis side. Around twenty-seven million Soviet citizens lost their lives.

World War II had a different character from earlier wars in that it became a total war. There was no distinction between military and civilian endeavour: everything was subordinated and geared to the war effort. The technological development of transport systems and the range of the weapons used meant that the arenas of war were very large. It was inevitable that civilian populations would fall as casualties. Towns and villages were destroyed, sometimes as collateral damage, sometimes deliberately. Almost two-thirds of those who died in the war were civilians. More than ten million of those who died were innocent civilian victims of the Holocaust, a sinister war-within-a-war waged on selected minority groups, the Jewish populations in particular. Most of the victims of the Holocaust died in Eastern Europe.

The Holocaust itself had repercussions in the post-war world. Something had been known by the Allied powers about the concentration camps, though perhaps not the scale of the cruelty and the killing that went on there. After the war there were pangs of conscience that nothing had been done sooner to relieve the victims. As part of the expiation of that guilt, the Allies backed the founding of the state of Israel as a homeland for the surviving Jewish refugees, and that in its turn has had ongoing repercussions for conflict in the Middle East. Many Jews had been displaced from their homes in central and eastern Europe; now Palestinians in their turn were displaced to make living space in Palestine for incoming Jews.

Hitler escaped the consequences of his actions by committing suicide immediately before his likely capture by the Soviet army as it entered Berlin. But there were other war leaders who survived and with them the question of how to deal with them. The Allies had made the decision as early as 1942 to put them on trial for war crimes. In fact Churchill had to be dissuaded by the Americans from a policy of summary execution. In 1943, Stalin, typically, said he wanted to execute 50,000 to 100,000 German staff officers; Roosevelt, thinking Stalin must be joking, said he thought 49,000 would be enough, while Churchill, who knew Stalin was not joking, denounced the idea. The final plan for a Trial of European War Criminals was the brainchild of US Secretary of War Henry Stimson and it was approved by President Truman. The twenty-four most important captured Nazi leaders were tried before an International Military Tribunal at the Nuremberg Palace of Justice in

1945–46; Nuremberg, the scene of the great Nazi rallies, was chosen as being especially symbolic.

The main war criminals were indicted for participating in a plan to initiate and wage wars of aggression, for war crimes and crimes against humanity. One committed suicide before the trial. The others charged were Martin Bormann (in absentia), Hans Frank, Wilhelm Frick, Hermann Goering, Alfred Jodl, Ernst Kaltenbrunner, Wilhelm Keitel, Joachim von Ribbentrop, Alfred Rosenberg, Fritz Sauckel, Arthur Seyss-Inquart, Julius Streicher (all sentenced to death); Walter Funk, Rudolf Hess, Erich Raeder (life imprisonment), Baldur von Schirach, Albert Speer (twenty years); Konstantin von Neurath (fifteen years); Karl Döenitz (ten years); Franz von Papen (eight years); Hans Fritsche and Hjalmar Schacht (acquitted). Those sentenced to death were hanged, apart from Goering who managed to commit suicide the day before his execution.

There was some disquiet at the time about the possible illegality of the Nuremberg trials. It was argued, for instance, by an English law professor that the judges were appointed by the victors and therefore not impartial, and an American judge went so far as to describe Nuremberg as 'a high-grade lynching party'. The trials were nevertheless to have a profound influence on the development of international criminal law, leading to the Genocide Convention, the Universal Declaration of Human Rights, the Geneva Convention on the Laws and Customs of War and eventually an International Criminal Court.

War crimes trials were also conducted in the Far East in 1946–48, but they received far less attention in the West. The Nazi leaders were more recognisable as personalities – charismatic, even – and had become infamous throughout Europe and the United States, whereas the Japanese leadership was, or appeared to be, relatively anonymous. This was in part the result of Allied propaganda, which took care not to vilify the Japanese emperor or demand his removal. Because of the emperor's special position in Japanese culture, that demand might have stiffened Japanese resistance and prolonged the war. The Allies were in a cleft stick. Emperor Hirohito was the head of state and therefore ought to have suffered a similar fate to the Nazi leaders, but the Allies feared that this would make the maintenance of peace and order in the Far East more difficult.

Hirohito's role in the conduct of the War in the Pacific was and still is unclear. He has been represented as ineffectual, a puppet king, but evidence emerged in the 1990s to show that he was active in planning the war. It could be argued that failing to bring Hirohito to trial for war crimes was a failure of international justice; he nevertheless was not brought to trial. Those put on trial and executed in Japan included Hideki Tojo, General Masaharu Homma, Tomoyuki Yamashita and five others who were convicted of committing atrocities during the war. Around eastern Asia, 900 other men were executed for murdering prisoners or instigating the war.

The Japanese claimed that they were only subjected to this treatment because the Nazi leaders were being put on trial, and that they were being found guilty by association. But evidence eventually emerged in the 1970s that the Japanese (especially Unit 731 operating in China) had committed some terrible atrocities, including using biological, chemical and thermal tests on their prisoners, dropping bubonic plague on Chinese cities, freezing Soviet prisoners in refrigerators. The Japanese were also guilty of enforcing sexual slavery on hundreds of thousands of women.

A continuing issue is the bias inherent in the war crimes trials. There were no war crimes trials relating to crimes committed by the Allies. The saturation bombing of civilian populations in cities like Dresden and the nuclear bombing of Hiroshima and Nagasaki could easily have been the subject of war crimes trials.

The Allied victory meant that the United States and the Soviet Union emerged as the two most important powers in the world. The rivalry between them immediately triggered a new conflict, the Cold War. The countries of Western Europe saw a measure of economic integration (at least – and some wanted more than that) as a way of ensuring that a European war would not break out again. The seeds of the European Union were sown when the European Coal and Steel Community was set up in the wake of the Treaty of Paris in 1951; the next fifty years would be spent expanding and extending that into a full-scale economic and political confederation.

In an attempt to ensure that any future conflicts would be small in scale, the United Nations was formed in 1945.

The war and its ending speeded up the progress of many colonies towards independence. Both British and Dutch colonies achieved their independence in the wake of the war, notably India and Indonesia. The Philippines, too, became independent. As that movement towards independence gained momentum it brought with it networks of new diplomatic, political and economic relationships among the new nations. The map of the world changed radically, with many new nations and new names; as the Gold Coast became independent, it changed its name to Ghana. France attempted to hang onto its colonies, with disastrous results. Within Europe, Britain and the United States colluded with the Soviet Union over Soviet hegemony in Eastern Europe. The Western powers were so grateful to Stalin for his determined resistance to Hitler, that they gave him everything he asked for. This appeasement of Stalin became known in Eastern Europe as the Western betrayal. Churchill even agreed to force Soviet refugees sheltering in Britain to return to the Soviet Union. Many committed suicide rather than return to certain death; those that returned were shot on arrival. The division of Europe into two camps did much to foster the atmosphere of mutual distrust that generated the Cold War.

In the Far East, the Chinese civil war resumed, but because the Nationalist Army had been so weakened by the war it fled to Taiwan in 1949, where it for a long time maintained a kind of government in exile. On the mainland of China, Mao was able to set up his communist state, the People's Republic of China.

World War II led directly to the development of the nuclear bomb. The bombings of Hiroshima and Nagasaki are (still) the only attacks by nuclear weapons ever to have been made. They nevertheless had a profound effect on subsequent decades. The decision to drop nuclear bombs on mainly civilian populations has remained hugely controversial. The argument at the time was that the Japanese were unlikely to surrender without a terrific fight. The battle for Okinawa showed that the invasion of the Japanese mainland (which was actually planned for November 1945) was likely to result in huge loss of life, especially among American troops. An estimate given to the American Secretary of War was that there would be between 1.4 and 4 million Allied casualties in the invasion and conquest of Japan. Whether the figures given were well-founded we shall never know, but they helped Truman to make the decision that dropping atom bombs on Japanese cities, however horrific, was going on balance to save lives. It was the more humane, the more life-saving, of the two options open to him.

The threat of the nuclear bomb and the fear of a nuclear attack were an integral part of the Cold War. The energy released in a nuclear reaction was also harnessed to make an entirely new and controversial form of energy at a time when governments were becoming aware that fossil fuels were not going to last for ever.

8

POST-WORLD WAR II CONFLICTS

THE COLD WAR
(1945–1991)

BEGINNINGS OF THE COLD WAR

Not all conflicts entail open fighting, battles and bloodshed. Some, as we saw with the struggle between Galileo and the Church, are conflicts of mindset, of *mentalité*, of attitude, *mores* or faith – and these conflicts are the most difficult to resolve. The Cold War was one of these phases of extreme tension and a very destructive and enduring one, lasting almost half a century. It was fundamentally a conflict between Communism and capitalism, between East and West, and above all between two global superpowers, the Soviet Union and the United States. Inevitably, as with armed conflicts, the superpowers brought into their orbit their allies, friends, slaves and satellites, so the Cold War was every bit as much a world war as the 1914–18 or 1939–45 wars. It was in a sense World War III that many people were expecting to break out at any moment.

The vivid phrase 'Cold War' was coined by the author George Orwell in a 1945 essay entitled *You and the Atomic Bomb*. It was invented at about the same time that in a speech in the United States Churchill coined the phrase 'Iron Curtain' to describe the unwelcome barrier that the Soviets had thrown across Europe from Stettin to Trieste. The idea had been around before, though. In the thirteenth century, Don Juan Manuel used the Spanish phrase '*guerra fria*' to describe the ideological tension between Christianity and Islam in medieval Spain.

Throughout the half century of the Cold War there was intense suspicion and rivalry between the superpowers. The rivalry was enacted in many different arenas: military and political coalitions, ideology, psychology, espionage, industrial and technological development (notably the space race) and also in spending on a nuclear arms race.

There was never an open war between the superpowers, never any direct military engagement between them, but there were several proxy wars, in which one power supported one minor player and the other gave military support to its enemy. Above all or beneath all of this, was an atmosphere of fear and foreboding, a sense that at any time the tension could escalate into all-out nuclear war. Neither side wanted that, as both knew that it meant destruction for both sides. This nuclear deterrent was the argument used repeatedly by Western governments against the many protesters who wanted to see a movement towards disarmament. The best assurance against annihilation, governments argued, was the certainty of mutual destruction if nuclear weapons were launched.

Towards the close World War II, tension between the Soviet Union and the United States began to increase. The Soviets suspected that the Americans had allowed the Russians to bear the brunt of the war effort, sustaining all the serious losses in manpower, so that they (the Americans) could sweep in at the last minute with minimal cost to themselves yet gain the most advantage out of manipulating the peace. There may be some truth in this, though at least some historians argue that the timing of the landings for the Normandy invasion were made on the basis of other tactical considerations.

The real beginnings of the Cold War were in the disagreement over the way Eastern Europe should be reconstructed after the destruction of Nazism. During World War II there was broad agreement between the United States and the Soviet Union that Nazism had to be destroyed, and that agreement had brought the two powers together as allies. But the rehabilitation of Germany and the adjacent states was seen in very different ways. Because Russia had been invaded several times during the course of history, the Soviets naturally thought of the desirability of developing Eastern Europe as a belt of buffer states that would remain sympathetic to them.

Serious differences emerged between the Americans and the Soviets at the Potsdam Conference regarding the future development of Germany and Eastern Europe. Only a week later, the Americans dropped atomic bombs on Japanese cities, which added to the Soviets' distrust of the United States. Stalin used the post-war instability as an opportunity to occupy many states in Eastern Europe, converting them to communism. More spectacularly still, he converted East Germany, accentuating the split by dividing the capital city of Berlin as well.

In response to this the United States adopted a rigorous policy of containment, launching an almost religious campaign to contain the spread of communism throughout the world. This in turn led to a strategy of more or less unlimited interference, overt and covert, in the administration of many countries round the world. There were repeated political and military crises that threatened to escalate into an overt World War III, because of the intense participation of the two superpowers, but none of them did: the Korean War of 1950–53, the Vietnam War of 1959–75, the Cuban Missile Crisis of 1962 and the Soviet-Afghan War of 1979–89. But there were, conversely, lulls in the Cold War when both powers were working towards *détente*.

CONTAINMENT AND KOREA (1947–53)

By 1947, US President Truman became concerned that time was running out if Soviet strategies in Europe were going to be curtailed or countered. He was worried that the Soviets were hoping in an atmosphere of political and economic confusion to weaken the United State's position. He was pushed into a formal announcement of a policy of 'containment' when the British said they could no longer finance the Greek monarchy and its military regime; failing to support the military regime meant accepting a communist-led coup. The United States interpreted the purely domestic squabble of the Greek civil war in terms of Soviet destabilisation. The 'Truman Doctrine' unveiled in March 1947 was that the United States would 'support free peoples who are resisting attempted subjugation by armed minorities or outside pressures.' On the strength of this statement, a huge sum of US money was allocated for intervention in the Greek Civil War. This set a precedent for successive US governments to give financial support to regimes that requested help in fighting communism – however corrupt and repressive those regimes might be.

Side by side with this was another kind of aid. The Marshall Plan was a promise of economic aid in the rebuilding of Western European political and economic systems, which had been severely damaged by World War II. That included the reconstruction of Germany's industry. Earlier ideas that no help should be given to Germany, as a punishment, were rejected; order and prosperity in Europe depended on a stable and productive Germany. A lesson had been learned from the Treaty of Versailles.

As a result of the Truman Doctrine and the Marshall Plan, billions of dollars in aid flooded into Europe. The United States consolidated its new-found role as leader of the Western world, and formally allied itself to the free states of Western Europe by becoming a signatory to the North Atlantic Treaty in 1949; this founded the North Atlantic Treaty Organization, NATO.

Stalin countered this move by linking the economies of the Eastern bloc together in a comparable way, aided by a Soviet version of the Marshall Plan, the Council for Mutual Economic Assistance, COMECON. As a show of strength, the first Soviet atom bomb was exploded in August 1949.

In 1949, the Americans consolidated the three Western zones of occupation in Germany into a new state, West Germany, and by 1955 the rehabilitated West Germany was awarded full membership of NATO. The Soviets responded by declaring the fourth zone, the Soviet-occupied zone, a new state, too, to be called the German Democratic Republic.

The Americans extended their containment policy across Asia, Africa and Latin America. At the same time, they made a formal alliance with Japan, in exchange for several long-term military bases. Truman worked towards creating new alliances with other states, such as Australia, New Zealand and Thailand.

Stalin was surprised when Truman sent US troops to drive back the North Koreans. In many countries that were US's allies, public opinion was divided over the Korean War. In 1953 the Korean War ended without any clear result. Unfortunately no lesson was learnt from this misguided political and military intervention in the Far East, and it was not long before the Americans were committing themselves to a similar lost cause – supporting the South Vietnamese government against North Vietnam, which was backed by China and the Soviet Union. The

Vietnam War was a classic proxy war. Had it been left as a local war, it might have ended sooner and killed fewer people. With the huge investment of personnel, technology and money by the superpowers, the Vietnam War was escalated and prolonged, causing untold misery to the Vietnamese people.

NEW LEADERS – CRISIS AND ESCALATION (1953–62)

The year 1953 brought a change of leadership in both superpowers. Truman was replaced by Eisenhower; Stalin died and was replaced by Khrushchev. In the Soviet Union there was a welcome move away from Stalinist terror. In the United States, there was a determination to reduce spending on conventional military intervention, while waving the nuclear threat more overtly in order to deter the Soviets. This was the 'New Look' that was given to the containment strategy; it also entailed threatening the Soviets with massive retaliation in response to any Soviet aggression. It is thought that this threat prevented a Soviet intervention in the Suez Crisis of 1956.

The situation in Germany remained at stalemate, with American troops stationed apparently for ever in West Germany and Soviet troops similarly stationed in the countries of Eastern Europe. Moscow firmed up the relationship between the Eastern European states and the 'mother country' by setting up the Warsaw Pact Treaty Organisation in 1955, in an attempt to mirror NATO. But the Warsaw Pact countries were not willing captives and in 1956 a brief Hungarian Revolution was stamped out by direct Russian intervention. In a similar spirit, in 1961 the East German authorities were obliged to build the Berlin Wall across Berlin – to prevent East Berliners escaping to the West.

In the United States, fear and hatred of communism reached new depths with a Wisconsin senator, Joseph McCarthy, alleging a communist conspiracy to take over the government of the United States. This led to a remarkable witch-hunt for communists in all walks of life.

The Third World became another arena for Cold War rivalry. As the West European colonial powers relinquished control over their former colonies, the newly independent states were available to be influenced, educated, bought or subverted by either of the superpowers. Presents were made of expensive hi-tech projects such as hydro-electric dams in exchange for friendship and alliance. The process was hard for the former colonial powers to watch, as they could see huge mistakes being made. Often the new nationalist governments were socialist in leaning. The US government used the CIA to support friendly Third World regimes – and to subvert or remove the others. This high level of interference in foreign countries has become second nature to US governments and their agents, and they have frequently expressed surprise that the United States is unpopular round the world. The CIA was used to overthrow Iran's first democratically elected government, led by Mohammed Mossadegh, in 1953; it was used again to remove the democratically elected president of Guatemala, Jacobo Guzmán, in 1954. The Soviets meanwhile courted Egypt and India.

Many of the newly independent nations rejected the pressure to choose sides in the Cold War. In 1955, at the Bandung Conference, many Third World governments made the decision to remain aloof from the power struggle between the superpowers. This led on to the setting up of a Non-Aligned Movement in 1961. Significant political leaders of Non-Aligned states included Nehru (India), Nkrumah (Ghana), Nasser (Egypt), Tito (Yugoslavia) and Sukarno (Indonesia).

A major increase in tension in the 1950s was created by nuclear bomb testing. Both superpowers were developing nuclear bombs and long-range missiles to carry them. Testing them was a show of strength, a flexing of muscles. At the same time, the Soviet Union suffered a severe weakening with the breakdown of its alliance with China; there was bitter rivalry between them for leadership of world communism.

The nuclear arms race brought the world close to nuclear war. Khrushchev made an alliance with Fidel Castro following the Cuban Revolution of 1959. Khrushchev intended to plant nuclear missiles on Cuba – a clear threat to the security of the United States. As the installation got under way in 1962, President Kennedy responded vigorously with a naval blockade of Cuba and a demand that a ship approaching Cuba, apparently laden with a cargo of missiles, must turn back. Khrushchev backed down at the last moment. Kennedy played a dangerous game, but it turned out that neither country really wanted to push the world over the brink into nuclear war; neither would use nuclear weapons against the other for fear of an annihilating retaliation.

The Cuban Missile Crisis led directly to the first attempts at discussing nuclear disarmament. There were those who argued that while such weapons existed, there was a distinct danger that they would be used. Early warning systems were in place, so that each country would have some warning of the imminent arrival of intercontinental ballistic missiles – and have the last-minute opportunity to retaliate in kind. However, these systems were vulnerable. One alert was triggered by a major earthquake, interpreted from a seismograph as a nuclear explosion.

A PERIOD OF *DÉTENTE* (1962–79)

The superpowers tried to adjust to a new, more sophisticated pattern of international relations in the 1960s and 1970s. There was a recognition that the world was not separated into two clearly opposed blocs. Both Japan and Western Europe made recoveries from the damage inflicted by World War II, becoming significant powers in their own right. The 1973 oil crisis underlined the fact that the oil-rich countries of the Middle East were also powerful, and that their power was independent of American or Soviet patronage. The Organisation of Petroleum-Exporting Countries (OPEC) emerged suddenly as a world power. Less powerful non-aligned countries also proved less susceptible to bullying or persuasion by the superpowers. New Soviet leaders, Kosygin and Brezhnev, were persuaded that warmer relations with the West would be productive.

The process of *détente* was interrupted. US President Johnson sent thousands of troops into the Dominican Republic in order to avert a Cuban-style revolution there. In Eastern Europe, the Soviets stamped out a political reform movement that threatened to take Czechoslovakia out of the Warsaw Pact. But behind the scenes, Brezhnev was worried about the weakening Soviet economy; one cause of its decline was excessive expenditure on military adventures and weapons. Tensions between the superpowers were beginning to ease. The most startling development was US President Nixon's 1972 visit to China to meet Mao Zedong and Chou En-Lai; rapprochement was under way. The next year, Nixon had the first Strategic Arms Limitation Talks (SALT) with Brezhnev in Moscow; there was an agreement to foster closer economic ties.

It was unfortunate that political crises in several parts of the world brought the movement towards *détente* to an end. The Yom Kippur War, the Chilean coup, the Angolan Civil War, the Iranian Revolution, the revolution in Nicaragua and the Soviet intervention in Afghanistan all combined to raise levels of distrust between the superpowers.

A SECOND COLD WAR (1979–85)

Yuri Andropov's short period in power in Moscow was a dangerous low point in relations between the Soviet Union and the United States. There was one lighter moment, in 1982, when a ten-year old American girl called Samantha Smith wrote to Andropov to tell him she was frightened of nuclear war and asking him to work towards peace. Andropov answered her letter and invited Samantha to go to Russia, which she did. It was one of the few attempts to improve relations.

There was a sharp reawakening of Cold War tensions. It was brought about by the new leaders in Britain and the United States, Thatcher and Reagan, denouncing the Soviet Union in severe ideological terms that were reminiscent of the opening of the Cold War back in the 1940s. Reagan also installed cruise missiles in Europe and unveiled an experimental Strategic Defence Initiative, intended to shoot down missiles in mid-flight; this initiative was nicknamed 'Star Wars', which did nothing to heighten a sense of political or military reality. US interference in the internal affairs of independent sovereign foreign states continued – the Lebanese Civil War, Grenada, Libya, Nicaragua. Meanwhile the Soviets were even more bogged down in Afghanistan than the Americans had been in Vietnam. Worse still, the Soviet economy was disintegrating. One American observer remarked that the Soviet system seemed to be expending more energy on simply maintaining its equilibrium than on improving itself.

THE END OF THE COLD WAR (1991)

The Cold War came to a gradual end during the late 1980s, as the Soviet leader Mikhail Gorbachev negotiated with US President Ronald Reagan. This was driven by the Soviet desire to reduce spending on arms, because of the country's weakening economy. The signs were there as early as 1980 that the Soviet Union was in serious difficulty. Though classified as a More Economically Developed Country, the Soviet Union had run up huge international debts, which can usually be taken as indicating a very weak and unstable economy. Those who noticed this statistic thought it was an anomaly, but it was actually a sign that the Soviet Union was collapsing.

The Soviet armed forces were also the largest in the world according to many measures, such as numbers and types of weapons, numbers of troops, size of the military-industrial base. These statistics led many US observers to overestimate the power of the Soviet Union. The statistics told the outside world nothing about quality, nor about the grotesque overspend on the military compared with the underfunding of other aspects of Soviet life. By 1980, because of the pressures of the Cold War itself and the need of politicians to establish their own power bases, the Soviet Union had developed its military to the point where it consumed twenty-five per cent of the Soviet Union's gross national product, which was excessive. It meant that there were areas of dire need in the civilian sector of the economy.

Gorbachev said that he wanted to wind down the arms race. Many experts in the Unites States doubted whether he was sincere in this, but as time passed it became clear that Gorbachev was so seriously concerned about reversing the decline in the Soviet economy that he really did not want to continue running an arms race with the United States. Gorbachev made some major military and political concessions, and in return Reagan agreed to discuss scaling down the arms race. The tensions that had escalated in the 1970s now subsided.

By 1988, the Soviet Union formally undertook never to intervene in the affairs of its satellite states in Eastern Europe; there would be no repeat of Hungary or Czechoslovakia. The following year the Soviet troops were withdrawn from Afghanistan.

The end of the Cold War came with an unexpected rush as internal reform programmes within the Soviet Union led to demands for more and more self-determination by member states. In December 1989, Gorbachev and US President Bush (Senior) met at a summit meeting in Malta and formally declared the Cold War over. The Soviet alliance system was crumbling; the Communist leaders of the Warsaw Pact countries had had their power undermined. Gorbachev attempted to reform the Communist Party within the Soviet Union to prevent the Party from resisting his reforms, but it was the Communist Party and its ideology that had been holding the Union together. The Soviet Union was in a state of collapse. By February 1990, the Communist Party had to surrender its monopoly on power over the state. In December 1991, the Union itself was formally dissolved, breaking up into fifteen independent states.

LEGACY

Although the Cold War was on the surface bloodless, it was fought at a high cost in proxy wars, revolutions and counter-revolutions around the world. It cost the United States the lives of 100,000 of its own people in Korea and Vietnam, and an estimated eight trillion dollars. The cost to the Soviet Union was even higher in relation to the state's gross national product. The many local civil wars generated or aggravated along the way left millions of people dead.

The collapse of the Soviet Union has left a political and ideological vacuum across a great swathe of Europe and Asia. The long-time dependence on the Communist Party left the Soviet Union institutionalised and dogma-dependent. The great military-industrial sector employed twenty per cent of Soviet citizens; its collapse has left millions unemployed and caused a huge economic downturn. The ending of the Cold War has been replaced by a period of profound uncertainty, regrouping, rehabilitation, searching for new directions.

There is one positive feature of the ending of the Cold War. The shadow of the bomb, the fear of all-out nuclear war, receded the moment the Cold War was over.

THE CHINESE CIVIL WAR

(1945–49)

BACKGROUND

The Chinese Civil War really had its beginnings in 1911, when the Qing dynasty collapsed leaving China in the grip of several warlords. The anti-monarchist and unificationist Nationalist Party, under its leader Sun Yat-sen, tried to get help from foreign powers to get rid of the warlords who had seized control, especially in northern China. The Western democracies ignored Sun Yat-sen, which they may later have regretted, and he then turned to the newly formed Soviet Union. The Soviets decided to support both the Nationalist Party and the new Communist Party in China, though they hoped that the Communists would succeed. It was in this way that a long protracted power struggle between Nationalists and Communists got under way.

A joint statement by Sun Yat-sen and the Soviets was issued in Shanghai in 1923. This was a pledge of Soviet help to achieve the unification and independence of China. There was also a Manifesto, issued by Sun Yat-sen and the Soviet representative, Adolph Joffe, setting up an alliance between the Nationalist and Communist parties. Soviet advisers started arriving in China in 1923 to help reorganise the Chinese Nationalist Party along the lines of the Soviet Communist Party. The Chinese Communist Party was under instructions to collaborate with the Nationalist Party; its members were even encouraged to join the Nationalist Party. The result of this co-operation was an alliance called the First United Front.

Sun Yat-sen had a major problem in dealing with the warlords: he commanded no army. So, in 1923, Sun Yat-sen sent one his lieutenants,

Chiang Kai-shek, to study politics and military matters in Moscow for several months. When Chiang Kai-shek returned he helped set up a military academy outside the city of Guangzhou, the Nationalist-Communist alliance's seat of government. The next year, Chiang was made head of the academy. He was a committed and inspiring instructor, who built personal bonds with the students and officers who would become the core of his army. His rise to prominence soon made him Sun Yat-sen's natural heir as leader of the Nationalists. The Soviets provided a great deal of information on military organisation and munitions for the purposes of study in Chiang's academy. In this way an army of the party was created, one that Sun Yat-sen hoped would be able to topple the warlords.

There were also Communists teaching at the academy, many of them political commissars whose aim was to instil a commitment to the idea of national revolution. The Chinese Communist Party was very small in those early days, growing from a membership of only 300 in 1922 to 1,500 in 1925. The Nationalist Party, by contrast, had 150,000 members in 1922. The party-within-party structure, together with the Soviet interference in Chinese politics, irritated Chiang Kai-shek. This was why the purge began, and the civil war.

Just after Sun Yat-sen died in 1925, Chiang Kai-shek set out on the long-planned Northern Expedition. The purpose of this military expedition was to defeat the northern warlords, unite China and establish Nationalist Party control. But by this stage factions had developed within the Nationalist Party and the communist contingent in it was growing. Chiang finally launched the expedition from Guangzhou in July 1926.

In 1927, after the Northern Expedition, the right wing of the Chinese Nationalist Party (or Kuomintang) under the leadership of Chiang Kai-shek purged the Communists and Socialists from an alliance of the Chinese Nationalist Party and the Chinese Communist Party. There was an ideological rift between the Nationalists and Communists which developed into a civil war. This continued intermittently until it was interrupted by the Second Sino-Japanese War, and that required an organised and united resistance to invasion by the Japanese; the internal disagreements were shelved in order to deal with the external threat. The Japanese attack was apparently opportunistic, seizing a moment when China was seriously vulnerable because of its inner turmoil.

PREPARING FOR THE SHOWDOWN

The defeat of Japan in August 1945, which marked the end of World War II, also marked the resumption of the Chinese Civil War. Chiang Kai-shek tried to resolve the warlord problem and simultaneously wipe out Communism. This was a mistake. Chiang did not have sufficient troops or time to carry out the purge of warlords in the regions formerly under Japanese control. As a result, compromises had to be made, and the warlords were given titles and ranks in the Nationalist army, then given instructions to keep order in the areas they controlled and if necessary fight off Communists. Chiang's hope was that the warlords could hold off the Communists until he was able to deploy his own troops in the region. He reasoned that even if the Communists gained the ascendancy in the warlords' areas the result would still be beneficial to China because the warlords' power would be reduced and it would be easier for Chiang and his troops to take control. The battles that followed between warlords and Communists resulted in victories for the Communists and the power of the warlords was indeed reduced.

But there was a price to pay. The Nationalists lost popular support in the Japanese-dominated areas where the warlords flourished. People simply resented Chiang Kai-shek and the Nationalists. The first peace negotiation after the end of World War II was held at Chongqing (August-October 1945) and attended by Chiang Kai-shek and Mao Zedong. It did nothing to stop the fighting in the north until January 1946.

General Marshall arrived in China from the United States to try to broker a ceasefire between the Nationalists and Communists. The idea was that this would lead to a coalition government incorporating all the political and military groups in China. But neither the Nationalists nor the Communists were ready to compromise on key issues; nor were they ready to give up territories they had managed to acquire as the Japanese surrendered.

In accordance with the Marshall Mission, the Nationalists demobilised 1.5 million troops. But most of these men belonged to warlords, not Chiang's own troops. This cause a great deal of resentment, especially among the ordinary soldiers discharged from service with the warlords. They protested and rioted in Chongqing, because they were out of work and nothing was being done to help them to integrate into civilian life. They turned against Chiang and the Nationalist government; some of them turned to banditry; most of them joined the Communists. There was a huge Nationalist defection in Manchuria, where 500,000 discharged Nationalist soldiers joined the Communist army, which had previously only numbered 50,000. The demilitarisation of the Nationalist soldiers also provided the Communists with weapons, which they desperately needed. This diversion of weaponry was even more serious because of Japan's wartime policy of stockpiling their own weapons – enough to supply 700,000 troops – in secret caches in remote areas in Manchuria. Soviet troops had found and requisitioned a large quantity of Japanese weapons, but most of them remained untouched. The Nationalists knew about the stocks of Japanese weapons, but ignored them because they imagined the Communists were too uneducated to work out how to use them. The Nationalists therefore made little effort to find, still less destroy, the stores of Japanese weapons.

The Communists in Manchuria then had the vast supplies of weapons left behind by the Japanese; they also had the discharged Nationalist soldiers joining them en masse, soldiers who were able to train them in the use of the weapons they were finding. This was just as well, as the Soviets did not give the Chinese Communists the level of support that had been expected. Lin Biao wrote to Stalin in 1947 asking for Japanese weapons found by the Soviets to be turned over to the Chinese Communists, but Stalin did not even bother to reply. Lin Biao wrote to Stalin again six months later and again received no answer from Moscow. In the circumstances, it was lucky that the Chinese Communists were able to locate the caches of Japanese weaponry, because they gave them enough supplies to last them through two years of fighting. The influx of discharged Nationalist troops meant that not only was the Communist army now much bigger, it was ninety per cent professionally trained and technically skilled.

The Communists were now better equipped than the Nationalists, who had only three-quarters of the weapons the Communists had. Curiously, the Nationalists did not notice this critical shift in their relative strength; they went on underestimating the Communists. One reason for their complacency was that the Nationalists had American weapons, which were superior to the Japanese, but not so superior as to justify ignoring the larger volume of weapons and the larger number of troops now weighting the Communist cause.

The Communists nevertheless also reduced their troops by one million, in order to be seen to be going along with the Marshall Mission. But there was another reason, which was ideological. Many of the discharges were a result of Mao Zedong's theory of class struggle; people were discharged for political reasons. Even at this early stage the Chinese Communists were conducting 'rectification' campaigns and persecuting people whose political views were considered unsatisfactory. Many of those purged from the Communist force were people from the land-owning or middle classes; they were considered to be unreliable. These unfortunate people were in many cases imprisoned, executed or forced to kill themselves. As a result, simply for personal safety, many Communists with middle-class backgrounds defected to the Nationalists. Mao admitted that in one area where the persecution was particularly brutal more than 300,000 Communists were driven to defect to the Nationalist side. The violent persecutions and purges of this phase were kept very quiet by the Chinese government until Mao's death; only then did the awful scale of the killing emerge in the Chinese newspapers.

RESUMPTION OF HOSTILITIES

A full-scale war broke out between the Communists and Nationalists in June 1946. The United States supported the Nationalists with large volumes of new military equipment, which was surplus now that World War II was over. The United States also airlifted Nationalist troops from central China into Manchuria. The Soviet Union provided a modest amount of aid to the Communists, but it included 700 tanks, 900 planes and 12,000 machine guns, all liberated from Japanese arms depots. More aid came from the Soviets in the form of tens of thousands of Japanese prisoners of war. They were sent to help the Chinese Communists handle the unfamiliar weaponry. Many of them also joined in the fighting on the Communist side. North Korea was used as a Communist sanctuary, a place where Manchurian railway equipment and bridges could be sent to be repaired.

Too late, the Nationalists tried to win the hearts and minds of the ordinary people. But local government corruption and the general economic chaos rendered this exercise totally ineffective. At the local level, all people were aware of was the corruption of their officials, and that stifled any support the Nationalists might have won. By the end of 1948, the Nationalists were clearly losing the civil war. They had already taken an enormous amount of punishment, undertaking the front-line fighting against the Japanese in World War II. The Communists had fought, too, but in the main it had been guerrilla warfare. The Nationalists became demoralised and were unable to halt the advance of the Communists and their People's Liberation Army.

With the decisive Liaoshen campaign, the Communists seized control of Manchuria. When they captured big Nationalist units, they acquired more tanks, heavy artillery and other equipment to help them in their vigorously assertive campaign to the south of the Great Wall of China. In the Huahai campaign at the end of 1948 and the beginning of 1949, the Communists took central China. The Beijing campaign, also at the beginning of 1949, resulted in Beijing and the rest of northern China falling to the Communists. Three months after that, the Communist forces crossed the Yangtze and captured Nanjing. This was a significant moment, as Nanjing was the Nationalists' capital city.

The progress of the Communists was very fast, because the rural areas had already come under Communist influence. The People's Liberation Army had only to take the cities. By the end of 1949, the People's Liberation Army was chasing remnants of the Nationalist army southwards, out of southern China. Chiang Kai-shek crossed from mainland China to the island of Taiwan with 600,000 Nationalist soldiers and two million civilian refugees. On 1 October 1949, Mao Zedong proclaimed the creation of the People's Republic of China, with its capital at Beijing. Two months later, on 1 December, Chiang Kai-shek proclaimed Taipei the temporary capital of the Republic of China, and continued to act as if his government was the legitimate and only government of China. But the struggle was almost over. The fighting came to an end in May 1950, as the Communists conquered the island of Hainan.

No treaty or peace was ever signed ending the civil war in China, and the two governments continued in hostile co-existence, one a real government of China, the other a phantom government (though supported by the United States). The level of killing and destruction in this civil war is hard to imagine, but the bare statistics give an idea of the scale. Between July 1946 and June 1950, in just four years, the Communists captured 4.6 million Nationalist troops and killed about another 4 million. During the same period, 260,000 Communist troops were killed, one million wounded and 20,000 captured by the Nationalists.

Aftermath

The most important consequence of the Chinese Civil War was the founding of the People's Republic of China under Mao Zedong. But there were other consequences too. Many observers expected the government in exile on Taiwan to fall within weeks. The most likely eventuality was a Communist invasion of Taiwan. To begin with, the United States showed no interest in preventing this from happening and it is hard to understand why Mao did not follow the rapid conquest of China through to its logical conclusion in a single sweep. But the opportunity was missed. The situation changed significantly in June 1950 when North Korea invaded South Korea, starting the Korean War. Because of this, a complete annihilation of Chiang Kai-shek by Mao became politically unacceptable in the United States. President Truman ordered an American fleet into the Taiwan Straits to prevent a Communist invasion of Taiwan.

The Communist takeover of such a huge country had a profound effect on the United State's psyche. Anti-Communism became a major force in Cold War America. The situation made it possible for Joseph McCarthy to purge the China experts from the US State Department – in case they were Communist sympathisers. That in turn meant that there were no real East Asia experts in the administration to advise John F. Kennedy when it came to framing a policy with regard to Vietnam. Maybe, if the old 'China hands' had been left in post, Kennedy would have received more pragmatic advice, and warned him not to involve the United States in the Vietnam War.

THE INDEPENDENCE AND PARTITION OF INDIA

(1947)

BACKGROUND

The conflict accompanying the partition of India was part of a long and painful process, the struggle for independence. Many Indian agitators had been trying to win independence from Britain, formally from as early as 1857, informally from much earlier. It was quite natural that the indigenous peoples of the Indian subcontinent should have wanted to manage their own affairs and be free of interference from the European incomers.

In 1757, at the Battle Plassey the British army under Robert Clive defeated the Nawab of Bengal. After that, the British East India Company established itself as an informal British government in India. This development is usually seen as marking the start of the British Raj. In 1765, following the Battle of Buxar, the Company gained the right to administer Bengal, Orissa and Bihar. Then, in 1849, after the First and Second Anglo-Sikh Wars, the Company annexed Punjab.

During the eighteenth and nineteenth centuries, the British Parliament passed a series of laws to facilitate the administration of the new provinces. Gradually the administration by the East India Company under licence from the British government became formal administration by the British government itself. There was a deliberate and conscious process of Anglicisation. In 1835, English was formally declared the medium for education. Hindu elites educated in the West began to reform controversial social and cultural practices such as the caste system, child marriage and suttee. European traditions such as debating societies and the open political discussion that went with them were adopted. Some of the colonial cultural traits therefore ultimately fed and fuelled the movement towards independence.

The colonial movement that started with the activities of the British East India Company met resistance from the middle of the eighteenth century. The modernisation or westernisation process was not by any means popular in India. Some sectors of Indian society deeply resented it. The arrogant assumption by the British that they were better and knew better how to run India for the Indians was despised. In addition there were conspicuous abuses for which the Indians justifiably hated the British. Henry Ouvry, a British army officer, wrote in his memoirs of many 'a good thrashing' dished out to Indian servants who were careless or lazy. A British spice merchant wrote home that tales of mistreated servants were not exaggerated. He knew people who kept servants 'purposely to thrash them'. Sometimes the abusive behaviour was larger in scale, involving public flouting of Indian customs. The British danced to brass band music on the terrace at the Taj Mahal; used whips to make way for themselves through bazaars; held parties in mosques. Behaviour like this was extremely provocative, and bound to fuel demands for independence.

THE INDIAN REBELLION (1857)

Before 1857 there were several intermittent local mutinies and rebellions. The Indian Rebellion of 1857 was different in terms of its geographical scale. About half of the land area of the subcontinent, especially in the north and centre, was in rebellion that year. One factor provoking rebellion was the indifference and lack of deference shown towards Indian rulers like the Mughals. Another was the friction caused by cultural differences between Indian soldiers and their British officers.

Often in conflicts there are many background factors that contribute to mounting tension over a long period, then one particular and maybe quite trivial event triggers the open conflict. This is the case in very large-scale conflicts like World War I, which with hindsight we may think was way out of proportion in relation to the triggering event, the assassination of an aristocrat in the Balkans. It is also what often happens in very small-scale conflicts, such as marital disputes; an overlooked domestic chore or an unwise purchase, perceived as 'the last straw', may be the trigger that precipitates divorce proceedings. The specific trigger that fired the Indian Rebellion of 1857 was the rumour that cow and pig fat had been used in the manufacture of cartridges for Enfield rifles. Because soldiers had to break the cartridges with their teeth before loading them, Hindu and Muslim soldiers were put in a position where they thought they might be consuming small amounts of taboo animal fat unintentionally.

In February 1857, Indian soldiers serving in the British army refused to use the cartridges. The British authorities said they had replaced the cartridges, which were now fat-free, and attempted to persuade the soldiers to make their own grease using vegetable oil and beeswax. The rumour would not go away. Then, a few weeks later, Mangal Pandey, an Indian soldier stationed in Barrackpore, attacked his sergeant and wounded another soldier. General Hearsay observed that Pandey was in a 'religious frenzy' and ordered another Indian soldier to arrest him. The second soldier refused to obey. On 7 April, both soldiers were hanged and the whole regiment, the 34th Native Infantry, was disbanded as a general punishment. There was consternation. On 10 May, the 11th and 20th Cavalry broke rank and turned on their officers. The next day the rebel Indian soldiers (known as sepoys) reached Delhi, where they were joined by more sepoys.

The residence of Bahadur, the last Mughal emperor, was captured by the sepoys and they demanded that Bahadur should reclaim his throne. The Mughal emperor was unwilling to comply, but after badgering he agreed and became the rebels' leader. The rebellion spread from Delhi widely through northern India, breaking out in towns like Lucknow, Kanpur, Meerut and Jhansi. The British authorities did not respond immediately, but when they did it was with force. Regiments were transferred from the Crimean War and other forces that had been heading for China were diverted to India.

The British army engaged in battle with the rebel army near Delhi, drove them into Delhi and then laid siege to the city during the months of July and August. After some street fighting, the British took the city. The last major battle was at Gwalior on 20 June 1858, but sporadic fighting went on for several months more.

The rebellion was an historic watershed. The British did away with the British East India Company and put India under the direct rule of the British government. A viceroy was appointed to function as Queen Victoria's representative in India. Indians were promised that from then on they would be treated as equals with the British under British law, but the deeply ingrained distrust remained. Indians were allowed into the civil service, but the relative numbers of Indians serving in the army were reduced; only British soldiers were allowed to handle artillery. Bahadur Shah, the rebellion's reluctant leader, lived out the rest of his life in exile at Rangoon in Burma. In 1876, as if to signal a new phase in India's history, Queen Victoria was given the title Empress of India – conspicuously not by the Indians but by her prime minister, Disraeli. The previous owner of the title Emperor of India was Bahadur Shah, who was by then dead.

THE INDIAN NATIONAL CONGRESS

Towards the end of the nineteenth century the anti-colonial movement was increasingly led by the Indian National Congress. This had moderate leaders who campaigned for dominion status within the empire. The period following the Indian Rebellion was one of growing political awareness, increasing political debate and increasing political organisation. In 1867, the East India Association was founded by Dadabhai Naoroji. In 1876, the Indian National Association was founded by Surendranath Banerjea. Then in 1885 came the formation, inspired somewhat surprisingly by a British civil servant, of the Indian National Congress; seventy-three Indian delegates, mostly Westernised and from the professions, met in Bombay to form the Congress. At first the Congress had no preconceived political ideology, but acted as a debating forum passing resolutions on relatively marginal issues. The resolutions were sent to the Viceroy and sometimes to the British

Parliament. The Congress was fairly ineffectual, except in creating a forum for discussion, and because of the restricted backgrounds of the participants it was far from representative.

There were other groups that were interested in reforms of Indian society and religion. It became increasingly clear that religious and social reforms were going to be important elements in any drive towards autonomous nationhood.

The Congress emerged as a pan-Indian organisation by 1900, but it had so far completely failed to attract Muslims. Muslims had a particular grievance at that time, which was that they were inadequately represented in government service. The activities of Hindu reformers were also going on outside the Congress. An attempt was made in 1875 to create a movement for Muslim regeneration, emphasising the compatibility of Islam with Western culture, but ultimately it failed because of the wide diversity of view among Muslims.

Gradually, nationalism began to creep into the Congress agenda. The desire was expressed for representation on government bodies. The Congressmen were still seeing themselves as loyal to the Raj, but they did want to play an active part in the government of their own country. One member who pursued this issue was Dadabhai Naoroji, who stood for election to the British Parliament, won his seat and became the first Indian in the House of Commons.

Bal Gangadhar Tilak was a prominent Indian nationalist. He opposed the British education system imposed in India because of its biased tendency to defame the culture and history of India. He attacked the ordinary Indians' deprivation of any voice in the government of the country. Tilak was seen by many as an extremist. He wanted Indians to attack the Raj and abandon British ways of doing things. He was supported in this by other nationalists such as Bipin Chandra Pal and Lala Lajpat Rai and under their leadership Indian nationalism developed strongly. There were also moderates, such as Gopal Krishna Gokhale, who wanted to negotiate with the British authorities, to have a political dialogue. Gokhale condemned Tilak for promoting and encouraging acts of violence. In the end, in 1907 Tilak and his supporters were forced out of the Congress for their extremism.

Muslims became alarmed at the aggressiveness of Tilak's Hindu nationalism and they were already feeling excluded from the National Congress which was Hindu-dominated. So, in 1906 they founded their own All India Muslim League. A deputation of Muslims tried to negotiate with the Viceroy regarding consideration of Muslims for government service and the number of offices reserved for Muslims was duly increased in 1909.

THE PARTITION OF BENGAL (1905)

In 1905, the Viceroy decided to partition the province of Bengal. The reason was mere administrative convenience, and it incensed the people of Bengal, not least because the drastic measure was taken without any consultation with the people. It also appeared to be a classic case of 'divide and rule'. There were disturbances in the streets and there was agitation in the press. The Congress encouraged people to boycott British products. This was tremendously successful in socio-political terms in that it brought a focus on British penetration of Indian life, and aroused the hostility of ordinary Indians to the British.

The British responded by announcing some constitutional reforms in 1909, and appointed a few moderates to various councils. The British made an extra goodwill gesture too. In 1911, George V travelled to India to attend a durbar. This was a grand ceremonial occasion in which subjects publicly and formally expressed their feudal loyalty to the ruler. It was very much a two-edged treat. Nationalist Indians were no doubt flattered that the king had come to India to see them, less pleased that the durbar was a demand for subservient obedience. But there was icing on the cake. At the durbar George V announced that the partition of Bengal was to be scrapped and that the capital was to be transferred from Calcutta to a new and more central site immediately south of Delhi. It would later be called New Delhi.

WORLD WAR I

Indian nationalists could easily have seen the outbreak of World War I as an opportunity to break away from British rule. It was an obvious moment for rebellion, and the British government was expecting it. Instead, there was initially a generous outpouring of goodwill and support for Britain, and in the most practical terms; 1.3 million Indians served in the various theatres of war between 1914 and 1918 and generous gifts of food, money and ammunition were sent.

There were, even so, centres of rebellion. Bengal in the east and Punjab in the north were foci of anti-colonial terrorist activity. There was an attempt by expatriate Indians headed by the Ghadar Party to instigate a rebellion along similar lines to the 1857 rebellion. The Ghadar Party was helped by subversive elements from Ireland, Germany and Turkey in the planning of this revolt, which has come to be known as the Hindu-German Conspiracy. The result was a series of failed local revolts, and they were scotched mainly as a result of a well-organised counter-intelligence operation.

The aftermath of World War I hit India very hard. The casualty rate had been high, and this was compounded by the impact of the Spanish flu pandemic. Trade was disrupted by the war and there was high inflation. Indian soldiers managed to smuggle weapons into India with the idea of raising an armed insurrection against British rule. The Congress managed to forge a temporary alliance (the Lucknow Pact) with the Muslim League.

The British trod very carefully, fully recognising the enormous support India had given Britain in World War I. In 1917, the Secretary of State for India announced an historic change in British policy towards India. There would be 'increasing association of Indians in every branch of administration and the gradual development of self-governing institutions, with a view to the progressive realisation of responsible government in India as an integral part of the British Empire.' This very careful wording did not mention or promise independence as such, though it implied it. The 1917 announcement was followed by the 1919 Government of India Act, which gave the detailed means by which this 'responsible government' was to come about. There was to be a dual administration, a diarchy in which power would be shared between elected Indian legislators and appointed British officials. The Government of India Act also extended the franchise; in other words

India would become more democratic. The diarchy brought about some real and significant changes in the provinces, where responsibility for agriculture, health, education, public works and local government were handed over to Indians. More sensitive matters like finance, taxation, law and order were still dealt with by the British administrators.

THE AMRITSAR MASSACRE (1919)

The Government of India Act was enlightened, imaginative and showed a clear and orderly path forward to self-government. Unfortunately it was undermined immediately by the Rowlatt Act, also of 1919. This was based on a report from the Rowlatt Commission on seditious conspiracy. The act gave the Viceroy's government special powers to deal with sedition by a variety of measures. It would be able to censor the press, detain political activists without trial, arrest without warrant anyone suspected of sedition. There was a national strike against these measures which marked the start of widespread discontent.

The unrest following the Rowlatt Act reached its climax in 13 April 1919, at the Amritsar massacre in Punjab. There was a demonstration at Jallianwala Bagh, a walled courtyard, in defiance of the ban on political demonstrations. The British commander, Brigadier-General Dyer, contained the crowd of 5,000 unarmed demonstrators in the enclosure, blocking the exits to prevent them from dispersing and ordered his men to open fire on them. The government version of events has 379 Indians killed, but it is likely that three times that number died; 1,137 were wounded. This pointless atrocity showed the Indian people that in spite of all that was said the British authorities still had no respect for the Indian people. The British officer who was believed to be the key figure responsible for the massacre was assassinated by an Indian in 1940.

GANDHI AND NON-CO-OPERATION

When World War I ended the Congress adopted non-violent strategies which included agitation and civil disobedience. The various organisations striving for independence were all partisan and represented sectional interests of one kind or another. It was really only with the arrival of Mohandas Gandhi that a genuine all-India approach emerged.

Gandhi was a prominent leader of the movement against apartheid in South Africa – a battle finally won by Nelson Mandela. There, Gandhi was an opponent of racial discrimination and abusive treatment. Before arriving in India, he had perfected his style of passive resistance by non-co-operation. In South Africa he had been very successful, with oppressive legislation repealed and political prisoners released from prison.

When Gandhi arrived in India, after being away for twenty years, he was concerned initially to support economic and educational development along European lines as the best way to solve a great many of India's problems. The veteran Congressman Gopal Krishna Gokhale became Gandhi's adviser. To begin with, Gandhi's strategies of non-violent civil disobedience seemed impractical and alien to many Indians. Yet, when he applied his technique, called satyagraha, in the anti-Rowlatt Act protests in Punjab, millions of people were inspired by what they saw. It was so effective that in quite a short time a small-scale sectional struggle was turned into a national struggle involving everybody. In Bihar, west of Calcutta, the Congress Party took up the cause of extremely poor share croppers, who were being bullied into paying excessively heavy taxes and being made to grow cash crops instead of the subsistence crops that would have given them food.

The movement gained wide popular support and created widespread and unparalleled public disorder. It was a major challenge to foreign rule, and a far more serious one than the 1857 rebellion. But when an angry mob killed twenty policemen at a demonstration, Gandhi, ever the man of high principle, called the movement off.

The Congress reorganised itself in 1920, with the specific goal of independence for India and with a mass participation membership and mass national appeal. Gandhi was sentenced to a term of six years' imprisonment in 1922, but served only two. On his release he set up a newspaper, *Young India*, and worked to reform Hindu society, specifically relieving the plight of the rural poor and the untouchables. At the same time a new generation of activists was emerging, the Indians who would become key figures in the Indian Independence Movement: Vallabhbhai Patel, Subhash Chandra Bose and Jawaharlal Nehru.

An all-party conference in Bombay in 1928 was intended to engender Indian resistance to British fending-off measures. It set up a committee to draft a constitution for India. The Calcutta meeting of the Indian National Congress called on Britain to give India dominion status (a sort of halfway house to complete independence) by the end of 1929. If not, it threatened, there would be a countrywide campaign of civil disobedience. But in the Congress generally there were increasing demands for total and unconditional independence. In its Lahore session in December 1929, with Nehru as its president, the INA called for complete independence.

Gandhi emerged from a period of seclusion and inaction at this point, to undertake a high-profile march. He walked 400 km (250 miles) from his commune in Ahmedabad to Dandi on the Gujarat coast (March-April 1930). The march was in protest against the British tax on salt. Once they reached the sea at Dandi, Gandhi and his followers symbolically made their own salt from sea water, flagrantly breaking the law in the process. In that same month, far away in Calcutta, there were some large-scale street riots in which demonstrating crowds came into conflict with the police. In all, in 1930 and 1931, more than 100,000 people were thrown into prison as a result of the civil disobedience campaign. At the Qissa Khwani bazaar massacre, in Peshawar, one of the peaceful demonstrations so inflamed and infuriated the authorities that the demonstrators were fired upon.

Gandhi himself was in prison when in November 1930 the first Round Table Conference about India's future was held in London. The Indian National Congress was excluded from it. Gandhi and others were released from prison in January 1931. Two months later a pact was agreed with Gandhi, and the government agreed to release all political prisoners. But some high-profile revolutionaries were not released and the death sentence on Bhagat Singh and two others were not rescinded. In return for the release of prisoners, Gandhi had to agree to stop the civil disobedience movement and take part in discussions as the sole representative of the Congress in the second session of the Round Table

Conference. This met in London in September-December 1931 and ended in failure. Disillusioned, Gandhi went back to India determined to reopen the civil disobedience campaign in January.

The deadlock between India and Britain over India's future continue, year after year. A Government of India Act was arrived at in 1935, but by that stage there were acrimonious disagreements between the Congress and the Muslim League. The Muslim League understandably disputed the right of the (Hindu-dominated) Congress to represent all the people of India. Congressmen countered with the argument that the Muslim League did not even represent the views of all Muslims. The Government of India Act sketched a loose federation that would give provincial autonomy and provide safeguards for minorities. The federal structure was intended to unify the princedoms and British India, but in the end it was not implemented because it was not clear what safeguards there would be for the privileges of the princes. Even so, a measure of provincial autonomy was achieved in February 1937, when elections were held. The Congress became the dominant elected political party; the Muslim League on the other hand performed badly in the elections.

Another major British gaffe was made in 1939, when the viceroy declared that India was joining World War II – without even the courtesy of consulting the provincial governments. It was in effect the same mistake that was being made over and over again, and the Indian people would not be content until the British were out of India altogether. The Congress asked all elected congressmen to resign from government in protest against this transgression.

Jinnah, the Muslim League president, meanwhile agitated in a different direction altogether. He persuaded a Muslim League session held at Lahore to adopt what became known as the Lahore Resolution. This was a momentous request to divide the subcontinent of India into two states, one Hindu and one Muslim. The idea of creating a separate Muslim state, Pakistan, had been floated nine years earlier, but few people had taken any notice of it. Now the volatile political climate and, probably, the disappointing performance of the Muslim League in the elections suddenly made the idea of a completely separate Muslim state more attractive. Once the Muslims had their own state, the competition and rivalry between Hindu and Muslim might end.

WORLD WAR II

Indians were strongly divided over World War II, not least because of the incredible mistake that Linlithgow, the viceroy, had made over committing them to it without consultation. Many of the congressmen who had resigned over Linlithgow's behaviour were at heart British loyalists and they wanted to support Britain in the war. The British Indian Army was in fact to be one of the biggest volunteer armies of the war. Gandhi was ambivalent. He resisted the calls for large-scale civil disobedience campaigns. He said he did not want to win India's freedom from the ashes of a destroyed Britain.

By 1942, Gandhi had changed his mind. He called for determined but passive resistance in his speech *Do or Die*, which was given on 8 August at the Gowalia Tank Maidan in Bombay. The place has since been renamed the August Revolution Ground. The All India Congress Committee met in Bombay, on the same day as Gandhi's speech, and passed a resolution for the British to *Quit India*. If they did not, the resolution continued, a huge civil disobedience campaign would follow. The government clamped down at once. The Japanese were moving west, towards India, and had reached the Burmese border of India; internal disruption could not be tolerated. Most of the leaders of the Congress were imprisoned within twenty-four hours of Gandhi's speech, many of them spending the rest of the war in prison. Gandhi himself was imprisoned at the Aga Khan Palace in Pune. The national leadership of the Congress Party was arrested all together and imprisoned all together at the Ahmednagar Fort. The Congress Party was banned.

In response, there were major protests and demonstrations all over India. There were strikes and widespread acts of sabotage. The British responded with speed and weight. Over 100,000 people were arrested across India. Demonstrators were subjected to public flogging. None of this, of course, did anything to persuade the Indian people that they wanted to be ruled by the British.

The war saw a new force developing in the final stages of the long struggle towards independence. This was the Azad Hind movement led by Netaji Chandra Bose, which sought support from the Axis Powers. Bose had nursed the ambition to raise a liberation army to get the British out of India by force. But the events of the war took Bose out of India altogether and into Japanese-occupied South-East Asia. There he set up what was called the Azad Hind Government as the Provisional Free Indian Government in exile. With the help of the Japanese, he organised an Indian National Army composed of Indian prisoners-of-war and other Indian expatriates. The idea was to return to India with a fighting force that could feed on the general resentment felt against the British to inflict a military defeat on the British Raj.

Bose's Indian National Army was a failure for a variety of reasons: poor weapons, poor supplies from the Japanese, lack of support, poor training. Bose himself disappeared. He is supposed to have died, but his true fate is uncertain. When the Japanese surrendered, the INA troops were captured and returned to India. Some of them were made to stand trial for treason. This was poor PR, as the audacity, indeed the very idea of Bose's pocket army, had caught the popular imagination of India. The soldiers of the British Indian Army might have been expected to regard the INA captives as collaborators and traitors, but they tended to support them for opposing the Raj. There was a strong groundswell of opposition to the British presence in India.

The trials of the INA soldiers in 1945 were potentially so dangerous in terms of inspiring revolt that the British government censored the BBC. The BBC was not allowed to report the story, but the press nevertheless reported the summary execution of INA soldiers at the Red Fort. Mutinies duly erupted in the British Indian Army and Royal Indian Navy, and there was popular support for these major mutinies. The Royal Indian Navy vessels symbolically hoisted three flags tied together: the flags of the Congress Party and the Muslim League and the Red Flag of the Indian Communist Party. The gesture showed very clearly how the ordinary people of India were thinking. Some historians argue that it was the INA trials and executions – and the mutinies that followed – that finally drove India to formal independence in 1947.

Certainly Clement Attlee, who was the British prime minister when Independence finally came, believed so. He thought that the *Quit India* campaign was of negligible importance, by comparison with the revolts and mutinies, in driving the British towards the decision to leave.

On 3 June 1947, Lord Mountbatten, the last British Governor-General of India, announced that British India was to be partitioned to create a secular India and a Muslim Pakistan. It was Jinnah's dream come true, but shortly to turn into a nightmare. Pakistan was declared a (Muslim) nation in its own right on 14 August, and India was declared a nation on 15 August.

Aftermath

The immediate aftermath was an outbreak of appalling violence as Hindus and Muslims carried out atrocities against one another. Separating the Muslim state of Pakistan from the rest of India was intended to resolve the friction, but instead it generated further major conflict among Hindus, Muslims and Sikhs. The new Prime Minister of India, Nehru, and his Deputy Sardar Patel asked Mountbatten to stay on as Governor-General of India. Mountbatten tried to help the subcontinent through this traumatic transition, and was replaced in 1948 by Chakravarti Rajagopalachari. Patel began the difficult task of unifying 565 princely states, which in some cases could only be achieved by force. The conflict was by no means over.

The independence movement and the achievement of independence was an important catalyst to the process of decolonisation worldwide. The independence of India was the first and most important step in the dismantling and disintegration of the British Empire. It was also an important step towards the replacement of the British Empire with the Commonwealth.

Gandhi's strategy of non-violent passive resistance was also an inspiration for the Civil Rights movement in the United States, led by Martin Luther King Jr. It was a model for the drive towards democracy in Burma led by Aung San Suu Kyi and for the African National Congress's fight against apartheid in South Africa led by Nelson Mandela, though that was not entirely non-violent.

The creation of a two-part Muslim state, with West Pakistan over on one side of India and East Pakistan on the other, was unlikely to have worked. There was serious rivalry between the two, which eventually erupted into civil war in 1970–71, a war which led to East Pakistan hiving off as a completely independent country in its own right, re-creating itself as Bangladesh. The circumstances surrounding Independence and Partition carried with them the seeds of future conflict, a long-term regional conflict which is a long way from being over.

THE CHINESE INVASION OF TIBET (1950–51)

THREATS AND NEGOTIATIONS

When the Communists came to power in China under Mao Zedong on 1 October 1949, they lost no time in claiming Tibet for China. Radio Beijing announced that 'the People's Liberation Army must liberate all Chinese territories, including Tibet, Xinjiang, Hainan and Taiwan.' This was rightly felt in Tibet as a clear and imminent threat. In order to clarify the situation and also to sort out some long-standing disputes with China over borders, on 2 November 1949 the Tibetan Foreign Office wrote to Mao Zedong, the Chinese leader, to propose negotiations to settle the territorial disputes.

In order to signal Tibet's anxiety about China's intentions, copies of this letter were sent to the governments of India, Britain and the United States. The governments of these three countries were concerned about the spread of Communism, and regarded its spread as a threat to the stability of Asia. They nevertheless gave Tibet no assurances of support, still less military aid in the event of invasion. Instead they advised the government of Tibet to negotiate directly with the government of China; any other course of action might provoke military action. The West knew, well before the end of 1949, a year before it happened, that China was going to take Tibet – it was first on the list of territories for conquest – and it was going to do nothing about it. Tibet was being hung out to dry.

The government of Tibet decided it would be best to negotiate on neutral territory. They wanted to send two officials, Tsepon Shakabpa and Tsechag Thubten Gyalpo, to meet Chinese officials in a third country, perhaps Singapore or Hong Kong. The two Tibetan officials would take up the issue of the menacing Chinese radio announcements (then still being repeated) about the imminent 'liberation of Tibet'. They would get assurances from the Chinese that the territorial integrity of Tibet would be respected. They would confirm that Tibetans would not tolerate interference.

The two Tibetan delegates went to Delhi to apply for visas to travel to Hong Kong for the meeting. There they were told that the new Chinese Ambassador to India would arrive in Delhi very soon and that they should negotiate through him. The Chinese Ambassador was Yuan Zhong-xian. He demanded that the two Tibetan representatives accept his Two-Point Proposal. It was that Tibetan defence would henceforth be the responsibility of China and that Tibet was to be recognised as part of China. Once that Proposal was accepted they were to go to Beijing to confirm the agreement. They passed these alarming proposals back to Lhasa. The government of Tibet told them to reject them. The negotiation ceased.

THE INVASION OF TIBET

The invasion of Tibet was massive, determined, relentless, swift. On 7 October 1950 a force of 40,000 Chinese troops under Wang Qiemi attacked the town of Chamdo, the provincial capital of Eastern Tibet. The attack came from eight directions and the small Tibetan army, about 8,000 troops in all, stood no chance at all. About half of them were killed in this initial attack.

The invasion came as a severe shock in India. On 26 October the Indian Foreign Ministry wrote a note to Beijing: 'Now that the invasion of Tibet has been ordered by the Chinese government, peaceful negotiations can hardly be synchronised with it and there will naturally be fear on the part of the Tibetans that negotiations will be under duress. In the present context of world events, invasion by Chinese troops of Tibet cannot but be regarded as deplorable and, in the considered judgement of the Government of India, not in the interest of China or peace.' It is unclear why the India government waited three weeks before reacting. Other countries also responded, including Britain and the United States, but all of them had made it clear long before that they were not going to do anything whatever about the invasion: it was only diplomatic support.

In November 1950, there was an emergency session of the Tibetan National Assembly. It met to request the sixteen-year-old Dalai Lama to assume authority as head of state and, at the same time, strangely, he was asked to leave Lhasa and go to Dromo on the Indian border, so that he would be in a position to escape to safety if necessary. The Tibetan Foreign Office issued a statement: 'Tibet is united as one man behind the Dalai Lama, who has taken over full powers. We have appealed to the world for peaceful intervention in this clear case of unprovoked aggression.' On 7 November the Tibetan government appealed to the United Nations to intervene. Part of the letter ran, 'Tibet recognises that it is no position to resist the Chinese advance. It is thus that it agreed to negotiate on friendly terms with the Chinese government. Though there is little hope that a nation dedicated to peace will be able to resist the brutal effort of men trained to war, we understand that the United Nations has decided to stop aggression wherever it takes place.' Ten days later El Salvador asked for the invasion of Tibet to be added to the agenda for discussion in the General Assembly. But the discussion did not take place because of a suggestion from the Indian delegation; the Indians said that a peaceful solution advantageous to Tibet, China and India might be reached among themselves. The Tibetans wrote again in December asking for UN intervention, but to no effect.

There was clearly going to be no help of any kind from outside, so the Dalai Lama and the Tibetan government sent five delegates to Beijing to put forward the Tibetan position and hear what the Chinese had to say. It was not given any powers to conclude agreements. The team was led by Kalon Ngapo Ngawang Jigme.

The negotiations opened in Beijing on 29 April with the leader of the Chinese delegation presenting the Tibetans with a draft agreement. The Tibetans rejected this out of hand. Then the Chinese offered a modified draft agreement, which was equally objectionable. The Chinese delegates, Li Weihan and General Zhang Jin-wu, announced that these were the final terms. The Tibetans were insulted, confined and threatened with violence. They were prevented from contacting their government for advice. They had to sign the so-called Agreement or take responsibility for an immediate Chinese advance on Lhasa. It was under these impossible conditions that the unfortunate Tibetan delegates agreed to the 'liberation' of Tibet. They insisted that they signed in their personal capacity and warned that the Tibetan government was not bound by their signatures.

The Chinese organised a signing ceremony, even forging official seals to make it look like an agreement between nations. The Seventeen Point Agreement authorised the entry into Tibet of the Chinese army and empowered China to manage Tibet's foreign affairs. It did offer safeguards such as the preservation of the existing political system including the status and powers of the Dalai Lama and Panchen Lama. There was to be regional autonomy and the regional culture and religion would be conserved. Any internal reforms would be voluntary and made after consultation. The safeguards turned out to be worthless.

The details of the Agreement were broadcast from Beijing on 27 May 1951. The Dalai Lama (in Dromo) and his government (in Lhasa) heard the news in a state of shock and disbelief. The Tibetan government sent a message of reprimand to its delegates for signing the Agreement without consultation. The delegates telegraphed to say that they were returning home and that General Zhang Jin-Wu was on his way to Dromo. In August, the Dalai Lama returned to Lhasa in the hope of negotiating a better treaty with China.

Above all, the Agreement confirmed China's sovereignty over Tibet. It was presented as a voluntary surrender on the part of Tibet, though of course it was not: it was surrender under duress. The Dalai Lama recalls that Lukhangwa, the Prime Minister of Tibet, told the Chinese General Zhang Jin-wu in 1952, 'It was absurd to refer to the terms of the Seventeen-Point Agreement. Our people did not accept the agreement and the Chinese themselves had repeatedly broken the terms of it. Their army was still in occupation of eastern Tibet; the area had not been returned to the government as it should have been.'

In September 1951, 3,000 Chinese soldiers entered Lhasa, soon to be followed by another 20,000. Now all the major towns of Tibet were under military occupation. Now in a position of unassailable military (though not moral) strength, China had no need to consider re-opening negotiations with the Dalai Lama, who had lost the power to accept or reject any agreement.

The Chinese introduced land reforms, religious reforms and social reforms in what amounted to a radical transformation of a highly traditional feudal society. They turned it into a province of a uncompromising communist state. Highways were built from China into Tibet, as far as Lhasa and then on to the borders with India, Nepal and Pakistan. To begin with, the Chinese were prepared to tolerate the lamas, but during the 1950s that tolerance wore off. The approach became more oppressive and uncompromising, and the lamas came to realise that their power, which was social and political as well as religious, would shortly be ended by the Communist authorities.

By the middle of the 1950s, Tibetans were beginning to resist the Chinese interference, especially in areas where land reforms had been implemented most rigorously. The rebellions spread. Then in 1959 came the so-called Great Leap Forward in China. At this time of cultural shift, the Chinese no longer troubled to show any circumspection towards the Dalai Lama; instead they treated him with open disrespect. In some areas of Tibet the Chinese attempted to set up rural communes along the lines of those being established throughout China. These developments provoked riots in Lhasa, and led to a large-scale rebellion.

The Tibetan resistance movement was the culmination of a lot of small local revolts. With support in the form of finance and organisation from the American CIA, there was at first some considerable success. At the end of the 1950s, large areas of southern Tibet were in the hands of the rebels. But the early success was reversed when the Chinese occupied Lhasa and the resistance fighters had to pull back across the border into Nepal. Resistance operations continued from outside Tibet's borders, deploying a force of 2,000 rebels, many trained in the United States.

By 1969, when the US government was for the first time since the Communist takeover making diplomatic overtures to the People's

Republic of China, the liberation of Tibet was suddenly of subordinate importance to the United States. As Henry Kissinger was about to open the all-important dialogue with Beijing, the CIA's support for the Tibetan Resistance was withdrawn. The government of Nepal oversaw the dismantling of the operation.

Resistance in Lhasa was quickly extinguished, though resistance in the provinces went on for several years. The Dalai Lama fled to India to begin a long life in exile. The Chinese set up the Panchen Lama as a state figurehead in the Dalai Lama's absence, claiming that he was the legitimate head of government. The Panchen Lama was less than a puppet – he was virtually a captive.

In 1965, the region that had been ruled by the Dalai Lama before 1959 was renamed the Tibet Autonomous Region. This 'autonomy' included the provision that the head of government would be an ethnic Tibetan. On the other hand, the real power in the TAR is wielded by the Communist Party general secretary, who until now has always been a Chinese – from outside Tibet.

At this time the monastic estates were dismantled and children's education became secular in emphasis. During the Chinese Cultural Revolution, a time of violent extremism, Red Guards organised campaigns of vandalism that had Tibet's cultural past as their target. It is believed that at this time more than 6,000 Tibetan monasteries were destroyed. Only a small number of monasteries now remain relatively undamaged. During this purge, thousands of Buddhist monks and nuns were imprisoned, tortured or killed.

Since the excesses of the Cultural Revolution, Chinese policies in Tibet have been more moderate. Officially at any rate, there is a fair degree of religious freedom, though the lamas are well advised not to challenge the authority of the People's Republic.

Aftermath

Tibet became and still remains part of China, though on the basis of what can be seen as a false treaty, a treaty signed under duress and by delegates who had not been empowered by their government to do so. From the global point of view, one major significance of the invasion and occupation of Tibet is that other countries were prepared to stand by, watch it happen, and do nothing. The Chinese announced in 1949 that they were going to take Tibet. In the year that passed before it actually happened, nothing had been done by the world powers to prevent it. India, Britain and the United States expressed disapproval but took no action.

The episode was a rite of passage for the scarcely fledged United Nations. The UN was created to intervene in just such a situation, the violation of international law, but it did not. It was exposed right at the very outset as a powerless talking shop or, as the Chinese themselves would have called it, a paper tiger.

THE SUEZ CRISIS
(1956–57)

ORIGINS OF THE WAR

The Suez Crisis or Suez War was one of those small-scale and apparently minor conflicts that turn out to have major global significance because of the issues involved. It is a very revealing conflict to study because of the way in which it arose out of sharply differing perceptions. The different countries involved had different views of the situation and in some cases quite misplaced expectations about the way other countries would behave. The British were bitterly disappointed and traumatised when they discovered that they did not as they expected have the support of the United States; there was a profound sense of betrayal in Britain. The American administration was exasperated when it found that its ally, Britain, was doing in Egypt exactly what it condemned its enemy, the Soviet Union, for doing in eastern Europe. The French were disappointed and angry when they found that they had been abandoned in a war zone by their allies, the British.

The focus of this extraordinary conflict was the Suez Canal. This important waterway was opened in 1869, designed by the French engineer Ferdinand de Lesseps. It was a short-cut between the Mediterranean and the Indian Ocean avoiding the long, time-consuming and expensive circumnavigation of Africa. Just 163 km (101 miles) long, it ran and still runs from Port Said on the Mediterranean coast at the eastern side of the Nile Delta to the Gulf of Suez at the northern end of the Red Sea. The corridor of territory occupied by the canal remained sovereign Egyptian territory and the company operating the canal, the Suez Canal Company, was an Egyptian-chartered company.

From the very beginning, the Suez Canal held overwhelming strategic importance to the British, who saw it as a short sea link to its colonies in the East, in particular to India and Australia. Because of this, in 1875 the British government under Disraeli bought the Egyptian share (the controlling share) in the Suez Canal Company. Then, in 1882, during an intervention in Egypt, Britain took over control of the canal completely. The Convention of Constantinople of 1888 clarified the new situation: the canal was an internationally neutral zone under British protection. The Ottoman Empire, which at that time incorporated Egypt, ratified the convention and agreed to allow international shipping to pass through at any time – in war or peace. As the successor of the Ottoman Empire, the government of Egypt was believed (by the British) to be bound by the treaty, though after World War II the newly independent Nasser government thought differently. It was this crucial difference of perception that caused the later conflict.

During the decades that followed, the Suez Canal proved its strategic value again and again, because it offered a huge saving in time in steaming from European ports to ports in the Indian Ocean or the Far East. It was an invaluable political and strategic link in both World Wars I and II. Once World War II was over and India was given its independence, the original rationale began to slip away. India became independent in 1947, then other colonies, one by one. But the political use of the canal was immediately replaced by an economic use that was equally pressing. The Suez Canal stopped being a highway of empire and became a highway of oil. By 1955, the year before the crisis, half of the canal's freight was oil; two-thirds of the oil imported and consumed by Europe passed through.

THE CRISIS

In 1952, there was a revolution in Egypt. King Farouk, a British ally, was deposed by army officers. The new military regime asserted a set of vigorously nationalistic policies emphasising Egypt's Arab identity. The Suez Canal crisis was already under way, as the Egyptians had closed the canal to Israeli shipping in contravention of the 1888 Constantinople Convention. The issue was debated at the United Nations Security Council, where it was argued that there should be free movement for shipping, with no vestiges of the wartime blockade remaining. In August 1951, the British Foreign Minister Anthony Eden argued that that Israel must be free to use the canal; this condition was implicit in the armistice between the two countries. Eden's argument persuaded the UN. On 1 September 1951, the Security Council passed Resolution 95, which condemned Egypt's closure of the canal an abuse and an unjustified interference with the rights of countries to travel and trade freely. Egypt was called upon to end the restrictions on the passage of international shipping. Under pressure, Egypt eased the restriction, but in 1952 it gradually reintroduced it again.

Then the trouble between Britain and Egypt began. In 1936, Britain had confirmed its control of the canal in the Anglo-Egyptian Treaty. Egypt renegued on that treaty in 1951, declaring it null and void. Britain, perhaps surprisingly, agreed to withdraw from the canal zone in 1954.

Then, on 26 July 1956, the government of Egypt decided to nationalise the Suez Canal Company. British banks and companies held a forty-four per cent stake in the company. This provocative decision was motivated by Egyptian pique at Britain's (and the United State's) withdrawal of an earlier offer to fund the building of the Aswan High Dam on the River Nile. Britain and the United States withdrew the offer after Egypt bought tanks from Czechoslovakia, arms from Russia and gave formal diplomatic recognition to the People's Republic of China. These gestures of friendship towards communist countries were seen by the British and American governments as gestures of hostility to the West.

Anthony Eden, now Prime Minister of Britain (1955–57), decided to go to war against Egypt to reclaim the Suez Canal. It was a terrible mistake. He was still in a World War II mindset and he tried to excite patriotic feelings in the British public by comparing Colonel Gamal Nasser, Egypt's head of state, with Mussolini and Hitler. The Labour Party opposition leader, Hugh Gaitskell, drew similar parallels. In the run-up to World War II, Eden had opposed appeasement and now he opposed it again. Nasser's militarism had to be curbed, by force if necessary. Eden's policy towards Egypt was not just about the canal: it was about Israel. Egypt was attempting to blockade Israel, and Eden wanted to show support for Israel.

In August, there was a three-sided meeting in London, in which Robert Murphy, the US ambassador, and Christian Pineau, the French foreign secretary, met Selwyn Lloyd, the British foreign secretary. Shortly after this, the French and British prime ministers, Guy Mollet and Anthony Eden, formed an alliance. Efforts were made from August through to October 1956 to try to defuse the situation, to reduce the possibility of war. A secret meeting was arranged at Sèvres, near Paris, in which Britain and France tried to get Israel's support for an anti-Egypt alliance. It was agreed in the Protocol of Sèvres that Israel would invade the Sinai Peninsula, which lay immediately to the east of the Suez Canal. Britain and France would intervene as if in the role of peacemakers, ordering both Israeli and Egyptian forces to pull back to lines 16 km (10 miles) from the canal. The British and French would be able to argue that Egypt was unable to secure the safety of this strategic route and that it must pass under Franco-British control.

Eden deliberately avoided discussing this devious protocol with the Americans, assuming that once the events unfolded as planned the Americans would go along with the outcome. It proved to be a very rash assumption, in fact a huge miscalculation.

THE INVASION

The Israeli invasion of Sinai, codenamed Operation Kadesh, was a major operation which had several military objectives. One thing the Israelis hoped to achieve was the clearing of training grounds for Fedayeen groups from the Gaza Strip. The invasion, planned and carried out by Major-General Moshe Dayan, began on 29 October 1956. Initial assaults on the coast of the Gulf of Aqaba were very successful as the Egyptians were taken by surprise.

In a controversial action in the mountains, the commander of the Israeli 202nd Brigade, Ariel Sharon, sent his lightly armed paratroopers along with ground forces against Egyptian forces who were alleged to be occupying the Mitla Pass. No scouts or reconnaissance planes had reported seeing Egyptian forces there, but Sharon reported to his superiors that he was expecting an enemy thrust from the pass, which would endanger his troops. He asked permission to attack several times and was refused. He was allowed to 'check the status' of the pass, and on the strength of this limited permission Sharon went ahead and took the pass. In the ensuing action, thirty-eight Israeli soldiers were killed. It later emerged that Sharon had used scouts to goad the Egyptians into fighting; he provoked a battle in order to take the Mitla Pass. Stories like this were to haunt Sharon in his later political career.

At the same time, Israel's Border Police militarised the eastern border with Jordan and this resulted in the killing of forty-eight Arab non-combatants. This incident, known as the Kafr Qasim massacre, took place on the day the invasion started.

The invasion was supported by the deployment of large air forces on Malta and Cyprus. The two air bases on Cyprus became so crowded that a third airfield had to be brought into action to cater for French aircraft. The RAF base on Malta was also overcrowded with British bombers. These air bases were supplemented by aircraft carriers. The British sent HMS *Eagle, Albion* and *Bulwark*, while the French sent the *Arromanches* and the *Lafayette*. British helicopters were deployed from HMS *Ocean* and *Theseus*. The attack by helicopter was to be historic – the first ever wartime helicopter assault.

On 30 October, France and Britain gave Egypt an ultimatum, and the next day they started bombing. On 3 November French fighters launched from the *Arromanches* and *Lafayette* attacked the airfield at Cairo. Nasser responded by scuttling the forty ships he had already positioned in the canal, making it completely impassable. This spectacular gesture, which was seen on newsreel footage around the world, vividly conveyed to the international community that he was not to be trifled with and that he meant to control the Suez Canal.

On 5 November British parachutists were dropped at the El Gamil airfield, where they cleared the area and set up a secure base on Egyptian soil for support aircraft. The next day Royal Marine commandos stormed the beaches using World War II landing craft. Ships offshore gave covering fire which damaged Egyptian shore batteries and gun emplacements. The town of Port Said was very severely damaged in this attack. Big oil storage tanks at Port Said were hit. They went up in flames, covering Port Said in a pall of smoke for several days. The Egyptians fell back easily in some places, strongly resisted in others. British commandos attacked in helicopters, some of which were hit by Egyptian shore batteries. Friendly fire from aircraft flying in from British aircraft carriers was responsible for inflicting heavy casualties on the commando units.

From the military point of view, the Anglo-French operation to take the canal was extremely well planned and successful in its outcome. But it was a political disaster. The Anglo-French alliance was in effect betrayed by the Americans. Eden had for some reason understood or assumed that the Americans would support the military intervention, but they did not. It remains unclear what was said by American diplomats to Eden in private, but he was undoubtedly severely shaken when support was withheld. A problem was that the United States was at the same moment dealing with a Soviet-Hungarian crisis. The Russians had invaded Hungary and the United States was strongly critical of this intervention. The Americans were embarrassed that its two main European allies were, at that very moment, invading another country and had to dissociate itself from their action. Critically, the United States saw that there was a distinct possibility of the Suez crisis escalating when Khrushchev, the Soviet leader, threatened to intervene in Egypt on the side of the Egyptians. Khrushchev also threatened to launch 'all types of weapons of destruction' against London and Paris.

Clearly, to avoid the escalation of the Suez crisis into World War III, the Anglo-French invasion of Egypt had to be halted. The Americans humiliated France and Britain by forcing them to agree a ceasefire, which it had earlier told them it would not do. The United States sponsored a resolution in the United Nations Security Council to order the cease-fire, and Britain and France vetoed the resolution. Then the United States appealed to the UN General Assembly with exactly the same request. The General Assembly passed the resolution and Britain and France were forced to accept it. Behind the scenes, the Eisenhower administration applied financial as well as political pressure on Britain. President Eisenhower threatened to sell US reserves of British money, which would have caused a catastrophic devaluation of British currency, crippling the

British economy. It was blackmail. The United States was really using every ounce of its power to force Britain to do what it wanted. In addition, Saudi Arabia refused to sell oil to France and Britain, and the Americans refused to supply the oil deficit, again unless France and Britain agreed to pull out. Britain was also reproved by the prime ministers of two of its largest Commonwealth allies, Canada and Australia.

Eden was psychologically destroyed by this change of events. He had assumed American support, and instead was subjected to a barrage of hostile threats and ultimata. It was disorientating and humiliating. Eden was plunged into a nervous breakdown. He announced a ceasefire on 6 November, without warning either Israel or France beforehand. The British and French withdrawal from Suez began at once and was completed within a few days. The Israelis had no choice but to withdraw from Sinai in March 1957.

Before the Anglo-French withdrawal from Suez, the Canadians suggested creating a UN Emergency Force which would keep the peace in the border zone between Egypt and Israel until a political solution could be worked out. This proposal was accepted by the United Nations and within a few days, after some difficult negotiations, a neutral force was agreed, one that would include no troops from the United States, Britain, France or the Soviet bloc. This was sent to Suez with Colonel Nasser's agreement. Lester Pearson, the Canadian who proposed the formation of the Emergency Force, was awarded the 1957 Nobel Peace Prize. It marked the creation of UN peace-keeping forces.

Aftermath

The Suez invasion was a major landmark in British history. It was the last time that Britain would try to use military force to impose its will overseas – without US support. The episode showed that Britain's foreign policy would for the foreseeable future be tied to American foreign policy, a feature of the political landscape which subsequently became a source of tension as Britain increasingly turned towards Europe. The ending of Britain's role as a freely acting world power brought into even sharper relief the polarisation of power in the hands of the two super-powers, the United States and the Soviet Union. It also emphasised the deficiency of NATO, which was at that time thinking and planning too narrowly within the European theatre, oblivious to the global implications of its actions.

The Suez invasion has been seen as the last gasp of British imperialism. The crisis and its resolution left Nasser's standing in the Arab world enormously enhanced, and indeed the self-image of the Third World generally was enhanced. The remaining colonies of both the French and the British were to agitate for their independence during the following years. It is hard to single out one event as a factor, but it does look as if Suez significantly accelerated the decolonisation process.

In Britain, the political landscape was changed, too. There was a significant regime change. Eden had been Winston Churchill's appointee and heir, and he had failed. Harold Macmillan was Chancellor of the Exchequer in Eden's government, and in later years he vividly described how Eden went into shock after the Americans betrayed him, how he was completely unable to function in cabinet meetings. Eden resigned and went away to convalesce. Macmillan, who was Eden's successor, was just as determined to curb the power of Nasser, but having learned the cruel lesson from Suez took care to court American support. Macmillan did a great deal to foster at least the image of the 'special relationship' between Britain and the United States with John F. Kennedy.

Suez had a profound effect in France, too. General de Gaulle saw the Suez fiasco as a demonstration that France could not depend on its allies. On Eden's instructions, British troops had been withdrawn in the middle of a war without any warning to France. Immediately after Suez, de Gaulle took France along a much more independent route. In 1957, France launched its own nuclear bomb testing programme in the Sahara. Within a few years, de Gaulle had taken France out of the integrated military command. De Gaulle was also famously to say 'Non' to Britain's membership of the European Economic Community (later to become the European Union). In France, the treachery of Britain was neither forgotten nor forgiven.

THE TURKISH INVASION OF CYPRUS (1974–ONGOING)

BACKGROUND

Because of its size and strategic geographical location in the Eastern Mediterranean, Cyprus has been fought over, seized and occupied many times. The Ottoman Turks seized the island in 1571, but allowed the mainly Greek population to continue practising their own culture and religion for 300 years. Then, in 1878, Cyprus was leased to Britain. In spite of this, the population was subject to a process of islamification and turkification driven from Turkey. When the Ottoman Empire entered tWorld War I on the German side, Britain annexed Cyprus, which later became a formal British colony. In 1923, the Treaty of Lausanne terminated any Turkish claims to Cyprus.

A tendency for polarisation of Greek Cypriot and Turkish Cypriot populations was perhaps intensified by British administrative policies, which set the two populations against one another. When Greek Cypriots rebelled in the 1950s, the British colonial administrators set up an Auxiliary Police force, recruited from Turkish Cypriots, to control the Greek Cypriots. It is easy to see how an exasperated colonial administration might have thought it was appropriate to make the native population sort out things among themselves, but the effect was to exacerbate inter-communal hostility.

The British hung onto Cyprus longer than to some of its other colonies. This may have been because of its strategic position, making it an ideal naval and air base for any operations in the region. It may alternatively have been because they were anxious about what might happen if they relinquished it. In a Cold War situation, there was a fear that Cyprus might fall into Communist hands and become to Europe what Castro's Cuba became to the United States. There was also a fear that Turkey would once again seize the island, which was clearly inappropriate and undesirable given the high proportion of Greek Cypriots living there. The British government may have decided to stay in control there for as long as possible to prevent either of these undesirable things happening.

Naturally there was Cypriot resistance to the continuing British occupation of the island. EOKA, the National Organisation of Cypriot Fighters (Ethniki Organosis Kyprion Agoniston), had as its aim the removal of the British and the integration of Cyprus with mainland Greece (summarised by the Greek word *enosis*). EOKA members murdered Turkish Cypriots who were seen to be collaborating with the British authorities, but EOKA as an organisation had Britain as its target. EOKA mounted a bombing campaign, beginning in April 1951. Secret negotiations about integrating Cyprus with Greece began in July 1952, under the chairmanship of Archbishop Makarios. These meetings led to the founding of a Council of Revolution in March 1953 and secret shipments of weapons from mainland Greece to Cyprus began in 1954. A former Greek army officer, Lieutenant Georgios Grivas, landed on Cyprus in November 1954 and this marked the launching of a major EOKA campaign to resist the British colonial presence.

The EOKA campaign was unfortunately not just directed against the British, but against Turkish Cypriots. In June 1955, for instance, a Turkish policeman in the service of the British was killed. The Turkish government retaliated by instigating a pogrom (a violent demonstration) against Greeks living in Istanbul. Between 3,000 and 4,000 shops owned by Greeks were vandalised, and thousands of ethnic Greeks left Istanbul during 1955.

EOKA attacks resumed in 1956. Because of the focus on Turkish Cypriots, a Turkish resistance organisation, TMT, began attacking Greek Cypriots – but also Turkish members of trade unions. In June 1958, TMT murdered eight Greek Cypriot civilians who had been transported to the Turkish Cypriot village of Geunyeli. The situation escalated in a series of tit-for-tat killings and bombings.

The British hung onto the troubled colony of Cyprus until 1960, when independence was declared. Under the London-Zurich-Agreements, a Republic of Cyprus was founded by the Turkish Cypriot and Greek Cypriot communities. EOKA's declared aims of getting rid of the British and enosis with Greece had been something of a smokescreen for attacks on Turkish Cypriots. Now that the autonomy of Cyprus had been settled, the communal violence continued. In December 1963, there were massacres of Turkish Cypriots. These led to retaliation by the Turkish government; the residence permits of 12,000 Greeks living in Istanbul were cancelled and their property was confiscated.

At about the same time, the Cypriot leader threatened to amend the 1960 constitution in respect of the guarantees of rights of Turkish Cypriots. This produced further acts of violence. After that the guarantors of the settlement of Cyprus's independence, Britain, Greece and Turkey, wanted to send in a NATO force under General Young.

A problem was the Turkish Cypriot municipal councils that the British had allowed to be set up in 1958, just prior to independence. Many Greek Cypriots feared that these separate councils were a first step towards a partition of the island – and they did not want partition. There was also resentment among Greek Cypriots that the Turkish Cypriots had been given a larger share of government posts than their population justified. This meant that Turkish Cypriot interests were unduly prominent in legislation and administration. So it was that in 1963, after repeated deadlocks in the legislative process and budget-setting, President Makarios proposed constitutional amendments to allow government to run smoothly.

THE COUP

Early in 1974, Cypriot intelligence officers discovered that EOKA was organising a coup. Makarios was to be deposed. A significant feature of the coup was that it was instigated by the military junta in Athens. 'The Colonels' had seized power in Greece in 1967 in a military coup that was condemned throughout Europe as anti-democratic. There was a student rebellion in November 1973 against the military junta, and the response to this was the replacement of the military junta by an even more repressive military junta, led by the Chief of the Military Police.

In July 1974, President Makarios wrote an open letter to the new Greek head of state, President Gizikis. In it, he openly complained about the Greek military regime's interference in Cyprus and in particular about its support for and direction of the activities of the EOKA terrorist organisation. The Greek government's response was to order the coup to go ahead. On 15 July 1974, units of the National Guard of Cyprus overthrew Makarios's government. Makarios himself narrowly escaped being assassinated in this attack. He left his presidential palace, escorting a party of visiting schoolchildren out of the building, hailed a taxi and went to Pafos. There he was rescued by the British, who flew him out of Cyprus in an RAF fighter. Meanwhile, Nikos Sampson was made president of the provisional government.

INVASION, OCCUPATION AND COLONISATION

Turkey launched an invasion of Cyprus by sea and air land on 20 July 1974, after trying and failing to enlist support for intervention by the third guarantor of Cyprus's independence, Britain. This military intervention was Turkey's response to the coup by the Cypriot National Guard to topple President Makarios of Cyprus. Because the coup was instigated in Athens rather than by the people of Cyprus, the Turkish government felt justified in launching an invasion to restore constitutional order. Turkey had earlier refused to recognise President Makarios or his government, but pointed out that the 1960 Treaty of Guarantee stipulated that Greece, Turkey and Britain were to ensure the independence of Cyprus as a sovereign state; under Article Four of that treaty it had the right to intervene. Turkey's position has not been ratified by any international body, because Article Four mentions only intervention, not military intervention, still less invasion and permanent occupation. Military intervention in another state is not permissible except with the consent of the UN Security Council. The Cyprus government called, from the beginning, for Turkey to take the case to the International Court of Justice at The Hague; the Court should decide whether Turkey's invasion of Cyprus was legal. Turkey has refused to do this.

Heavily armed Turkish troops landed before dawn at Kyrenia on the north coast. After the initial invasion, the first wave, constitutional order was restored. The UN Security Council succeeded in imposing a ceasefire within three days of the invasion (on 22 July) and at that point Turkish troops occupied three per cent of the island's land area and 5,000 Greek Cypriots had abandoned their homes. The Turkish forces had secured a narrow corridor of land between Kyrenia and Nicosia. During the next few days they succeeded in widening that corridor, violating the ceasefire as they did so.

These events sent shock waves through Greece as well. On 23 July, as a direct result of the events in Cyprus, the Greek military regime collapsed, and the next day Constantine Karamanlis returned to Athens from Paris to be sworn in as Greek Prime Minister.

Glafkos Cliridis (or Klerides), the leader of the Cyprus Parliament, took on the role of interim president of Cyprus until Makarios returned. In spite of these developments in Greece and Cyprus, which signalled a return to greater stability and normality on the island, Turkey launched the second wave of its invasion. There was a conference on 14 August, at which Turkey demanded that the Cyprus government accept partition, population transfer and thirty-four per cent of the land area to be under Turkish Cypriot control. Acting President Cliridis asked for forty-eight hours in which he could consult Athens and the Greek Cypriot leaders, but the Turkish foreign minister refused on the grounds that it was playing for time. Just ninety minutes after the conference broke up, the Turkish military attack resumed.

By August 1974, Turkish troops had occupied thirty-seven per cent of the island, in effect the northernmost one-third. This was in contravention of a series of resolutions passed by the UN Security Council and General Assembly requiring an end to military action in Cyprus. The situation then was the creation of a *de facto* Turkish Cypriot break-away state under Turkish military occupation. Because of the Turkish military occupation, more than 160,000 Greek Cypriots who were living in the north, and who had been the majority population there, were obliged to leave. The polarisation of control and the rising political temperature also meant that the 50,000 Turkish Cypriots who were living in the south were displaced to the north, into the area under Turkish military control. They settled in the properties that had been abandoned by the displaced Greek Cypriots.

The process of double displacement was naturally full of bitterness and hostility on both sides. None of these people wanted to leave their homes. Some were violently forced out and there were atrocities on both sides, though it is hard to find objective reports of them. In 2004, a documentary film, *Voice of Blood*, was made by a Greek Cypriot film-maker, Antonis Angastiniotis. It examined the 1974 massacres of Turkish Cypriots at the villages of Aloa, Sandalari and Maratha. There were also massacres of Greek Cypriots by Turkish Cypriot civilians and Turkish soldiers at the villages of Palaikythro and Achna and in prisoner-of-war camps. A British naval officer reported the killing of twenty-seven Turkish Cypriots in Nicosia General Hospital by Greek Cypriots – and that was as early as 1964. From what has emerged since it is likely that some at least of these stories are disinformation, and they have been released in order to whip up tension. If the number of atrocities against Turkish civilians can be exaggerated, strenuous reaction by the Turkish government – even an invasion – might seem to be justified.

Here we come back to one of the frequently recurring themes in conflict – that exaggeration, deception and lies are integral and inescapable elements of conflict. In human conflict, truth is always the first victim.

Aftermath

The unhappy division of the island of Cyprus between the two hostile communities continues. The partition was imposed and driven by the Turkish government, and one might therefore have expected that the situation favoured the Turkish Cypriots, but the Turkish Cypriot occupation of the north has not gone smoothly or happily, and it is hard to see how anyone has benefited by the wrenching change. The north still suffers from isolation because of ostracism by the international community.

Negotiations to try to find a mutually acceptable solution to the problems have been going on continually, ever since the trauma of partition. Between 1974 and 2002, it was generally the Turkish Cypriot side that was seen to be turning its back on a balanced solution. But since 2002, the situation has reversed. Now it is the Greek Cypriot side that is obstructing. The latest proposal, the Annan Plan, is a plan to reunify the island, which most people outside Cyprus see as the best long-term solution. The Annan Plan has been approved and supported by the United States, Britain and Turkey; it has also, significantly, been accepted by the Turkish Cypriots, who made their wish known in a referendum. But in a parallel referendum in the south, the Greek Cypriots rejected it. The Greek Cypriot leaders and the Greek Orthodox Church leaders both urged them in the run-up to the referendum to vote 'No'.

The situation has improved to the extent that Turkish Cypriots have freedom of movement and settlement rights throughout the island. But Greek Cypriots are still being stopped from returning to their homes in the Turkish-occupied area.

In 1976 and 1983, the European Commission of Human Rights found Turkey guilty of repeated violations of the European Convention of Human Rights. 'Having found violations of a number of Articles of the Convention, the Commission notes that the acts violating were exclusively directed against members of one of two communities in Cyprus, namely the Greek Cypriot community. It concludes that Turkey has thus failed to secure the rights and freedoms set forth in these Articles without discrimination the grounds of ethnic origin, race, religion as required by Article 14 of the Convention.' The 20,000 Greek Cypriots in the enclave of the Karpass Peninsula whose human rights were being violated in this way in 1975 were unable to endure the way they were being treated. By 2001, only 600 of them were still there. In 2001, the European Court of Human Rights found Turkey guilty of the violation of fourteen articles of the European Convention of Human Rights. At the same time, Turkey was found guilty of violating the rights of Turkish Cypriots by exposing civilians to trial by a military court. Turkey has also been found to have violated Article 49 of the Geneva Convention by bringing a large number of Turks from Turkey (perhaps as many as 37,000) to occupy the former homes of displaced Greek Cypriots.

THE FALKLANDS WAR
(1982)

THE ARGENTINE INVASION OF THE FALKLANDS

This was a war fought over disputed territory in the South Atlantic: the Falklands Islands, South Georgia and the South Sandwich Islands. Argentina for a long time claimed ownership of the Falkland Islands because the islands lie off the Argentinian coast, albeit 640 km (400 miles) offshore, the distance between England and Denmark. The British government also claimed sovereignty over the islands.

The war was triggered by an Argentinian occupation of South Georgia on 19 March 1982. A group of scrap metal merchants was hired to make the landing and raise the Argentine flag there. This symbolic action was not taken seriously by the British government and no action was taken. The failure of the British to respond was taken as a signal that there would be no response to an occupation of the Falklands either. A blind eye would be turned by the Foreign Office. So the token occupation of South Georgia was followed about two weeks later by a military occupation of the Falkland Islands.

It represents the most recent invasion of British territory by a foreign power, though Argentina saw it as re-occupation of Argentinian territory. The Argentinian government's motive in staging the invasion was to distract the attention of the people of Argentina from major domestic problems. There was a serious economic crisis and also large-scale civil unrest directed against the unpopular and repressive military regime that had been in power since 1976. The Falklands War was a diversion, set up by the military regime headed by General Leopoldo Galtieri with a view to retaining political power by tapping long-standing Argentinian aspirations regarding the islands.

The occupation of the Falklands was taken very seriously in London, and a substantial task force was sent to the South Atlantic to reclaim the territory for Britain.

THE RETAKING OF THE FALKLANDS

By the middle of April, an RAF air base had been set up on the island of Ascension in the middle of the South Atlantic. The naval task force also called at Ascension to prepare for war.

A small force was sent ahead to retake South Georgia. An initial landing of British Special Air Servicemen on 21 April had to be withdrawn because of severe weather and two helicopter crashes. Two days later the Argentine submarine *Santa Fe* was detected in the area and attacked with torpedoes, gunfire and missiles. The submarine was so badly damaged that her crew abandoned her at the jetty at King Edward Point on South Georgia. Then Major Sheridan landed seventy-six men and the Argentine forces on the island surrendered without a fight. The Union flag was raised again on South Georgia.

Then came Operation Black Buck – five bombing raids on the Falklands, launched from 1 May onwards from Wideawake air base on Ascension. These raids were probably ineffective. The damage done to the runways at Port Stanley was not serious (repaired with the day) and the damage inflicted on radar installations was also quickly repaired. British post-war propaganda argues that the Black Buck raids persuaded Argentina to withdraw its Mirage III aircraft and deploy them in a defence zone round Buenos Aires. It may be that the RAF were keen to run high-profile raids in order to forestall threatened cuts in defence spending. The raids were nevertheless a landmark. At 12,875 km (8,000 miles), and with a sixteen-hour round trip, these were the longest-range bombing range in history, and only surpassed in the 1991 Gulf War. Some Sea Harriers were launched from the deck of HMS *Invincible*. The BBC reporter Brian Hanrahan was forbidden to reveal how many planes were involved, and he annoyed the military authorities by reporting neutrally, 'I counted them all out and I counted them all back.' In relation to another phase of the war, Admiral Woodward later blamed reporting by the BBC World Service for giving away information about the faulty detonation of Argentine bombs; he thought the BBC was more interested in seeking out the truth than in the lives of British servicemen. Colonel H. Jones made a similar complaint about the BBC when the BBC announced that there would be an attack on Goose Green. Colonel Jones threatened to have senior officials at the BBC prosecuted for treason, but he was shortly afterwards killed in action. The role of journalists both in and out of war zones has always been tricky.

Even though the paved Stanley runway was repaired, it was too short for the Argentine Air Force's fast jets, so these had to be launched from the mainland. Because they had to travel so far, they were able to spend only a short time in the Falklands before returning. This compelled them, later, to fly over British forces to reach the islands. The Argentines sent a strike force of thirty-six planes on 1 May. They also used decoy planes. A squadron of unarmed civilian jets simulated strike aircraft about to attack the British fleet. The decoys were naturally regarded as legitimate targets by the British, and on one flight a decoy jet was shot down killing Air Vice Commodore Rodolfo de la Colina, the highest-ranking Argentine officer to be killed in the war.

THE SINKING OF THE *GENERAL BELGRANO*

The *General Belgrano* originally saw action in World War II as USS *Phoenix*, when she had survived the attack on Pearl Harbour in 1941. The nuclear-powered British submarine HMS *Conqueror* under Captain Christopher Wreford-Brown torpedoed and sank the *Belgrano* on 2 May. As a result of the sinking, 323 Argentine crew members died; more than 700 were rescued from the open ocean, in spite of the storm conditions. The losses in the *Belgrano* sinking account for just over half the Argentine losses in the Falklands War. The *Belgrano* is the only ship ever to have been sunk by a nuclear submarine in combat.

There was concern in Britain about inappropriate reporting of the sinking. The *Sun* newspaper ran its notorious headline 'GOTCHA' above an early report that the *Belgrano* had been attacked, before it was realised that the ship had sunk with the loss of 323 lives. There was a more serious question about the ethics or legality of the *Conqueror*'s attack on the *Belgrano*. Britain had declared a large exclusion zone round the Falklands, issuing the clear warning that Argentine vessels trespassing inside this zone could find themselves under attack. But the *Belgrano* was outside the exclusion zone and steaming away from the Falklands. Mrs Thatcher was asked to explain this subsequently, but the decision to sink the *Belgrano* was never satisfactorily explained. Commander Wreford-Brown informed the British Admiralty four hours before the attack that the cruiser had changed direction and was heading away from the exclusion zone, but the information was not passed on to the Ministry of Defence or Rear-Admiral Woodward, commander of the RN task force. An attempt was made to suggest that a false location was supplied to *Conqueror*, with information coming from a Soviet satellite via Norwegian intelligence, but the *Conqueror* had been shadowing the *Belgrano* for several days and knew both its own location and the *Belgrano*'s with some precision.

The sinking of the *Belgrano* was a tactical error in that it gave ammunition to those in Britain who were campaigning against the war. It also hardened the Argentine position at a moment when a comprehensive peace plan had been put forward by the Peruvian president Fernando Terry. After the *Belgrano* sinking, these diplomatic efforts could not succeed. The loss of the *Belgrano* had a profound military effect. The entire Argentine fleet returned to port for the rest of the war.

THE SINKING OF THE *SHEFFIELD*

Two days after the *Belgrano* was sunk, the British destroyer HMS *Sheffield* was sunk. It was engulfed in fire after being hit by Exocet missiles launched from about 40 km (25 miles) away by an Argentine aircraft. The missiles were detected by radar before they struck but there had been many false alarms already that morning. HMS *Hermes* thought the detection was spurious, but HMS *Glasgow* continued to send the coded warning 'Handbrake': Exocet radar detected. The *Sheffield*'s own detection system was temporarily deafened because the satellite communications terminal was in use at the time. It is not known why the *Sheffield*'s crew did not respond to the warning from the *Glasgow*, but no chaff was fired. The watchkeeper, Lieutenant Walpole, only gave a shipwide warning of attack a matter of seconds before the missiles arrived, when he actually saw the rocket trails.

The *Sheffield* was struck amidships, igniting fierce fires that killed twenty crew and severely injuring twenty-four more. After a few hours the ship had to be abandoned, and the fires went on burning for nearly a week. HMS *Sheffield* sank while being towed out of the exclusion zone by the *Yarmouth*.

In the second half of May, there were active initiatives by the United Nations to mediate a peace. The British were unwilling to break off the campaign once begun, not least because of the cost of keeping the task force in the South Atlantic. It was also important to bring the matter to a conclusion before the winter storms.

At night on 21 May, Commodore Clapp led the Amphibious Task Group in a landing on the beaches of San Carlos Water on the west coast of East Falkland. The bay was nicknamed Bomb Alley by the British, because of the repeated attacks by Argentine jets. The British secured a beachhead, from which they could capture Darwin and Goose Green before going on to Port Stanley. The vulnerability of the British to Argentine air attack was becoming more obvious. After the destruction of the *Sheffield*, HMS *Ardent*, HMS *Antelope* and MV *Atlantic Conveyor* were sunk; HMS *Argonaut* and HMS *Brilliant* were badly damaged. The loss of all the equipment on the *Atlantic Conveyor* was especially serious logistically.

On 27–28 May, the British attacked Darwin and Goose Green, which was held by the Argentine 12th Infantry Regiment. The fighting was fierce: seventeen British soldiers and fifty-five Argentine soldiers were killed and 1,050 Argentine soldiers were captured. The BBC World Service announced the capture of Goose Green before it happened. Colonel H. Jones, VC, lost his life during the attack.

Another 5,000 British troops arrived and on 1 June the new British Divisional commander, Major General Jeremy Moore, was able to plan an offensive that would take Port Stanley. The Welsh Guards were sent in to support a dashing advance along the southern approach to Port Stanley. The advance was hasty, unco-ordinated and hard to organise. There was considerable confusion as many parts of the operation had to be altered and improvised at the last minute. Landing craft were available to bring troops ashore to capture Stanley, but there was confusion and bickering over the choice and designation of the landing places – Fitzroy and Bluff Cove. The confusion caused dangerous delays, as the vessels in Port Pleasant bearing waiting troops were sitting targets for two waves of Argentine Skyhawks. The disaster at Port Pleasant (usually known as Bluff Cove) gave some of the darkest images of the war, with British helicopters hovering in thick smoke as they winched survivors from burning landing ships.

On the night of 11 June, British forces attacked the Argentine-defended ring of high ground round Port Stanley. There were simultaneous co-ordinated assaults, all successful. Two nights later the second phase of attacks started, and Wireless Ridge and Mount Tumbledown were captured. These were the last natural defences, and the Argentine forces in Stanley began to falter. On 14 June, the commander of the Argentine garrison in Port Stanley, Brigade General Mario Menendez, surrendered to Major Jeremy Moore, and 9,800 Argentine soldiers were taken prisoner – over 4,000 of them were repatriated to Argentina on the liner *Canberra* alone.

On 20 June, the British recaptured the South Sandwich Islands.

Aftermath

It was a small war by most standards – 258 British deaths, 649 Argentine deaths, three Falklander deaths – but it had major political reverberations, generating waves of patriotic feeling in both countries.

The military victory strengthened the government of Margaret Thatcher, helping her to win the 1983 election, the outcome of which had before the war seemed uncertain. Although Thatcher did well out of the war, several members of her government felt sufficiently compromised by what had happened to resign, notably Foreign Secretary Lord Carrington; he resigned because his department had failed to anticipate the war.

The Argentine defeat strengthened protests against the military regime and hastened its downfall. The Falklands have remained under British control, though Argentina has given no indication that it intends to relinquish its claim.

In military terms, the war was clearly a success from the British point of view, but there were many terrible mistakes and many avoidable fatalities. A British victory was by no means a certainty, especially with the South Atlantic winter closing in on a task force a very long way from home. As Admiral Woodward said afterwards, 'It was a damned close run thing.'

9

POST-COLD WAR CONFLICTS

THE GULF WAR

(1990–91)

The Gulf War was a major and epoch-making conflict between Iraq and a thirty-five-nation coalition force led by the United States and authorised by the United Nations. Its purpose was simple – to liberate Kuwait from Iraqi occupation.

The war had complex origins, developing out of a war between Iraq and Iran. The United States was already concerned about Iraq's aggressive stance towards Israel and Iraq's disapproval of the move towards a peace between Israel and Egypt. The United States also condemned Iraq for supporting militant Palestinian groups and this led the Americans to name Iraq as a state sponsor of international terrorism in a formal name-and-shame list compiled in 1979.

As war broke out between Iraq and Iran, the United States remained officially neutral. By 1982, Iran was mounting a successful counter-offensive against Iraq, while the United States worked hard to stop Israel from involving itself in the conflict. The Americans wanted to develop better diplomatic relations with Iraq and so decided to remove it from the list of state sponsors of terrorism. Officially this was justified because the Iraqi record had improved, but the US government was still convinced that Iraq was involved in terrorism. The real motive was to help Iraq to defeat Iran and to that end America started giving Iraq aid, selling 200 million dollars' worth of arms to Iraq between 1983 and 1990, which even so amounted to just one per cent of Iraq's arms purchases during that period. The United States also gave unknown amounts of covert aid to Iraq; it is known that the Americans supplied battlefield intelligence to Saddam Hussein, the military dictator who was Iraq's head of state.

The United States also supplied economic aid to Iraq, for the same reason. The war with Iran seriously disrupted Iraq's oil export trade and the US economic support enabled Saddam Hussein to go on fighting the war with Iran in spite of this. Iraq was in receipt of five billion dollars' worth of export credit guarantees between 1983 and 1990, by way of the US Department of Agriculture. In 1985, the United States gave Iraq over 680 million dollars in credits in order to enable Iraq to build an oil pipeline.

So, during the Iraq-Iran War there is no question about it; the United States was an ally of Iraq, and gave Saddam Hussein several different kinds of aid to help him win that war. This was in spite of American reservations about the Iraqi regime's stance in regard to Israel and to terrorist organisations. But once the Iraq-Iran War was over there was a distinct cooling in the relationship between the United States and Iraq. The US Congress made moves to apply diplomatic and economic pressure on Iraq, because of concerns over alleged violations of human rights, general hostility towards Israel and its dramatic military build-up. There was no unanimity among American politicians about the right way to treat Iraq, but there were those who thought it had been a poor idea to support the Saddam Hussein regime in the first place.

The formal diplomatic relationship between the United States and Iraq remained unchanged until a specific event, which could be seen as Saddam Hussein's worst mistake – his invasion of Kuwait. As late as October 1989, President George W. Bush signed a secret directive that stated, 'Normal relations between the United States and Iraq would serve our [American] long term interest and promote stability in both the Persian Gulf and the Middle East.' This is quite a remarkable statement in view of later events: the Gulf War and, even more so, the Iraq War. Following the Iraqi invasion of Kuwait, the United States found reasons for cooling its relationship with Iraq. The countries of the West had a very direct interest in maintaining their own access to oil supplies from the Middle East. America realised that it was not in the interests of the West in general or the United Sates in particular for Iraq to retain control of a high proportion of the Middle East oil. The United States did not want a Middle East dominated by Iraq.

THE IRAQI INVASION OF KUWAIT

When the Iraq-Iran War ended in August 1988, Iraq was heavily in debt to Kuwait and Saudi Arabia. Defying the quotas for oil productions set by OPEC, Kuwait had increased its own rate of oil production by forty per cent. The resulting drop in oil prices had a disastrous effect on the economy of Iraq. The government of Iraq described what Kuwait had done as tantamount to economic warfare. It also accused Kuwait of slant-drilling across the border and pirating oil from the Rumaila oilfield, which belonged to Iraq.

These were the seeds of conflict. The situation was made worse by the poor quality of the maps that defined the borders of Kuwait. There was room to dispute the location of its borders, and they had never been mutually agreed anyway. Negotiations between Iraq and Kuwait broke down in July 1990. Then Saddam Hussein moved troops to the borders of Kuwait and summoned the American ambassador, April Glaspie. According to transcripts of the meeting, Saddam Hussein listed his grievances against Kuwait, threatened invasion, but promised to hold off invasion until another round of negotiations was held. The American ambassador made it clear that the United States had no interest in Arab-Arab conflicts, which was a remarkable assertion in view of the country's many-sided support of Iraq against Iran, which Saddam knew about better than anyone. The ambassador went on to give an 'American' view of what Iraq was doing that now seems hopelessly at odds with the American view of the situation not long afterwards.

'My assessment after twenty-five years' service in this area is that your [Saddam Hussein's] objective must have strong backing from your Arab brothers. I now speak of oil. But you, Mr President, have fought through a horrific and painful war. Frankly, we can see only that you have deployed massive troops in the south. Normally that would not be any of our business. But when this happens in the context of what you said on your national day, then when we read the details in the two letters of the Foreign Minister, then when we see the Iraqi point of view that the measures taken by the United Arab Emirates and Kuwait is, in the final analysis, parallel to military aggression against Iraq, then it would be reasonable for me to be concerned. And for this reason, I received an instruction to ask you, in the spirit of friendship – not in the spirit of confrontation – regarding your intentions.'

Some observers have understandably seen this curiously roundabout and emollient statement as giving Saddam Hussein the green light to invade Kuwait. Nowhere is he told to stop or pull back. It is possible that this statement and other signals like it may have been taken by Saddam Hussein as mild approval to proceed, and an indication that the United States would not bother to intervene. The United States had after all done nothing about the reunification of Germany, which simply involved wiping out an internal border. All Saddam Hussein thought he was doing was wiping out an internal border. Some observers believe that Saddam Hussein was not under these illusions at all, but simply underestimated the weight of the American military response, which when it came was mighty indeed.

Then, in a very ill-judged public relations exercise, Saddam Hussein detained a group of Western civilians as informal hostages, and had himself shown on television with them (23 August 1990), smiling and patting the six-year-old Stuart Lockwood. He said, 'We hope your presence as guests here will not be for too long. Your presence here, and in other places, is meant to prevent the scourge of war.' This did nothing to reassure the West that Saddam Hussein was harmless. The hostages were clearly being used as a human shield.

Just hours after Saddam Hussein moved his troops into Kuwait, the United Nations Security Council passed a resolution condemning the invasion and demanding withdrawal. The Arab League passed a resolution to solve the problem from within, and warned against foreign (ie Western) intervention. Then the UN imposed economic sanctions on Iraq. The West decided to fight and push back the Iraqis because they feared an attack on Saudi Arabia, which was perceived as a far more important matter – to the West.

The Iraqi invasion moved easily to within striking distance of Saudi Arabia's main mineral resource, the Hama oilfields. If the Iraqis gained control there, the way would be open to take Riyadh, the Saudi capital. Iraq bitterly resented the fact that it owed Saudi Arabia twenty-six billion dollars, and once his troops were inside Kuwait Saddam Hussein launched verbal attacks on the Saudis. Saudi Arabia was sponsored by the United States, he said, and not a legitimate guardian of the Muslim holy cities of Mecca and Medina.

OPERATION DESERT SHIELD

President George W. Bush announced that the United States would send a 'wholly defensive' mission to stop Iraqi troops from invading Saudi Arabia. US troops entered Saudi Arabia on 7 August 1990. The next day, Saddam Hussein bullishly declared Kuwait to be part of Iraq.

On 11 September 1990, President Bush said, 'Within three days, 120,000 Iraqi troops with 850 tanks had poured into Kuwait and moved south to threaten Saudi Arabia. It was then that I decided to act to check that aggression.' This was said to be based on satellite photos showing the build-up of Iraqi forces along the border. An investigative journalist checking the story obtained a commercial Russian satellite photo, and showed it to expert analysts. They found that the photo did not match the claims made by President Bush at all. There was very little evidence of activity in the crucial border area. Either President Bush had not told the truth, or the Russians had deliberately or accidentally sent a non-recent photo. As would happen several times during this and the later conflict (the Iraq War), doubts were expressed about the rationale offered by the Bush administration for going to war.

The Americans sent two naval battle groups to the area, the aircraft carriers USS *Dwight D. Eisenhower* and USS *Independence* with their escorts. To curb any further Iraqi activity, forty-eight US fighter planes landed in Saudi Arabia to begin air patrols of the Saudi-Kuwait-Iraq borders. Two more naval groups were sent, centring on the battleships USS *Missouri* and USS *Wisconsin*. After just 100 years of battleships, these were to be the last battleships to take part in a war. The US military build-up continued until there were 500,000 troops in the area. The build-up was nevertheless quite slow, and the Iraqis had a clear two month period in which they could have invaded Saudi Arabia if they had wanted to do so. There were only sufficient forces in the area from October onwards for the United States to have stopped Iraq.

The UN Security Council gave Saddam Hussein an ultimatum on 29 November 1990: withdraw from Kuwait by 15 January 1991 or force would be used. US Secretary of State James Baker built a coalition of military forces from thirty-four countries to support the US opposition to Iraq. Many of the coalition states were reluctant to join, either because they saw the war as a local Arab affair or because they saw the exercise as a means to increase American influence in Kuwait. US troops still made up three-quarters of the coalition force. Norway sent what looked like a token force of fifty personnel. Many of the waverers decided to join because of Iraq's bare-faced belligerence.

Senior officials discussed the possibility of invasion. Additional reasons for dealing a blow against Saddam Hussein were found: his history of human rights abuse, Iraq's possession of chemical and biological weapons, Iraq's aspiration to build nuclear bombs. Something more than the violation of Kuwaiti sovereignty was felt to be necessary to justify invasion – largely for the benefit of those many states who felt that the conflict should have been left as a local matter. As would happen later, the reasons for going to war were being beefed up in order to win support.

There were last-minute peace negotiations, but these were scotched by Iraq. Iraq wanted to make demands of its own, such as the withdrawal of Syrian troops from Lebanon and the withdrawal of Israeli troops from the West Bank, the Gaza Strip and the Golan Heights. Bush managed to persuade the Israelis to stay out of the coming hostilities by telling them that British Special Forces were already in Iraq, searching for the SCUD missile launchers that were being aimed at Israeli cities.

On 12 January 1991, the US Congress authorised the use of military force to drive the Iraqi troops out of Kuwait. The voting was nevertheless very close indeed, so even at this late stage the Gulf War might have been averted.

One day after the expiry of the ultimatum deadline, on 17 January 1991, the coalition forces launched a colossal air campaign codenamed Operation Desert Storm. Over 1,000 sorties were launched every day. Within a few hours, under cover of night, Stealth bombers bombed Baghdad, the capital of Iraq, at the same time as a cruise missile strike. The attack went on for hours causing widespread destruction of the capital's television stations, airfields, government buildings and presidential palaces. A major priority for the coalition was the destruction of the Iraqi air force and anti-aircraft facilities. Many of the weapons, such as 'smart bombs', found their targets because they were guided by computers. This was the first computer war.

Just five hours into the attacks, Saddam Hussein broadcast over the radio, 'The great duel, the mother of all battles, has begun. The dawn of victory nears as this great showdown begins.' His response to the coalition attack was to launch Scud missiles at Israel, apparently with the intention of goading Israel into joining in the conflict. This attack on Israel continued for six weeks and Israel showed remarkable restraint in not retaliating.

The coalition next attacked the Iraqi command and communications facilities. The Iraqi Air Force seems to have panicked. It fled to Iran. This mass exodus was a great surprise to the coalition, which had expected a defection but to a country friendly to Iraq, such as Jordan. In fact the coalition had positioned fighters over western Iraq in order to stop the Iraqi pilots reaching Jordan. This wrong guess meant that almost the entire Iraqi Air Force escaped; Iran never returned the aircraft, and kept the crews captive for several years. The Iraqi Navy tried to escape to Iran, too, but apparently only one small boat managed to get through.

In a move that was presumably intended as a diversion, Iraq released two billion litres of crude oil into the Gulf – the biggest oil spill in history, a terrible waste of fossil fuel and a grotesque act of vandalism. A possible motive was to prevent US Marines from getting ashore from their vessels.

A third and major phase of the coalition air campaign was the targeting of Iraqi military installations. These included Scud missile launchers, weapons research facilities, supposed weapons of mass destruction sites. There were also attacks on Iraq's infrastructure: dams, water pumping stations, power stations, port facilities, oil refineries, pipelines, bridges. Many of these installations were identified on satellite photographs, which in turn were referenced to the co-ordinates of the US Embassy in Baghdad. These co-ordinates were determined with great accuracy by an American air force officer visiting the US Embassy in August 1990. He used a Global Positioning System unit he was carrying in a briefcase; the exact position of the US embassy was relayed back to Virginia and used as the point of origin for a system of precise co-ordinates for all the targets. This was another dimension to the new style of computer warfare. GPS locations combined with smart weapons meant that many of the key facilities could be knocked out with ruthless accuracy. By the end of this very destructive war, Iraq's power production was down to four per cent of its pre-war level.

In spite of the super-accuracy of the coalition bombing, the Iraqis claimed that some civilian targets were hit. A blockhouse that US officials thought was a communications centre was said by the Iraqis to be an air raid shelter. Hundreds of civilians were killed when two laser-directed smart bombs hit it, the Iraqis claimed. It was a short-term propaganda victory for the Iraqis; after the war Iraqi military leaders were to admit that it had been a communications centre after all. On the ground, the forces of the two sides were more evenly matched than in the air, though the enormously effective coalition air campaign greatly hampered the Iraqi ground forces. To begin with, special coalition units landed behind Iraqi lines to gather intelligence. Then on 22 February, Iraq agreed to a ceasefire proposed by Russia. Under this the Iraqis agreed to withdraw to pre-invasion positions within six weeks of a total cease-fire. The coalition did not however accept these terms, and gave Iraq only twenty-four hours to start withdrawing.

On 24 February, the coalition forces began a major and rapid push into Iraq on the ground and in the air. This took the Iraqis by surprise. They began retreating out of Kuwait on 26 February, vengefully setting fire to the Kuwaiti oilfields as they went. A long straggling convoy of retreating Iraqi soldiers developed along the main highway from Kuwait back into Iraq. This was bombed so much that it was called the Highway of Death. The bombing of this road and everyone on it was highly controversial, as not all of the people on the road were military personnel. Coalition forces pursued the retreating Iraqis right across the border, across Iraq and only stopped 240 km (150 miles) short of Baghdad. On 27 February, President Bush declared that Kuwait had been liberated.

Aftermath

The war was a triumph of planning and execution by the coalition forces, resulting in just 358 coalition deaths, compared with about 30,000 Iraqis killed. The Pentagon had estimated before the war that there might be as many as 30,000 or 40,000 coalition casualties. Above all the war showed the tremendous effectiveness of some of the new laser- and computer-based weapons technology, making this the first of a new generation of super-modern wars. The coalition ground forces turned out to be far better equipped than the Iraqi army with its Soviet equipment and command style.

The spectacular swiftness of the coalition victory resulted in a comprehensive review of military strategy in China. A movement began to modernise the technology used by the Chinese army.

The war ended with optimistic talk of a rising in Iraq and the hope that Saddam Hussein would soon be toppled from power by his overwhelming military defeat. Kurdish leaders in the north of Iraq took heart at this thought. But the Kurds received no American support when they rebelled, Iraqi generals remained loyal to Saddam, and the Kurdish troops were annihilated. Millions of Kurds tried to flee across the mountains into Kurdish areas of Iran and Turkey. Incidents like these led to the establishment, by the coalition forces, of no-fly zones in the extreme north and south of Iraq in an attempt to stop Saddam Hussein persecuting his own people.

In Kuwait, more than 400,000 people were expelled from the country, including a large number of Palestinians who had supported and collaborated with Saddam Hussein.

One surprising outcome of the war was a non-outcome. The coalition forces were clearly powerful enough to drive on to Baghdad, where they could have overthrown the Saddam Hussein regime. Bush himself may have wanted to do just this, but such a course of action would probably have broken up the coalition – not least because regime change in Iraq had never been given as a reason for fighting the war or as an aspiration. Many people in the West, not just in the Bush administration, were disappointed to see that Saddam Hussein's grip on power in his own country was apparently undiminished.

Economic sanctions against Iraq were kept in place after the Gulf War ended, until such time as Iraq co-operated with weapons inspection. Iraq never fully co-operated with the inspectors, whom they accused, with some justification, of spying.

The economic sanctions against Iraq contributed substantially to the misery of the Iraqi people, increased the child mortality rate, and contributed to an increasingly negative image of the West in general and the United States in particular in the Arab world. UNICEF reported that the sanctions resulted in an additional 40,000 child deaths per year. The presence of American troops in Saudi Arabia, the invasion of Iraq and the economic blockade of Iraq were all to become grievances held against the United States by Osama bin Laden, and therefore led on to the 9/11 attacks, which in turn led to the War on Terror.

It would be the Iraqi government's persistent refusal to co-operate with weapons inspection that would spark the next war in the Middle East, the Iraq War, which was to a great extent a continuation of the Gulf War.

THE WAR ON TERROR
(2001–ONGOING)

The War on Terror announced by US President George W. Bush was a direct response to the spectacular terrorist attacks on the United States on 11 September 2001. The attacks, on different locations, were carefully co-ordinated and almost simultaneous, to create the maximum psychological impact on the West.

On the morning of 11 September, nineteen terrorists who were Islamic extremists affiliated to al-Qaeda hijacked four commercial jet airliners. Because they were undertaking internal flights, security was minimal, so it was possible for the armed hijackers to board the planes unimpeded. Each team of hijackers included one trained pilot. The hijackers deliberately flew two of the airliners, United Airlines Flight 175 and American Airlines Flight 11, into the twin towers of the World Trade Centre in New York. These deliberate high-energy impacts started massive fires in the towers, which weakened them and caused them to collapse shortly afterwards.

The hijackers intentionally crashed a third airliner, American Airlines Flight 77, into the Pentagon Building near Washington DC. The fourth airliner, United Airlines Flight 93, did not reach the target intended by the hijackers. One of the passengers picked up on her mobile phone news of what had happened to the other three hijacked planes. The passengers and crew made a desperate attempt either to regain control of the aircraft or to bring it down prematurely in open country without causing any deaths in an urban area. It came down in a field near Shanksville in Pennsylvania.

Three thousand people, nearly all of them civilians, died in the attacks. Al-Qaeda was responsible for the attacks. The organisation had its origins in the 1979 Soviet invasion of Afghanistan. Shortly after the invasion Osama bin Laden went to Afghanistan to help organize the Arab resistance to the Soviets; it was called Maktab al-Khadamat (MAK). When the Soviets withdrew from Afghanistan in 1989, MAK evolved into al-Qaeda, a rapid reaction force. It was during the course of the Afghan struggle for independence, in 1984, that the concept of *jihad*, the righteous war, was defined. It was decided that it was the duty, the obligation, of every Muslim to help the embattled Afghans to get rid of the Russian intruders. This strictly military concept of a holy war was developed after 1989 to mean something much wider. Some Muslims who were involved in the *jihad* against the Soviet troops invading Afghanistan are very unhappy about the way the *jihad* has been turned into a directionless and angry massacre of innocent civilians around the world; this is not how Islamic scholars were defining *jihad* in 1984.

Osama bin Laden became more radical. In 1996, bin Laden issued his first *fatwa*, calling for American troops to leave Saudi Arabia. A second *fatwa* issued two years later instructed his followers 'to kill Americans anywhere' – a long way from a righteous war. At least in the fatwa bin Laden gave his reasons: the continuing presence of American troops in Saudi Arabia after the Gulf War and American policy regarding Israel.

As more information emerged in the hours and days after the 9/11 attacks, many speculated that bin Laden was behind the attacks. For several years, the CIA had been aware that, as far as the United States was concerned, he was the most dangerous man in the world. Now, if he really was behind these attacks, he had proved it. Within hours of the attack, the FBI had discovered the identities of the hi-jackers; few of them had made any attempt to conceal their identities, and they were conspicuous because of their Arabic appearance and names. The luggage of Mohamed Atta, which for some reason was not transferred from an earlier flight onto American Airlines Flight 11, contained details of the identities of all nineteen hijackers, along with information about their plans and motives. Some communications were intercepted on the day of the attacks that pointed directly to bin Laden as the initiator of this terrible crime. The shock felt in the United States was even greater than that felt at the time of Pearl Harbour, when the Japanese attacked without first declaring war. 9/11 was the same, but worse – an undeclared war on a civilian population.

So far, only people at the edges of the conspiracy have been tried and convicted in connection with the attacks. Osama bin Laden, who at first denied, but later admitted, responsibility for organising them, has not been formally indicted and remains at liberty.

The international campaign against terrorism was launched in the wake of 9/11 by the US government under President George W. Bush. It incorporates a range of legal, political and military actions that are alleged to be motivated by a desire to 'curb the spread of terrorism'. The War on Terror was formally authorised by US Congress under an Authorization for Use of Military Force against Terrorists which was passed on 18 September 2001.

The first move after the authorisation was the freezing of assets of terrorist organisations. The UN Security Council passed a resolution obliging all states to criminalise any kind of support for terrorist activity. The Taliban rejected an ultimatum to surrender al-Qaeda operatives who were active in Afghanistan, so the United States and some of its NATO allies began air strikes against al-Qaeda targets in Afghanistan on 7 October 2001. Forces operating from within Afghanistan collaborated with the USA-NATO initiative and succeeded in capturing most of Afghanistan by early 2002.

This campaign was taken on to the Philippines, where US special forces fought with the Philippine army against al-Qaeda.

One of the most momentous episodes in the War on Terror was the decision, taken in March 2003, to expand the campaign into Iraq. The US government took the view that the regime of Saddam Hussein was sponsoring al-Qaeda, as well as continuing to develop weapons of mass destruction.

The War on Terror has developed into a large-scale undertaking, fought in several theatres of war. In the Horn of Africa, a force of 2,000 US personnel was posted at Djibouti, with the aim of stopping suspect shipments from entering north-eastern Africa from the Middle East. The situation there has become more complicated now that an Islamist faction in Somalia has campaigned for the establishment of Sharia Law; the al-Qaeda leader Osama bin Laden urged the Somalis to set up an Islamic state in July 2006, and warned the West to stay out. One side effect of the conflict has been the generation if a new war between Somalia and its neighbour, Ethiopia.

In the Mediterranean, NATO began checking shipping to prevent the movement of terrorists or weapons of mass destruction. The argument was that this would improve the security of shipping in general and reduce the rate of illegal immigration into Greece.

The Israeli army invaded southern Lebanon in July 2006, after Hezbollah killed two Israeli soldiers and captured two others. The war lasted over a month, causing the deaths of about 1,000 Lebanese and 163 Israelis. The UN arranged the terms of a ceasefire on 14 August 2006. This war was really part of the ongoing war between Israel and her Arab neighbours, but in the current international climate it has been possible for Israel to claim that it was fighting a war against terror, and that interpretation was ratified by President Bush.

In 2007, a conflict broke out in northern Lebanon between an Islamist militant organisation called Fatah al-Islam and the Lebanese army. The terrorist group has been described as a militant jihadist group inspired by al-Qaeda. During this conflict, the American government provided military aid to the Lebanese government.

In 2006 the Fatah-Hamas conflict started; this is a struggle between two Palestinian factions trying to gain political control over the Palestinian territories. Much of the fighting is in the Gaza Strip, which was taken over by Hamas in June 2007. Fatah is backed by the United States. Hamas is considered to be a terrorist organisation by the United States, UN and EU. On 12 May 2003, al-Qaeda terrorists bombed Riyadh in the Saudi Arabia.

India experienced a steady increase in Islamist terrorism during the 1990s. Several terrorist groups have emerged in Kashmir – Lashkar-e-Toiba, Hizbul Mujahideen and Jaish-e-Mohammed – creating serious problems, such as a series of massacres. Al-Qaeda has been giving both ideological and financial support to terrorist activities in Kashmir; bin Laden and his associates are keen to see a holy war waged against India. Islamic fundamentalists disseminate propaganda condemning the 'idol worshippers and Hindus' who 'occupy Kashmir'. In India itself there have been ten major terrorist attacks since 2001, including the Samjhauta Express bombings in 2007. The Indian government has taken a range of measures to combat terrorism, some of which have been criticised as infringing human rights, though it must be remembered that India has been the victim of terrorist attacks for far longer than the West. India's war against terror long precedes the American's. Tension has increased along the Pakistan-Indian border, though in 2002 President Musharraf of Pakistan gave a speech in which he tried to reduce the tension, yet reaffirmed Pakistan's claim to Kashmir.

In Indonesia, in 2002 and 2005, the island of Bali was hit by suicide and car bombings, killing more than 200 people. The Indonesian authorities suspect the Jemaah Islamiyah terrorist group of carrying both of these attacks. In 2004 a car bomb exploded outside the Australian embassy in Jakarta, killing ten Indonesians. The bombing was preceded by a message warning that the attack would take place unless Abu Bakar Bashir was released from prison; he had been imprisoned on a treason charge for supporting the Bali bombings.

In 2002, the United States sent a special operations unit to the Philippines to give advice and help to the Philippine Army on methods of combating terrorism. The focus was on removing the Abu Sayyaf

Group and Jemaah Islamiyah from their base on the island of Basilan.

The United States meanwhile pursues the organisation that attacked it on 11 September 2001 – and the regimes that have given it shelter. Within a week of the attacks, the US Congress had passed the authorisation 'to use all necessary and appropriate force against those nations, organisations, or persons [who] planned, authorised, committed, or aided the terrorist attacks that occurred on September 11, 2001.' This enabled the US government to invade Afghanistan, where Osama bin Laden then had his base. But it was not long before the US government was declaring that the Saddam Hussein regime in Iraq had also supported al-Qaeda, so there was an implicit 'thinking ahead' to a punitive invasion of Iraq. Once Iraq had been invaded, there were similar signals that Syria and Iran might be on the list for American invasion.

The War on Terror mindset had repercussions domestically, too. The 9/11 attacks were at least partly planned and organised within the United States. Those involved had to be brought to justice. This entailed extensive investigations. Thousands of people were detained, questioned, arrested. A great many people were investigated secretly, without their knowledge. Civil liberties groups allege that these and other domestic developments represent a dangerous encroachment on civil liberties.

There was a reorganisation of US government departments in order to create a new Homeland Security Department.

A multinational Combined Task Force 150 was created to deal with the War on Terror. Contributors to this force include the United States, Britain, France, Germany, Spain, Italy, Canada, Australia and New Zealand. This was used to support the war in Afghanistan.

CRITICISM OF THE WAR ON TERROR

The phrase 'War on Terror' has been widely criticised as being too vague and general; it has been roundly condemned because it appears to be a cover for action against any state or group acting against the interests of the United States and because it puts the United States into a state of perpetual, unending war. The phrase 'War on Terror' has, not least, been used to justify unilateral pre-emptive war and significant abuses of human rights. It was used as the justification for invading Iraq.

In the war in Iraq there have been several major examples of human rights abuse by American soldiers. The notorious photo of the US soldier Private Lynndie England gleefully humiliating a naked Iraqi prisoner serves as an icon of the abuses that went on in the Abu Ghraib prison. Prisoners of war taken captive in the Afghanistan war were taken to the Guantanamo Bay special camp, where many of them have been detained indefinitely without being brought to trial. This extrajudicial detention is a blatant abuse of basic human rights. It is something the US government not only condones but has actively and deliberately set up; extraordinarily, none of the United State's allies seems to be prepared to issue the Americans with an ultimatum regarding human rights abuses at Guantanamo Bay.

There is also criticism that the War on Terror is really a cover for other agendas. Participating governments are exploiting the need to deal with terrorism as a means of pursuing long-standing policy objectives; the United States' desire to depose Saddam Hussein is a clear-cut example. They – the participating governments – have also wanted to reduce civil liberties and infringe human rights in order to increase government control over populations; there have indeed been noticeable infringements including invasions of privacy in the West, and many of them introduced in the name of the War on Terror.

The phrase War on Terror is also objectionable. As in the 'War on Drugs', there is no enemy. Terrorism is not an enemy, it is a tactic, a method. Lumping together diverse political and military operations in different parts of the world and calling them the War on Terror in reality obscures the very real differences among the local and regional conflicts involved. They are not really all part of the same war at all.

In the year or so following 9/11, there was strong support in Russia, India, Japan, Britain, France and Germany for the American's War on

Terror. But by 2006, support for it among the electorates of those countries had fallen into the minority in each of those countries except Russia. It was down to forty-nine per cent in Britain (the highest level of support among all of the countries except one) and nineteen percent in Spain and China. It is only in India, the place where terrorism has been a serious problem for longest, that public support for the War on Terror has remained high and stable. Increasingly, there is scepticism about the motives of the key political leaders. Increasingly, there is an uneasy feeling that the War on Terror is a smokescreen for the long-term and deep-seated desire of the United States to control the Middle East oilfields and by so doing dominate the world economically and politically.

There is also the thought that the War on Terror may have backfired. The overthrow of the Taliban regime in Afghanistan may have benefited the terrorists' networks. The destabilisation of Iraq in the aftermath of the invasion has also led to its turning into a training ground for jihadists. Continuing meddling in the affairs of the Middle East could aggravate the terrorism by giving al-Qaeda and related organisations further justification for jihad strikes against the West. Seen in this light, military action against Iran by the United States and its allies could prove to be catastrophic.

THE IRAQ WAR
(2003–ONGOING)

THE DECISION TO GO TO WAR

All wars are controversial, either because of the way in which they are conducted or because of the motives of one or both of the protagonists. It is appropriate that as we reach the end of this long catalogue of wars we come to one of the most controversial of all – the Iraq War. This conflict is known by several different names, reflecting the different views of it held by different interest groups: Iraq War, Occupation of Iraq, Second Gulf War, Operation Iraqi Freedom.

The decision to wage this war was made by the US President Bush, UK Prime Minister Tony Blair and other heads of state who supported President Bush. The reason they gave publicly for waging war was Iraq's alleged possession and active development of weapons of mass destruction (WMD). These weapons, they said, constituted a direct threat to the United States, its allies and interests. Some heads of state and other diplomats did not believe that Iraq had WMD and did not believe the intelligence reports that were presented by the Bush administration; they expressed their opposition to the war from the outset. Bush was nevertheless determined to invade. In his 2003 State of the Union Address, he stated that the United States could not wait until there was an imminent military threat from Saddam Hussein, Iraq's head of state.

After the invasion, it gradually emerged that the intelligence documents were indeed suspect. They had been rewritten to make the threat seem greater. It also emerged that the Bush administration had made the decision to invade Iraq well before the WMD intelligence was gathered or created. The Pentagon had wanted for some time to wage war on Iraq. Iraq was no threat to the United States.

In the early stages of the War on Terror, the Central Intelligence Agency (CIA) led by George Tenet emerged as the most important agency in the war in Afghanistan. Tenet had personal meetings with President Bush and in these meetings he insisted that no connection existed between Iraq and al-Qaeda. But the president wanted to implicate Iraq. Tenet also informed Bush in September 2002 that there were no weapons of mass destruction. Again, this was not what Bush wanted to hear. The vice president, Dick Cheney, and the secretary of state, Donald Rumsfeld, instigated a secret programme to re-examine the evidence for Iraqi involvement with al-Qaeda (in other words, *find* some evidence), and by finding that evidence marginalise Tenet and the CIA. The agents produced the material that they were required by their masters to produce and this highly questionable intelligence was fed back to the Vice president and then released to the press. One technique for giving this material a fake objectivity and apparent validity was for the Vice president's office to leak it to major newspapers such as *The New York Times.* Cheney would then appear on political talk shows on television to discuss the intelligence, quoting *The New York Times* as a source.

Many observers have commented that the purpose of the carefully planned double attack (in 1990 and 2003) was ultimately commercial; its purpose was an imperialist one, to redistribute the markets and resources of the Middle East. The administrations of the two Presidents Bush, father and son, on behalf of the banks and oil corporations, wanted to dominate and control this strategic region. It was natural for the United States to do this in league with the former colonial powers of the region, Britain and France. The interests and wishes of the Iraqi people came nowhere.

It has always been the custom in such wars for the aggressor to mask the truth about its motive. This war was no exception, and a reason or excuse for the war that would find favour with the people of Britain in particular had to be found. There is evidence that the United States was planning the Iraq War even before the Iraqi invasion of Kuwait in August 1990.

In a similar way, the British Prime Minister, Tony Blair, explained that the goal of the invasion of Iraq was 'regime change'. Plainly that was not true, as there were plenty of other unsavoury régimes around the world under which human rights were being abused, and which Blair was not proposing to topple by force. Blair did not in any case think up regime change in Iraq for himself. Six months after the 9/11 attacks, Condoleeza Rice, who was at that time America's National Security Adviser, had a meeting with Tony Blair's chief policy adviser, David Manning. According to David Manning, Rice did not want to talk about Osama bin Laden, as he had naturally expected; she wanted to press for regime change in Iraq. Iraq was by then already the target, even though there was no known connection between Iraq and the attack on the World Trade Centre. It was mystifying.

The 'Downing Street memo' is another incriminating piece of evidence about the same issue. This memo, published in *The Sunday Times* on 1 May 2005, is a transcript of the minutes of a secret meeting on 23 July 2002 between Tony Blair, his advisers and Sir Richard Dearlove, the then head of MI6. At that meeting, which took place eight months before the invasion of Iraq, Sir Richard Dearlove explained current US policy in relation to Iraq. He said that Washington officials had made clear at a recent meeting that 'Bush wanted to remove Saddam through military action, justified by the conjunction of terrorism and WMD. But the intelligence and the facts were being fixed around the policy.' In other words President George W. Bush, the son of the President Bush who had ordered the 1990 attack on Iraq for invading Kuwait, had made the pre-emptive decision twelve years later to remove Saddam Hussein from power. Pretexts, reasons, justifications – and even facts – could be assembled later. More seriously still, the memo made it clear that, in spite of appearances to the contrary later, Blair knew perfectly well that the decision to invade Iraq had been made first and 'facts' to justify it would come later.

This raises the other reason given for invading Iraq by both Bush and Blair: that Iraq had caches of weapons of mass destruction with which it was about to attack the West. A pre-emptive strike against the mad and dangerous dictator was necessary. But Saddam Hussein did not have stores of such weapons, and Dr David Kelly was one of the people who knew this.

A British Foreign Office official wrote a memo to Foreign Secretary Jack Straw about the importance of winning popular and parliamentary support for a war against Iraq. 'We have to be convincing that: the threat is so serious/imminent that it is worth sending our troops to die for.' The Blair government then perjured itself by releasing an intelligence report which made the rash and unsubstantiated claim that the Iraqi government could launch a chemical or biological weapons attack (by the clearest implication against Britain) at forty-five minutes' notice. Across the Atlantic, Colin Powell was enmeshed in a similar game of misleading the United Nations abut Iraq's weaponry. In his address to the UN Security Council in the run-up to the invasion, Powell later admitted that he had presented an inaccurate case to the UN. The intelligence he was using was, he said, 'deliberately misleading'.

It came as little surprise to most people when, after the invasion, absolutely no evidence was found of weapons of mass destruction in Iraq. US officials had similarly claimed a connection between Saddam Hussein and the terrorist organisation al-Qaeda. No evidence of that was found either. What has emerged as the war has unfolded is that the invasion was based on carefully and strategically constructed lies. The Bush administration has been accused of falsely portraying intelligence gathered in the Middle East.

Iraq was badgered to allow inspectors in to check for caches of weapons of mass destruction. During 2002, the year before the invasion took place, President Bush pressed repeatedly for unhindered inspection with threats of military force. Complying with UN Security Council Resolution 1441, Iraq eventually agreed to new inspections towards the end of 2002. Significantly, these inspections yielded no evidence whatsoever of WMDs. But the Bush administration had decided long before, as we have seen, that Iraq was to be invaded.

In February 2002, the CIA sent Joseph Wilson, a former ambassador, to investigate a claim that Iraq had tried to buy yellowcake uranium from the African state of Niger. When Wilson returned, he told the CIA that the claim was 'unequivocally wrong'. In spite of this, the Bush administration went on referring to the alleged uranium deals as a justification for military intervention. President Bush even repeated the allegation, then definitely known to be wrong, in his January 2003 State of the Union Address, this time quoting British sources. In frustration, Wilson wrote a piece for *The New York Times* in June 2003 in which he repeated that the CIA had investigated the yellowcake uranium story and found that it was fraudulent. Shortly after this, in what looked like a classic political dirty trick in retaliation against Wilson, Wilson's wife Valerie Plame Wilson was identified in a newspaper as an undercover CIA agent. It is, in the United States, a felony to reveal the identity of a CIA agent, so an investigation by the Justice Department was launched. This revealed that the information was leaked to the press by no less a person than Richard Lee Armitage, Second in Command at the State Department. Armitage, a strong and committed supporter of the drive to remove Saddam Hussein from power, admitted to being the source of the leak. No legal action was taken against him.

The final authorisation for the war came from the US Senate in October 2002. To ensure that the vote went the way the Bush administration wanted, seventy-five senators were told in private that Saddam Hussein had the means of attacking the North-eastern Seaboard of the United States with chemical or biological weapons carried by unmanned aerial vehicles (UAVs). The administration wanted the Senate to believe that Saddam had the weapons, the reach and the intention to make a strike against cities like New York and Washington. It was a fiction, but it was enough to concentrate the minds of the senators to vote the required way. The Senate duly voted on 11 October 2002 to authorise the war. Then the Bush administration had the legal right to invade. In February 2003, Colin Powell developed the same UAV scenario in a presentation on Iraq's WMD to the Security Council. But behind the scenes the truth of these claims was disputed. The Defence Intelligence Agency denied that Iraq had the UAV capability to deliver these alleged weapons; the only vehicles that approximated to these UAVs were outdated drones that were for reconnaissance and could only carry a camera.

THE INVASION

The war began on 20 March 2003 with an invasion of Iraq by forces led by the United States. There were small contingents from forty other states, but ninety-eight per cent of the troops were American or British. It began in a surreal atmosphere of global disbelief. Many suspected that the Americans and the British had 'cooked up' the justification for going to war and there was no ethical justification for it at all. Anti-war groups around the world staged demonstrations. Several nations declared their opposition to it, France, Germany and Russia among them. The French foreign minister said, 'military intervention would be the worst solution.'

Under the US codename Operation Iraqi Freedom, the invasion started, led by General Franks. About 300,000 coalition soldiers were involved. There was criticism from military strategists who condemned the decision to send so few; they reckoned that 500,000 troops were needed to take, occupy and control Iraq. The Iraqi army was even so very quickly overwhelmed and on 9 April Baghdad fell to the coalition forces. A colossal iron statue of Saddam was toppled, symbolising the end of Saddam's 24 years of rule in Iraq. The problems began at once, with the outbreak of looting of government buildings and large-scale civil disorder. There was a massive increase in crime. Meanwhile the rest of Iraq was occupied. On 13 April, the last town not under coalition control, Saddam's home town of Tikrit, was taken. Two days later the coalition's military leaders stated that the war was as good as over. The invasion and conquest of Iraq had taken just over a month. Over 9,000 Iraqi soldiers and over 7,000 civilians had been killed; 172 US and British soldiers had been killed.

On 21 April 2003 the coalition set up a Coalition Provisional Authority with full powers to act as a temporary government of Iraq until a democratic regime could be set up. It was headed first by Jay Garner, then L. Paul Bremer. The Iraq Survey Group was also set up. This fact-finding team was to hunt for stockpiled weapons of mass destruction. In 2004, it published its report, with the devastating and inevitable conclusion that there were no weapons of mass destruction.

On 1 May 2003, President Bush visited the aircraft carrier USS *Abraham Lincoln* off San Diego to make a mission accomplished victory speech. This turned out to be premature, as factional fighting was about to break out, the huge damage to the Iraqi infrastructure had yet to be repaired, and Saddam Hussein was still at liberty. Then there was a gradually stepping up of the attacks on coalition forces, especially in the Sunni dominated region. The coalition forces found themselves waging an informal against 'insurgents', a convenient term apparently meaning exasperated Iraqis who want the invaders to leave their country. The situation was made more complicated still by the eruption of a civil war between (some) Sunni and Shia Iraqis. This new wave of guerrilla fighting was made possible by the hundreds of weapons caches prepared in advance of the invasion by the Iraqi army.

The coalition forces were very slow to restore basic services to normal, pre-war levels. The misery that this caused the civilian population greatly fuelled the mounting anger over the presence of the occupation armies and at the provisional government. Bush announced that American troops would stay in Iraq, challenging the insurgents with the unfortunate provocation, 'My answer is, bring 'em on.' This remark was widely condemned.

The coalition forces were keen to hunt down the leaders of the Saddam régime. On 22 July a coalition force killed Saddam Hussein's two sons, Uday and Qusay, and one of his grandsons. More than 300 top official in the former regime were either captured or killed. On 13 December 2003, Operation Red Dawn successfully captured Saddam Hussein on a farm near Tikrit.

Following Saddam's capture, elements that had been excluded from the CPA started to agitate for democratic elections and the creation of an Iraqi Interim Government. Conspicuous among the agitators was the Shia cleric Grand Ayatollah Ali al-Sistani. The CPA could have allowed democratic elections at this point but refused, preferring to wait for a time before handing over to an Interim Iraqi Government. Now that there was the possibility of gaining political power in an Iraqi government, the activities of the insurgents were stepped up, especially round the town of Fallujah and the poor Shia districts of cities from Baghdad to Basra.

In March 2004, serious fighting erupting in Fallujah, when Iraqi insurgents ambushed a US food convoy led by four American private military contractors. The four contractors were killed, dragged from their vehicles, set on fire and their burnt corpses hung on a bridge over the Euphrates. Photos of the incident were sent to news agencies, causing outrage in the United States and provoking an attempt at a 'pacification' of the city in April. This was the First Battle of Fallujah.

In November 2004, came the Second Battle of Fallujah, which was the bloodiest battle of the war so far. The US army described it as the heaviest urban combat since the Battle of Hue City in Vietnam. The American troops were confronted with a frightening array of Islamist extremists: Filipino gunners, Pakistani mortar men, Chechen snipers and Saudi suicide bombers. The Americans controversially used white phosphorus incendiaries against the insurgents. It was a fierce ten-day battle in which fifty-four Americans and about 1,000 insurgents died.

Civilian casualties were mercifully low as most had been evacuated before the battle.

Far from being won, the war was suddenly going against the coalition forces. In April 2004 there were revelations in the press that Iraqi prisoners had been abused by their American captors at Abu Ghraib. There were descriptive reports, but there were also decisively damning photographs of US military personnel in the act of humiliating prisoners. The war had been shakily justified at the outset. Now a body-blow had been delivered to the coalition. Ostensibly the only reason the armies of occupation had for being in Iraq was to protect the people of Iraq. Here were soldiers of those armies – abusing Iraqis. The opinion of the ordinary Iraqi people and the opinion of the world swung against the Americans. The war had reached a turning point. The military phase had begun promisingly well; now it looked as if the moral war was going to be lost.

In January 2005, Iraqis elected an Iraqi Transitional Government to draft a constitution. A couple of calm months followed, but then there was a wave of suicide bombing by despairing Sunnis and others, targeting Shia gatherings. Over 700 Iraqi civilians died in May 2005. A constitutional referendum in October was followed by the election of a national assembly in December. The construction of a democratic Iraq was under way at last, but the process was a painful one: there were more than 34,000 reported insurgent attacks in 2005.

Early 2006 brought more talks about the creation of an Iraqi government, more attacks on coalition troops and an eruption of sectarian violence. This new violence followed the bombing, probably by al-Qaeda, of the al-Askari mosque at Samarra. This was one of the holiest places in Shi'a Islam. The bomb injured no one, but seriously damaged the building and provoked a violent retaliation in which over 165 people were shot. Iraq was descending into civil war. An analysis of the death toll in Iraq from the start of the invasion to 2006 suggested that two-thirds of the violent deaths were accounted for by Iraqis killing other

Iraqis. The situation became so dangerous that huge numbers of Iraqis emigrated as refugees; 3.9 million Iraqis left the country during and after the invasion. There is no agreement about the death toll. The UN figures give 34,452 Iraqi civilian deaths in 2006 alone, which is twice the figure from the Iraqi government ministries. The Iraq Body Count gives almost 80,000 violent civilian deaths from the start of the war until 20 September 2007, but it also believes that this is an underestimate. An Opinion Research Business survey carried out in August 2007 estimated 1,220,580 violent civilian deaths due to the war, and half of these people were shot dead. A Lancet survey carried out a year earlier gave a figure of 654,965. The true figures will probably never be known.

The new Iraqi government sanctioned by the national assembly took office in May 2006, replacing the Iraqi Transitional Government. The sectarian violence continued regardless. In November, it escalated when Sunni-Arab militants deployed five suicide car bombs in Baghdad's Shiite slums to kill 215 people and injure another 257. The Shiites retaliated at once with mortar fire, releasing ten shells at the Sunnis' most sacred shrine in Baghdad. Several more rounds of mortar fire were aimed at the offices of the Association of Muslim Scholars, a major Sunni Muslim organisation, and this attack set fire to neighbouring houses. Neither the coalition nor the new government were unable to curb the violence.

In December 2006, the Iraq Study Group, led by James Baker and Lee Hamilton, released its report. Its conclusion was pessimistic; 'the situation in Iraq is grave and deteriorating. . . US forces seem to be caught in a mission that has no foreseeable end.' The report proposed increasing diplomatic efforts with Iran and Syria and investing more effort in training Iraqi troops. A separate report in the same month from the Pentagon was similarly pessimistic, noting that there were 960 Iraqi attacks on Americans and Iraqis per week – higher than ever.

Saddam Hussein was brought to trial, which lasted a year. He was found guilty of crimes against humanity by an Iraqi court and hanged on 30 December 2006. Immediately afterwards, at the beginning of 2007, Bush proposed sending 21,000 more soldiers to Iraq and a commitment to reconstruction, with a budget of 1.2 billion dollars. This injection of energy, a surge strategy, was designed to bring the Iraq War to a speedy close.

THE PROSPECT OF WITHDRAWAL

Public opinion in many countries increasingly favours the withdrawal of the coalition forces. The pressure on US troops was increased in 2007 by the announcement by Blair that Britain would be withdrawn from Basra. His successor as British prime minister, Gordon Brown, announced in the autumn of 2007 that the British forces remaining in Iraq would be withdrawn by the end of 2008. The Danish prime minister, Anders Rasmussen, announced the withdrawal of 441 of the 450 Danish soldiers in Iraq. In September 2007, General Petraeus, commander of the coalition forces in Iraq, addressed Congress, announcing the withdrawal of 30,000 US soldiers by the summer of 2008. This US draw-down is officially justified by the curtailment of violence. US military sources claimed that violence in Baghdad had dropped by 80 per cent by March 2007, but the figures for civilian casualties do not match those given by the UN, which relies on figures from the Iraqi Health Ministry and Iraqi mortuaries. The problems of instability and disorder had really not been resolved and the announced withdrawal from Iraq really amounted to giving up and leaving Iraq to descend into civil war.

On 22 August 2007, President Bush addressed the Veterans of Foreign Wars convention. In his speech he, perhaps surprisingly, compared the Iraq War with the Vietnam War, drawing attention to the problem of withdrawal. 'Then as now people argued the real problem was America's presence and that, if we would just withdraw, the killing would end.' He went on to point out that the United State's withdrawal from Vietnam led to the takeover of power in Cambodia by the Khmer

Rouge and in Vietnam by the Viet Cong, along with reprisals against the Vietnamese who had allied themselves with the Americans. Bush equally surprisingly pointed out that Osama bin Laden had made a similar comparison in an interview for a Pakistani newspaper following the 9/11 attacks, in which he, bin Laden, had said, 'the American people had risen against their government's war in Vietnam. And they must do the same today.' In his speech, Bush pointed out that there was a significant difference between the Vietnam situation and the one currently faced in Iraq. At the end of the Vietnam War, neither the Viet Cong nor the Khmer Rouge followed the Americans home. But Iraq would be different. 'If we withdraw before the job is done, this enemy will follow us home. And that is why, for the security of the United States of America, we must defeat them overseas so we do not face them in the United States of America.'

But it is no longer purely an American decision. The coalition's presence is no longer seen as beneficial by the Iraqi government. By late 2007 over half the members of the Iraqi parliament voted against the continuing occupation.

The internal sectarian violence continued uncontrolled. On 13 September 2007, Abdul Sattar Abu Risha was killed by a bomb in the city of Ramadi. Abu Risha was a major US ally, who led the Sunni Arab tribes when they rose against al-Qaeda. It was al-Qaeda who organised and carried out the assassination. On the internet a statement was published by the so-called Islamic State of Iraq, describing Abu Risha as 'one of the dogs of Bush' and his assassination as 'heroic'.

Consequences

The origins of the war were extremely controversial at the start and remained so throughout. There are major questions about the war's legality, and the Bush Doctrine of pre-emptive war. Secretary General of the UN Kofi Annan said that invasion of Iraq 'was not in conformity with the UN charter. From our point of view, from the charter point of view, it was illegal.' Where this puts the political leaders who instigated the illegal invasion remains to be seen, though the phrase 'war crime' has been used by several commentators.

Nor is the damage to Britain and the United States purely legal and ethical. There is a huge financial implication. The total cost of the war is likely to be in the area of two trillion dollars. There is also global disapproval to consider, and the long-term consequences of that are hard to guess. The BBC World Service carried out a poll of over 26,000 people in twenty-five different countries. The result indicated that three-quarters of the world's population disapproved of the American handling of the Iraq War.

During the Iraq War, tensions between the United States and the immediate neighbours of Iraq, Turkey and Iran, increased. Militants based in the Kurdish area in the north of Iraq, Kurdistan, harassed Turkish troops. The Turkish authorities stated a right (and implied intention) to cross the border to pursue militants. The Turks have even shelled Kurdish villages in Iraq.

Iraq itself has been terribly damaged by the war. What was before the war a mediocre and poorly maintained infrastructure has been severely damaged and disrupted, and it is still largely unrepaired. Five years after the invasion many ordinary Iraqi people are still living with unreliable supplies of clean water, electricity, petrol and cooking fuel. Over half of the Iraqis describe reconstruction efforts in their area as ineffective. Hospitals were damaged, and many doctors have left the country. The standard of Iraq's health care has deteriorated to what it was fifty years ago. Two-thirds of Iraqi children are suffering from psychological problems. About one-fifth of the Iraqi population, 4.2 million, have become refugees; half are displaced within Iraq, half have left altogether. The hated dictator has been removed, but in every other way the lives of the people of Iraq have been made worse by the war.

There were inexcusable human rights abuses on every side during the war. Even the coalition forces committed abuses, the forces invading (allegedly) on a crusade against an evil tyrant. The relationship between the Iraq War and the War on Terror is hard to see, as yet. President Bush evidently believed at the time of 9/11 that Iraq played some role in the al-Qaeda attacks on his country. But some counter-terrorism experts believe that the invasion of Iraq was, in relation to terrorism, a fatal mistake. The coalition's occupation of Iraq was a powerful recruitment pretext for jihadists. The invasion galvanised al-Qaeda and created a new arena for its activities. Iraq became a breeding colony and a training ground for a whole new generation of terrorists, who will take home with them whatever they have learnt there. The Iraq War has become a major cause for the jihadists, intensifying the already intense resentment of American interference in the Muslim world, and attracting new recruits to the global jihadist movement. The words of Osama bin Laden in October 2003 may prove to be prophetic indeed: 'Be glad of the good news: America is mired in the swamps of the Tigris and Euphrates. Bush is, through Iraq and its oil, easy prey. Here is he now, thank God, in an embarrassing situation and here is America today being ruined before the eyes of the whole world.'

The consequences and ramifications of the much-criticised and much-condemned Iraq War are hard to foresee, and that in itself has made many commentators see the decision to invade in the first place as an act of supreme irresponsibility. One of the lessons of history is that the outcome of a battle is very hard to predict. The outcome of a war is even harder to foresee. Some leaders in the past waged wars with an acute and intense sense of history. Julius Caesar, Alexander the Great, Napoleon, Nelson and Margaret Thatcher had that acute sense of history and were fired by dreams of glory as well as the calculated 'place in history' that a success in war would give them. But other leaders, and Bush and Blair appear to be among them, seem to lack a sense of history, to be dangerously innocent of the workings of past conflicts and what might have been learned from them regarding the consequences of a future war. And the long-term consequences of a war are very uncertain indeed.

FUTURE CONFLICTS

In the Introduction to a companion volume in this series, *Natural Disasters that Changed the World*, I commented that most disasters in the natural world follow patterns and cycles, and that it is becoming increasingly possible to predict the disasters of the future. The terrible disasters that will one day overtake Naples, Tokyo and San Francisco were mentioned in that book as example of disasters that are, quite literally, waiting to happen. The natural processes of the Earth's interior and its atmosphere and climate are cyclical in nature, so we can make forecasts. But what of human conflict? Is it possible to forecast future wars?

From the story as we have seen it unfolding so far it would seem that it is not. One reason is that conflict arises out of complicated interactions among groups of people at many different scales – families, dynasties, classes, political factions, regions, nations – and the patterns of interaction only become visible with the benefit of hindsight. Another reason is that individual people play key roles in precipitating wars or averting them. This where 'great men' history enters the picture in a big way. The Napoleonic Wars would not have happened but for Napoleon Bonaparte; the 1939–45 European War could not have happened without Adolf Hitler. On a lesser scale, the Anglo-Zulu War would not have happened but for Sir Henry Bartle Frere. While social, political and economic forces may repeat through history, human personalities never do; they vary infinitely. For that reason alone, future wars cannot be forecast.

One thing that can safely be forecast is that there will be conflict. This book has been laid out in sections to make it more accessible and easier to navigate. That style of presentation implies that wars are separate finite events lasting a certain number of months or years with well-defined beginnings and endings. But each war has its history; it arises out of a pre-existing conflict, just as a battle arises out of a war. When we look closely we can see that wars are part of a continuum, with major conflicts erupting like volcanoes from the huge simmering lava chambers of continuous low-level conflict.

The history of mankind is the history of continuous conflict, which is an inescapable part of the human condition. It seems that as a species we cannot live without it. We think we want peace, but cannot survive without strife.